A TIM SEELEY/STEFANO CASELLI PRODUCTION

HACK/SLASH™

—REVENGE OF THE RETURN PART 4—

LOVE STORIES

Written by **TIM SEELEY**

Art by **EMILY STONE**

Colors by **COURTNEY VIA**

Letters by **BRIAN J. CROWLEY**

DOUBLE DATE

Written by **TIM SEELEY**

Art by **FERNANDO PINTO,**
STEFANO CASELLI/TIM SEELEY & SPLASH!

Letters by **BRIAN J. CROWLEY**

TUB CLUB

Written by **TIM SEELEY**

Art by **REBEKAH ISAACS**

Colors by **ANDREW DALHOUSE**

Letters by **CRANK!**

LITTLE CHILDREN

Written by **TIM SEELEY**

Art by **EMILY STONE**

Colors by **COURTNEY VIA**

Letters by **BRIAN J. CROWLEY**

Book Design by **SEAN K. DOVE**

Edits by **MIKE O'SULLIVAN**

DEVILS DUE PUBLISHING:

DDP

www.devilsdue.net

PRESIDENT **JOSH BLAYLOCK**
C.E.O. **PJ BICKETT**
ASSISTANT PUBLISHER **SAM WELLS**
ART DIRECTOR **SEAN DOVE**
MARKETING MANAGER **BRIAN WARMOTH**
SENIOR EDITOR **MIKE O'SULLIVAN**

I.P. DEVELOPMENT **STEPHEN CHRISTY**
STAFF ILLUSTRATOR **TIM SEELEY**
STAFF ILLUSTRATOR **MIKE BEAR**
WEBSTORE MANAGER **IDRYS GRANT**
OFFICE ASSISTANCE **NORA HICKEY**
MANAGER OF FINANCE **DEBBIE DAVIS**

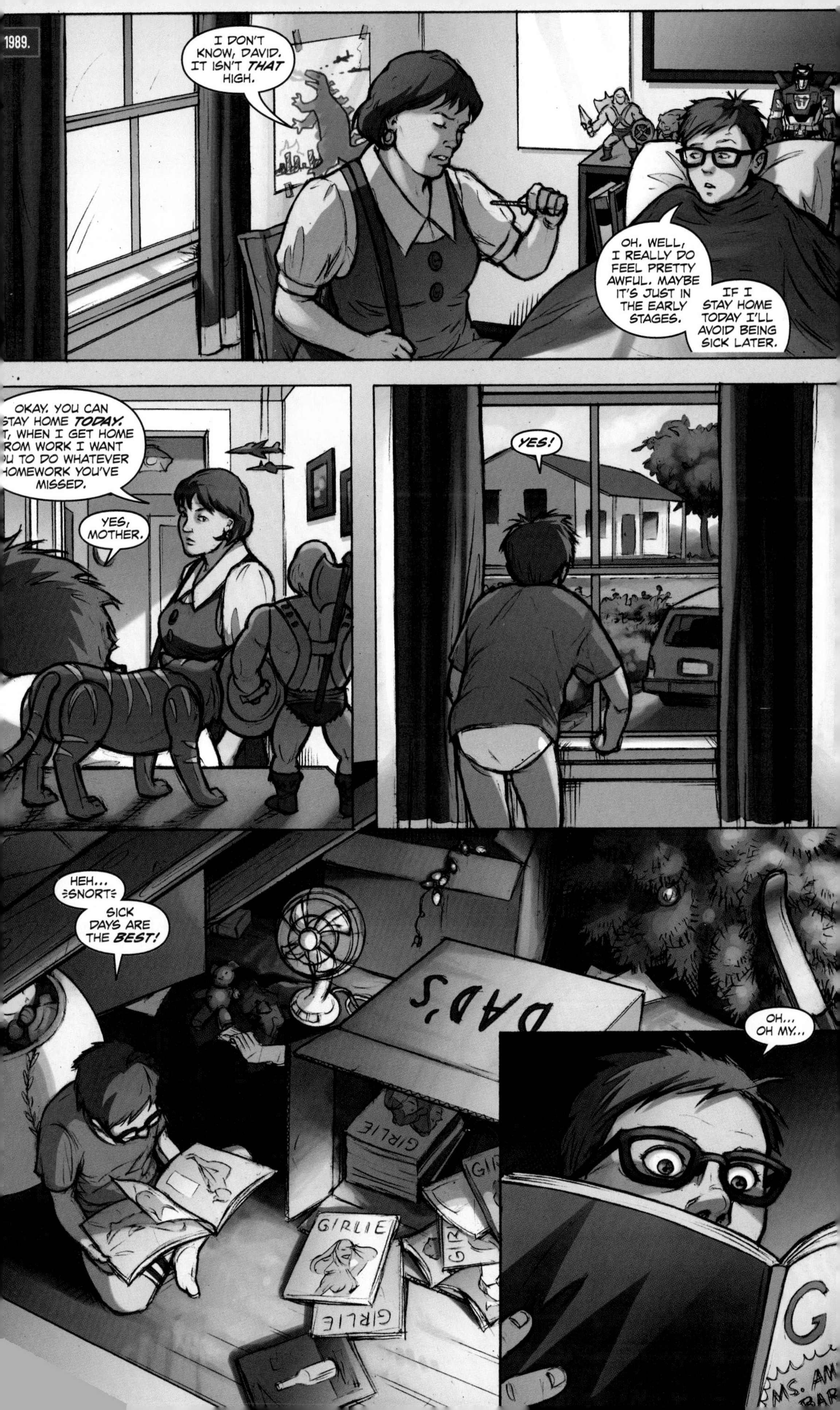
1989.
I DON'T KNOW, DAVID. IT ISN'T *THAT* HIGH.
OH. WELL, I REALLY DO FEEL PRETTY AWFUL. MAYBE IT'S JUST IN THE EARLY STAGES.
IF I STAY HOME TODAY I'LL AVOID BEING SICK LATER.
OKAY. YOU CAN STAY HOME *TODAY.* BUT, WHEN I GET HOME FROM WORK I WANT YOU TO DO WHATEVER HOMEWORK YOU'VE MISSED.
YES, MOTHER.
YES!
HEH... SNORT
SICK DAYS ARE THE *BEST!*
DAD'S
GIRLIE
GIRLIE
GIRLIE
OH... OH MY...

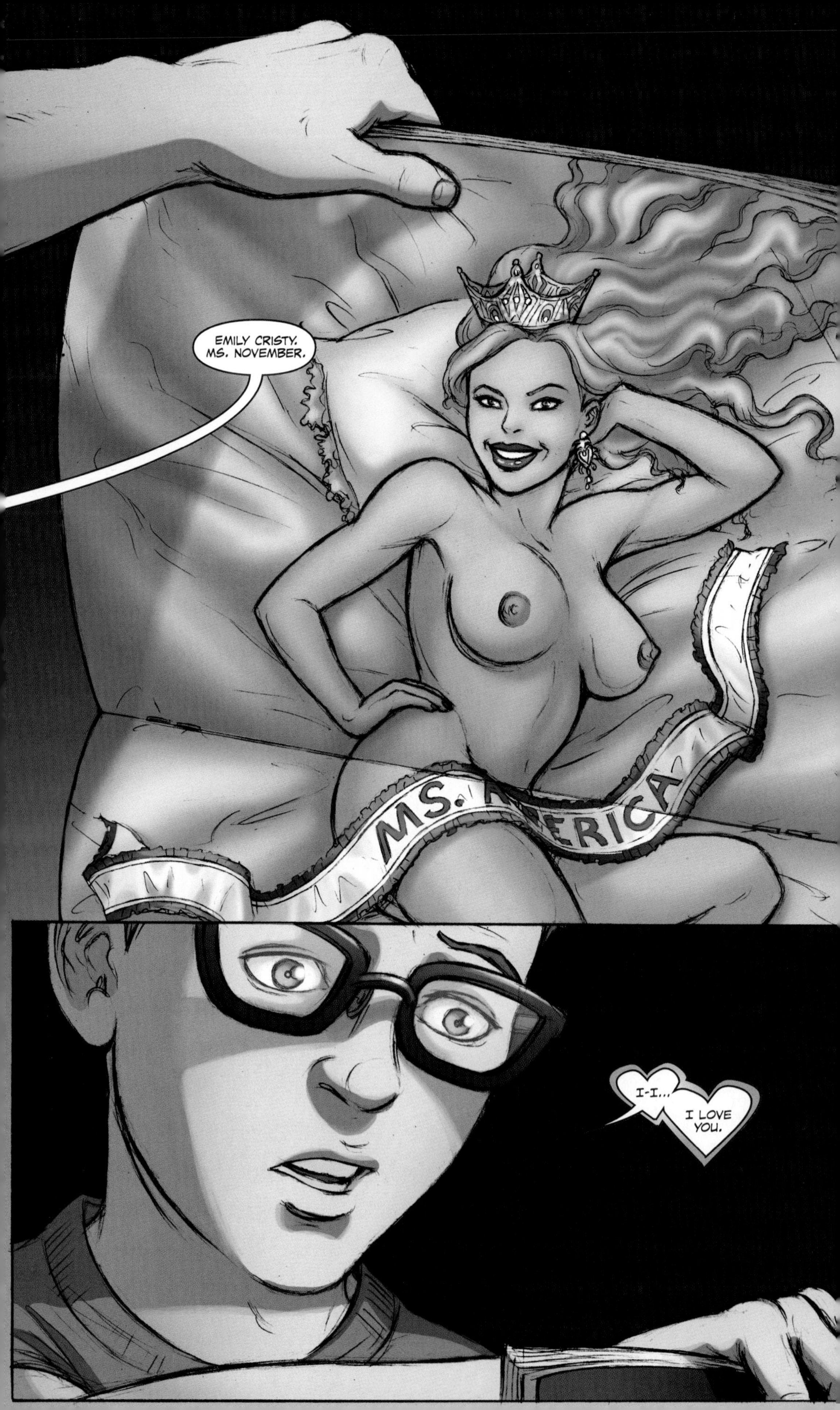
EMILY CRISTY. MS. NOVEMBER.
MS. AMERICA
I-I...
I LOVE YOU.

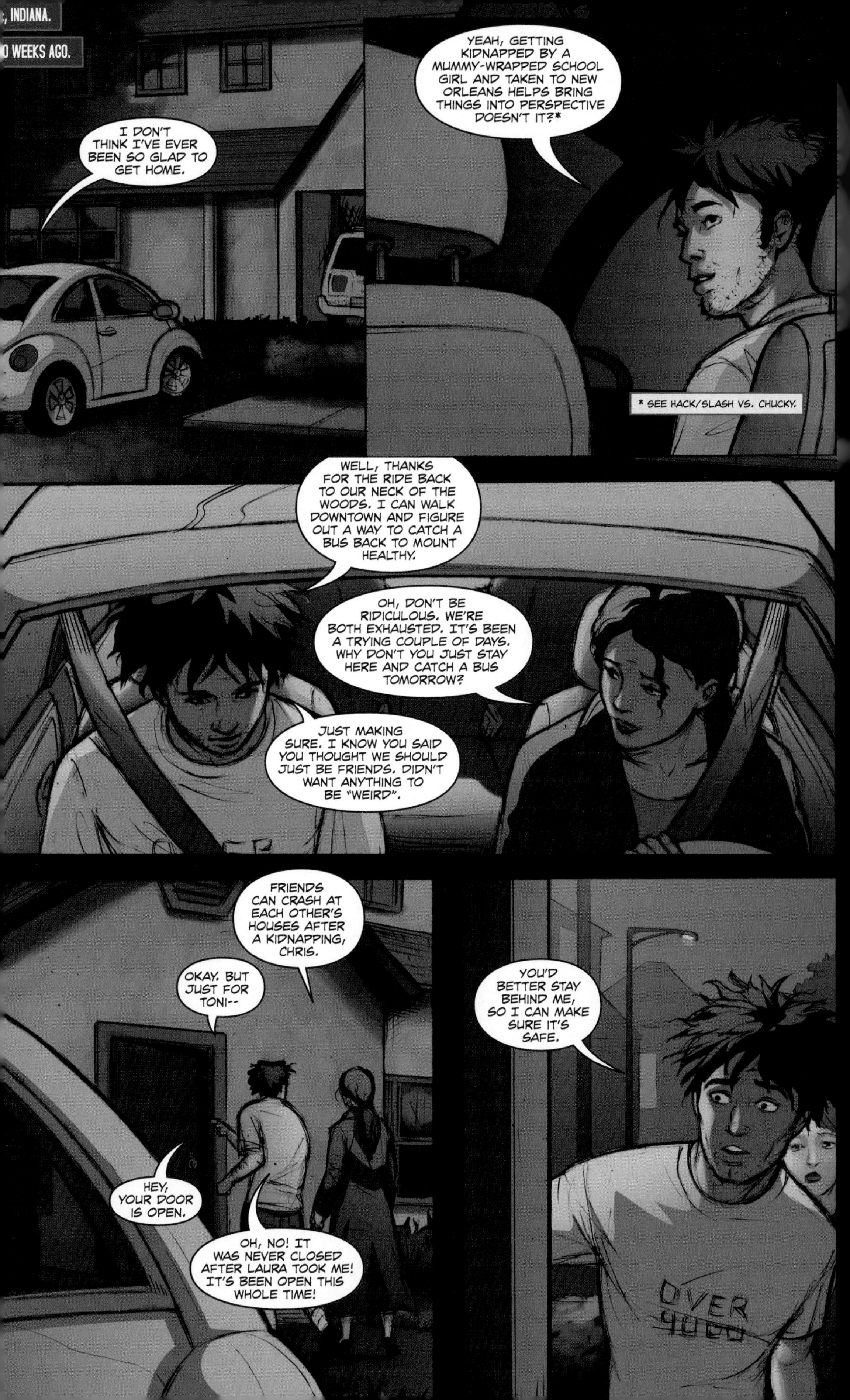
, INDIANA.
0 WEEKS AGO.
I DON'T THINK I'VE EVER BEEN SO GLAD TO GET HOME.
YEAH, GETTING KIDNAPPED BY A MUMMY-WRAPPED SCHOOL GIRL AND TAKEN TO NEW ORLEANS HELPS BRING THINGS INTO PERSPECTIVE DOESN'T IT?*
* SEE HACK/SLASH VS. CHUCKY.
WELL, THANKS FOR THE RIDE BACK TO OUR NECK OF THE WOODS. I CAN WALK DOWNTOWN AND FIGURE OUT A WAY TO CATCH A BUS BACK TO MOUNT HEALTHY.
OH, DON'T BE RIDICULOUS. WE'RE BOTH EXHAUSTED. IT'S BEEN A TRYING COUPLE OF DAYS. WHY DON'T YOU JUST STAY HERE AND CATCH A BUS TOMORROW?
JUST MAKING SURE. I KNOW YOU SAID YOU THOUGHT WE SHOULD JUST BE FRIENDS. DIDN'T WANT ANYTHING TO BE "WEIRD".
FRIENDS CAN CRASH AT EACH OTHER'S HOUSES AFTER A KIDNAPPING, CHRIS.
OKAY. BUT JUST FOR TONI--
HEY, YOUR DOOR IS OPEN.
OH, NO! IT WAS NEVER CLOSED AFTER LAURA TOOK ME! IT'S BEEN OPEN THIS WHOLE TIME!
YOU'D BETTER STAY BEHIND ME, SO I CAN MAKE SURE IT'S SAFE.
OVER

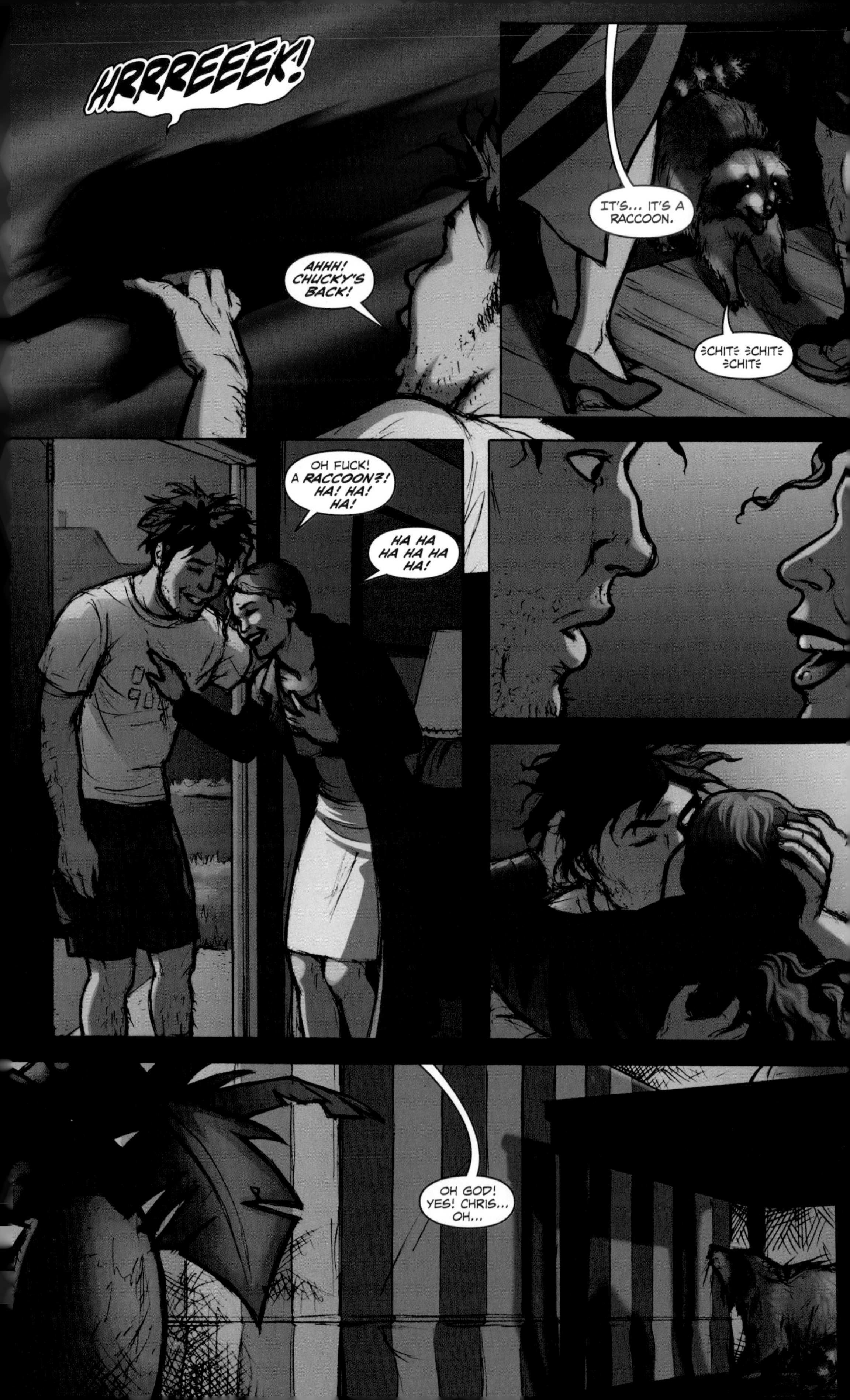
HRRREEEK!
AHHH! CHUCKY'S BACK!
IT'S... IT'S A RACCOON.
CHIT CHIT CHIT
OH FUCK! A RACCOON?! HA! HA! HA!
HA HA HA HA HA HA!
OH GOD! YES! CHRIS... OH...

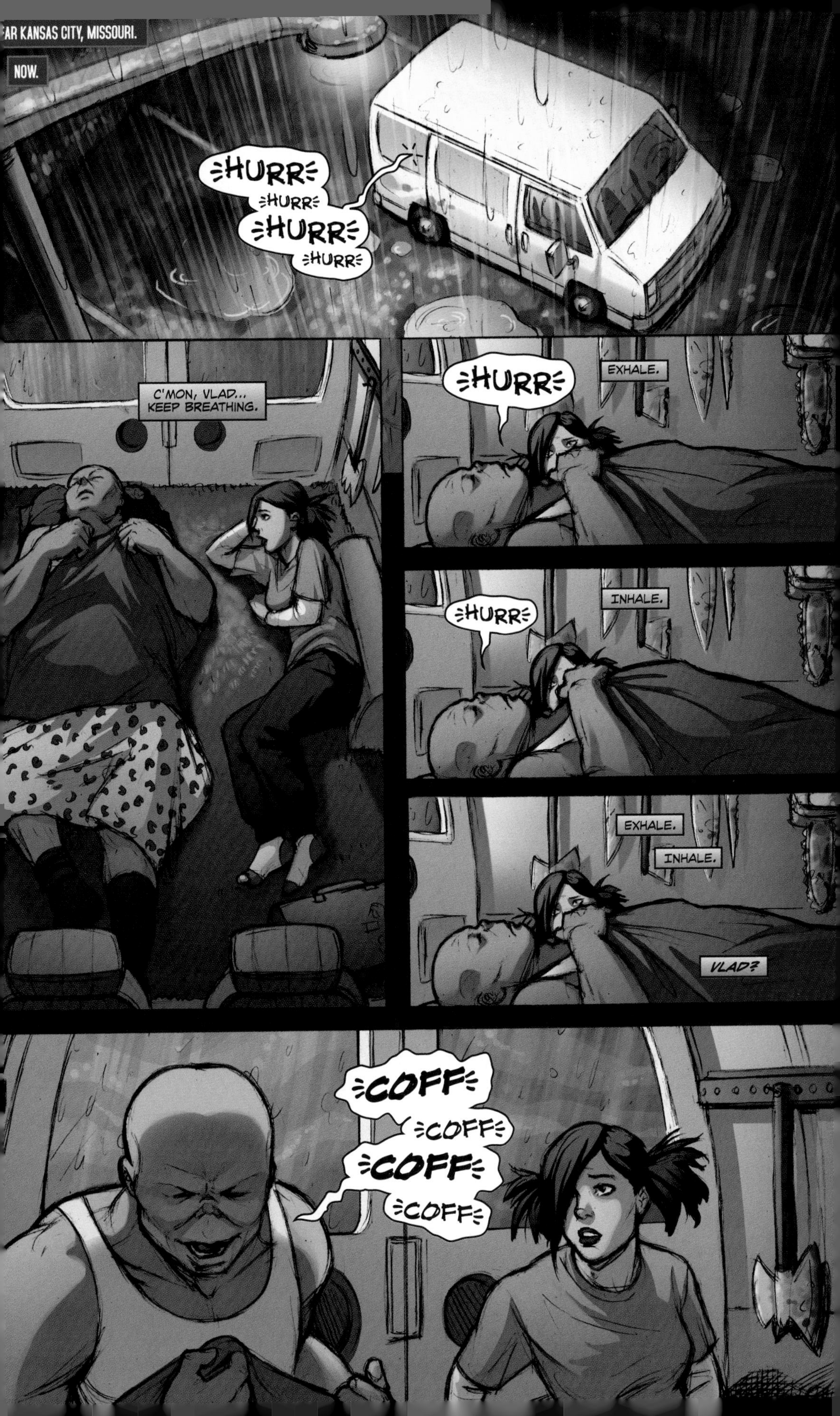
AR KANSAS CITY, MISSOURI.
NOW.
HURR
HURR
HURR
HURR
C'MON, VLAD... KEEP BREATHING.
HURR
EXHALE.
HURR
INHALE.
EXHALE.
INHALE.
VLAD?
COFF
COFF
COFF
COFF

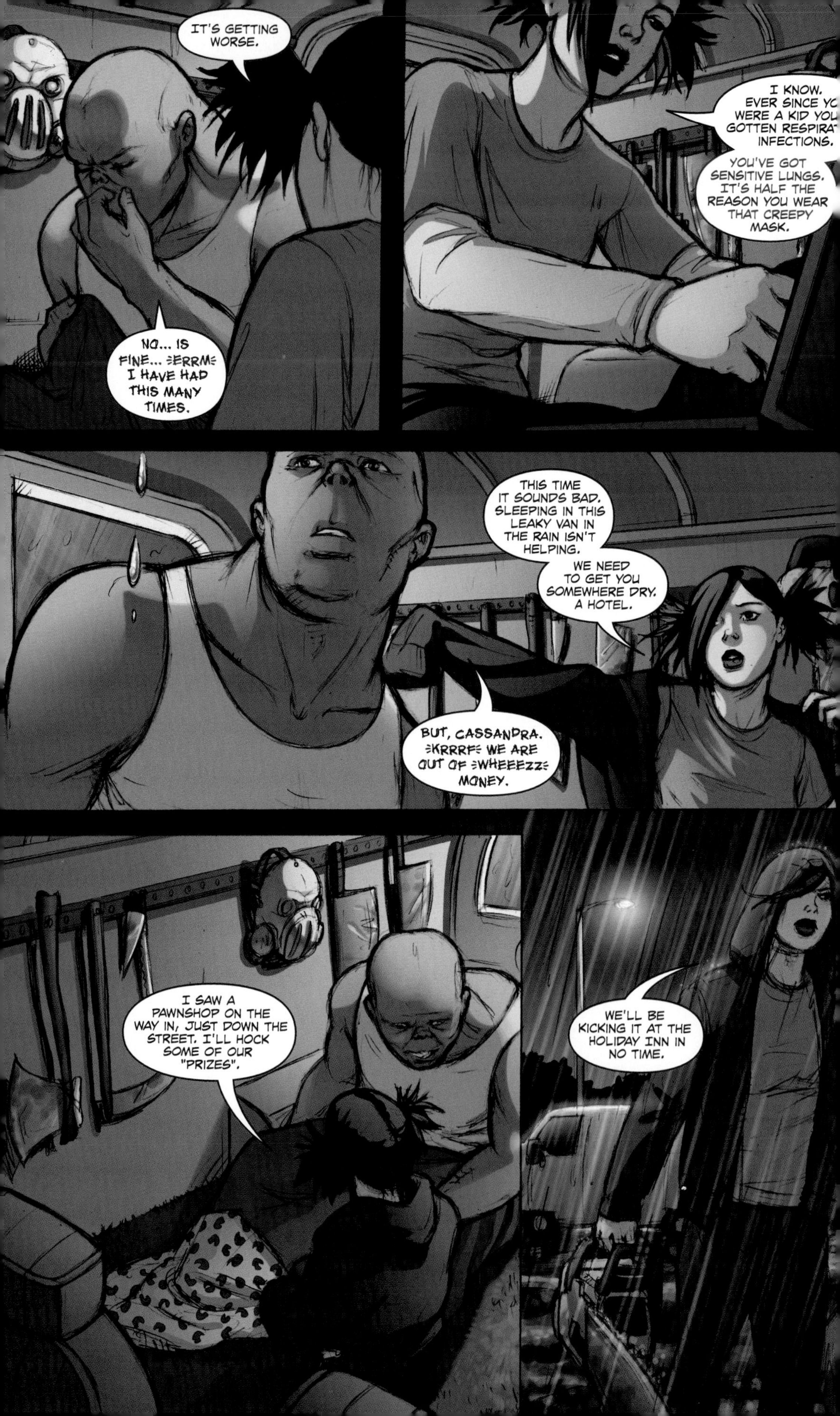
IT'S GETTING WORSE.
NO... IS FINE... =ERRM= I HAVE HAD THIS MANY TIMES.
I KNOW. EVER SINCE YO WERE A KID YOU GOTTEN RESPIRA INFECTIONS.
YOU'VE GOT SENSITIVE LUNGS. IT'S HALF THE REASON YOU WEAR THAT CREEPY MASK.
THIS TIME IT SOUNDS BAD. SLEEPING IN THIS LEAKY VAN IN THE RAIN ISN'T HELPING.
WE NEED TO GET YOU SOMEWHERE DRY. A HOTEL.
BUT, CASSANDRA. =KRRRF= WE ARE OUT OF =WHEEEZZ= MONEY.
I SAW A PAWNSHOP ON THE WAY IN, JUST DOWN THE STREET. I'LL HOCK SOME OF OUR "PRIZES".
WE'LL BE KICKING IT AT THE HOLIDAY INN IN NO TIME.

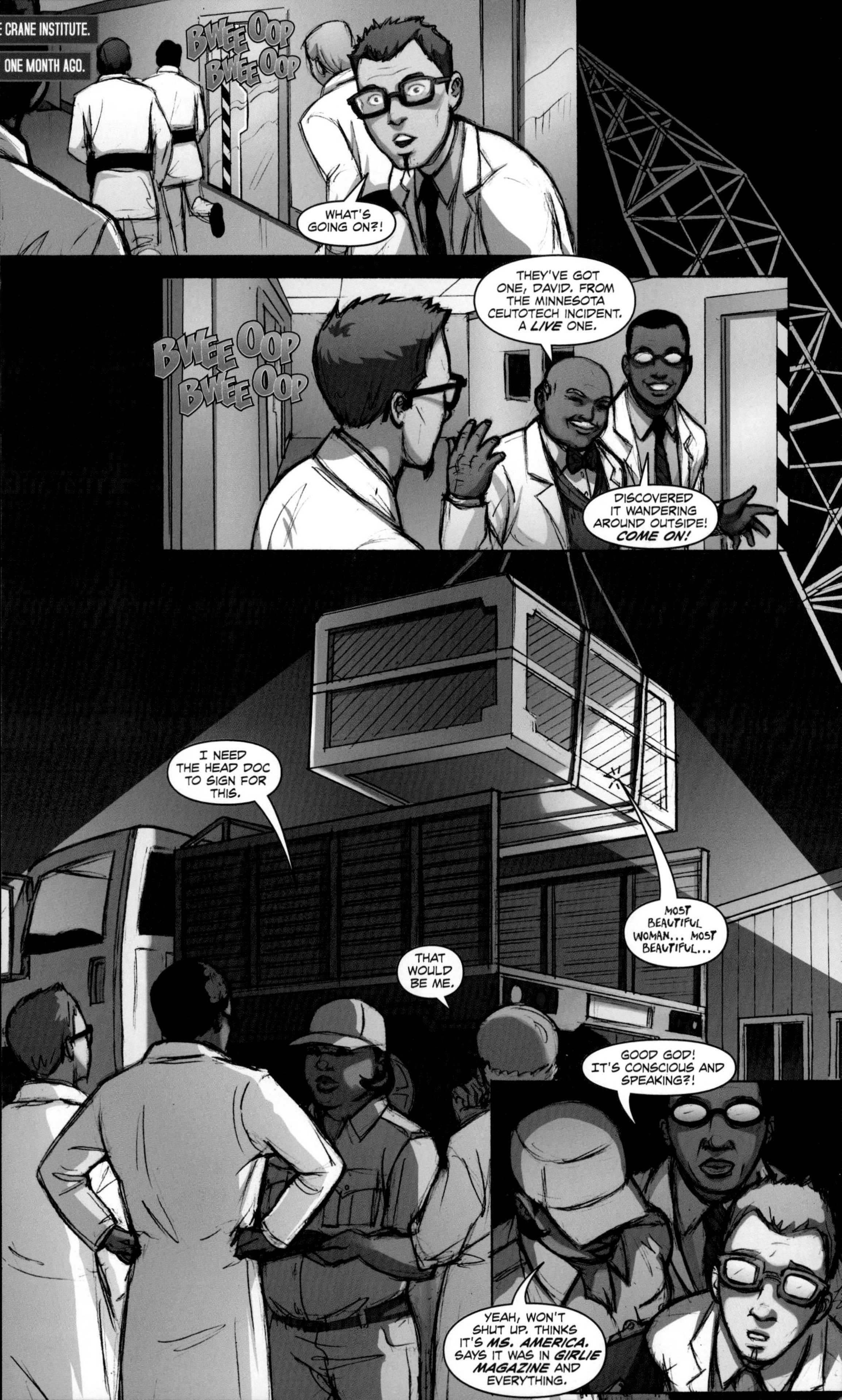
E CRANE INSTITUTE.
ONE MONTH AGO.
BWEE OOP BWEE OOP
WHAT'S GOING ON?!
BWEE OOP BWEE OOP
THEY'VE GOT ONE, DAVID. FROM THE MINNESOTA CEUTOTECH INCIDENT. A LIVE ONE.
DISCOVERED IT WANDERING AROUND OUTSIDE! COME ON!
I NEED THE HEAD DOC TO SIGN FOR THIS.
MOST BEAUTIFUL WOMAN... MOST BEAUTIFUL...
THAT WOULD BE ME.
GOOD GOD! IT'S CONSCIOUS AND SPEAKING?!
YEAH, WON'T SHUT UP. THINKS IT'S MS. AMERICA. SAYS IT WAS IN GIRLIE MAGAZINE AND EVERYTHING.

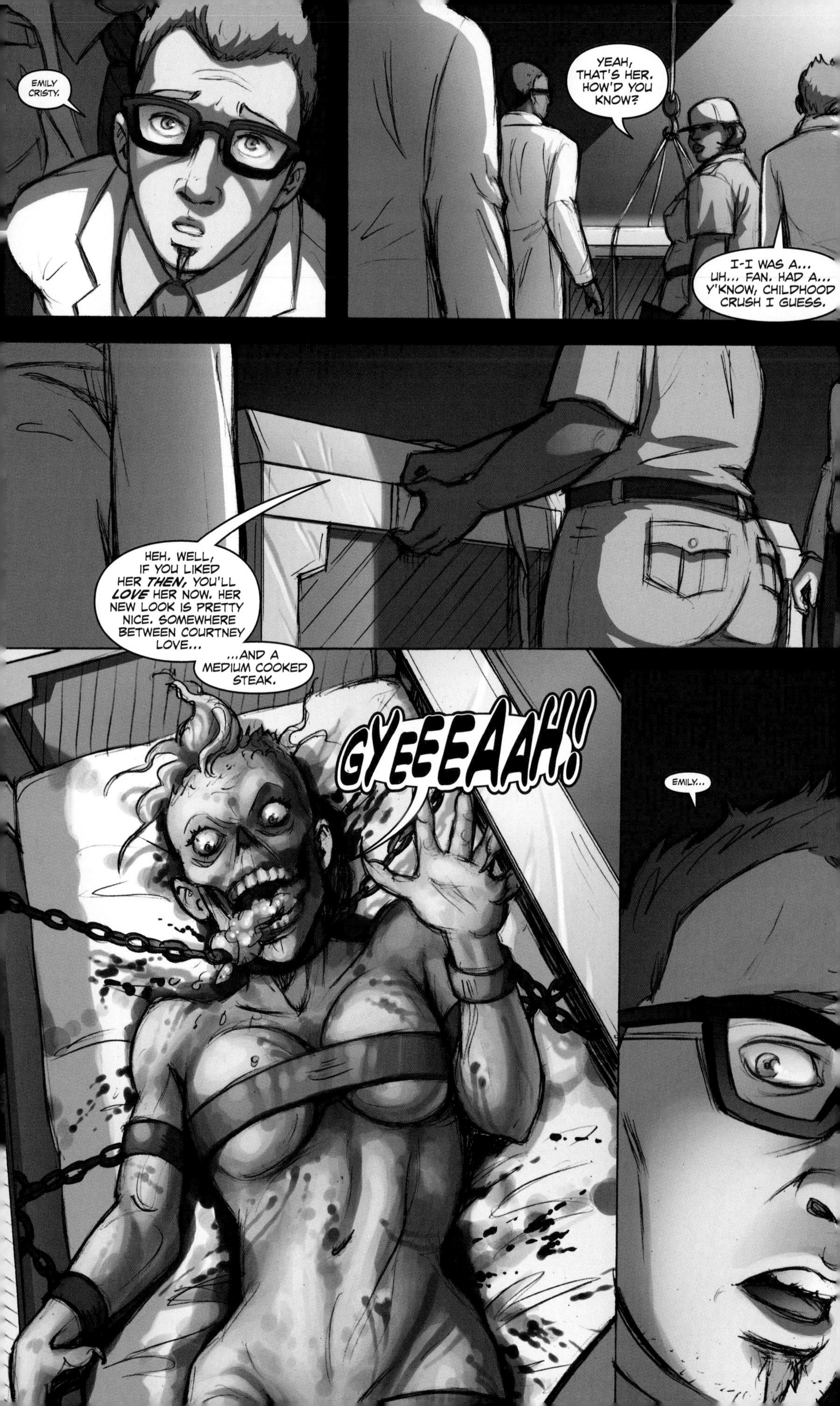
EMILY CRISTY.
YEAH, THAT'S HER. HOW'D YOU KNOW?
I-I WAS A... UH... FAN. HAD A... Y'KNOW, CHILDHOOD CRUSH I GUESS.
HEH. WELL, IF YOU LIKED HER THEN, YOU'LL LOVE HER NOW. HER NEW LOOK IS PRETTY NICE. SOMEWHERE BETWEEN COURTNEY LOVE...
...AND A MEDIUM COOKED STEAK.
GYEEEAAH!!
EMILY...

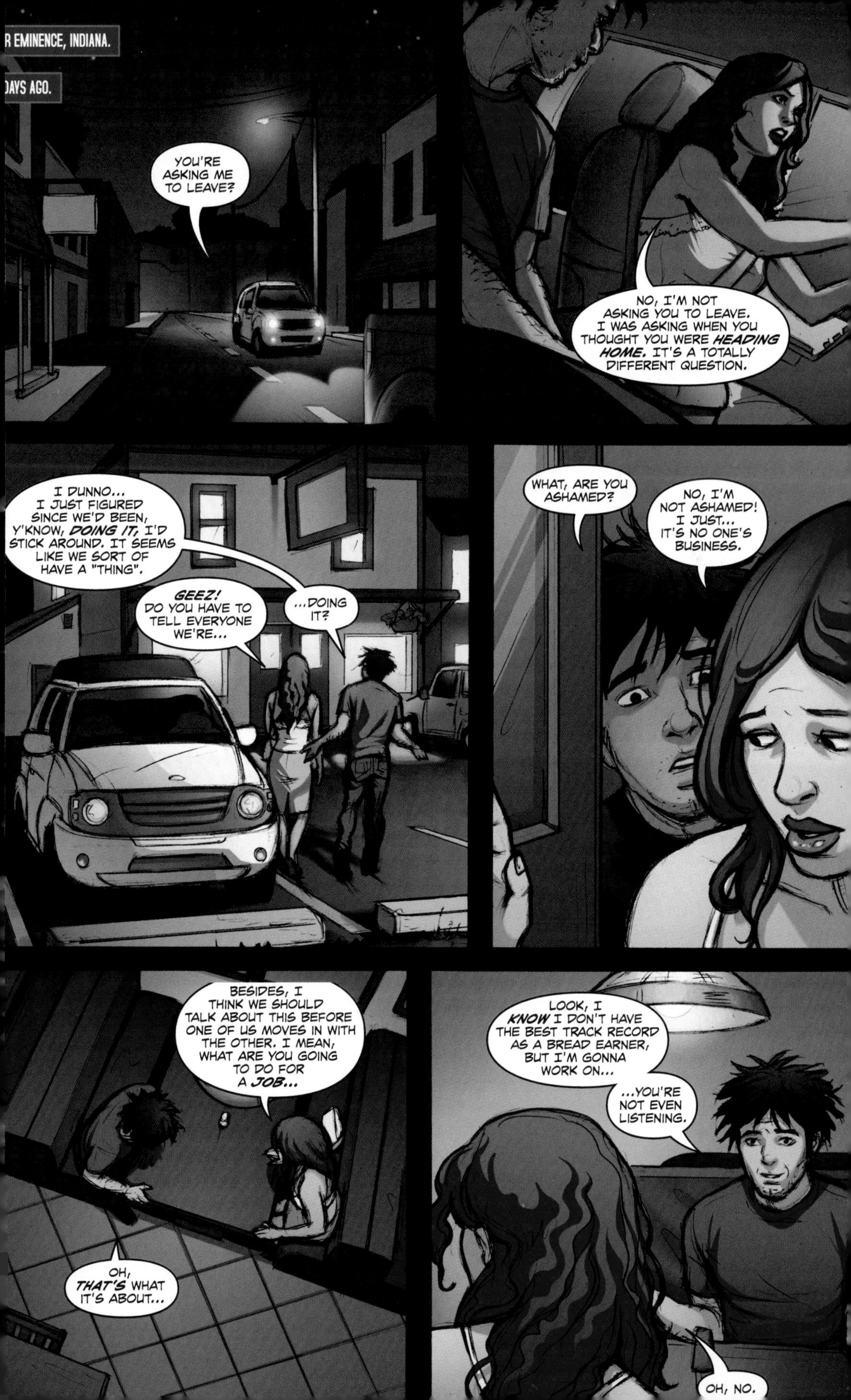
R EMINENCE, INDIANA.
DAYS AGO.
YOU'RE ASKING ME TO LEAVE?
NO, I'M NOT ASKING YOU TO LEAVE. I WAS ASKING WHEN YOU THOUGHT YOU WERE *HEADING HOME.* IT'S A TOTALLY DIFFERENT QUESTION.
I DUNNO... I JUST FIGURED SINCE WE'D BEEN, Y'KNOW, *DOING IT,* I'D STICK AROUND. IT SEEMS LIKE WE SORT OF HAVE A "THING".
GEEZ! DO YOU HAVE TO TELL EVERYONE WE'RE...
...DOING IT?
WHAT, ARE YOU ASHAMED?
NO, I'M NOT ASHAMED! I JUST... IT'S NO ONE'S BUSINESS.
BESIDES, I THINK WE SHOULD TALK ABOUT THIS BEFORE ONE OF US MOVES IN WITH THE OTHER. I MEAN, WHAT ARE YOU GOING TO DO FOR A *JOB...*
OH, *THAT'S* WHAT IT'S ABOUT...
LOOK, I *KNOW* I DON'T HAVE THE BEST TRACK RECORD AS A BREAD EARNER, BUT I'M GONNA WORK ON...
...YOU'RE NOT EVEN LISTENING.
OH, NO.

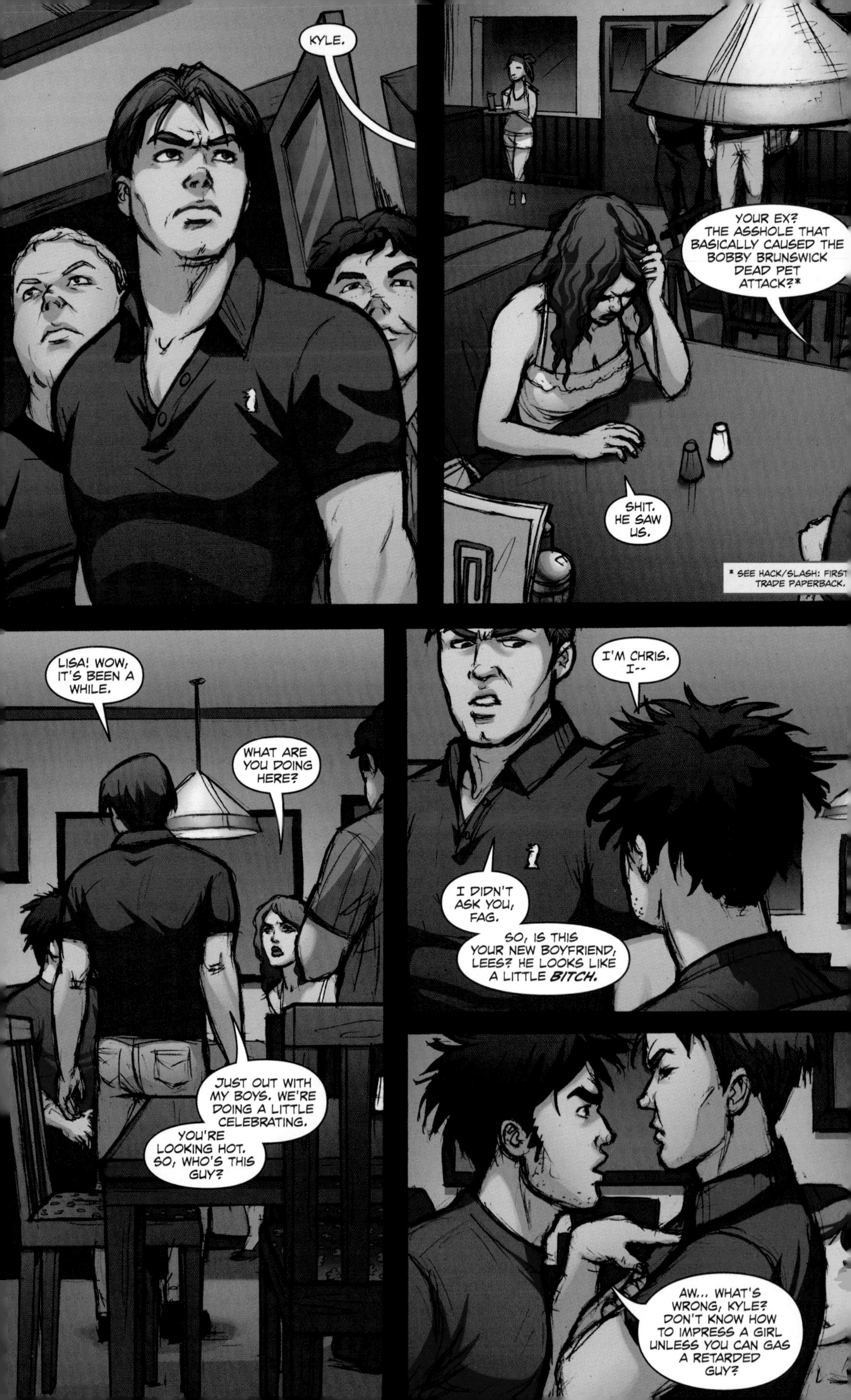
KYLE.
YOUR EX? THE ASSHOLE THAT BASICALLY CAUSED THE BOBBY BRUNSWICK DEAD PET ATTACK?*
SHIT. HE SAW US.
* SEE HACK/SLASH: FIRST TRADE PAPERBACK.
LISA! WOW, IT'S BEEN A WHILE.
WHAT ARE YOU DOING HERE?
JUST OUT WITH MY BOYS. WE'RE DOING A LITTLE CELEBRATING.
YOU'RE LOOKING HOT. SO, WHO'S THIS GUY?
I'M CHRIS. I--
I DIDN'T ASK YOU, FAG.
SO, IS THIS YOUR NEW BOYFRIEND, LEES? HE LOOKS LIKE A LITTLE *BITCH*.
AW... WHAT'S WRONG, KYLE? DON'T KNOW HOW TO IMPRESS A GIRL UNLESS YOU CAN GAS A RETARDED GUY?

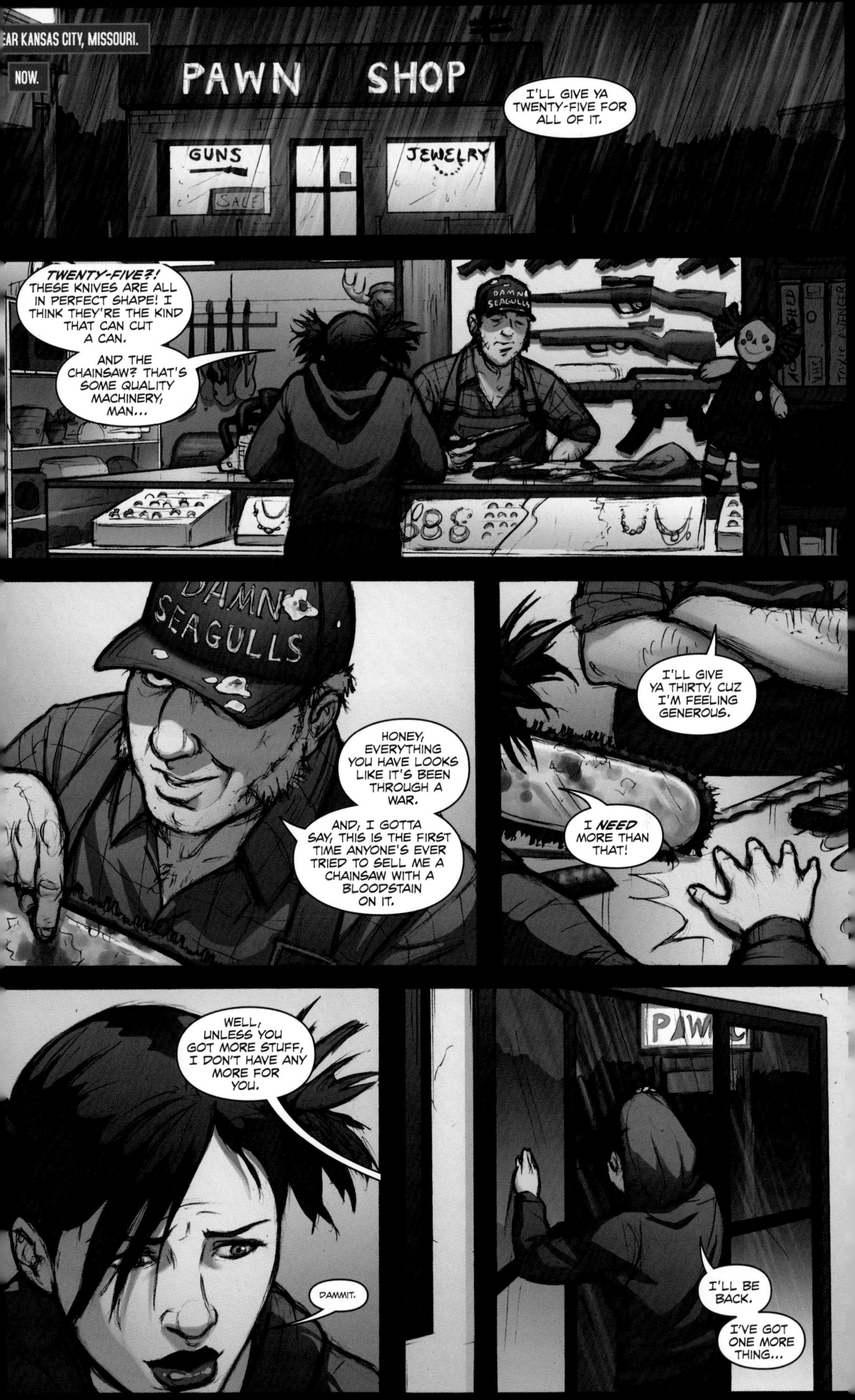
EAR KANSAS CITY, MISSOURI.
NOW.
PAWN SHOP
GUNS
SALE
JEWELRY
I'LL GIVE YA TWENTY-FIVE FOR ALL OF IT.
TWENTY-FIVE?! THESE KNIVES ARE ALL IN PERFECT SHAPE! I THINK THEY'RE THE KIND THAT CAN CUT A CAN.
AND THE CHAINSAW? THAT'S SOME QUALITY MACHINERY, MAN...
DAMN SEAGULLS
HONEY, EVERYTHING YOU HAVE LOOKS LIKE IT'S BEEN THROUGH A WAR.
AND, I GOTTA SAY, THIS IS THE FIRST TIME ANYONE'S EVER TRIED TO SELL ME A CHAINSAW WITH A BLOODSTAIN ON IT.
I'LL GIVE YA THIRTY, CUZ I'M FEELING GENEROUS.
I NEED MORE THAN THAT!
WELL, UNLESS YOU GOT MORE STUFF, I DON'T HAVE ANY MORE FOR YOU.
DAMMIT.
PAW
I'LL BE BACK.
I'VE GOT ONE MORE THING...

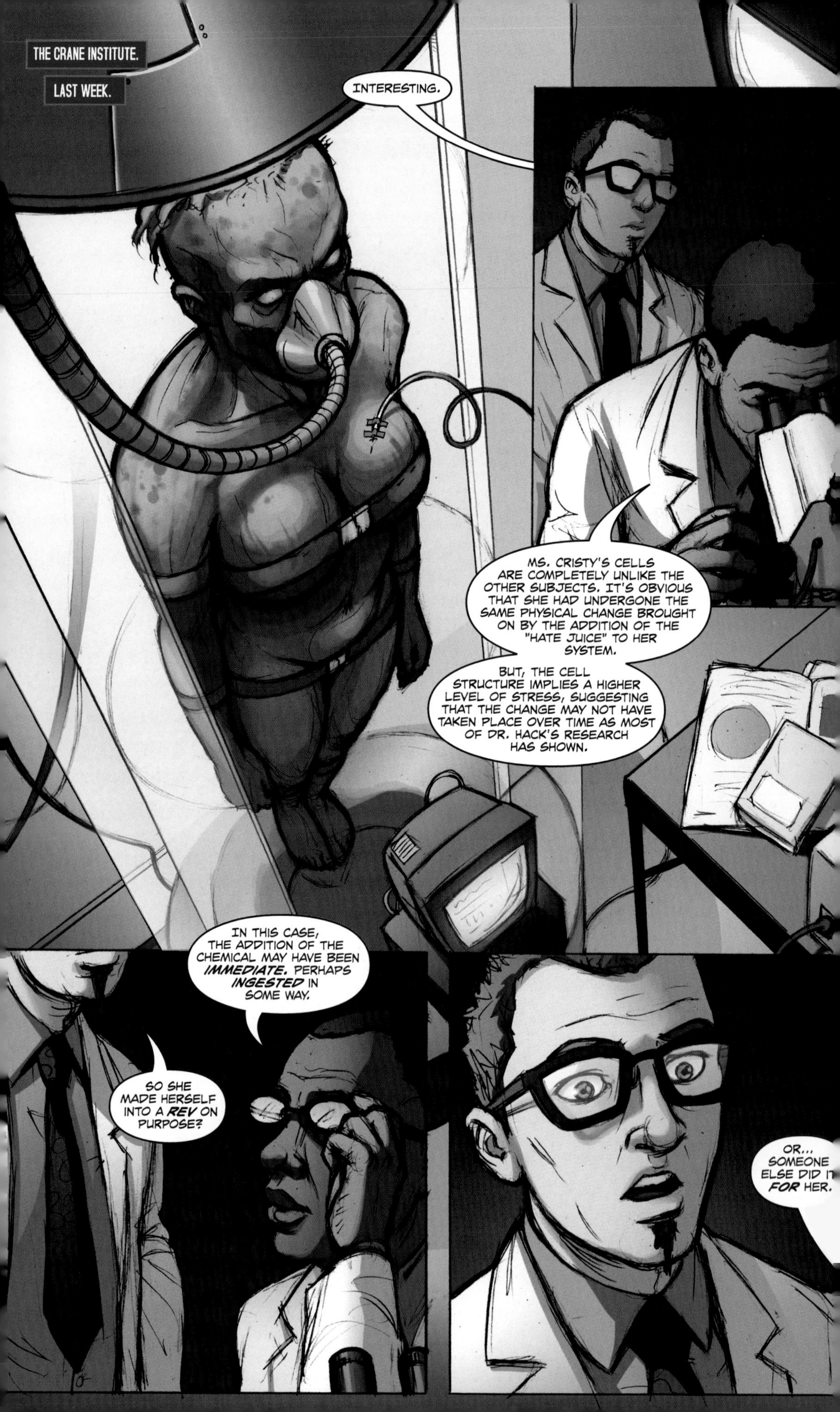
THE CRANE INSTITUTE.
LAST WEEK.
INTERESTING.
MS. CRISTY'S CELLS ARE COMPLETELY UNLIKE THE OTHER SUBJECTS. IT'S OBVIOUS THAT SHE HAD UNDERGONE THE SAME PHYSICAL CHANGE BROUGHT ON BY THE ADDITION OF THE "HATE JUICE" TO HER SYSTEM.
BUT, THE CELL STRUCTURE IMPLIES A HIGHER LEVEL OF STRESS, SUGGESTING THAT THE CHANGE MAY NOT HAVE TAKEN PLACE OVER TIME AS MOST OF DR. HACK'S RESEARCH HAS SHOWN.
IN THIS CASE, THE ADDITION OF THE CHEMICAL MAY HAVE BEEN *IMMEDIATE*. PERHAPS *INGESTED* IN SOME WAY.
SO SHE MADE HERSELF INTO A *REV* ON PURPOSE?
OR... SOMEONE ELSE DID IT *FOR* HER.

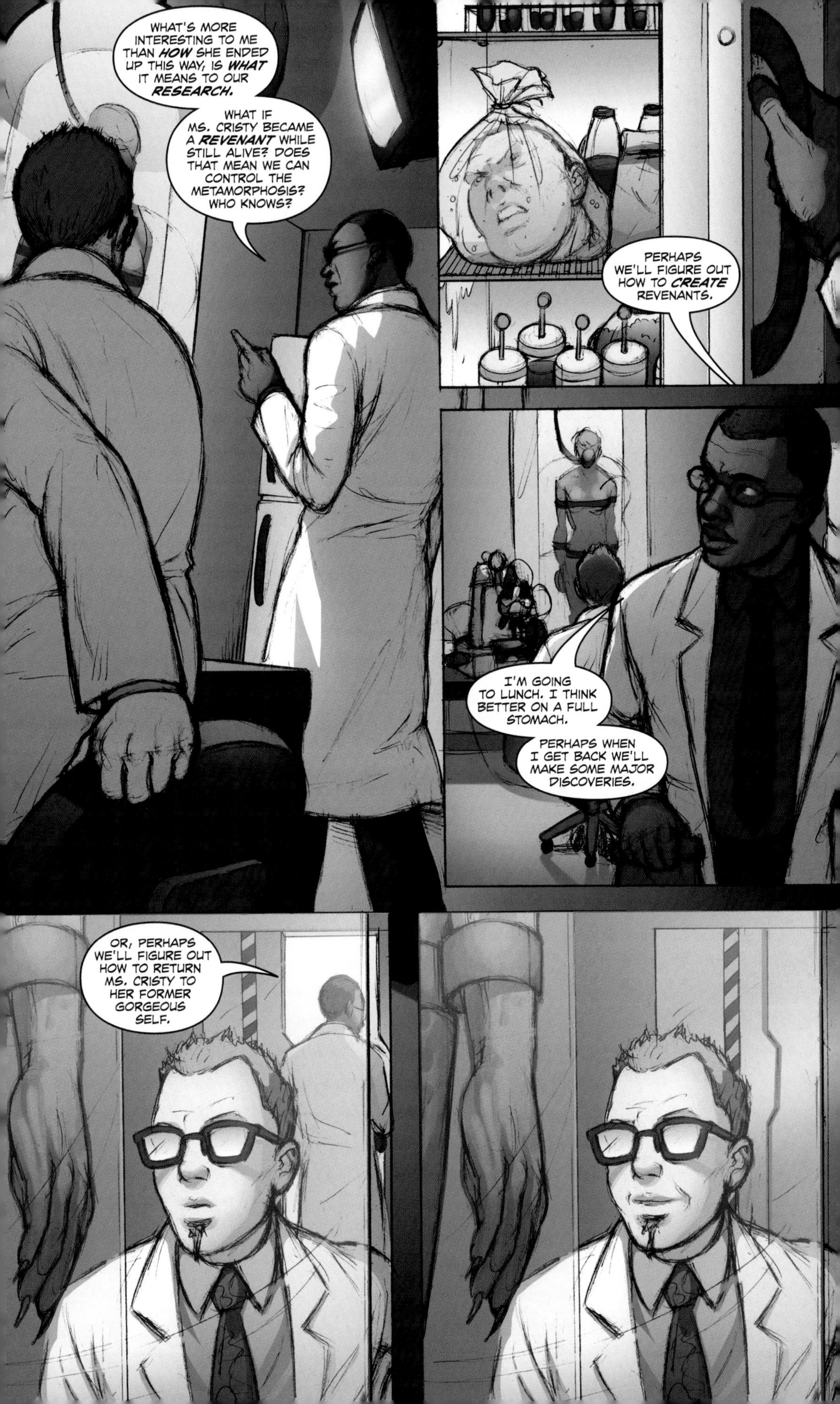
WHAT'S MORE INTERESTING TO ME THAN *HOW* SHE ENDED UP THIS WAY, IS *WHAT* IT MEANS TO OUR *RESEARCH.*
WHAT IF MS. CRISTY BECAME A *REVENANT* WHILE STILL ALIVE? DOES THAT MEAN WE CAN CONTROL THE METAMORPHOSIS? WHO KNOWS?
PERHAPS WE'LL FIGURE OUT HOW TO *CREATE* REVENANTS.
I'M GOING TO LUNCH. I THINK BETTER ON A FULL STOMACH.
PERHAPS WHEN I GET BACK WE'LL MAKE SOME MAJOR DISCOVERIES.
OR, PERHAPS WE'LL FIGURE OUT HOW TO RETURN MS. CRISTY TO HER FORMER GORGEOUS SELF.

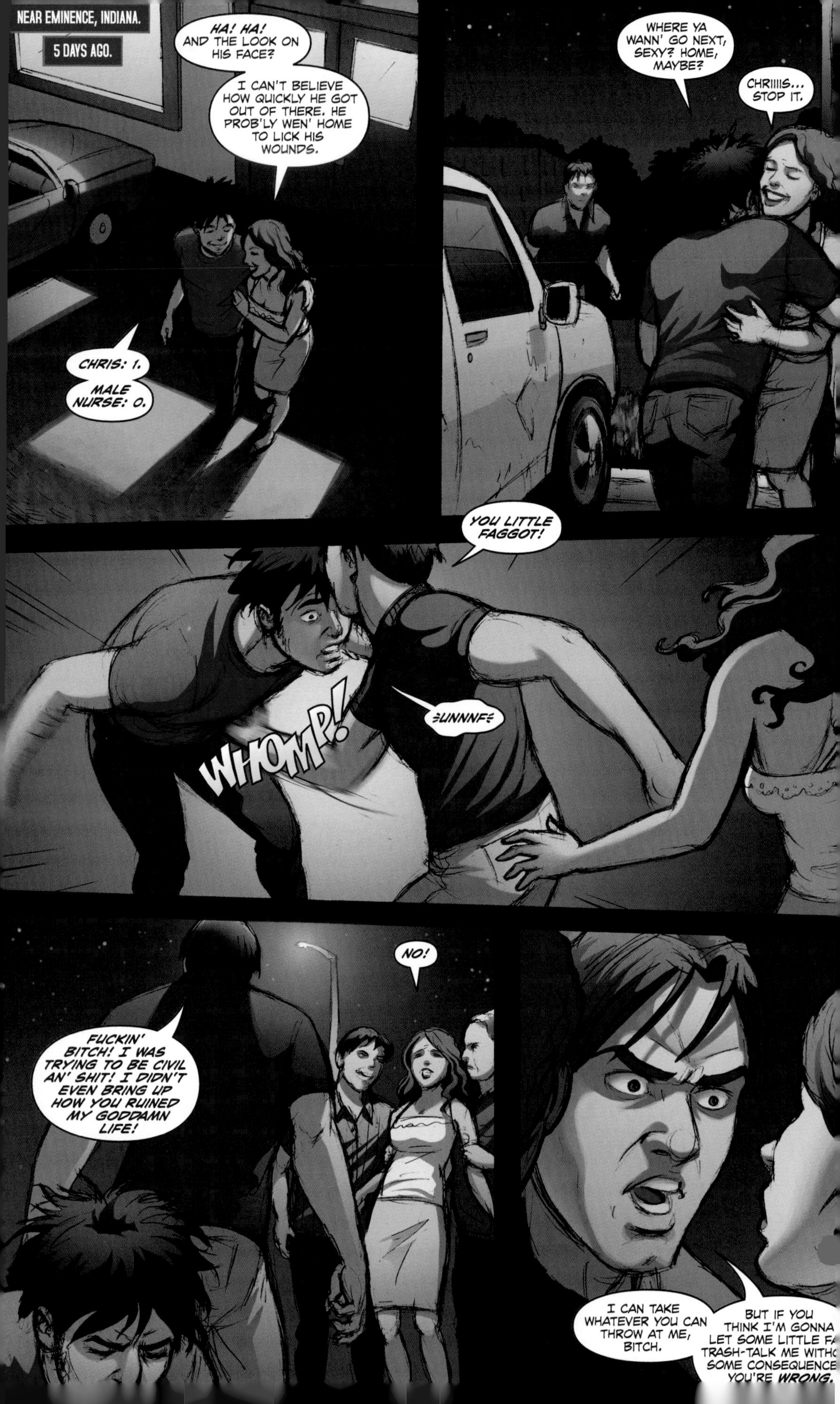
NEAR EMINENCE, INDIANA.
5 DAYS AGO.
HA! HA! AND THE LOOK ON HIS FACE?
I CAN'T BELIEVE HOW QUICKLY HE GOT OUT OF THERE. HE PROB'LY WEN' HOME TO LICK HIS WOUNDS.
CHRIS: 1.
MALE NURSE: 0.
WHERE YA WANN' GO NEXT, SEXY? HOME, MAYBE?
CHRIIIIS... STOP IT.
YOU LITTLE FAGGOT!
WHOMP!
=UNNNF=
NO!
FUCKIN' BITCH! I WAS TRYING TO BE CIVIL AN' SHIT! I DIDN'T EVEN BRING UP HOW YOU RUINED MY GODDAMN LIFE!
I CAN TAKE WHATEVER YOU CAN THROW AT ME, BITCH.
BUT IF YOU THINK I'M GONNA LET SOME LITTLE FA TRASH-TALK ME WITHO SOME CONSEQUENCE YOU'RE WRONG.

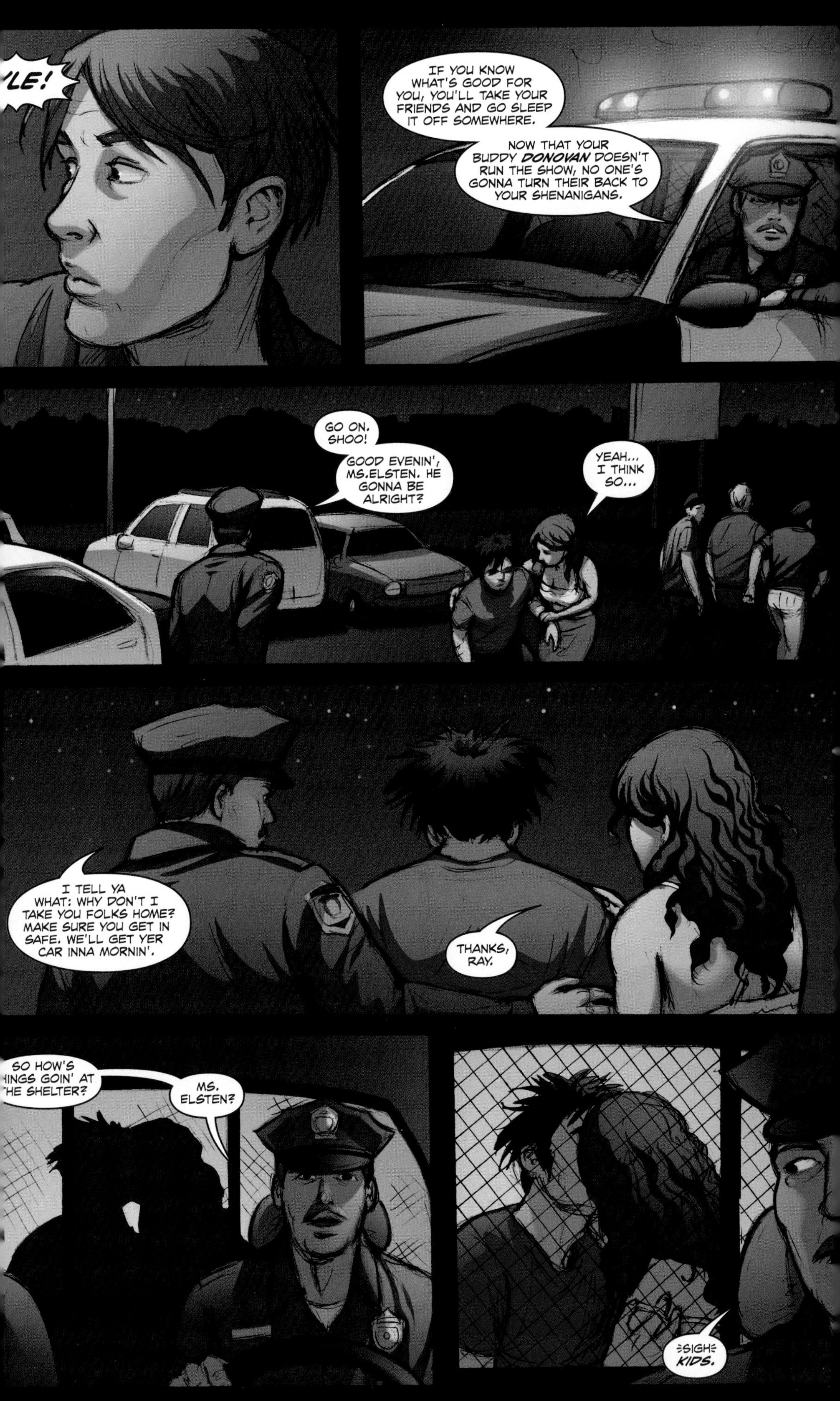
'LE!
IF YOU KNOW WHAT'S GOOD FOR YOU, YOU'LL TAKE YOUR FRIENDS AND GO SLEEP IT OFF SOMEWHERE.
NOW THAT YOUR BUDDY DONOVAN DOESN'T RUN THE SHOW, NO ONE'S GONNA TURN THEIR BACK TO YOUR SHENANIGANS.
GO ON. SHOO!
GOOD EVENIN', MS.ELSTEN. HE GONNA BE ALRIGHT?
YEAH... I THINK SO...
I TELL YA WHAT: WHY DON'T I TAKE YOU FOLKS HOME? MAKE SURE YOU GET IN SAFE. WE'LL GET YER CAR INNA MORNIN'.
THANKS, RAY.
SO HOW'S HINGS GOIN' AT HE SHELTER?
MS. ELSTEN?
SIGH KIDS.

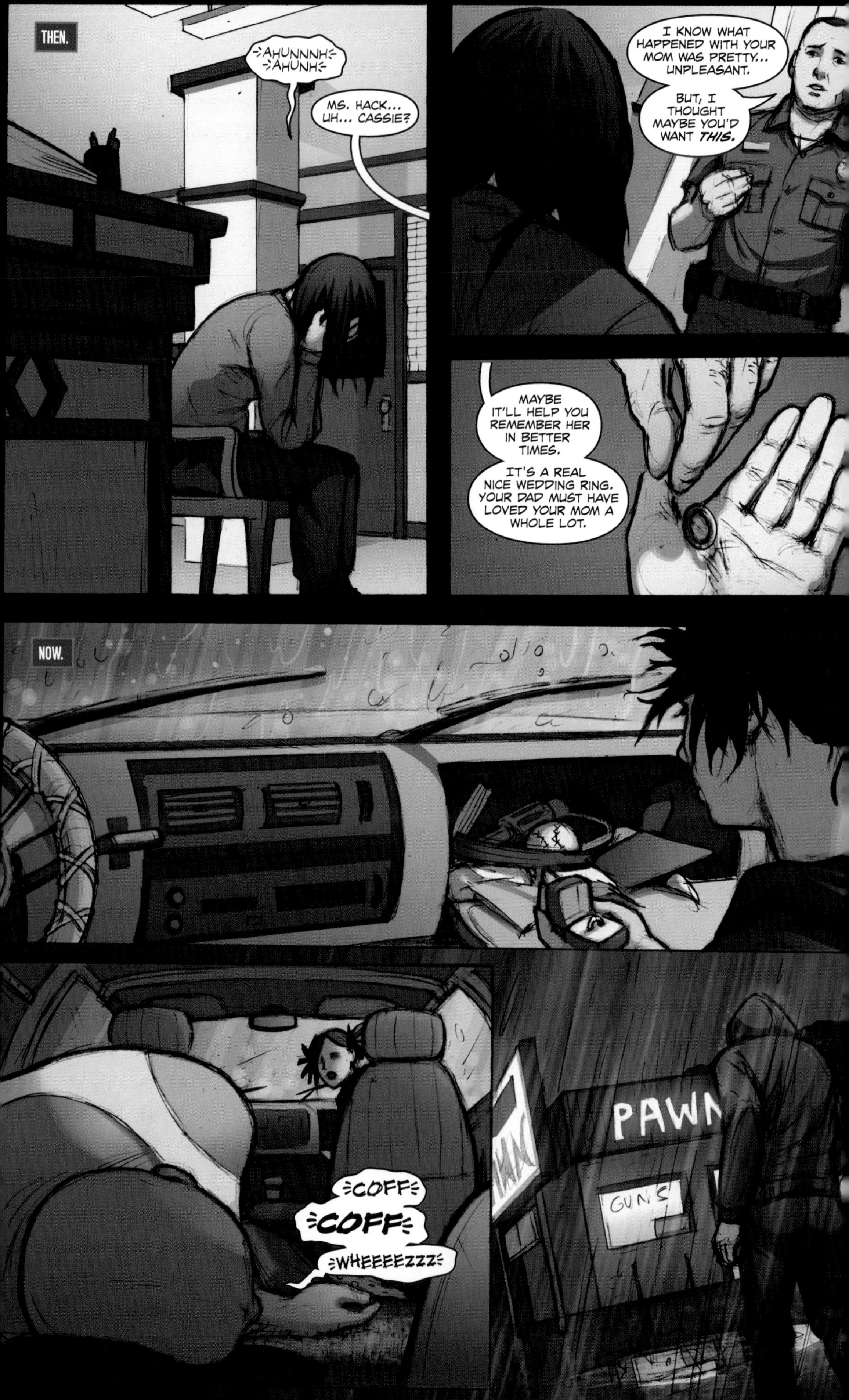

THEN.
AHUNNNH AHUNH
MS. HACK... UH... CASSIE?
I KNOW WHAT HAPPENED WITH YOUR MOM WAS PRETTY... UNPLEASANT.
BUT, I THOUGHT MAYBE YOU'D WANT THIS.
MAYBE IT'LL HELP YOU REMEMBER HER IN BETTER TIMES.
IT'S A REAL NICE WEDDING RING. YOUR DAD MUST HAVE LOVED YOUR MOM A WHOLE LOT.
NOW.
COFF
COFF
WHEEEEZZZ
PAWN
GUNS

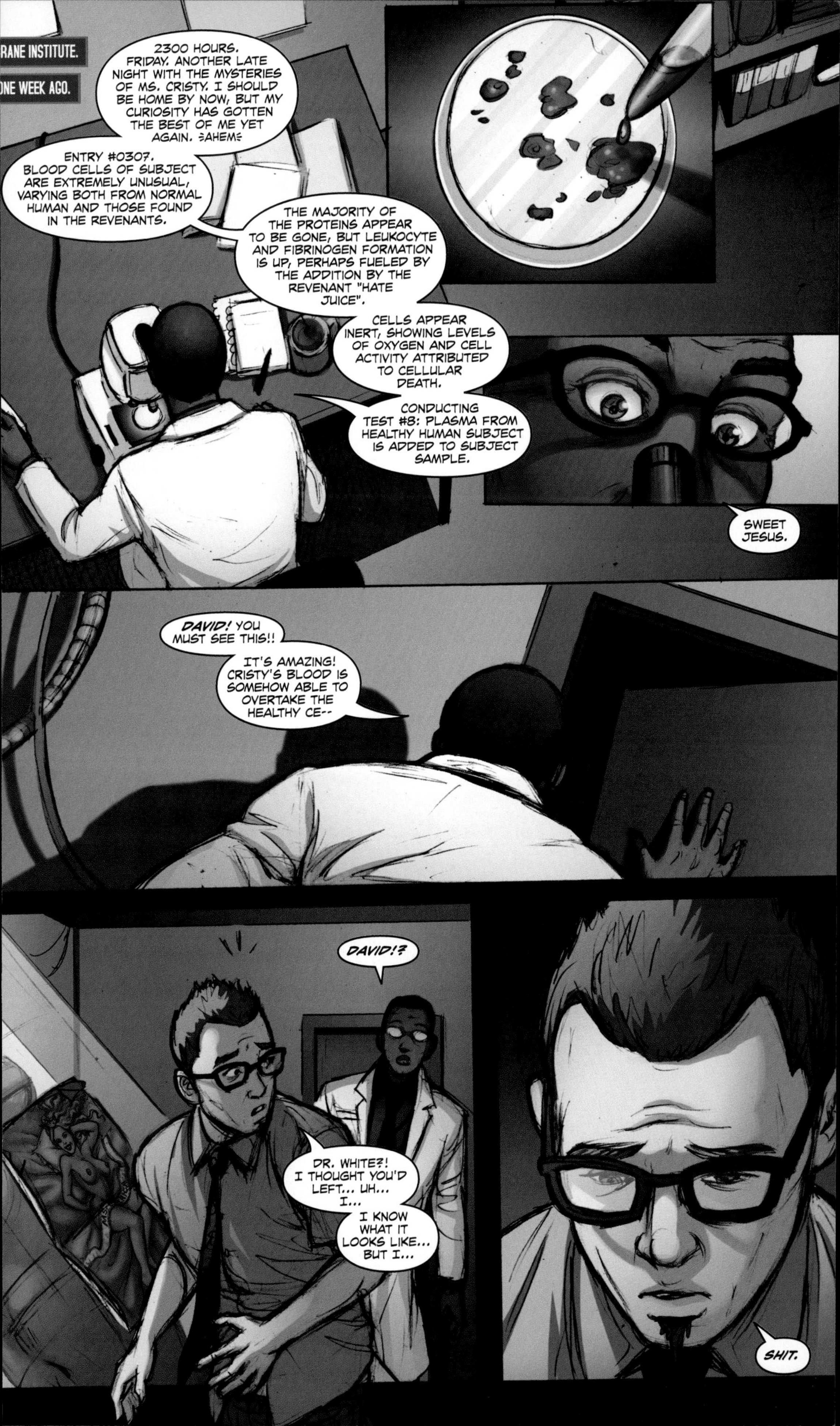

...RANE INSTITUTE.
ONE WEEK AGO.
2300 HOURS. FRIDAY. ANOTHER LATE NIGHT WITH THE MYSTERIES OF MS. CRISTY. I SHOULD BE HOME BY NOW, BUT MY CURIOSITY HAS GOTTEN THE BEST OF ME YET AGAIN. ≈AHEM≈
ENTRY #0307. BLOOD CELLS OF SUBJECT ARE EXTREMELY UNUSUAL, VARYING BOTH FROM NORMAL HUMAN AND THOSE FOUND IN THE REVENANTS.
THE MAJORITY OF THE PROTEINS APPEAR TO BE GONE, BUT LEUKOCYTE AND FIBRINOGEN FORMATION IS UP, PERHAPS FUELED BY THE ADDITION BY THE REVENANT "HATE JUICE".
CELLS APPEAR INERT, SHOWING LEVELS OF OXYGEN AND CELL ACTIVITY ATTRIBUTED TO CELLULAR DEATH.
CONDUCTING TEST #8: PLASMA FROM HEALTHY HUMAN SUBJECT IS ADDED TO SUBJECT SAMPLE.
SWEET JESUS.
DAVID! YOU MUST SEE THIS!!
IT'S AMAZING! CRISTY'S BLOOD IS SOMEHOW ABLE TO OVERTAKE THE HEALTHY CE--
DAVID!?
DR. WHITE?! I THOUGHT YOU'D LEFT... UH... I...
I KNOW WHAT IT LOOKS LIKE... BUT I...
SHIT.

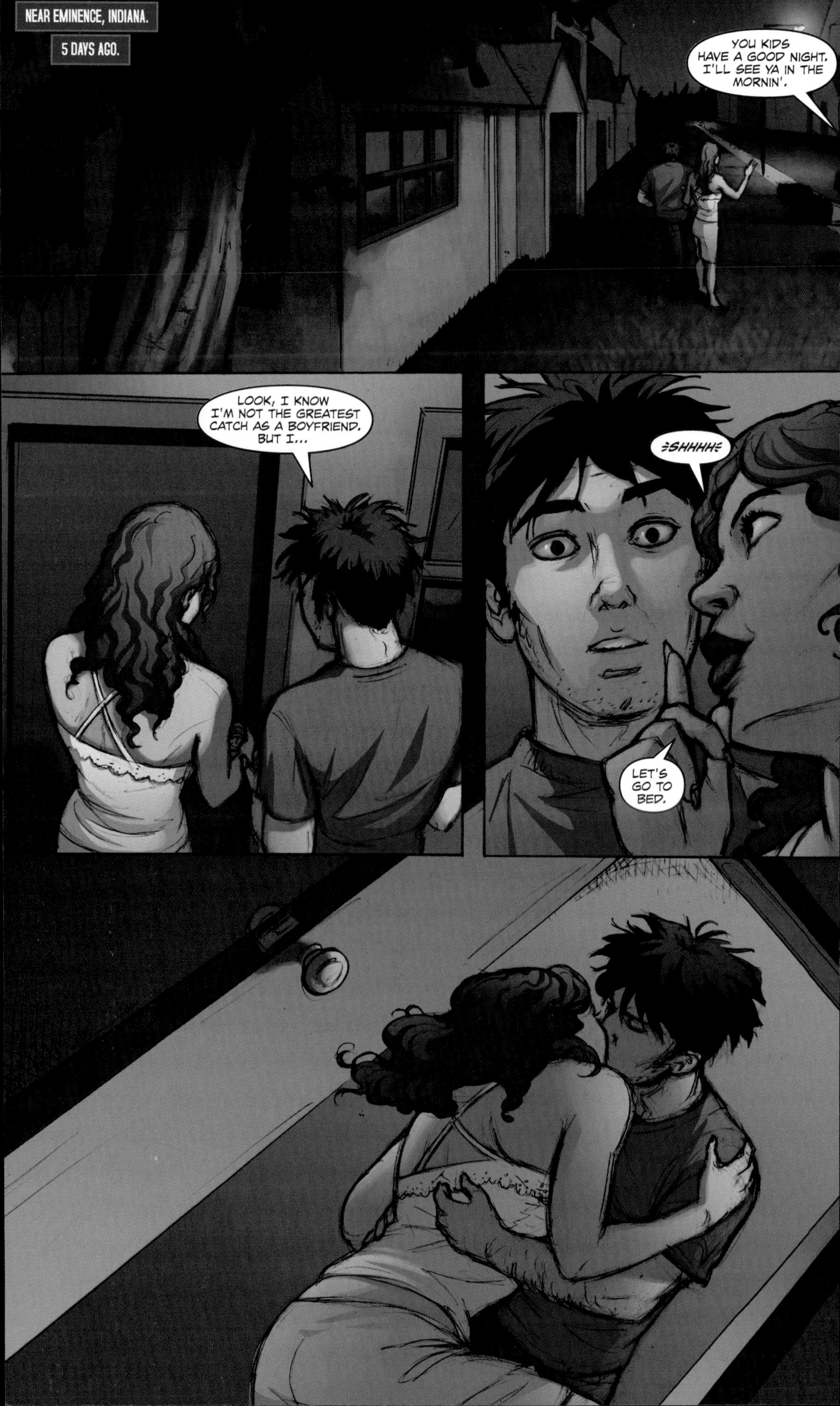

NEAR EMINENCE, INDIANA.
5 DAYS AGO.
YOU KIDS HAVE A GOOD NIGHT. I'LL SEE YA IN THE MORNIN'.
LOOK, I KNOW I'M NOT THE GREATEST CATCH AS A BOYFRIEND. BUT I...
SHHHH
LET'S GO TO BED.

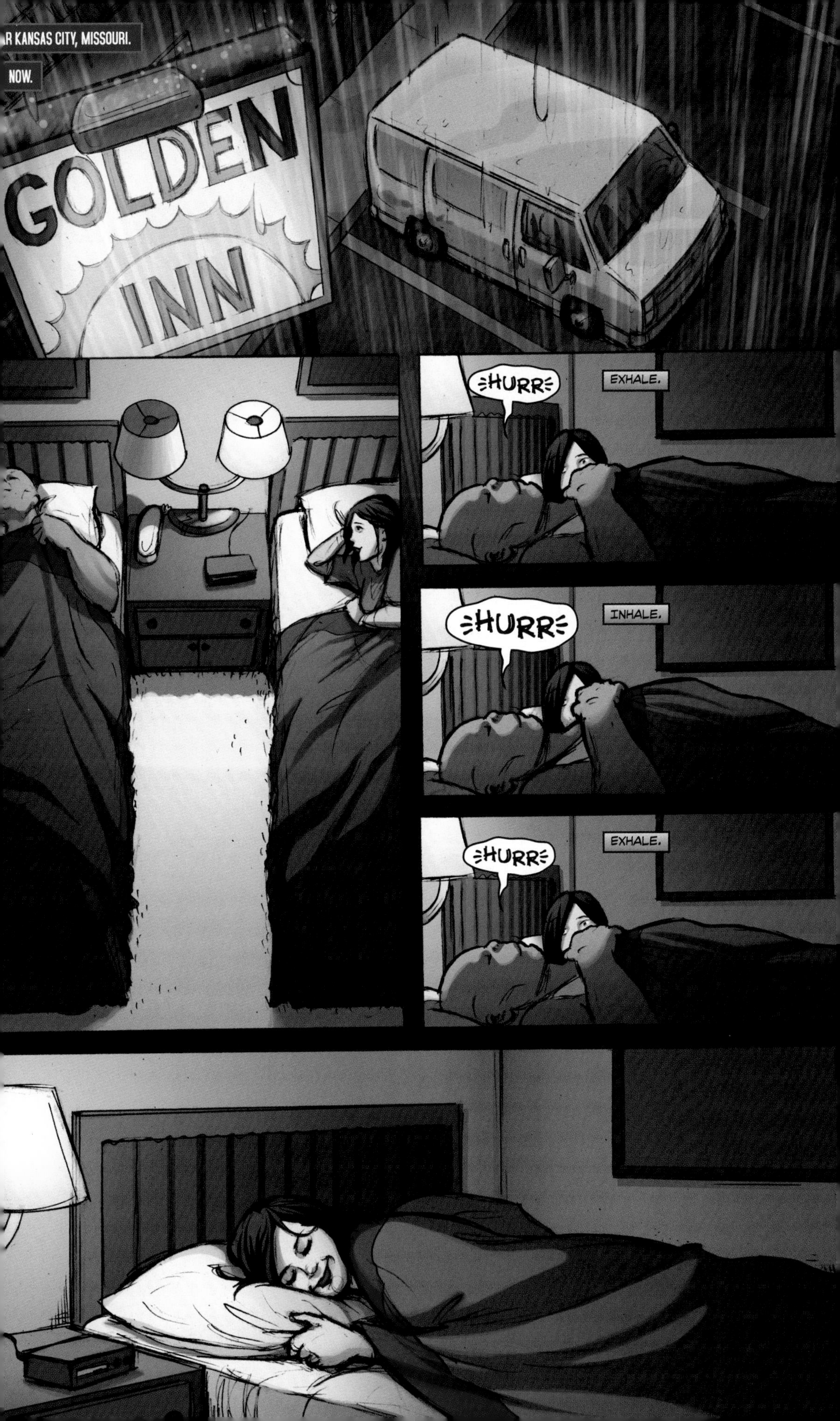
R KANSAS CITY, MISSOURI.
NOW.
GOLDEN INN
HURR
EXHALE.
HURR
INHALE.
HURR
EXHALE.

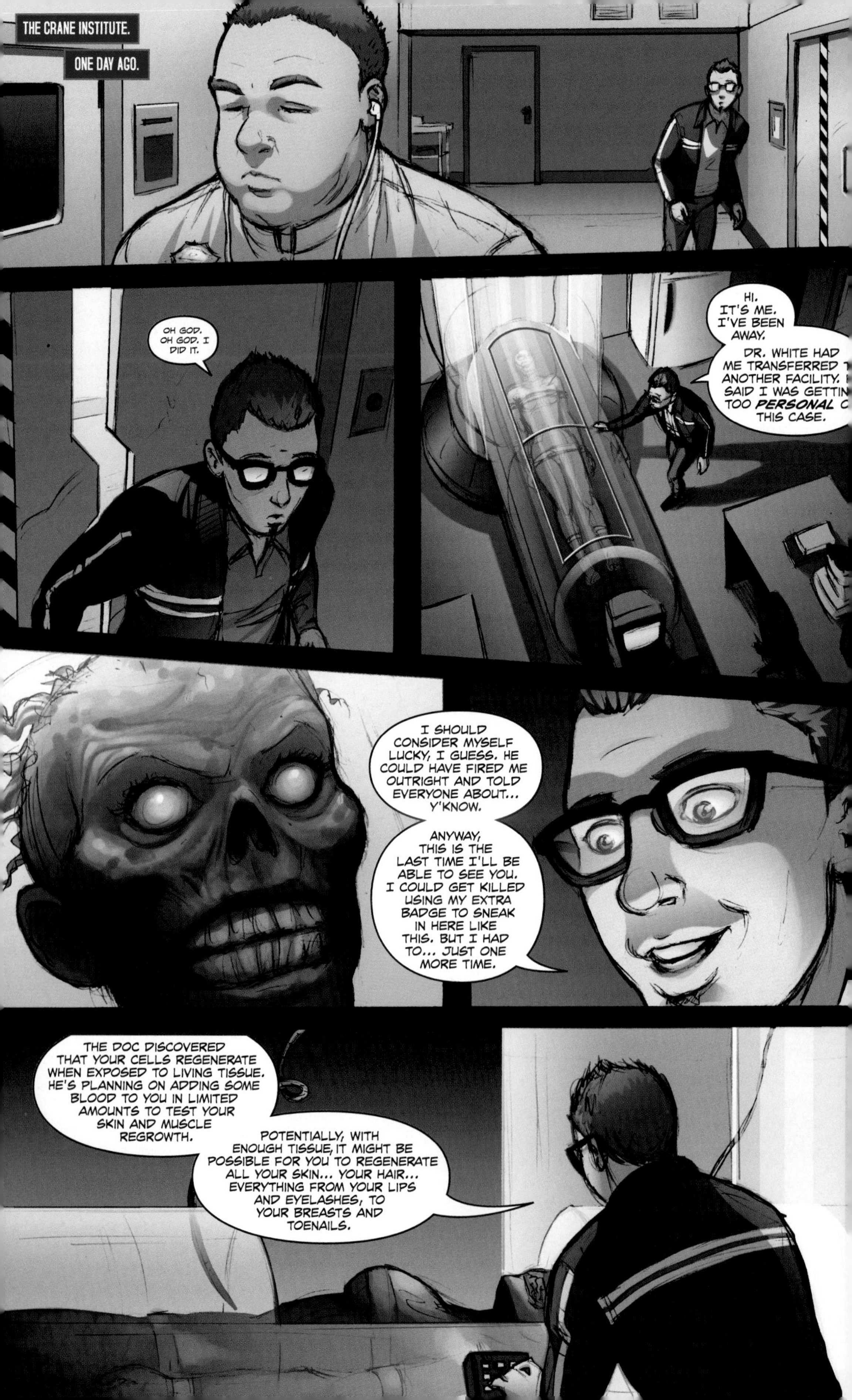
THE CRANE INSTITUTE.
ONE DAY AGO.
OH GOD. OH GOD. I DID IT.
HI. IT'S ME. I'VE BEEN AWAY.
DR. WHITE HAD ME TRANSFERRED T ANOTHER FACILITY. SAID I WAS GETTIN TOO *PERSONAL* C THIS CASE.
I SHOULD CONSIDER MYSELF LUCKY, I GUESS. HE COULD HAVE FIRED ME OUTRIGHT AND TOLD EVERYONE ABOUT... Y'KNOW.
ANYWAY, THIS IS THE LAST TIME I'LL BE ABLE TO SEE YOU. I COULD GET KILLED USING MY EXTRA BADGE TO SNEAK IN HERE LIKE THIS. BUT I HAD TO... JUST ONE MORE TIME.
THE DOC DISCOVERED THAT YOUR CELLS REGENERATE WHEN EXPOSED TO LIVING TISSUE. HE'S PLANNING ON ADDING SOME BLOOD TO YOU IN LIMITED AMOUNTS TO TEST YOUR SKIN AND MUSCLE REGROWTH.
POTENTIALLY, WITH ENOUGH TISSUE, IT MIGHT BE POSSIBLE FOR YOU TO REGENERATE ALL YOUR SKIN... YOUR HAIR... EVERYTHING FROM YOUR LIPS AND EYELASHES, TO YOUR BREASTS AND TOENAILS.

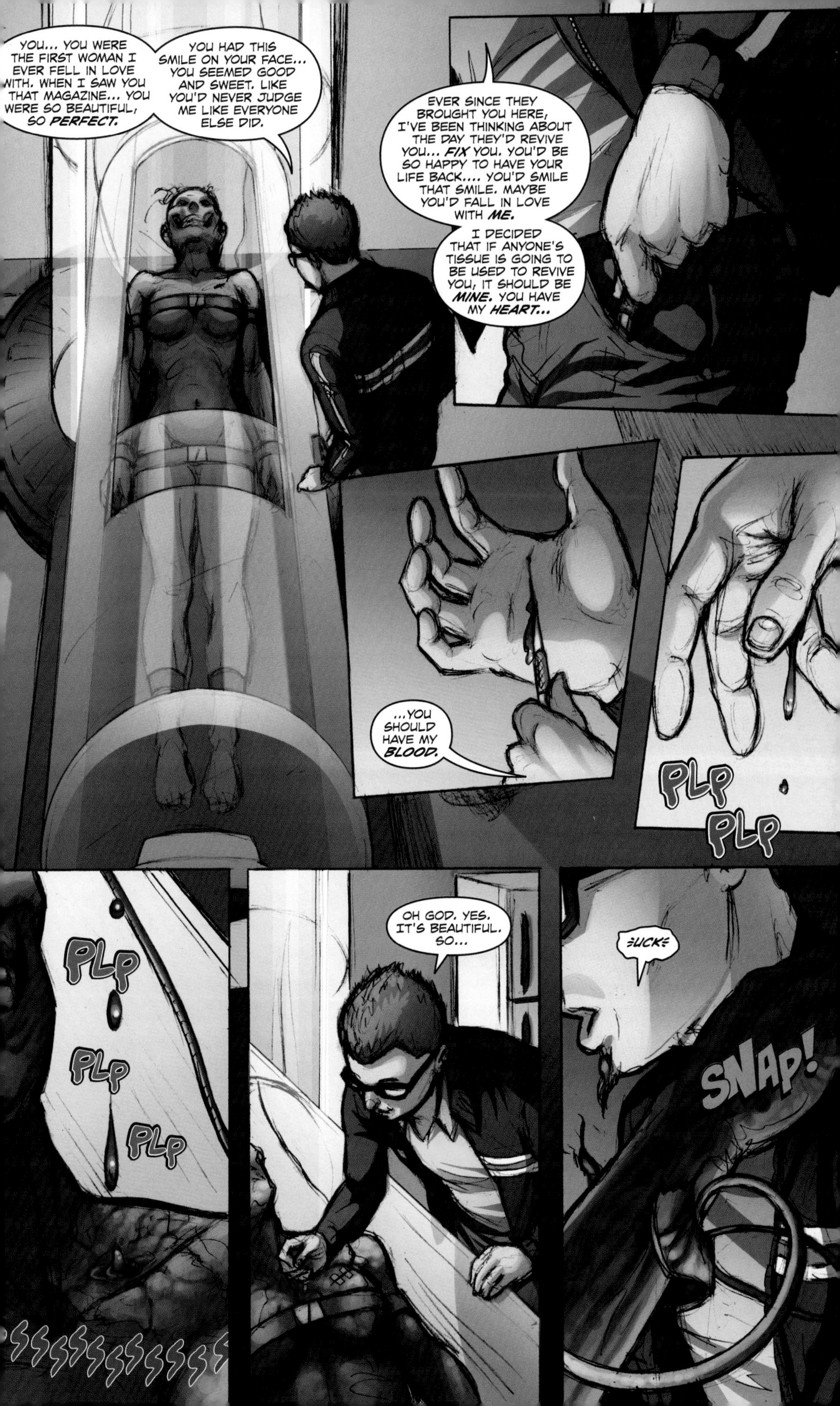
YOU... YOU WERE THE FIRST WOMAN I EVER FELL IN LOVE WITH. WHEN I SAW YOU THAT MAGAZINE... YOU WERE SO BEAUTIFUL, SO *PERFECT.*
YOU HAD THIS SMILE ON YOUR FACE... YOU SEEMED GOOD AND SWEET. LIKE YOU'D NEVER JUDGE ME LIKE EVERYONE ELSE DID.
EVER SINCE THEY BROUGHT YOU HERE, I'VE BEEN THINKING ABOUT THE DAY THEY'D REVIVE YOU... *FIX* YOU. YOU'D BE SO HAPPY TO HAVE YOUR LIFE BACK.... YOU'D SMILE THAT SMILE. MAYBE YOU'D FALL IN LOVE WITH *ME.*
I DECIDED THAT IF ANYONE'S TISSUE IS GOING TO BE USED TO REVIVE YOU, IT SHOULD BE *MINE.* YOU HAVE MY *HEART...*
...YOU SHOULD HAVE MY *BLOOD.*
PLP
PLP
PLP
PLP
PLP
SSSSSSSSSSSSS
OH GOD. YES. IT'S BEAUTIFUL. SO...
UCK
SNAP!

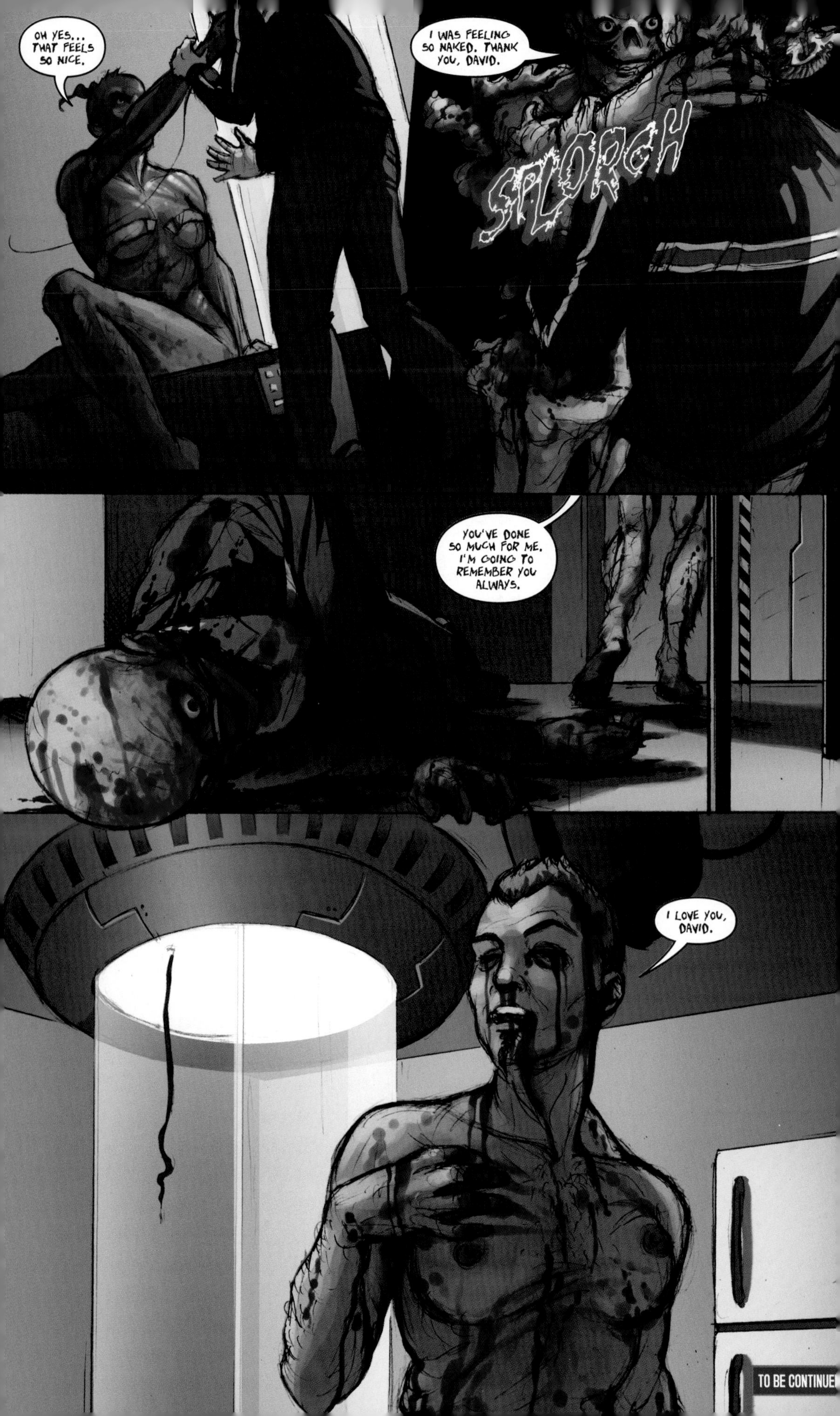
OH YES... THAT FEELS SO NICE.
I WAS FEELING SO NAKED. THANK YOU, DAVID.
SPLORCH
YOU'VE DONE SO MUCH FOR ME. I'M GOING TO REMEMBER YOU ALWAYS.
I LOVE YOU, DAVID.
TO BE CONTINUE

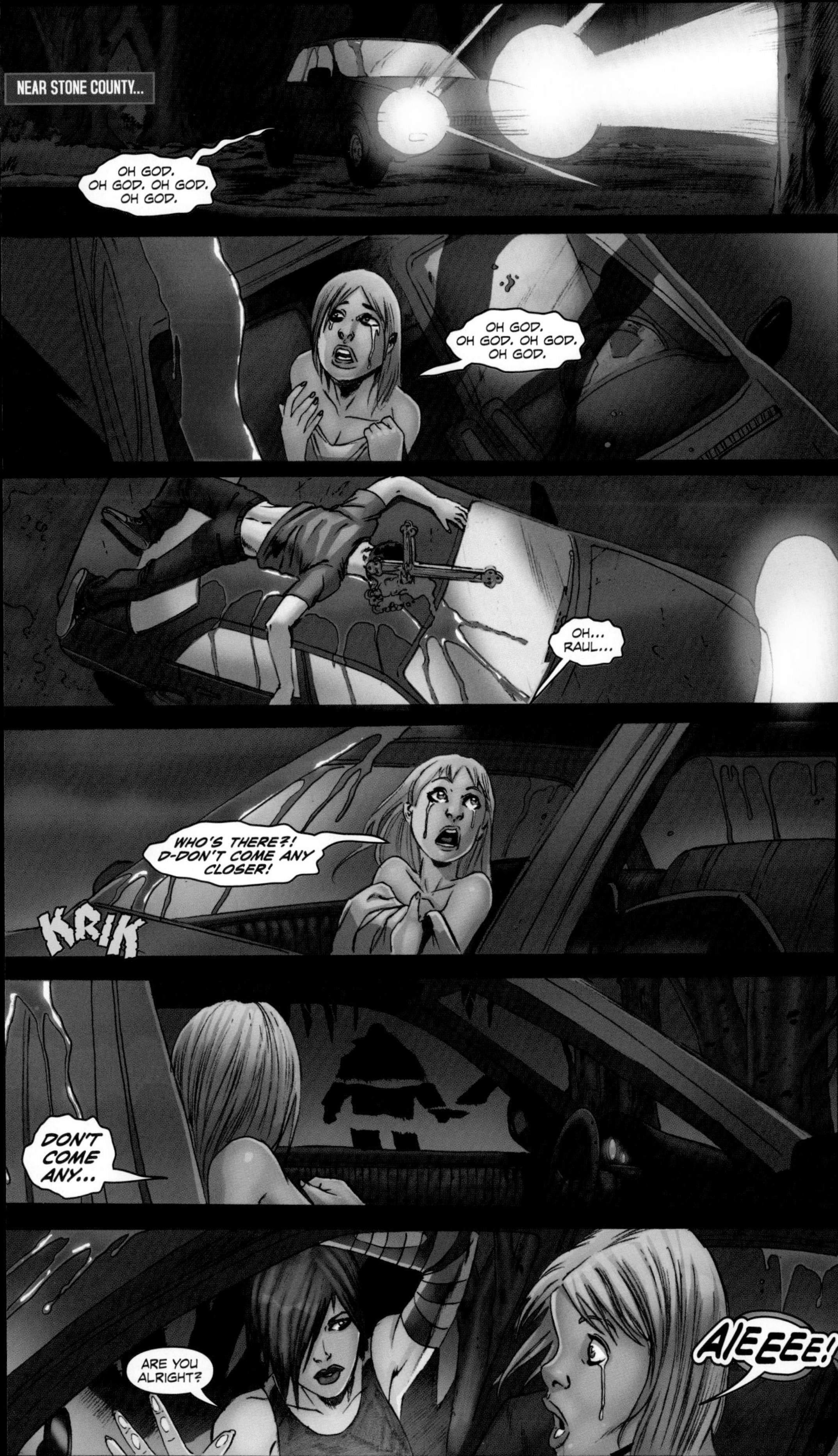
NEAR STONE COUNTY...
OH GOD. OH GOD. OH GOD. OH GOD.
OH GOD. OH GOD. OH GOD. OH GOD.
OH... RAUL...
WHO'S THERE?! D-DON'T COME ANY CLOSER!
KRIK
DON'T COME ANY...
ARE YOU ALRIGHT?
AIEEEE!

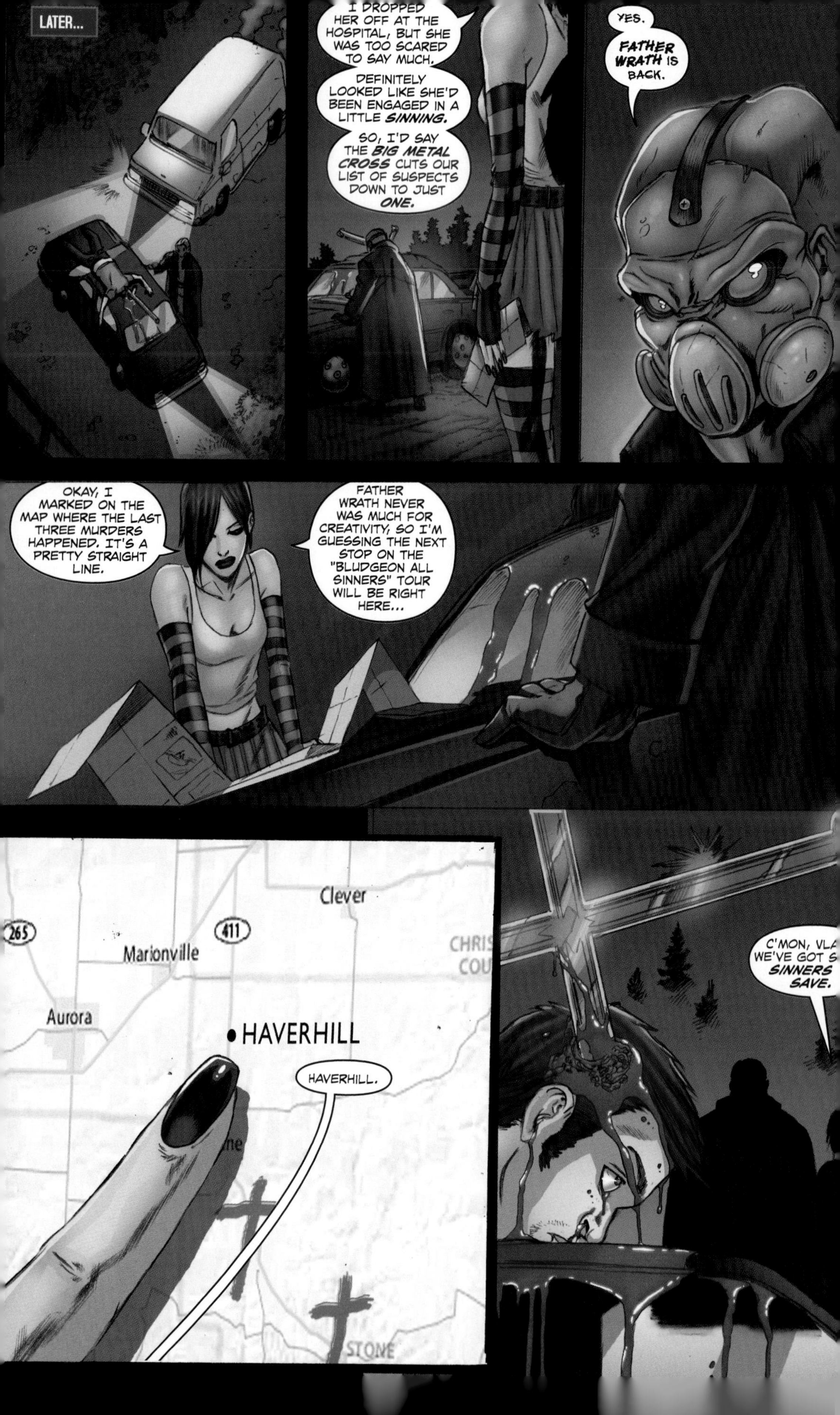
LATER...
I DROPPED HER OFF AT THE HOSPITAL, BUT SHE WAS TOO SCARED TO SAY MUCH.
DEFINITELY LOOKED LIKE SHE'D BEEN ENGAGED IN A LITTLE SINNING.
SO, I'D SAY THE BIG METAL CROSS CUTS OUR LIST OF SUSPECTS DOWN TO JUST ONE.
YES.
FATHER WRATH IS BACK.
OKAY, I MARKED ON THE MAP WHERE THE LAST THREE MURDERS HAPPENED. IT'S A PRETTY STRAIGHT LINE.
FATHER WRATH NEVER WAS MUCH FOR CREATIVITY, SO I'M GUESSING THE NEXT STOP ON THE "BLUDGEON ALL SINNERS" TOUR WILL BE RIGHT HERE...
Clever
265
411
Marionville
Aurora
HAVERHILL
HAVERHILL.
STONE
C'MON, VLA
WE'VE GOT S
SINNERS
SAVE.

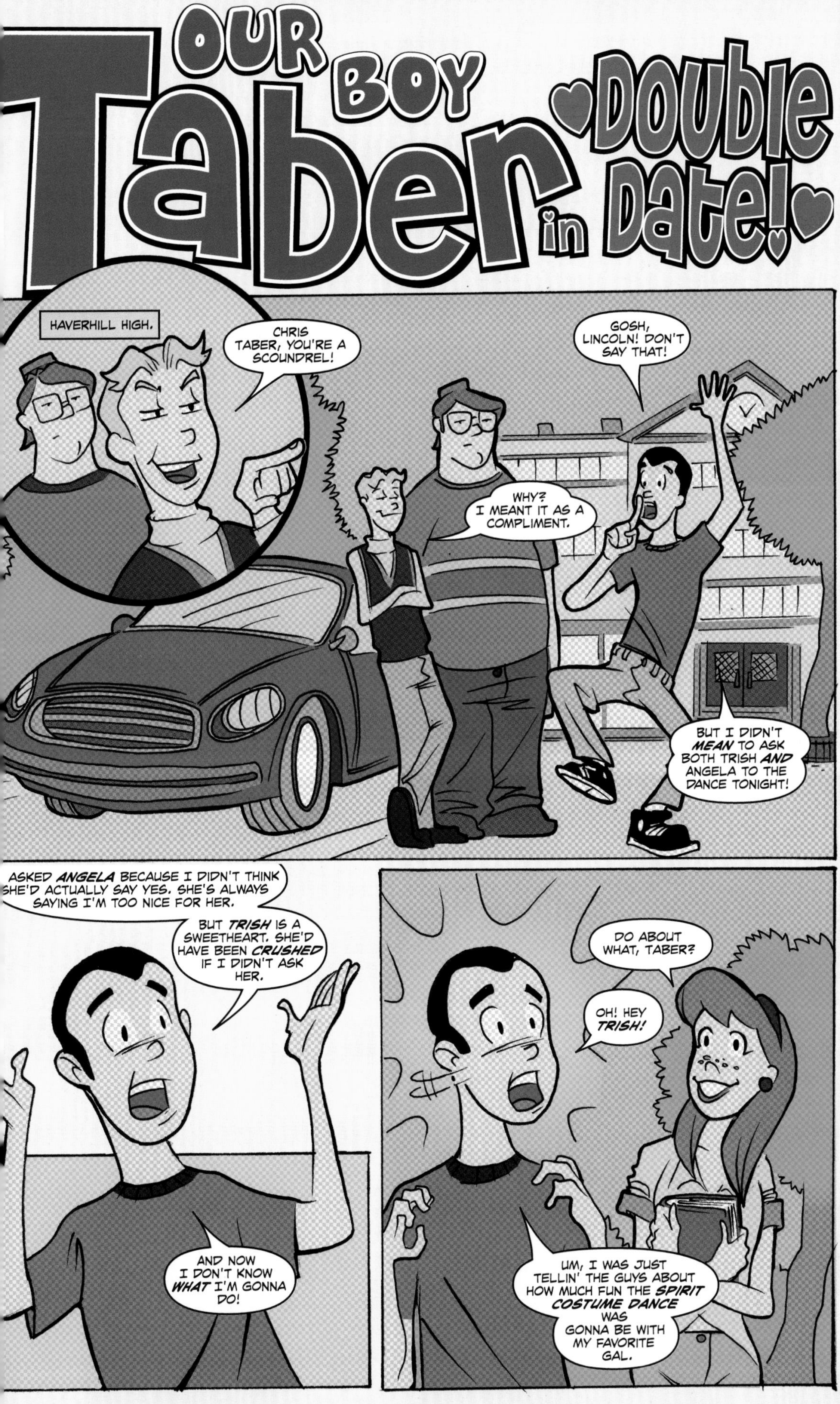
OUR BOY Taber in DOUBLE DATE!
HAVERHILL HIGH.
CHRIS TABER, YOU'RE A SCOUNDREL!
GOSH, LINCOLN! DON'T SAY THAT!
WHY? I MEANT IT AS A COMPLIMENT.
BUT I DIDN'T *MEAN* TO ASK BOTH TRISH *AND* ANGELA TO THE DANCE TONIGHT!
ASKED *ANGELA* BECAUSE I DIDN'T THINK SHE'D ACTUALLY SAY YES. SHE'S ALWAYS SAYING I'M TOO NICE FOR HER.
BUT *TRISH* IS A SWEETHEART. SHE'D HAVE BEEN *CRUSHED* IF I DIDN'T ASK HER.
AND NOW I DON'T KNOW *WHAT* I'M GONNA DO!
DO ABOUT WHAT, TABER?
OH! HEY *TRISH!*
UM, I WAS JUST TELLIN' THE GUYS ABOUT HOW MUCH FUN THE *SPIRIT COSTUME DANCE* WAS GONNA BE WITH MY FAVORITE GAL.

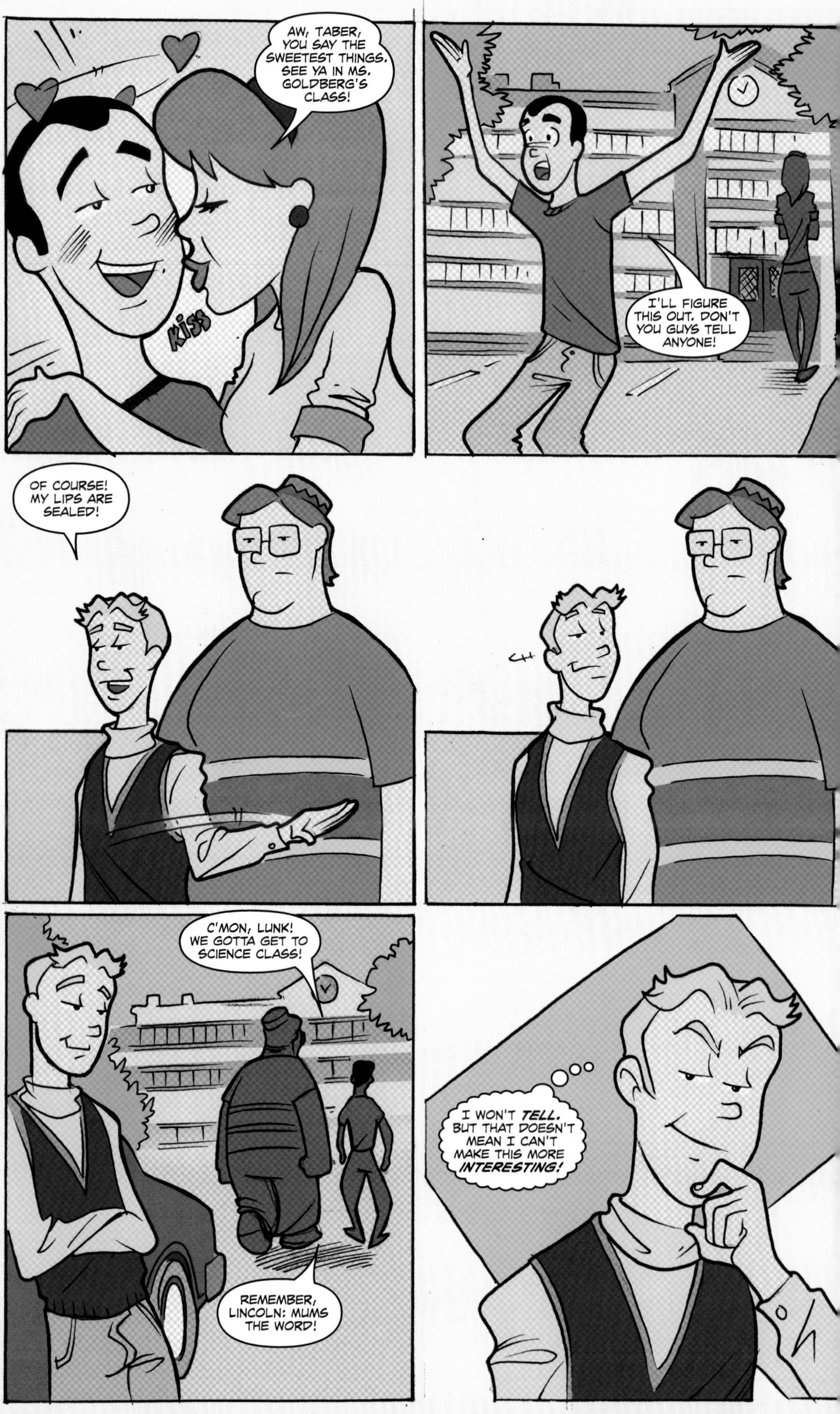
AW, TABER, YOU SAY THE SWEETEST THINGS. SEE YA IN MS. GOLDBERG'S CLASS!
KISS
I'LL FIGURE THIS OUT. DON'T YOU GUYS TELL ANYONE!
OF COURSE! MY LIPS ARE SEALED!
C'MON, LUNK! WE GOTTA GET TO SCIENCE CLASS!
REMEMBER, LINCOLN: MUMS THE WORD!
I WON'T TELL. BUT THAT DOESN'T MEAN I CAN'T MAKE THIS MORE INTERESTING!

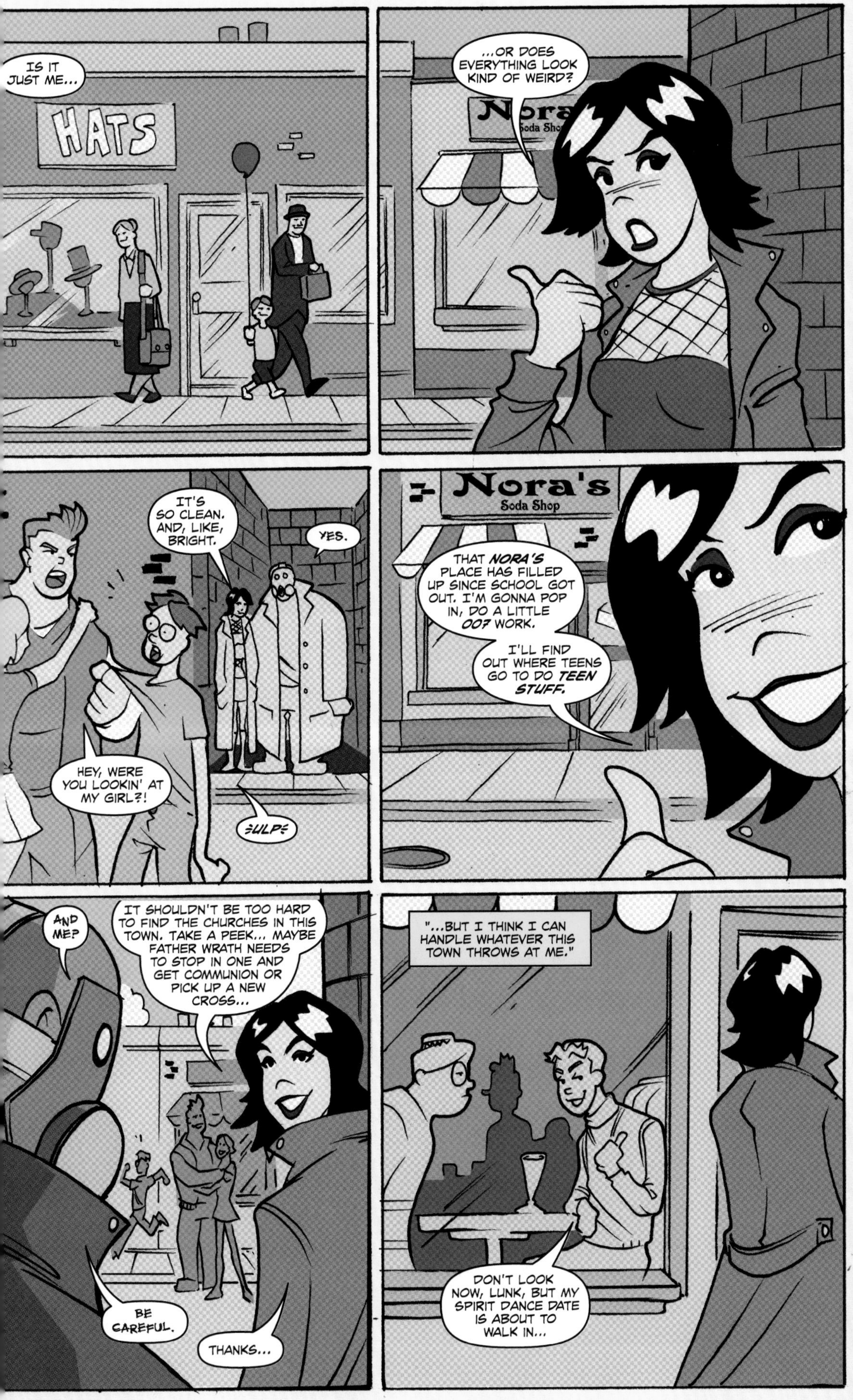
IS IT JUST ME...
HATS
...OR DOES EVERYTHING LOOK KIND OF WEIRD?
IT'S SO CLEAN. AND, LIKE, BRIGHT.
YES.
HEY, WERE YOU LOOKIN' AT MY GIRL?!
ULP
Nora's Soda Shop
THAT NORA'S PLACE HAS FILLED UP SINCE SCHOOL GOT OUT. I'M GONNA POP IN, DO A LITTLE 007 WORK.
I'LL FIND OUT WHERE TEENS GO TO DO TEEN STUFF.
AND ME?
IT SHOULDN'T BE TOO HARD TO FIND THE CHURCHES IN THIS TOWN. TAKE A PEEK... MAYBE FATHER WRATH NEEDS TO STOP IN ONE AND GET COMMUNION OR PICK UP A NEW CROSS...
BE CAREFUL.
THANKS...
"...BUT I THINK I CAN HANDLE WHATEVER THIS TOWN THROWS AT ME."
DON'T LOOK NOW, LUNK, BUT MY SPIRIT DANCE DATE IS ABOUT TO WALK IN...

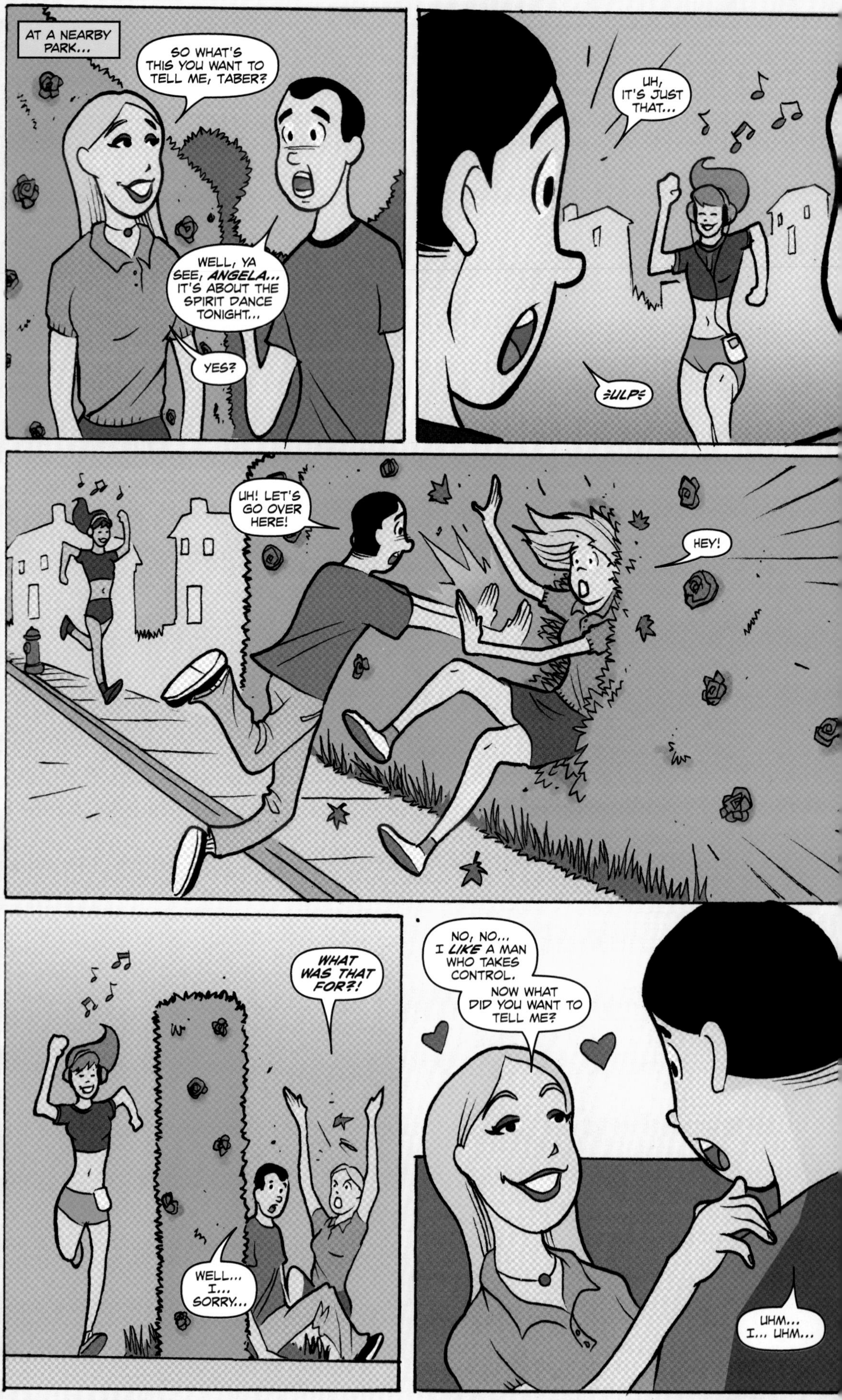

AT A NEARBY PARK...
SO WHAT'S THIS YOU WANT TO TELL ME, TABER?
WELL, YA SEE, ANGELA... IT'S ABOUT THE SPIRIT DANCE TONIGHT...
YES?
UH, IT'S JUST THAT...
GULP
UH! LET'S GO OVER HERE!
HEY!
WHAT WAS THAT FOR?!
WELL... I... SORRY...
NO, NO... I LIKE A MAN WHO TAKES CONTROL.
NOW WHAT DID YOU WANT TO TELL ME?
UHM... I... UHM...

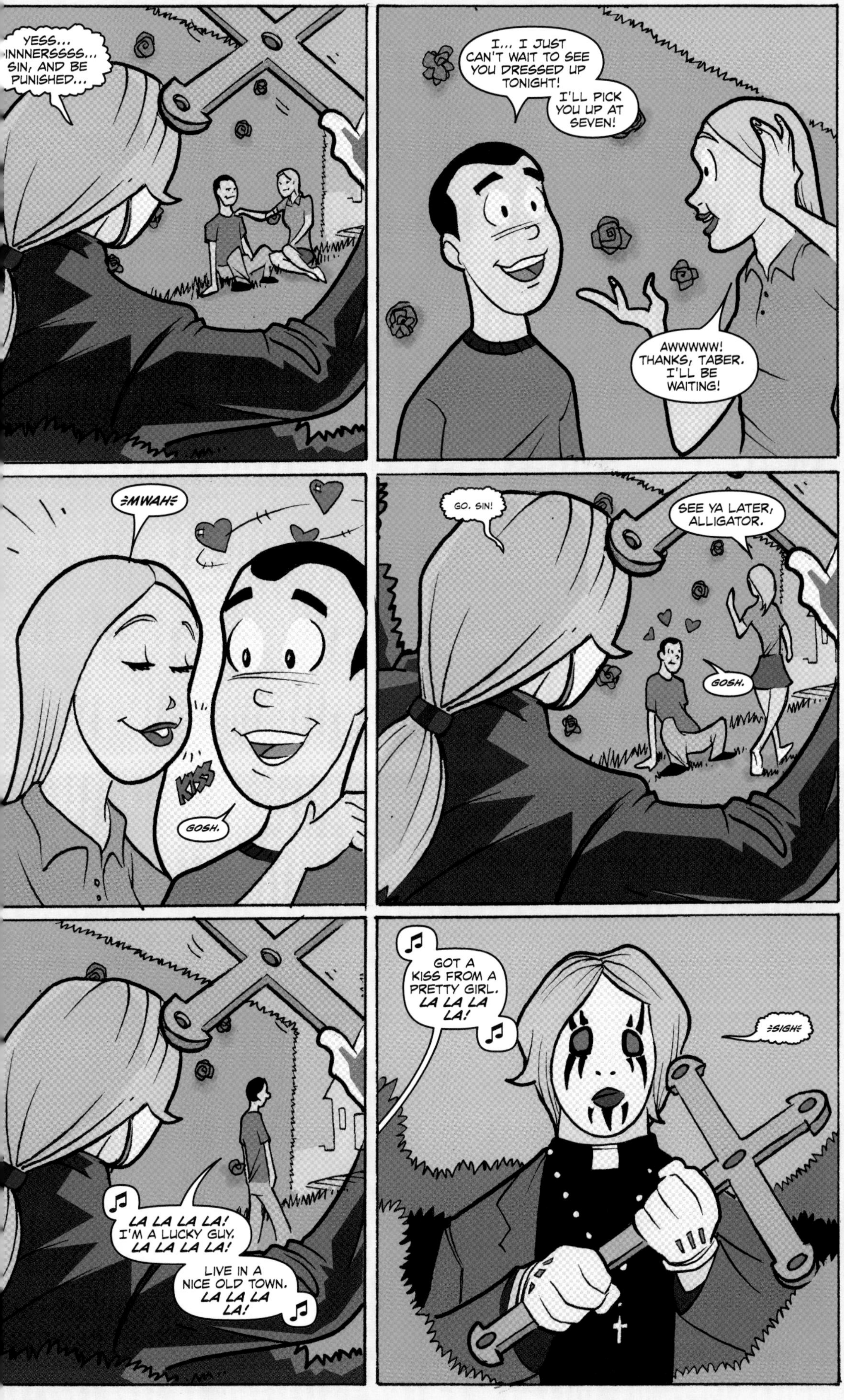
YESS... INNNERSSSS... SIN, AND BE PUNISHED...
I... I JUST CAN'T WAIT TO SEE YOU DRESSED UP TONIGHT!
I'LL PICK YOU UP AT SEVEN!
AWWWWW! THANKS, TABER. I'LL BE WAITING!
MWAH
KISS
GOSH.
GO. SIN!
SEE YA LATER, ALLIGATOR.
GOSH.
LA LA LA LA! I'M A LUCKY GUY. LA LA LA LA!
LIVE IN A NICE OLD TOWN. LA LA LA LA!
GOT A KISS FROM A PRETTY GIRL. LA LA LA LA!
SIGH

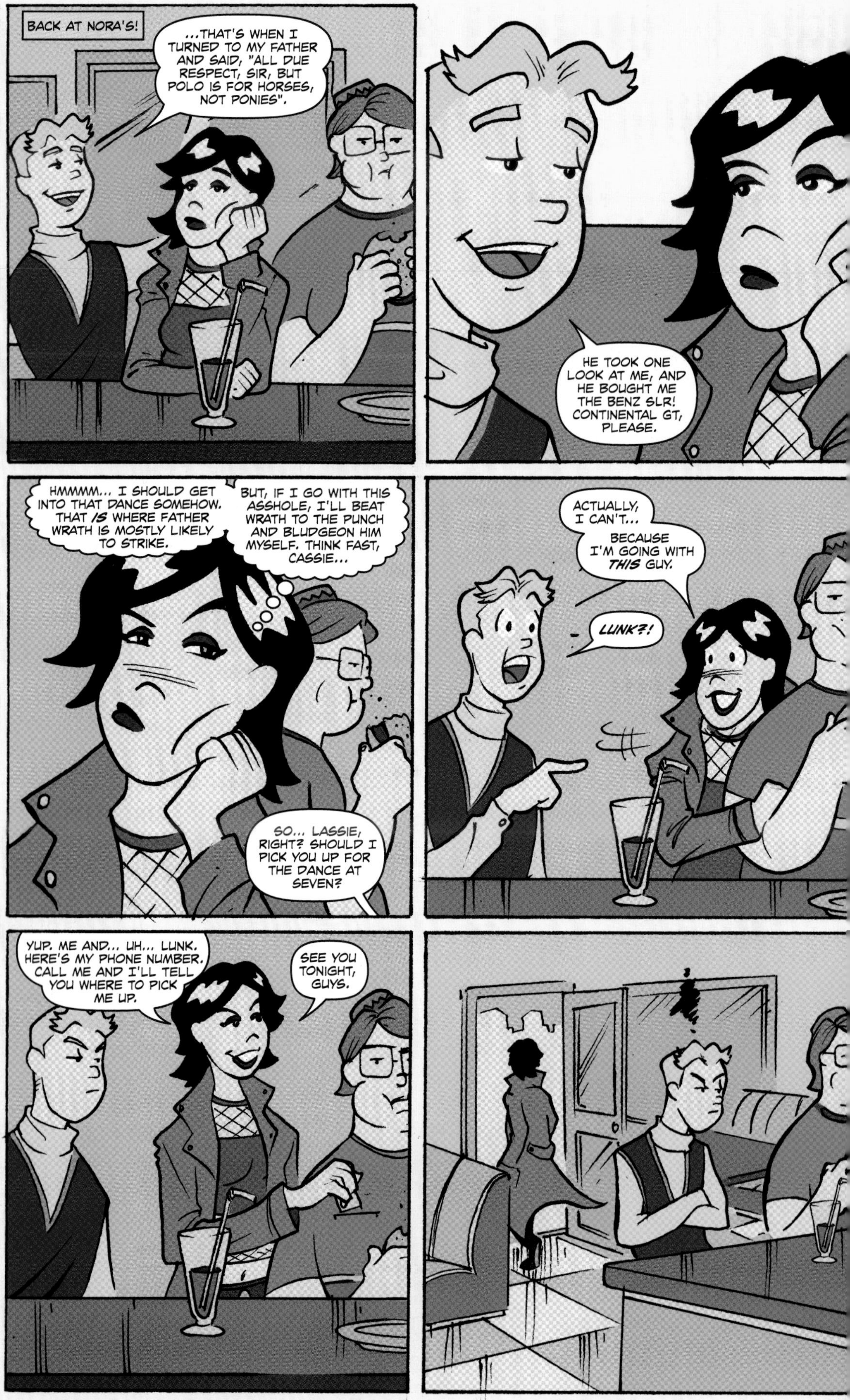
BACK AT NORA'S!
...THAT'S WHEN I TURNED TO MY FATHER AND SAID, "ALL DUE RESPECT, SIR, BUT POLO IS FOR HORSES, NOT PONIES".
HE TOOK ONE LOOK AT ME, AND HE BOUGHT ME THE BENZ SLR! CONTINENTAL GT, PLEASE.
HMMMM... I SHOULD GET INTO THAT DANCE SOMEHOW. THAT IS WHERE FATHER WRATH IS MOSTLY LIKELY TO STRIKE.
BUT, IF I GO WITH THIS ASSHOLE, I'LL BEAT WRATH TO THE PUNCH AND BLUDGEON HIM MYSELF. THINK FAST, CASSIE...
SO... LASSIE, RIGHT? SHOULD I PICK YOU UP FOR THE DANCE AT SEVEN?
ACTUALLY, I CAN'T...
BECAUSE I'M GOING WITH THIS GUY.
LUNK?!
YUP. ME AND... UH... LUNK. HERE'S MY PHONE NUMBER. CALL ME AND I'LL TELL YOU WHERE TO PICK ME UP.
SEE YOU TONIGHT, GUYS.

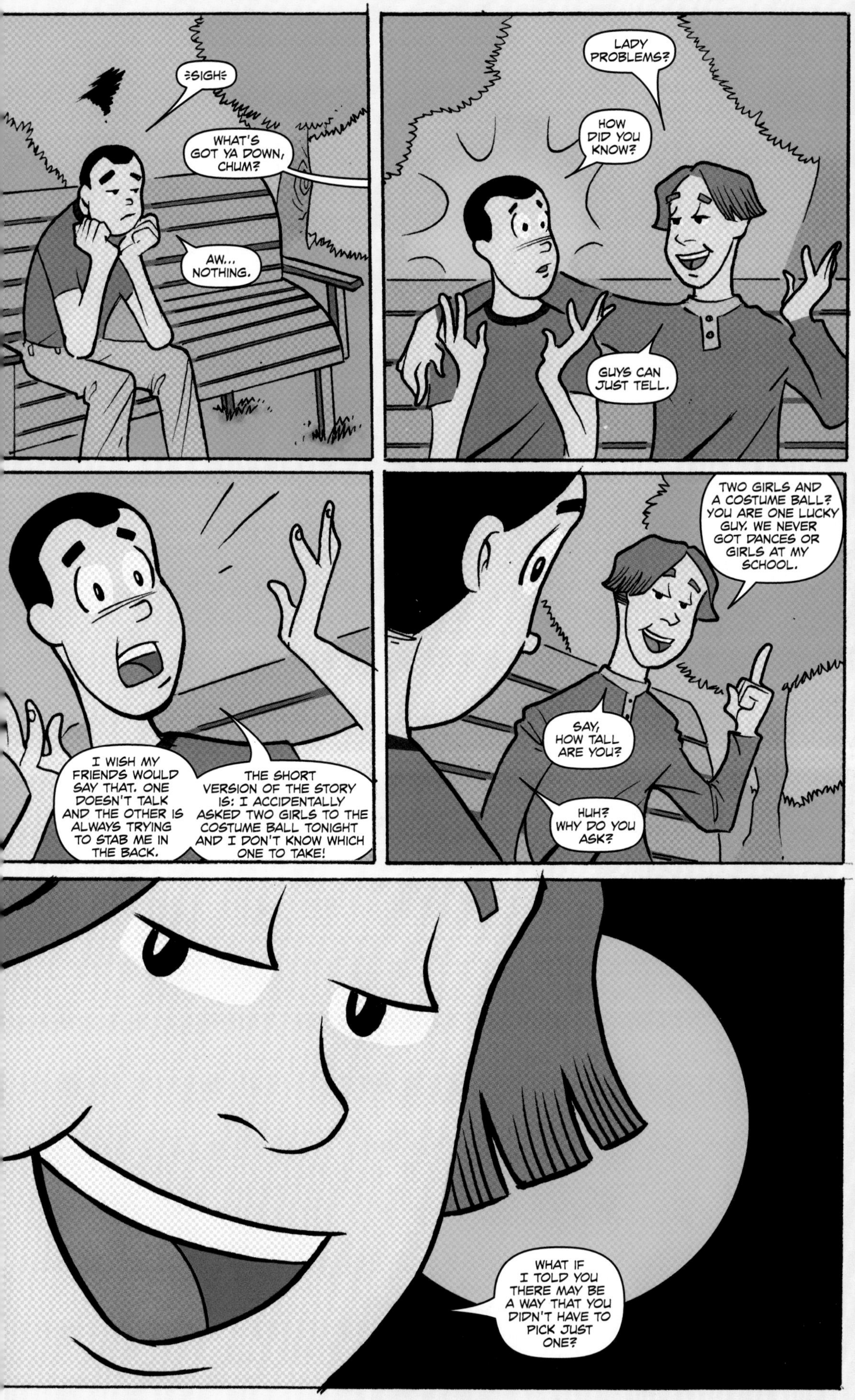

=SIGH=
WHAT'S GOT YA DOWN, CHUM?
AW... NOTHING.
LADY PROBLEMS?
HOW DID YOU KNOW?
GUYS CAN JUST TELL.
I WISH MY FRIENDS WOULD SAY THAT. ONE DOESN'T TALK AND THE OTHER IS ALWAYS TRYING TO STAB ME IN THE BACK.
THE SHORT VERSION OF THE STORY IS: I ACCIDENTALLY ASKED TWO GIRLS TO THE COSTUME BALL TONIGHT AND I DON'T KNOW WHICH ONE TO TAKE!
TWO GIRLS AND A COSTUME BALL? YOU ARE ONE LUCKY GUY. WE NEVER GOT DANCES OR GIRLS AT MY SCHOOL.
SAY, HOW TALL ARE YOU?
HUH? WHY DO YOU ASK?
WHAT IF I TOLD YOU THERE MAY BE A WAY THAT YOU DIDN'T HAVE TO PICK JUST ONE?

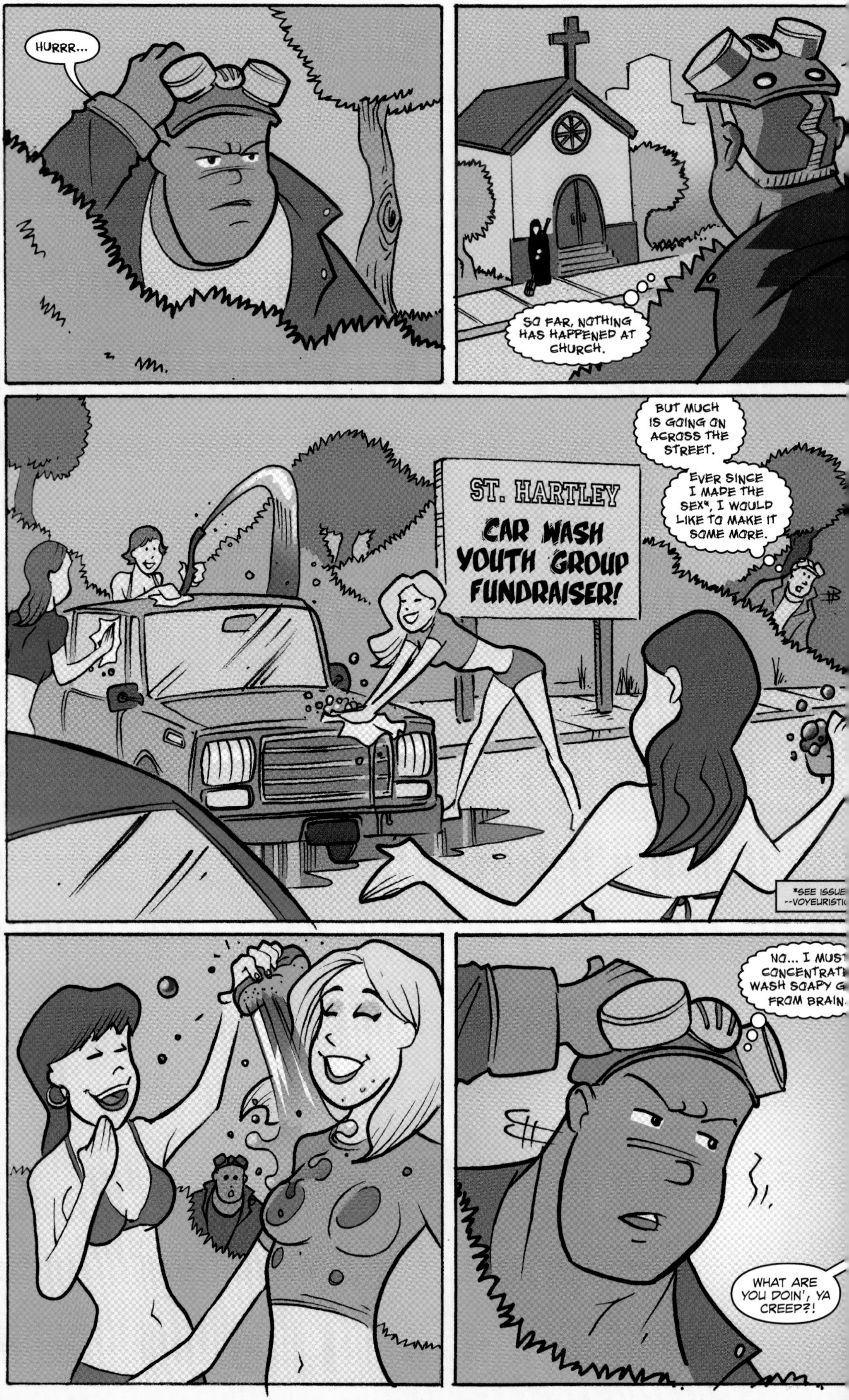
HURRR...
SO FAR, NOTHING HAS HAPPENED AT CHURCH.
BUT MUCH IS GOING ON ACROSS THE STREET.
EVER SINCE I MADE THE SEX*, I WOULD LIKE TO MAKE IT SOME MORE.
ST. HARTLEY
CAR WASH
YOUTH GROUP
FUNDRAISER!
*SEE ISSUE
--VOYEURISTI
NO... I MUST
CONCENTRAT
WASH SOAPY
FROM BRAIN
WHAT ARE YOU DOIN', YA CREEP?!

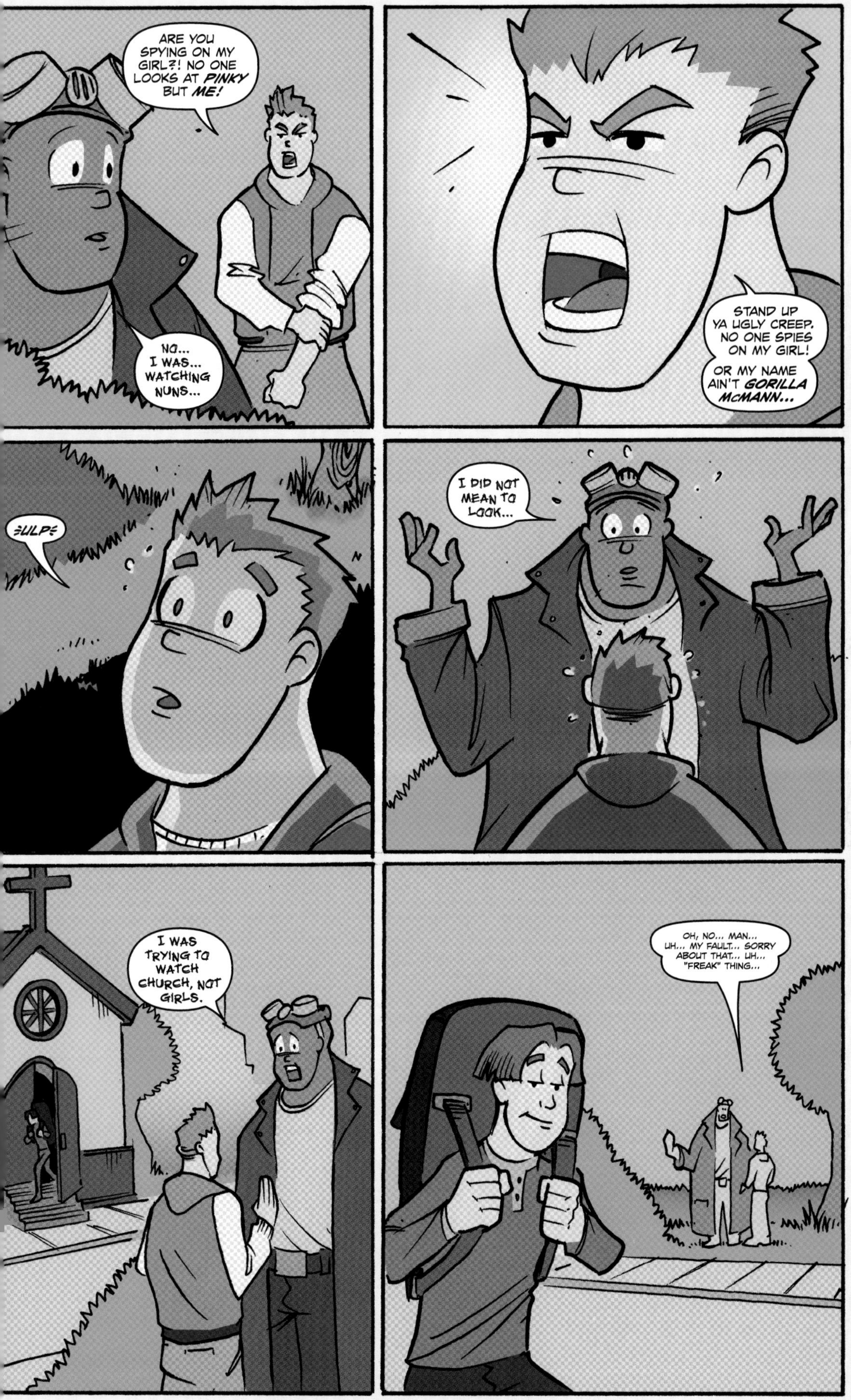

ARE YOU SPYING ON MY GIRL?! NO ONE LOOKS AT *PINKY* BUT *ME!*
NO... I WAS... WATCHING NUNS...
STAND UP YA UGLY CREEP. NO ONE SPIES ON MY GIRL!
OR MY NAME AIN'T *GORILLA McMANN...*
GULP
I DID NOT MEAN TO LOOK...
I WAS TRYING TO WATCH CHURCH, NOT GIRLS.
OH, NO... MAN... UH... MY FAULT... SORRY ABOUT THAT... UH... "FREAK" THING...

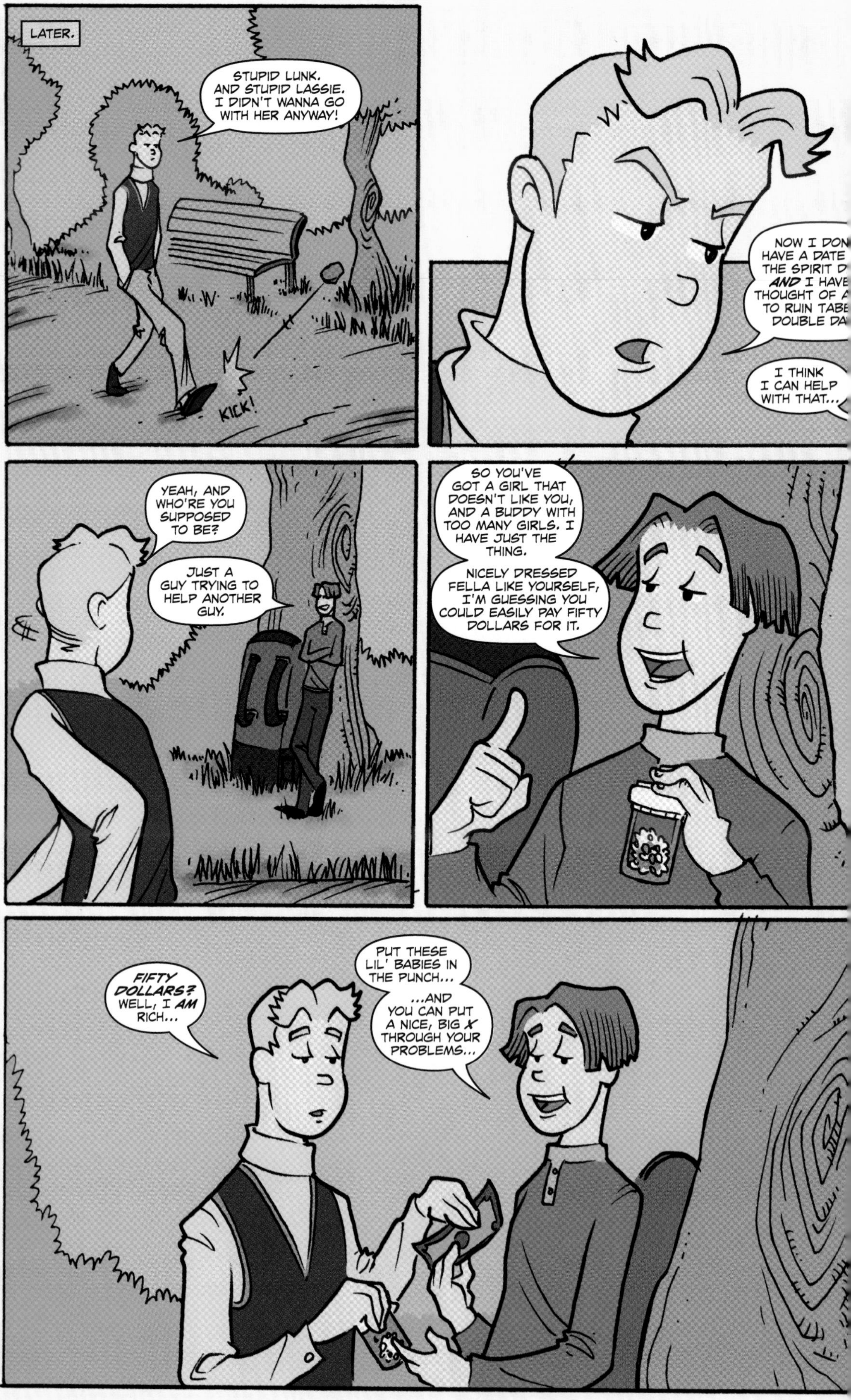

LATER.
STUPID LUNK. AND STUPID LASSIE. I DIDN'T WANNA GO WITH HER ANYWAY!
KICK!
NOW I DON HAVE A DATE THE SPIRIT D AND I HAVE THOUGHT OF A TO RUIN TABE DOUBLE DA
I THINK I CAN HELP WITH THAT...
YEAH, AND WHO'RE YOU SUPPOSED TO BE?
JUST A GUY TRYING TO HELP ANOTHER GUY.
SO YOU'VE GOT A GIRL THAT DOESN'T LIKE YOU, AND A BUDDY WITH TOO MANY GIRLS. I HAVE JUST THE THING.
NICELY DRESSED FELLA LIKE YOURSELF, I'M GUESSING YOU COULD EASILY PAY FIFTY DOLLARS FOR IT.
FIFTY DOLLARS? WELL, I AM RICH...
PUT THESE LIL' BABIES IN THE PUNCH...
...AND YOU CAN PUT A NICE, BIG X THROUGH YOUR PROBLEMS...

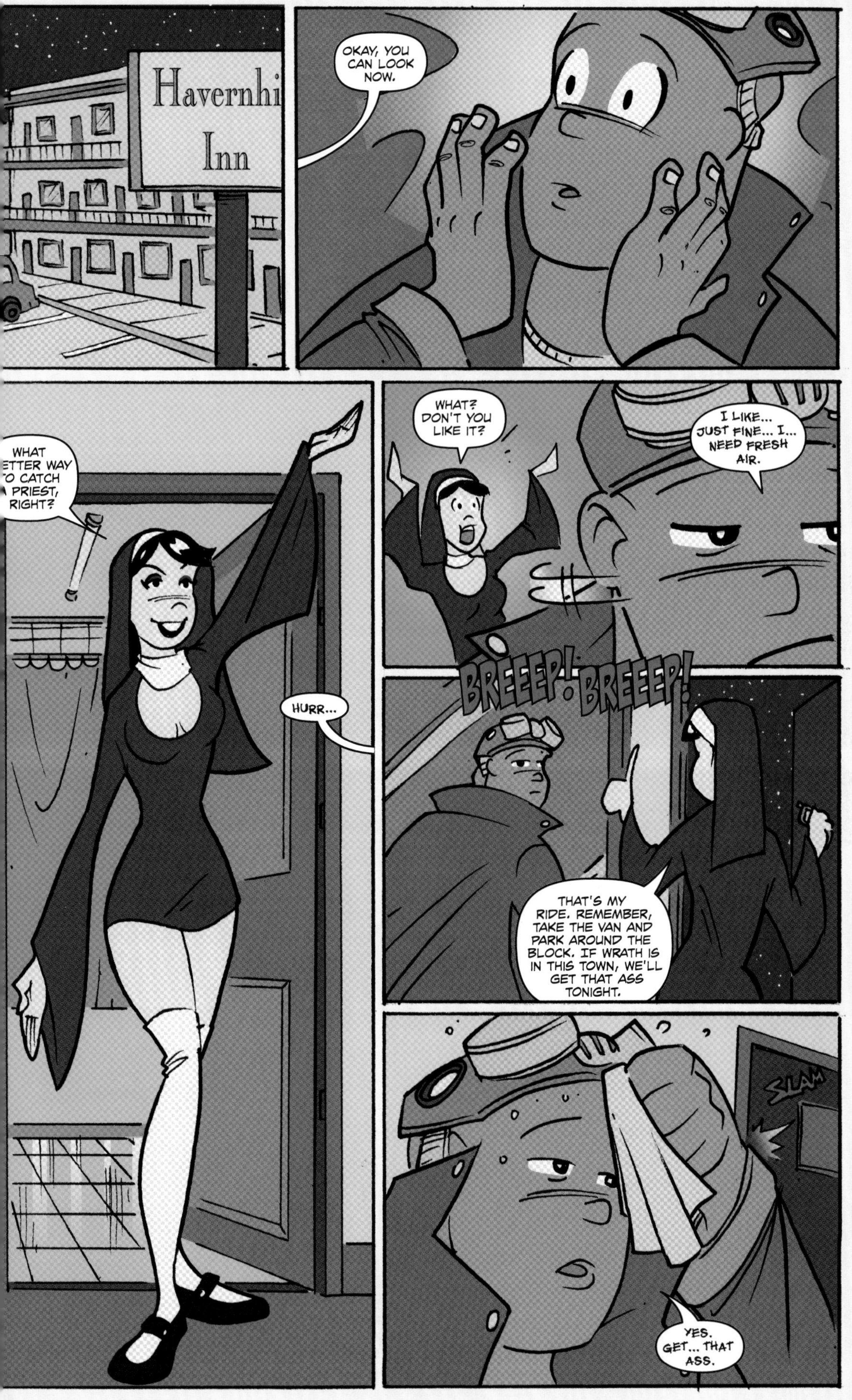
Havernhi
Inn
OKAY, YOU CAN LOOK NOW.
WHAT BETTER WAY TO CATCH A PRIEST, RIGHT?
HURR...
WHAT? DON'T YOU LIKE IT?
I LIKE... JUST FINE... I... NEED FRESH AIR.
BREEEP! BREEEP!
THAT'S MY RIDE. REMEMBER, TAKE THE VAN AND PARK AROUND THE BLOCK. IF WRATH IS IN THIS TOWN, WE'LL GET THAT ASS TONIGHT.
SLAM
YES. GET... THAT ASS.

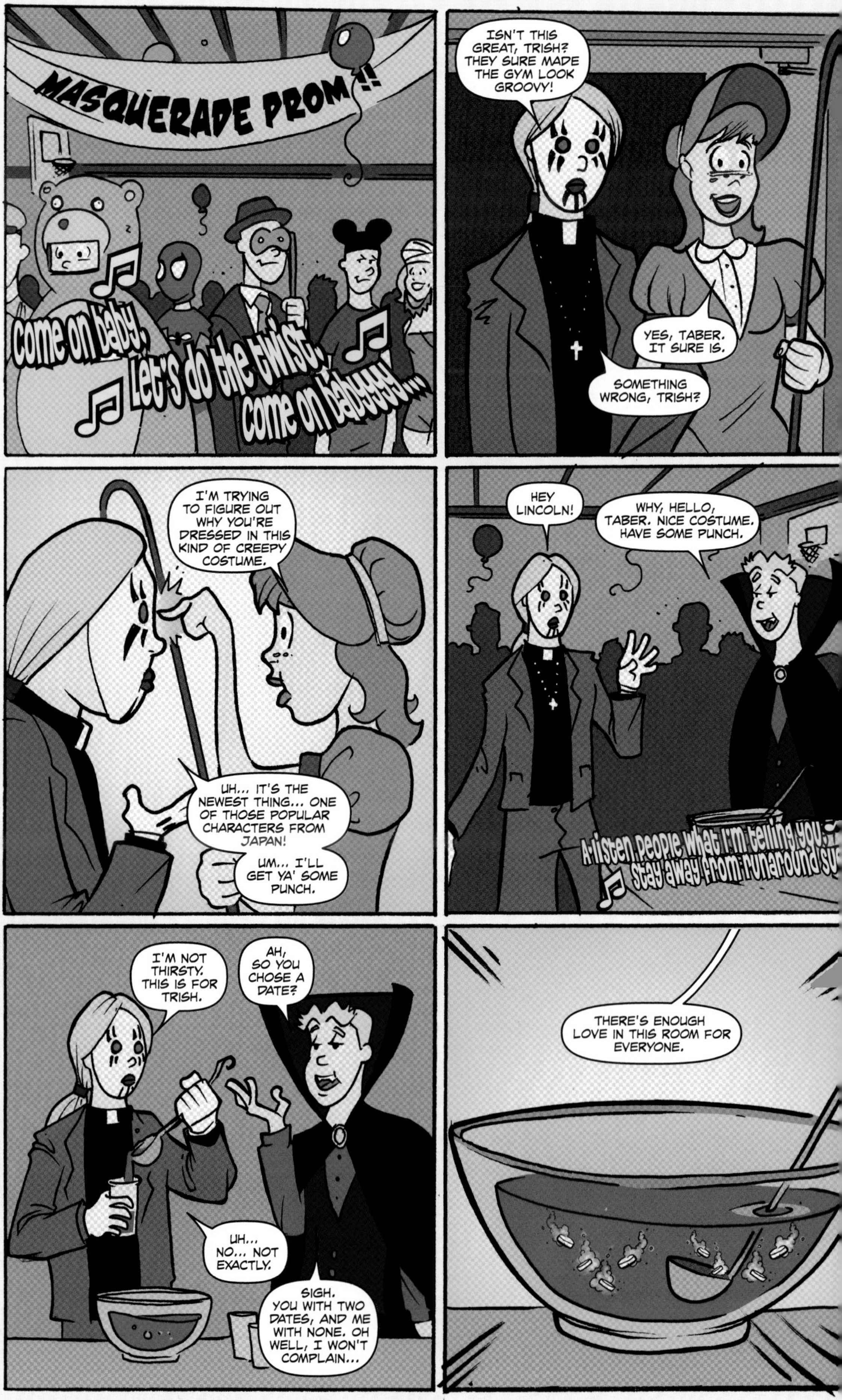
MASQUERADE PROM!!
Come on baby, Let's do the twist. Come on babyyy...
ISN'T THIS GREAT, TRISH? THEY SURE MADE THE GYM LOOK GROOVY!
YES, TABER. IT SURE IS.
SOMETHING WRONG, TRISH?
I'M TRYING TO FIGURE OUT WHY YOU'RE DRESSED IN THIS KIND OF CREEPY COSTUME.
UH... IT'S THE NEWEST THING... ONE OF THOSE POPULAR CHARACTERS FROM JAPAN!
UM... I'LL GET YA' SOME PUNCH.
HEY LINCOLN!
WHY, HELLO, TABER. NICE COSTUME. HAVE SOME PUNCH.
A-listen people what I'm telling you: stay away from runaround su
I'M NOT THIRSTY. THIS IS FOR TRISH.
AH, SO YOU CHOSE A DATE?
UH... NO... NOT EXACTLY.
SIGH. YOU WITH TWO DATES, AND ME WITH NONE. OH WELL, I WON'T COMPLAIN...
THERE'S ENOUGH LOVE IN THIS ROOM FOR EVERYONE.

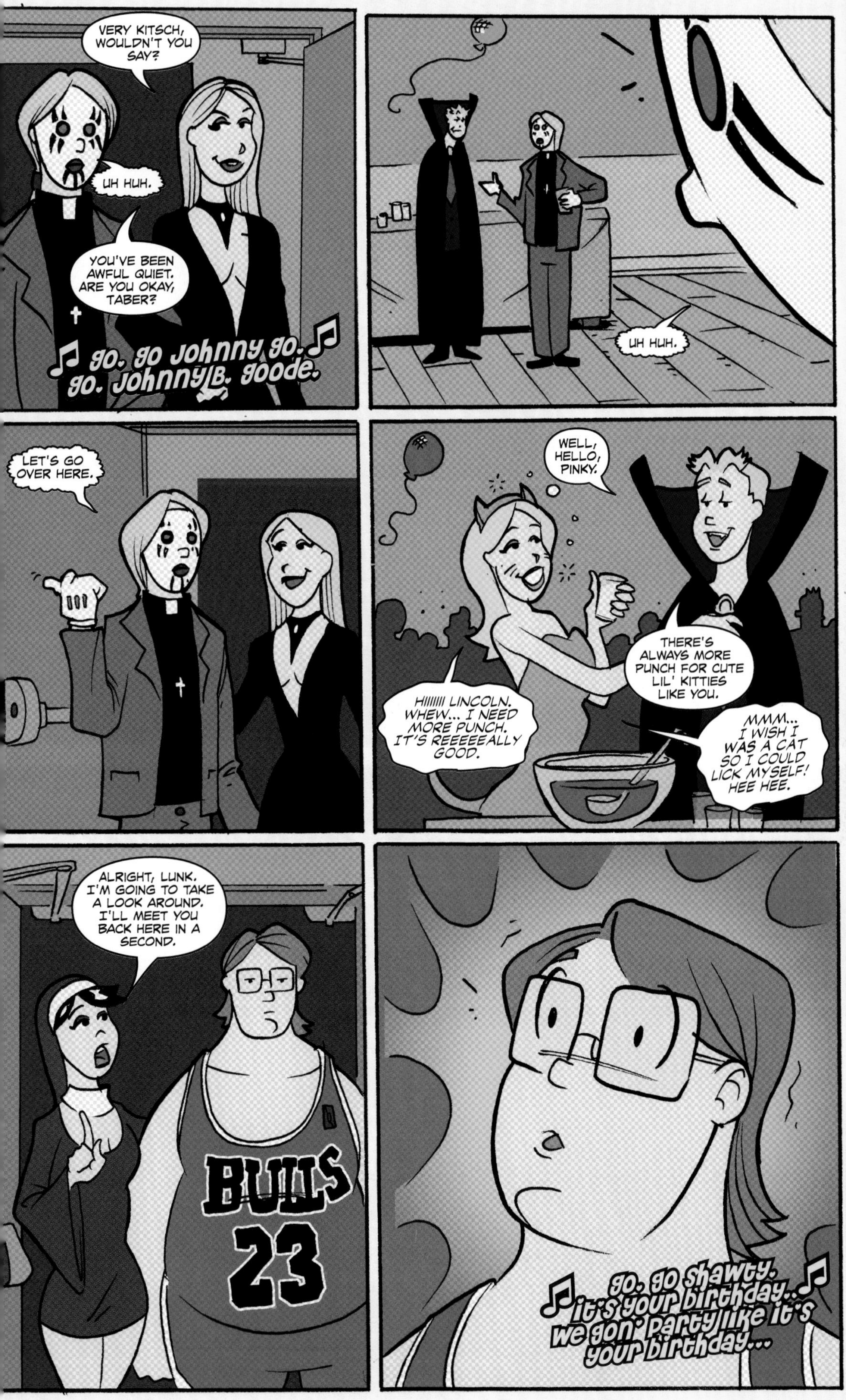
VERY KITSCH, WOULDN'T YOU SAY?
UH HUH.
YOU'VE BEEN AWFUL QUIET. ARE YOU OKAY, TABER?
go, go Johnny go. go, Johnny B. goode.
UH HUH.
LET'S GO OVER HERE.
WELL, HELLO, PINKY.
THERE'S ALWAYS MORE PUNCH FOR CUTE LIL' KITTIES LIKE YOU.
HIIIIIII LINCOLN. WHEW... I NEED MORE PUNCH. IT'S REEEEEALLY GOOD.
MMM... I WISH I WAS A CAT SO I COULD LICK MYSELF! HEE HEE.
ALRIGHT, LUNK. I'M GOING TO TAKE A LOOK AROUND. I'LL MEET YOU BACK HERE IN A SECOND.
BULLS
23
go, go shawty. it's your birthday... we gon' party like it's your birthday...

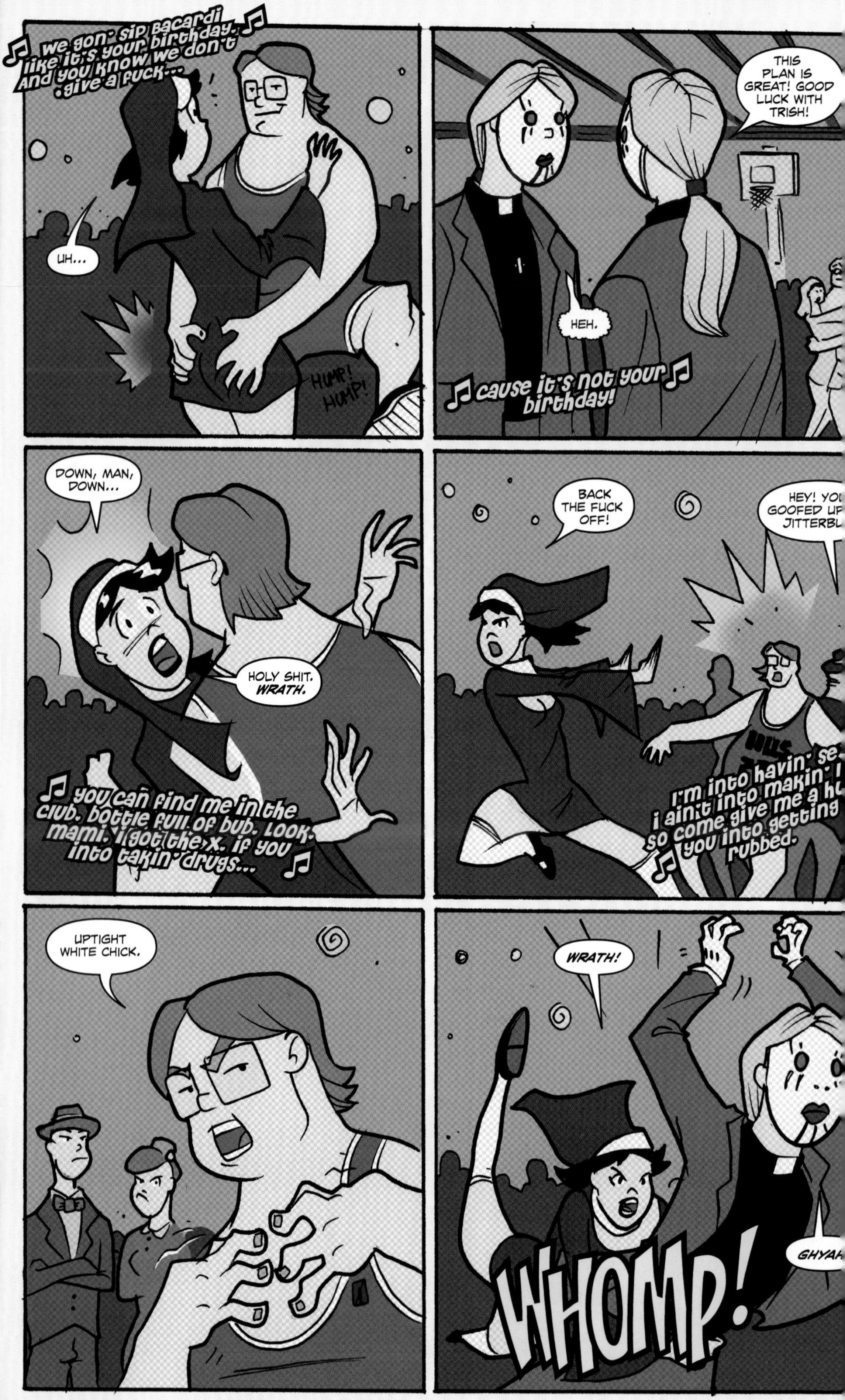

we gon' sip Bacardi like it's your birthday. And you know we don't give a fuck...
UH...
HUMP! HUMP!
THIS PLAN IS GREAT! GOOD LUCK WITH TRISH!
HEH.
cause it's not your birthday!
DOWN, MAN, DOWN...
HOLY SHIT. *WRATH.*
you can find me in the club. bottle full of bub. look. mami, i got the x. if you into takin' drugs...
BACK THE FUCK OFF!
HEY! YO GOOFED UP JITTERB
i'm into havin' se
i ain't into makin'
so come give me a h
you into getting rubbed.
UPTIGHT WHITE CHICK.
WRATH!
WHOMP!
GHYA

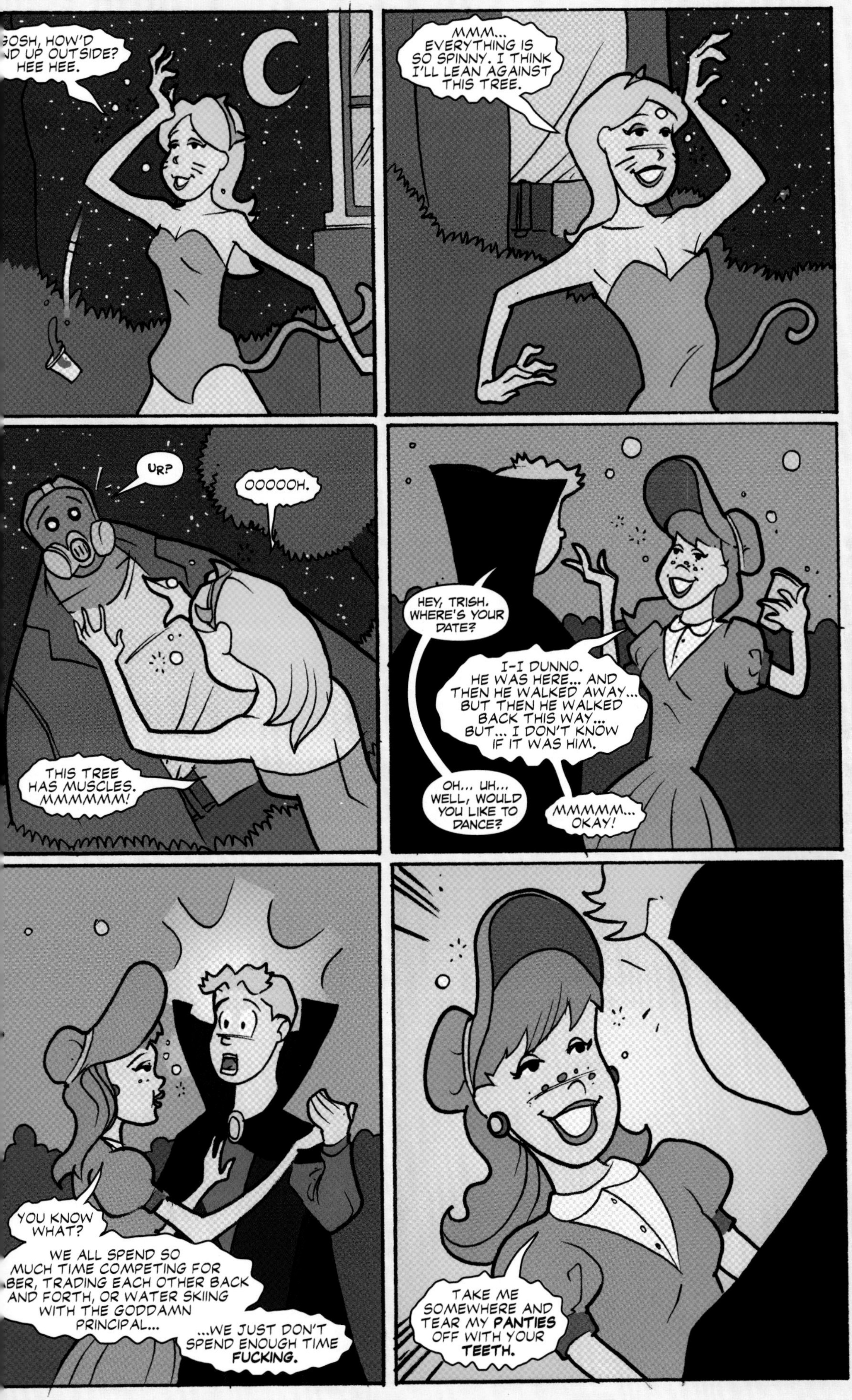
GOSH, HOW'D
ND UP OUTSIDE?
HEE HEE.
MMM... EVERYTHING IS SO SPINNY. I THINK I'LL LEAN AGAINST THIS TREE.
UR?
OOOOOH.
THIS TREE HAS MUSCLES. MMMMMM!
HEY, TRISH. WHERE'S YOUR DATE?
I-I DUNNO. HE WAS HERE... AND THEN HE WALKED AWAY... BUT THEN HE WALKED BACK THIS WAY... BUT... I DON'T KNOW IF IT WAS HIM.
OH... UH... WELL, WOULD YOU LIKE TO DANCE?
MMMMM... OKAY!
YOU KNOW WHAT?
WE ALL SPEND SO MUCH TIME COMPETING FOR
BER, TRADING EACH OTHER BACK AND FORTH, OR WATER SKIING WITH THE GODDAMN PRINCIPAL...
...WE JUST DON'T SPEND ENOUGH TIME **FUCKING.**
TAKE ME SOMEWHERE AND TEAR MY **PANTIES** OFF WITH YOUR **TEETH.**

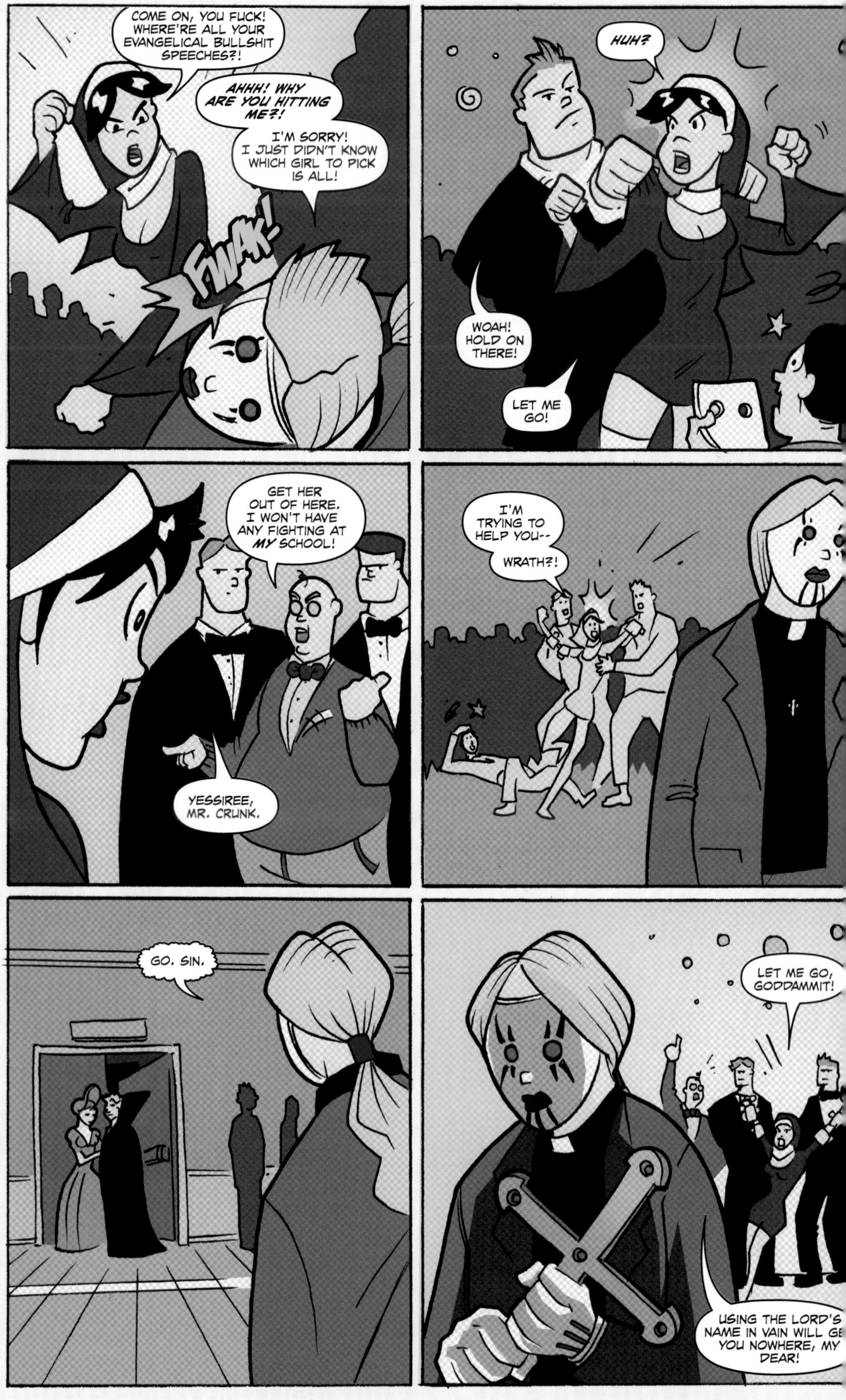
COME ON, YOU FUCK! WHERE'RE ALL YOUR EVANGELICAL BULLSHIT SPEECHES?!
AHHH! WHY ARE YOU HITTING ME?!
I'M SORRY! I JUST DIDN'T KNOW WHICH GIRL TO PICK IS ALL!
FWAK!
HUH?
WOAH! HOLD ON THERE!
LET ME GO!
GET HER OUT OF HERE. I WON'T HAVE ANY FIGHTING AT MY SCHOOL!
YESSIREE, MR. CRUNK.
I'M TRYING TO HELP YOU--
WRATH?!
GO. SIN.
LET ME GO, GODDAMMIT!
USING THE LORD'S NAME IN VAIN WILL GE YOU NOWHERE, MY DEAR!

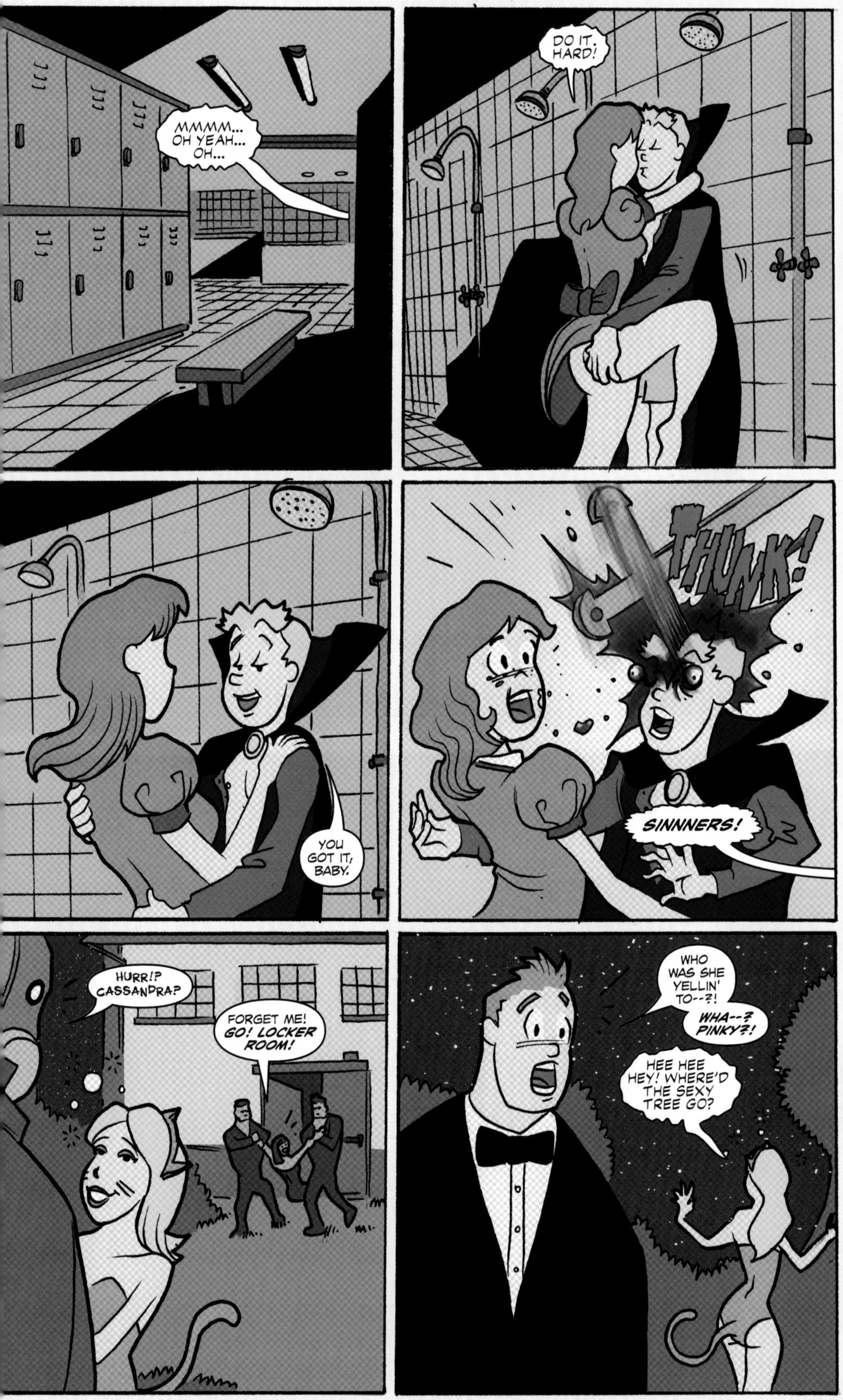
MMMM... OH YEAH... OH...
DO IT, HARD!
YOU GOT IT, BABY.
THUNK!
SINNERS!
HURR!? CASSANDRA?
FORGET ME! GO! LOCKER ROOM!
WHO WAS SHE YELLIN' TO--?!
WHA--? PINKY?!
HEE HEE HEY! WHERE'D THE SEXY TREE GO?

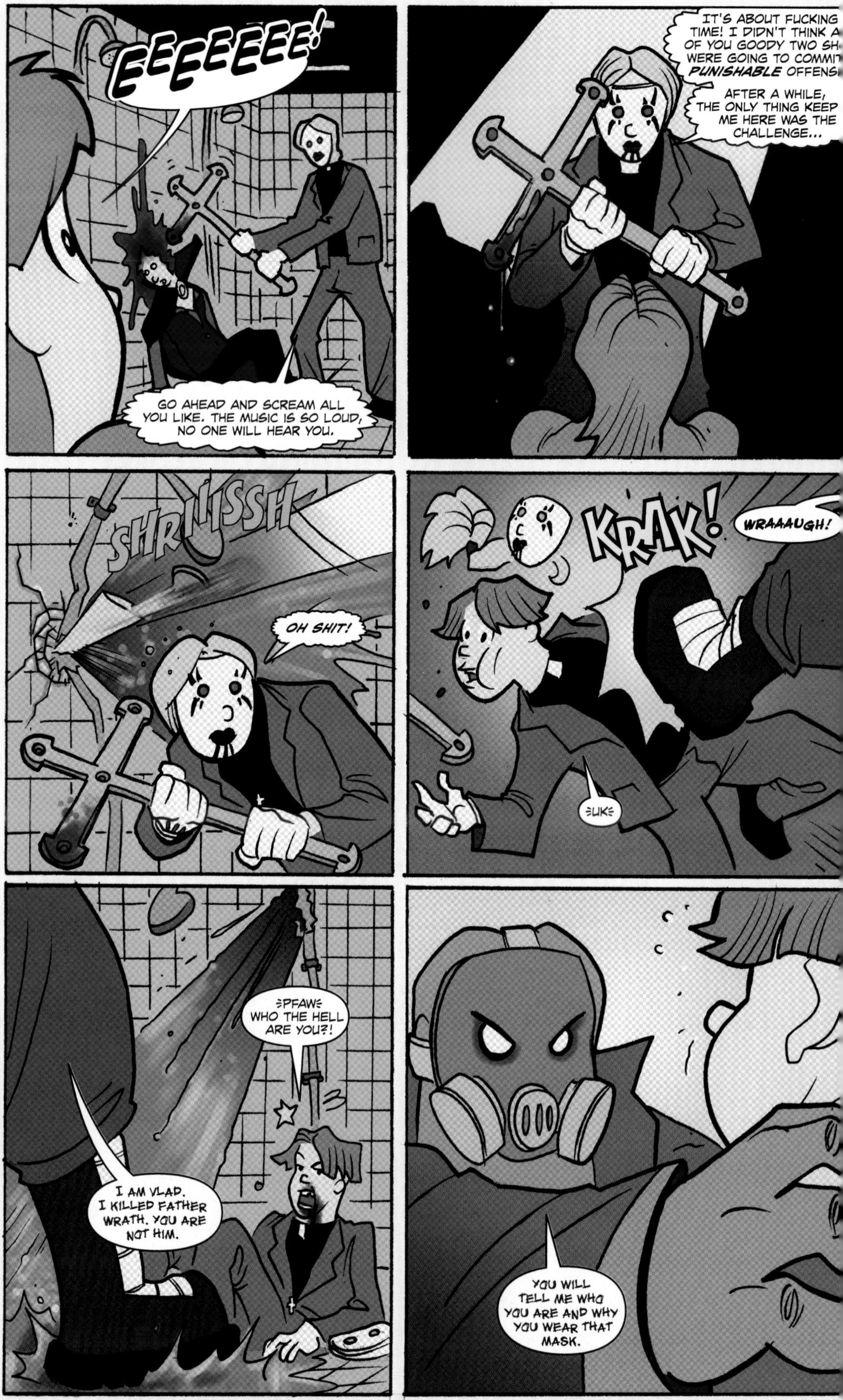
EEEEEEEE!
GO AHEAD AND SCREAM ALL YOU LIKE. THE MUSIC IS SO LOUD, NO ONE WILL HEAR YOU.
IT'S ABOUT FUCKING TIME! I DIDN'T THINK A OF YOU GOODY TWO SH WERE GOING TO COMMIT PUNISHABLE OFFENS
AFTER A WHILE, THE ONLY THING KEEP ME HERE WAS THE CHALLENGE...
SHRIIISSH
OH SHIT!
KRAK!
WRAAAUGH!
UK
PFAW
WHO THE HELL ARE YOU?!
I AM VLAD. I KILLED FATHER WRATH. YOU ARE NOT HIM.
YOU WILL TELL ME WHO YOU ARE AND WHY YOU WEAR THAT MASK.

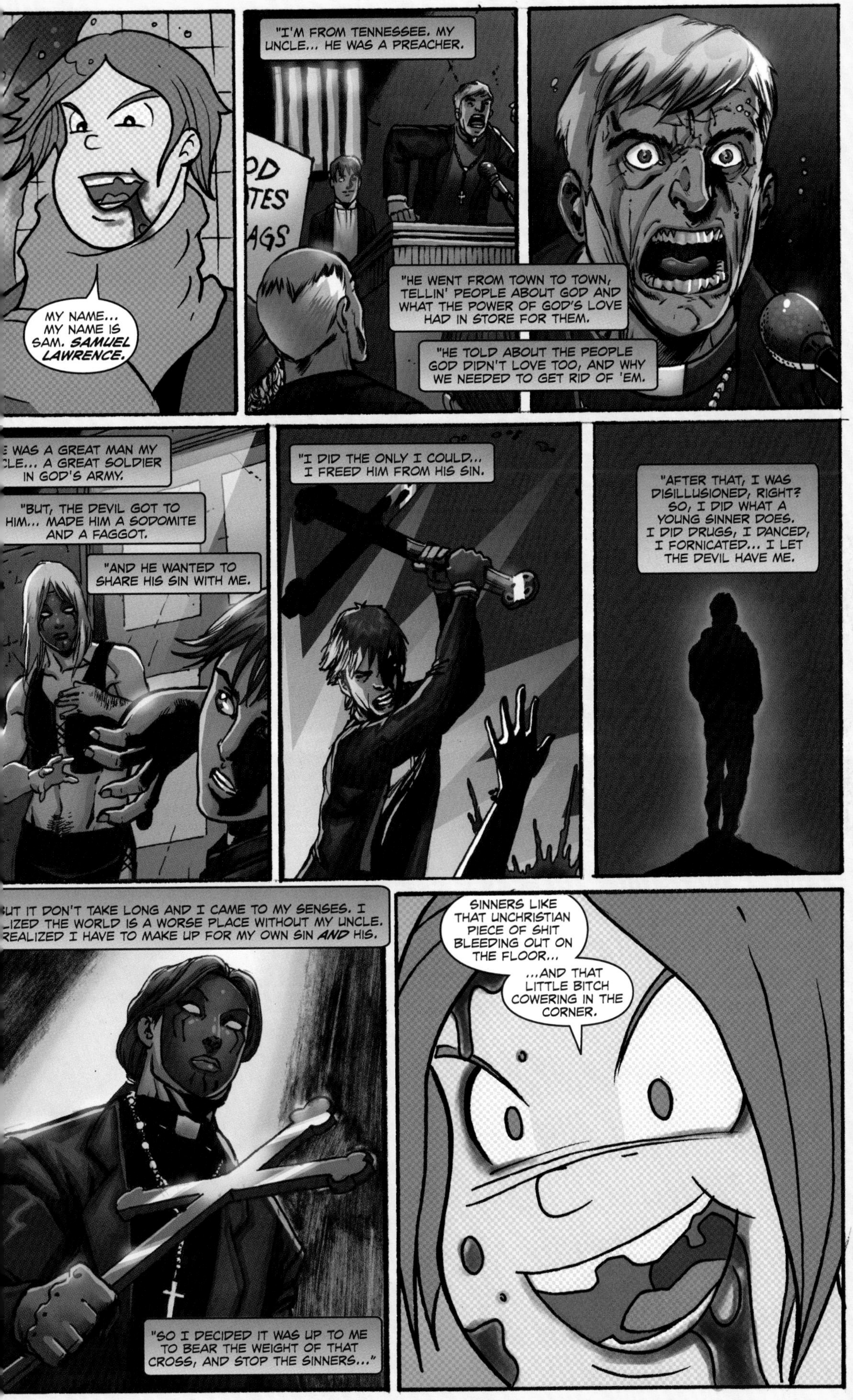

MY NAME... MY NAME IS SAM. *SAMUEL LAWRENCE.*
"I'M FROM TENNESSEE. MY UNCLE... HE WAS A PREACHER.
OD
TES'
AGS
"HE WENT FROM TOWN TO TOWN, TELLIN' PEOPLE ABOUT GOD AND WHAT THE POWER OF GOD'S LOVE HAD IN STORE FOR THEM.
"HE TOLD ABOUT THE PEOPLE GOD DIDN'T LOVE TOO, AND WHY WE NEEDED TO GET RID OF 'EM.
E WAS A GREAT MAN MY CLE... A GREAT SOLDIER IN GOD'S ARMY.
"BUT, THE DEVIL GOT TO HIM... MADE HIM A SODOMITE AND A FAGGOT.
"AND HE WANTED TO SHARE HIS SIN WITH ME.
"I DID THE ONLY I COULD... I FREED HIM FROM HIS SIN.
"AFTER THAT, I WAS DISILLUSIONED, RIGHT? SO, I DID WHAT A YOUNG SINNER DOES. I DID DRUGS, I DANCED, I FORNICATED... I LET THE DEVIL HAVE ME.
UT IT DON'T TAKE LONG AND I CAME TO MY SENSES. I LIZED THE WORLD IS A WORSE PLACE WITHOUT MY UNCLE. REALIZED I HAVE TO MAKE UP FOR MY OWN SIN *AND* HIS.
"SO I DECIDED IT WAS UP TO ME TO BEAR THE WEIGHT OF THAT CROSS, AND STOP THE SINNERS..."
SINNERS LIKE THAT UNCHRISTIAN PIECE OF SHIT BLEEDING OUT ON THE FLOOR...
...AND THAT LITTLE BITCH COWERING IN THE CORNER.

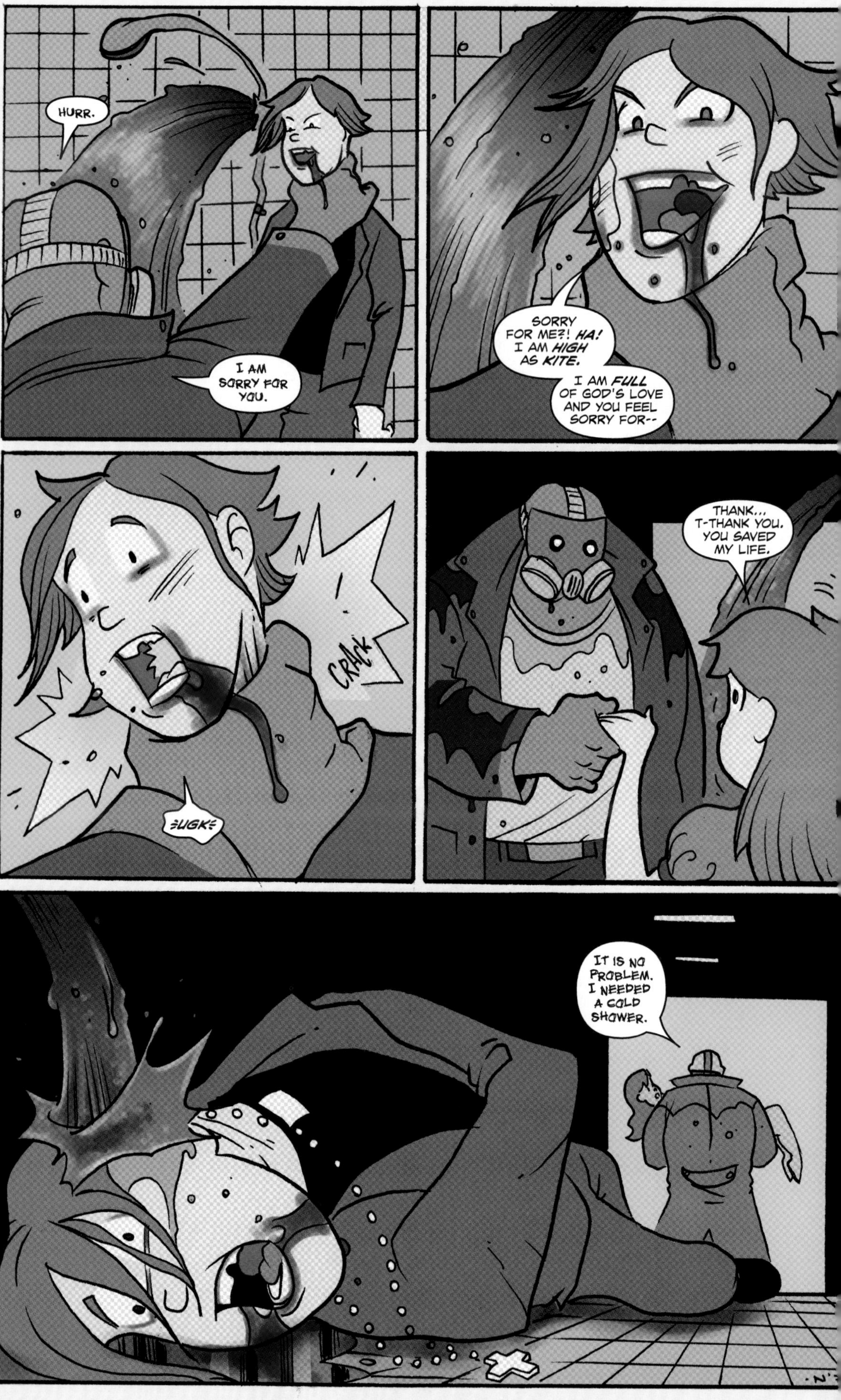
HURR.
I AM SORRY FOR YOU.
SORRY FOR ME?! HA! I AM HIGH AS KITE.
I AM FULL OF GOD'S LOVE AND YOU FEEL SORRY FOR--
CRACK
UGK
THANK... T-THANK YOU. YOU SAVED MY LIFE.
IT IS NO PROBLEM. I NEEDED A COLD SHOWER.

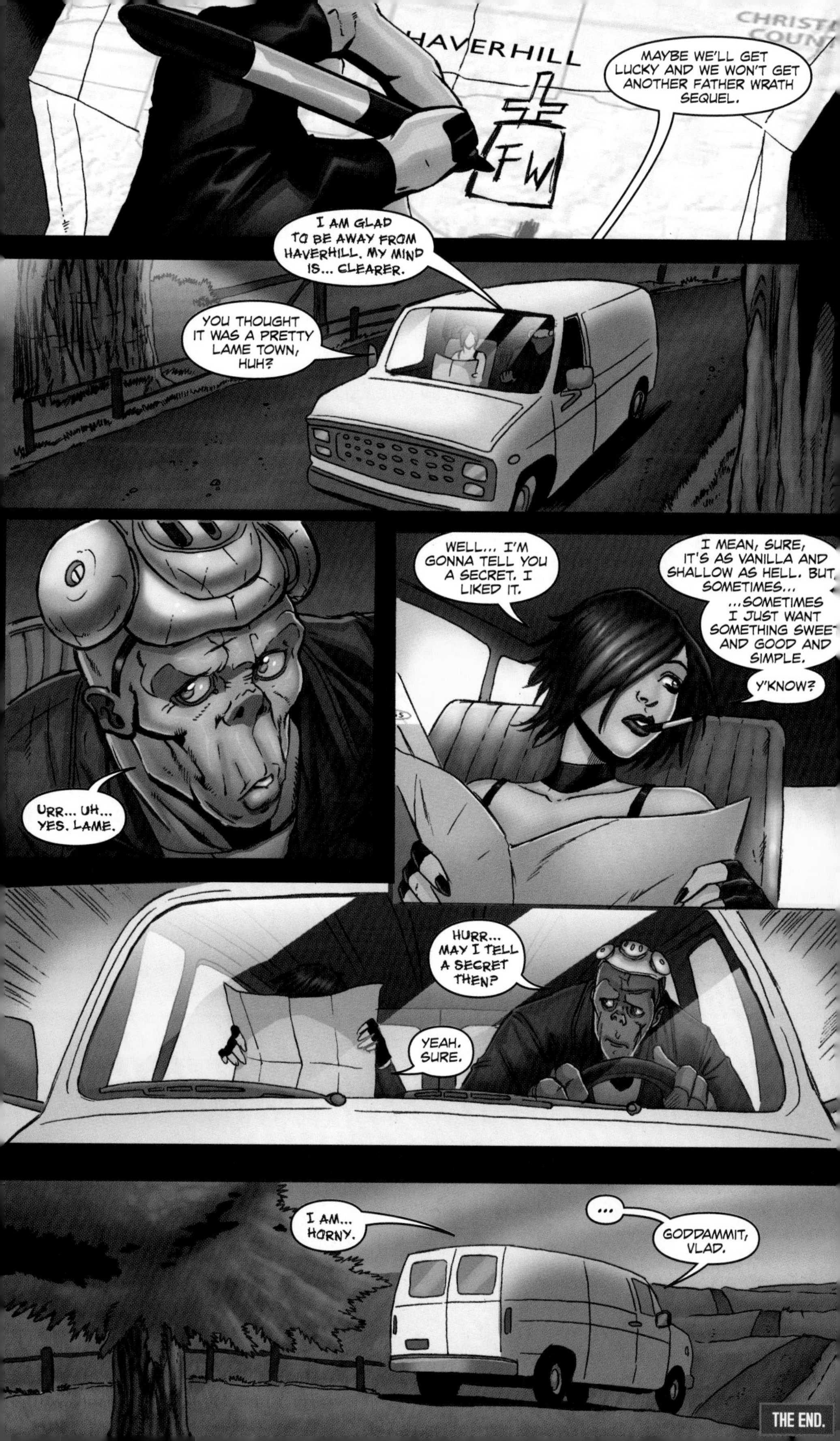
HAVERHILL
CHRIST COUN
FW
MAYBE WE'LL GET LUCKY AND WE WON'T GET ANOTHER FATHER WRATH SEQUEL.
I AM GLAD TO BE AWAY FROM HAVERHILL. MY MIND IS... CLEARER.
YOU THOUGHT IT WAS A PRETTY LAME TOWN, HUH?
URR... UH... YES. LAME.
WELL... I'M GONNA TELL YOU A SECRET. I LIKED IT.
I MEAN, SURE, IT'S AS VANILLA AND SHALLOW AS HELL. BUT, SOMETIMES...
...SOMETIMES I JUST WANT SOMETHING SWEET AND GOOD AND SIMPLE.
Y'KNOW?
HURR... MAY I TELL A SECRET THEN?
YEAH. SURE.
I AM... HORNY.
...
GODDAMMIT, VLAD.
THE END.

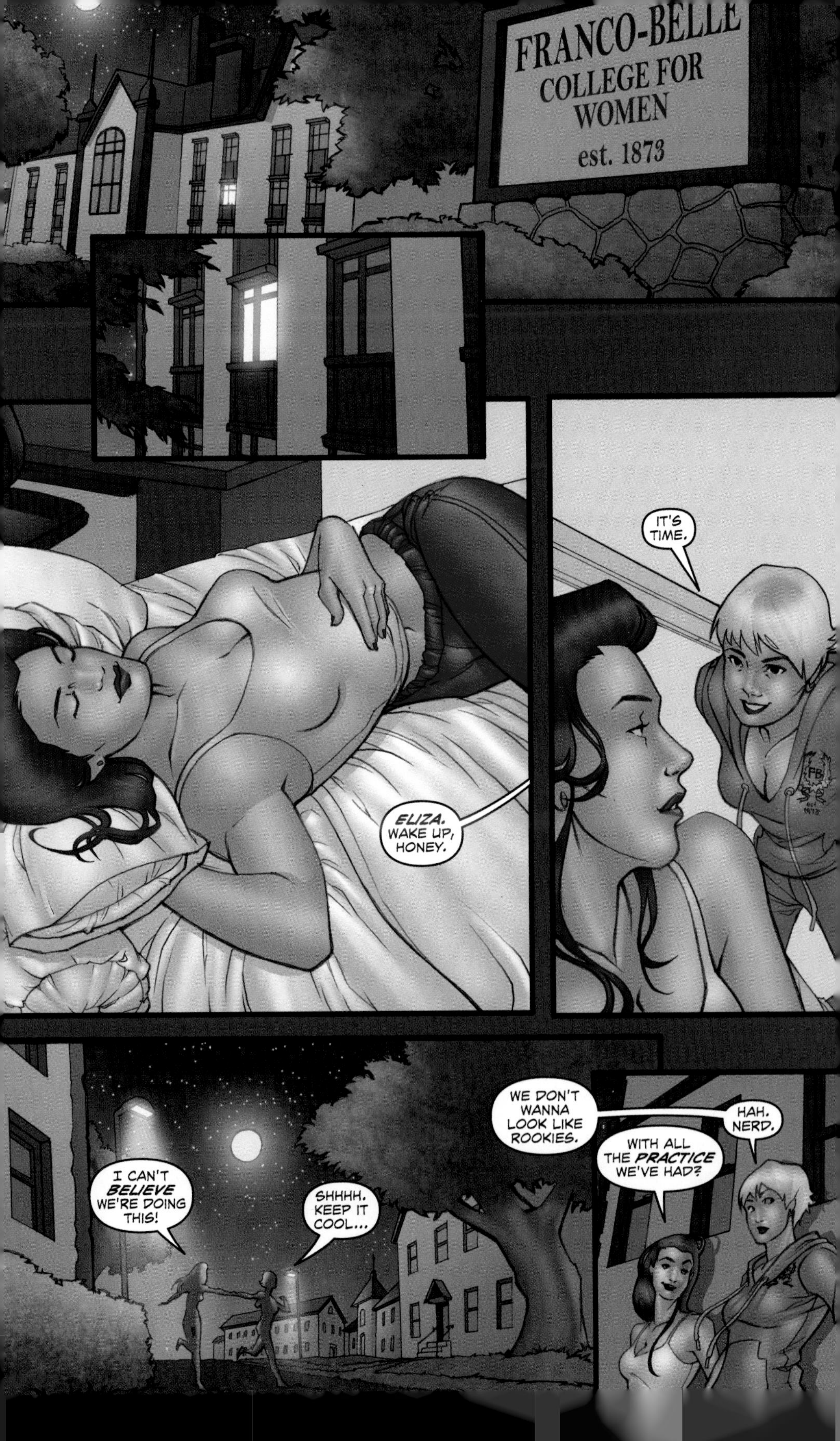
FRANCO-BELLE COLLEGE FOR WOMEN est. 1873
ELIZA. WAKE UP, HONEY.
IT'S TIME.
I CAN'T BELIEVE WE'RE DOING THIS!
SHHHH. KEEP IT COOL...
WE DON'T WANNA LOOK LIKE ROOKIES.
HAH. NERD.
WITH ALL THE PRACTICE WE'VE HAD?

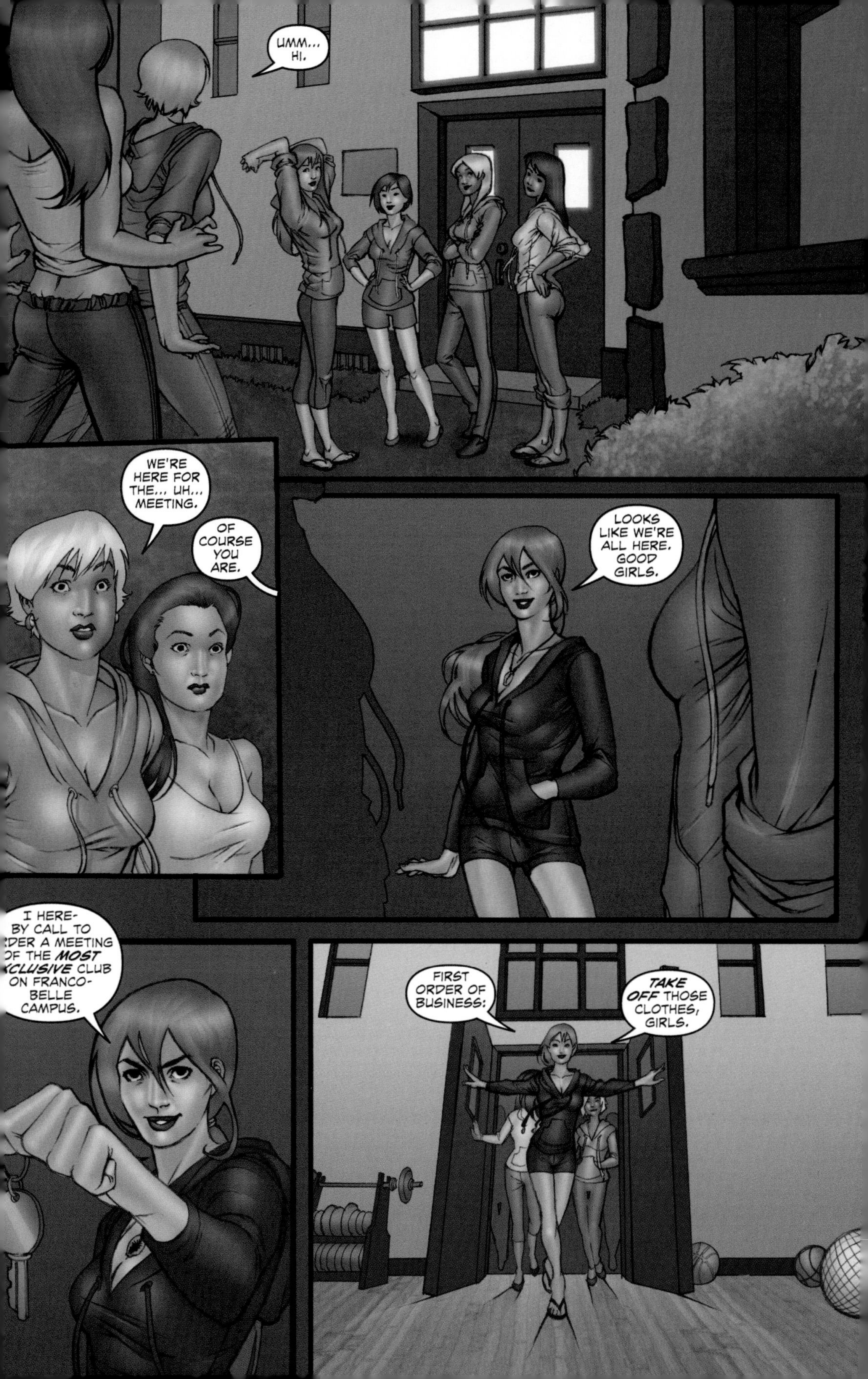
UMM... HI.
WE'RE HERE FOR THE... UH... MEETING.
OF COURSE YOU ARE.
LOOKS LIKE WE'RE ALL HERE. GOOD GIRLS.
I HERE-BY CALL TO
RDER A MEETING
OF THE MOST
CLUSIVE CLUB
ON FRANCO-BELLE CAMPUS.
FIRST ORDER OF BUSINESS:
TAKE OFF THOSE CLOTHES, GIRLS.

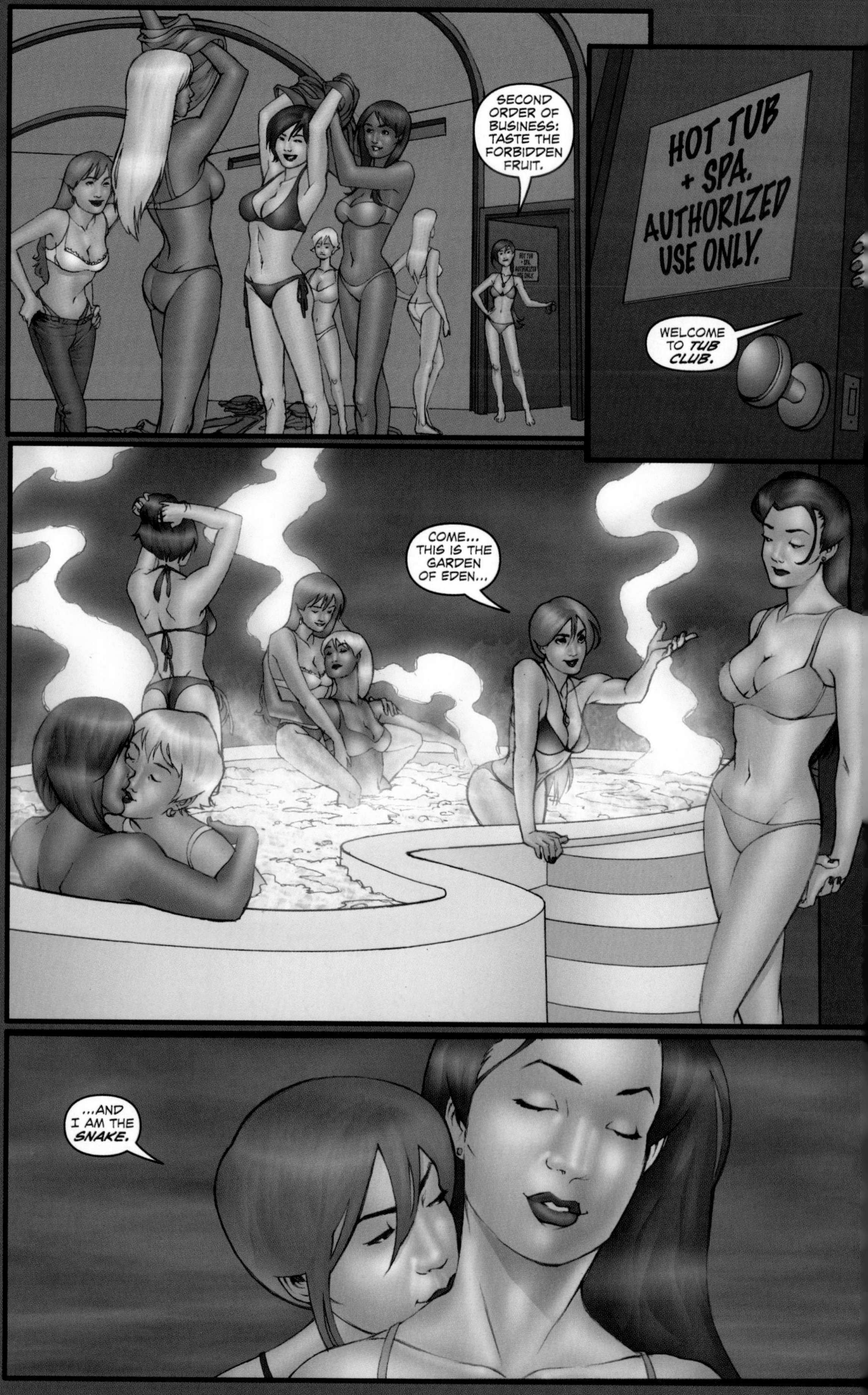
SECOND ORDER OF BUSINESS: TASTE THE FORBIDDEN FRUIT.
HOT TUB + SPA. AUTHORIZED USE ONLY.
WELCOME TO TUB CLUB.
COME... THIS IS THE GARDEN OF EDEN...
...AND I AM THE SNAKE.

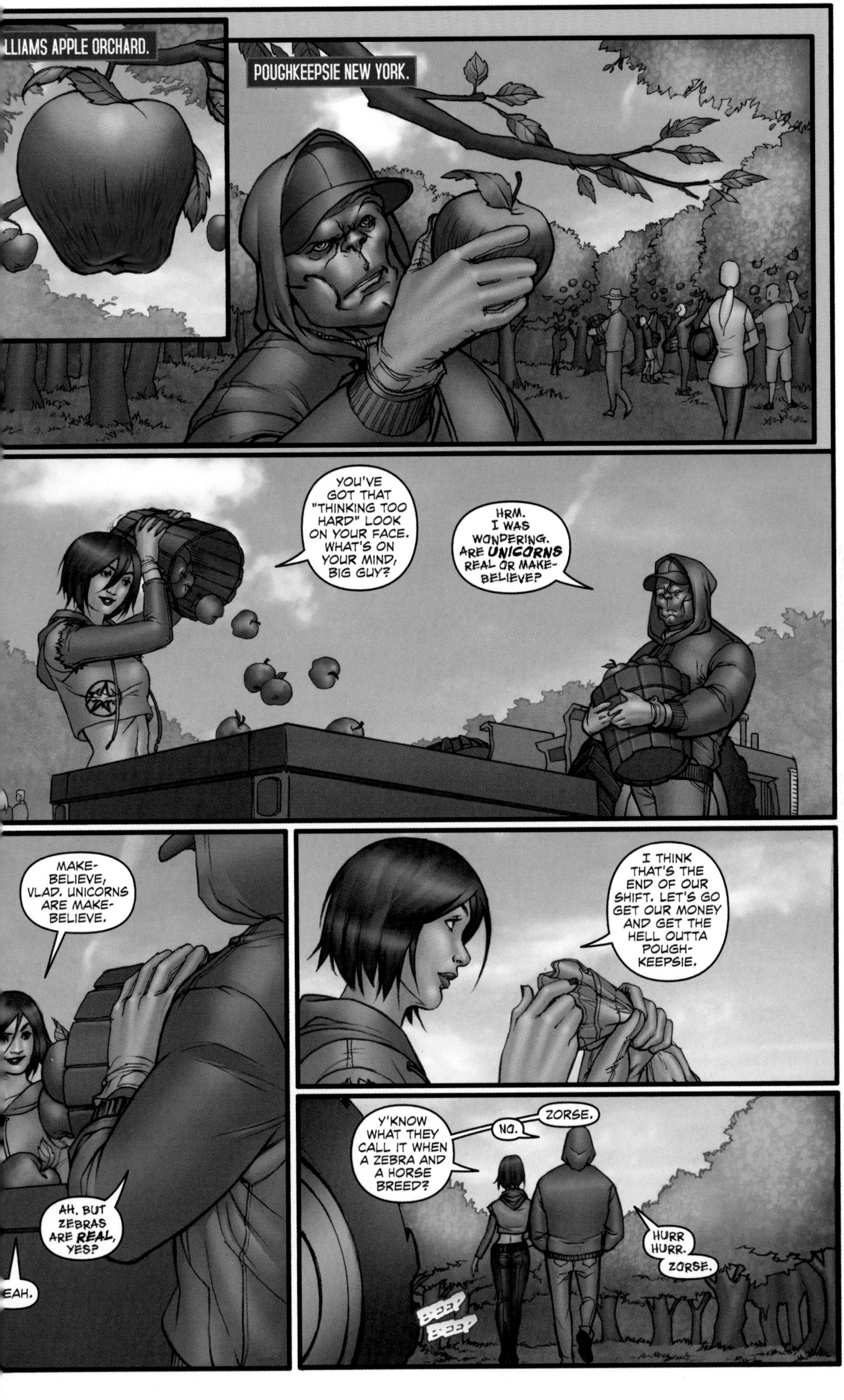

LLIAMS APPLE ORCHARD.
POUGHKEEPSIE NEW YORK.
YOU'VE GOT THAT "THINKING TOO HARD" LOOK ON YOUR FACE. WHAT'S ON YOUR MIND, BIG GUY?
HRM. I WAS WONDERING. ARE UNICORNS REAL OR MAKE-BELIEVE?
MAKE-BELIEVE, VLAD. UNICORNS ARE MAKE-BELIEVE.
AH. BUT ZEBRAS ARE REAL, YES?
EAH.
I THINK THAT'S THE END OF OUR SHIFT. LET'S GO GET OUR MONEY AND GET THE HELL OUTTA POUGH-KEEPSIE.
Y'KNOW WHAT THEY CALL IT WHEN A ZEBRA AND A HORSE BREED?
NO.
ZORSE.
HURR HURR. ZORSE.
BEEP BEEP

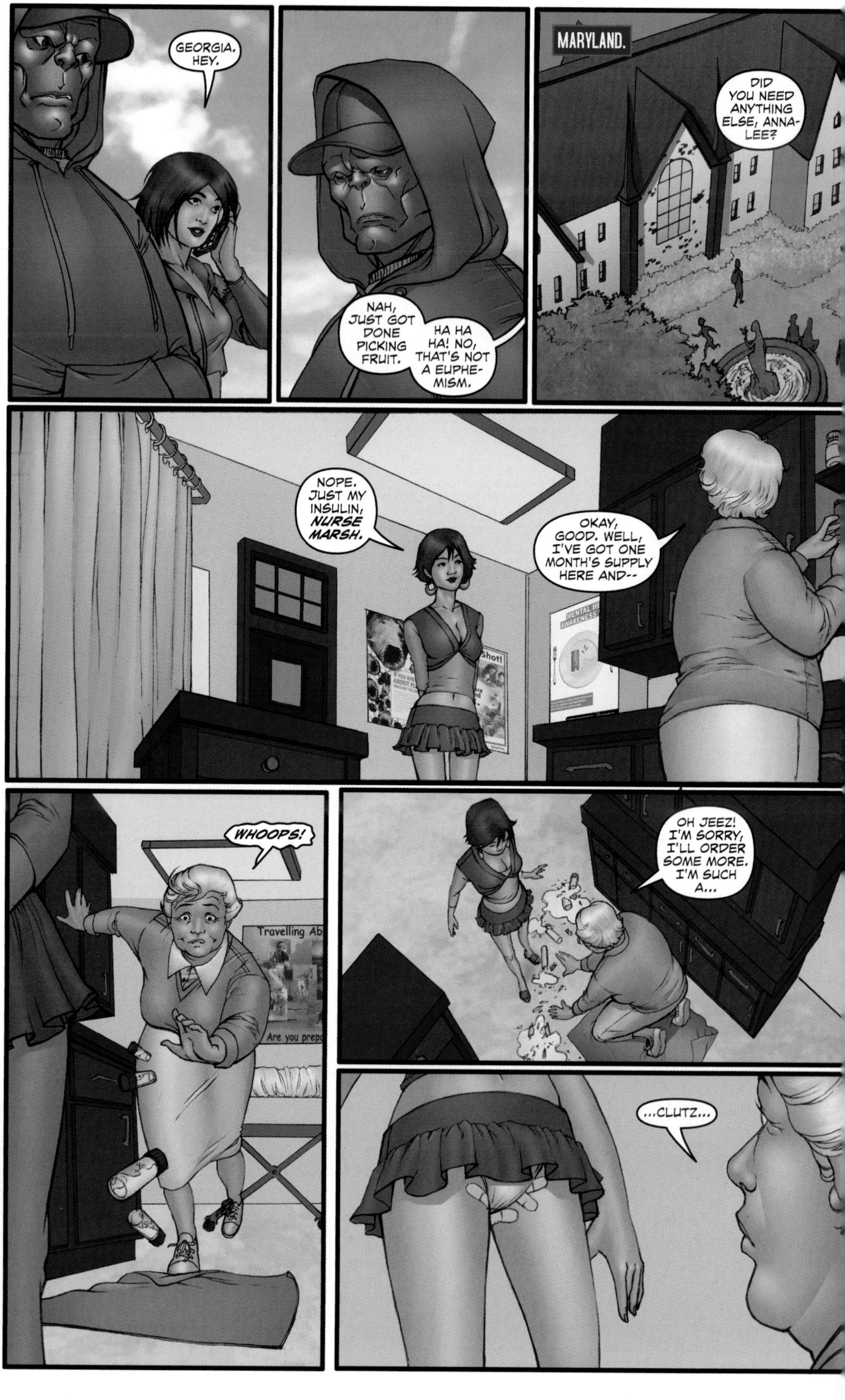
GEORGIA. HEY.
NAH, JUST GOT DONE PICKING FRUIT.
HA HA HA! NO, THAT'S NOT A EUPHEMISM.
MARYLAND.
DID YOU NEED ANYTHING ELSE, ANNA-LEE?
NOPE. JUST MY INSULIN, NURSE MARSH.
OKAY, GOOD. WELL, I'VE GOT ONE MONTH'S SUPPLY HERE AND--
MENTAL HE AWARENESS
Shot!
WHOOPS!
Travelling Ab
Are you prepa
OH JEEZ! I'M SORRY, I'LL ORDER SOME MORE. I'M SUCH A...
...CLUTZ...

EMINENCE, INDIANA.

NOW *THAT'S* ART.

HEH. YEAH... ART.

ORIGINAL *THUNDERGUARD* MAGAZINE SPECIAL EDITION *MAIL-AWAY* POSTER.

TOTALLY COLLECTIBLE. THESE THINGS GO FOR 300 BUCKS ON EBAY.

THAT'S GREAT, CHRIS.

YOU HATE IT.

NO... NO, IF YOU'RE GOING TO MOVE IN, AND PAY HALF THE MORTGAGE, IT'S ONLY FAIR THAT YOU SHOULD GET TO MAKE IT *YOUR* HOME TOO.

AND IF THE WAY YOU DO THAT IS BY PUTTING UP... *THIS...* THEN, THAT'S THE WAY IT'LL BE.

AW, LISA, YOU ARE THE GREATEST.

YEAH... WELL, LET'S AT LEAST KEEP THE ACTION FIGURES IN THE *HACK/SLASH INC.* OFFICE, OKAY?

THAT REMINDS ME! I HAD A MEDICAL EXAMINER IN ALBERT CITY WHO WAS GONNA EMAIL ME SOME PHOTOS OF A BIZARRE BODY. WANNA CHECK IT OUT?

I CAN'T THINK OF *ANYTHING* MORE ROMANTIC.

HEAR ANYTHING ELSE FROM THAT LADY MASSACHUSETTS?

YEAH. I THINK I HAVE ENOUGH TO SEND IT TO CASS IN THE MORNING.

THERE'S NO BODIES OR ANYTHING... JUST A LEGEND... BUT IT COULD BE SOMETHING.

COOL. WELL, LET'S TAKE A LOOK AT WHAT I GOT AND SEE IF *MINE'S* SOMETHING.

HERE WE GO. LET'S OPEN THIS UP...

SHIT!

THAT'S DEFINITELY SOMETHING

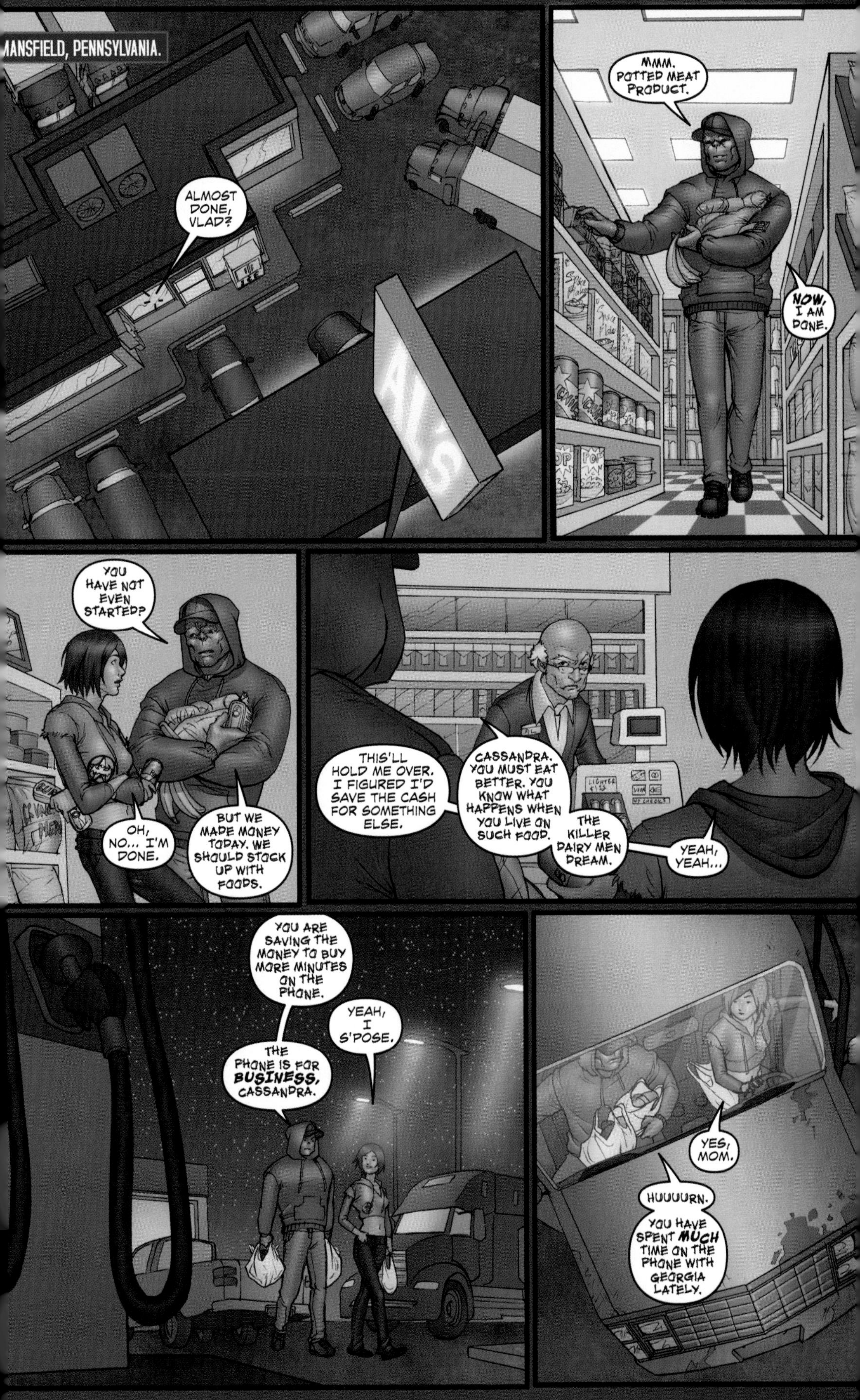
MANSFIELD, PENNSYLVANIA.
ALMOST DONE, VLAD?
AL'S
MMM. POTTED MEAT PRODUCT.
NOW, I AM DONE.
YOU HAVE NOT EVEN STARTED?
OH, NO... I'M DONE.
BUT WE MADE MONEY TODAY. WE SHOULD STOCK UP WITH FOODS.
THIS'LL HOLD ME OVER. I FIGURED I'D SAVE THE CASH FOR SOMETHING ELSE.
CASSANDRA. YOU MUST EAT BETTER. YOU KNOW WHAT HAPPENS WHEN YOU LIVE ON SUCH FOOD.
THE KILLER DAIRY MEN DREAM.
YEAH, YEAH...
YOU ARE SAVING THE MONEY TO BUY MORE MINUTES ON THE PHONE.
YEAH, I S'POSE.
THE PHONE IS FOR BUSINESS, CASSANDRA.
YES, MOM.
HUUUURN.
YOU HAVE SPENT MUCH TIME ON THE PHONE WITH GEORGIA LATELY.

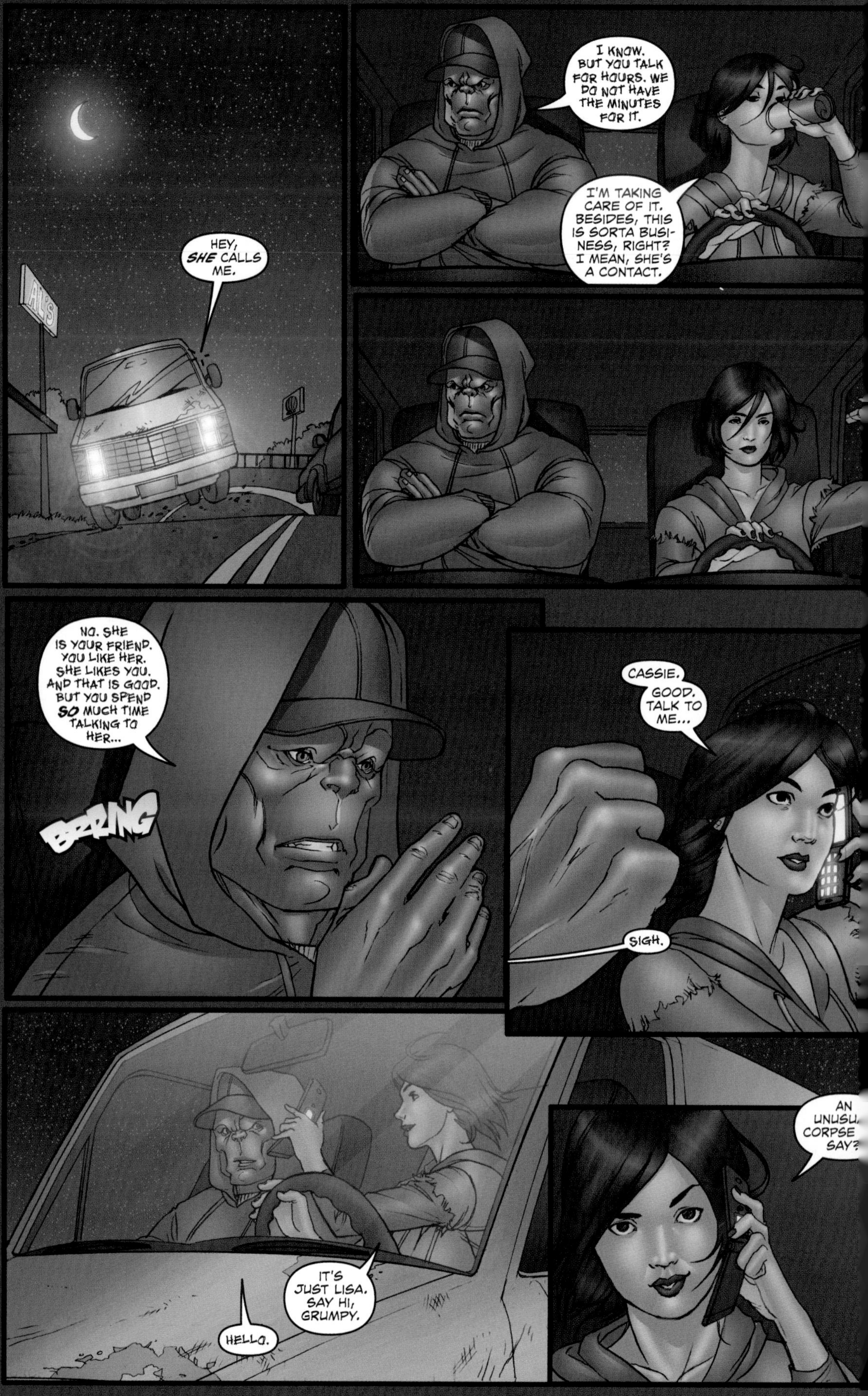
AL'S
HEY, SHE CALLS ME.
I KNOW. BUT YOU TALK FOR HOURS. WE DO NOT HAVE THE MINUTES FOR IT.
I'M TAKING CARE OF IT. BESIDES, THIS IS SORTA BUSINESS, RIGHT? I MEAN, SHE'S A CONTACT.
NO. SHE IS YOUR FRIEND. YOU LIKE HER. SHE LIKES YOU. AND THAT IS GOOD. BUT YOU SPEND SO MUCH TIME TALKING TO HER...
BRRING
CASSIE. GOOD. TALK TO ME...
SIGH.
IT'S JUST LISA. SAY HI, GRUMPY.
HELLO.

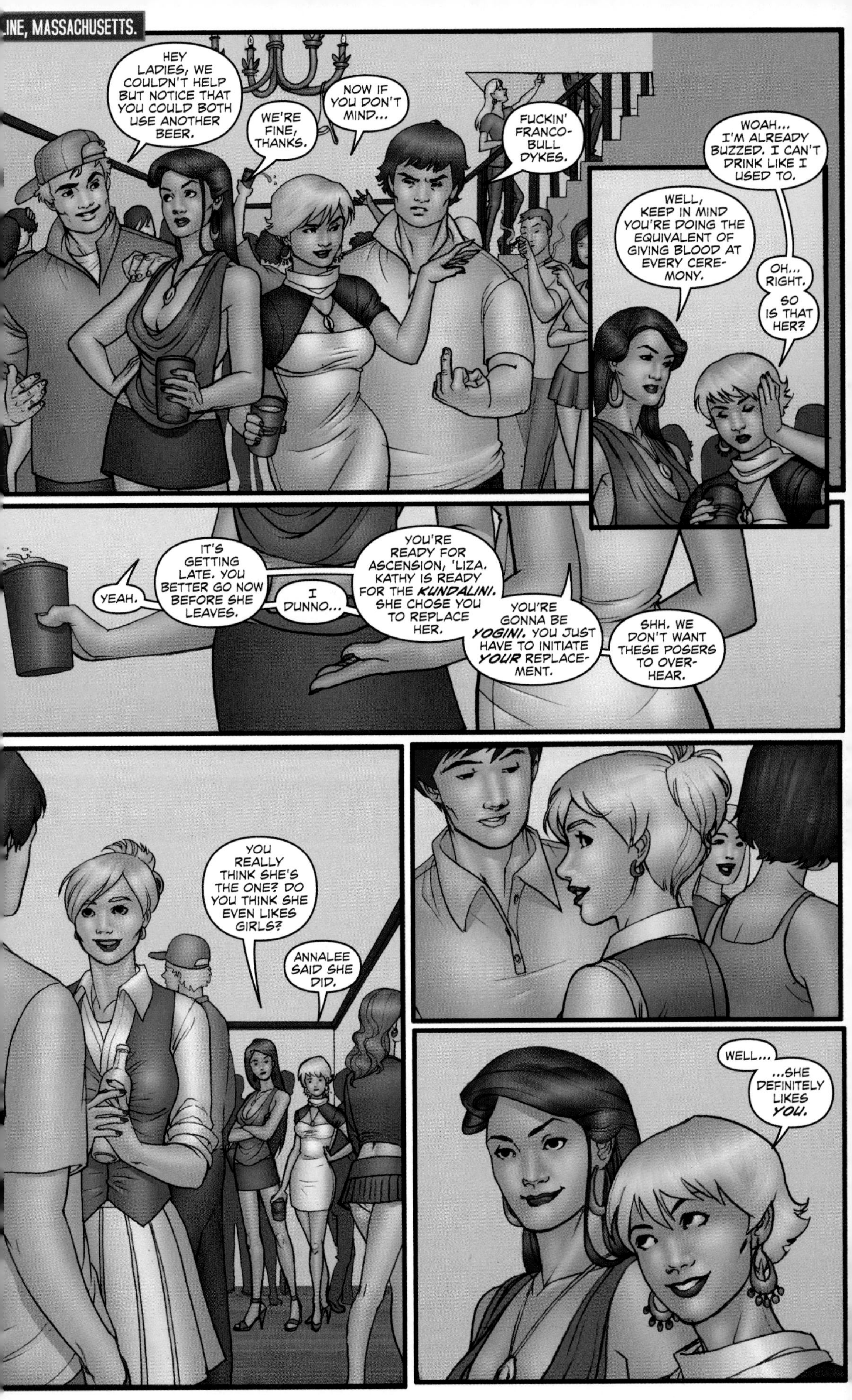
...LINE, MASSACHUSETTS.
HEY LADIES, WE COULDN'T HELP BUT NOTICE THAT YOU COULD BOTH USE ANOTHER BEER.
WE'RE FINE, THANKS.
NOW IF YOU DON'T MIND...
FUCKIN' FRANCO-BULL DYKES.
WOAH... I'M ALREADY BUZZED. I CAN'T DRINK LIKE I USED TO.
WELL, KEEP IN MIND YOU'RE DOING THE EQUIVALENT OF GIVING BLOOD AT EVERY CEREMONY.
OH... RIGHT.
SO IS THAT HER?
YEAH.
IT'S GETTING LATE. YOU BETTER GO NOW BEFORE SHE LEAVES.
I DUNNO...
YOU'RE READY FOR ASCENSION, 'LIZA. KATHY IS READY FOR THE KUNDALINI. SHE CHOSE YOU TO REPLACE HER.
YOU'RE GONNA BE YOGINI. YOU JUST HAVE TO INITIATE YOUR REPLACEMENT.
SHH. WE DON'T WANT THESE POSERS TO OVERHEAR.
YOU REALLY THINK SHE'S THE ONE? DO YOU THINK SHE EVEN LIKES GIRLS?
ANNALEE SAID SHE DID.
WELL...
...SHE DEFINITELY LIKES YOU.

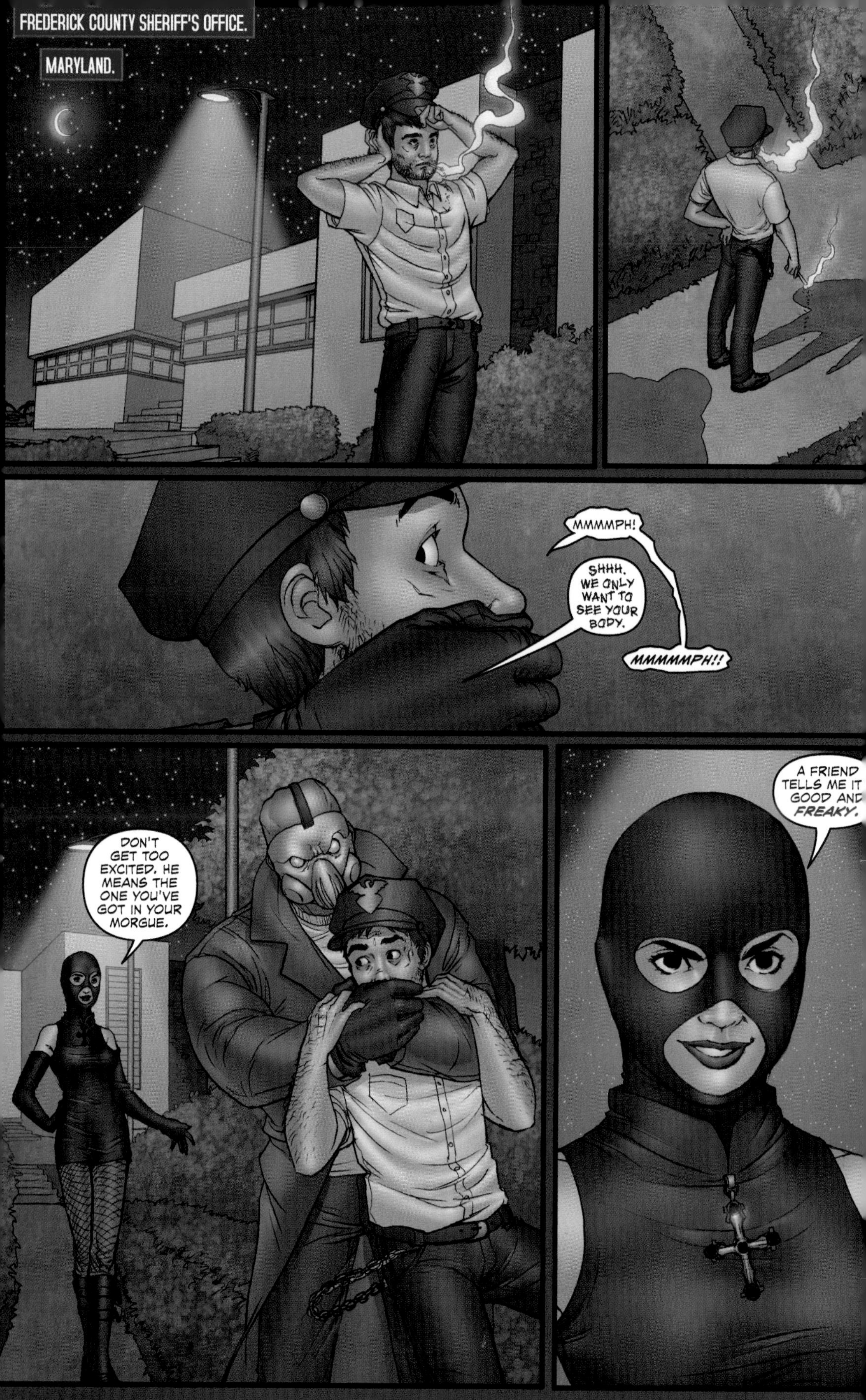
FREDERICK COUNTY SHERIFF'S OFFICE.
MARYLAND.
MMMMPH!
SHHH. WE ONLY WANT TO SEE YOUR BODY.
MMMMMPH!!
DON'T GET TOO EXCITED. HE MEANS THE ONE YOU'VE GOT IN YOUR MORGUE.
A FRIEND TELLS ME IT GOOD AND FREAKY.

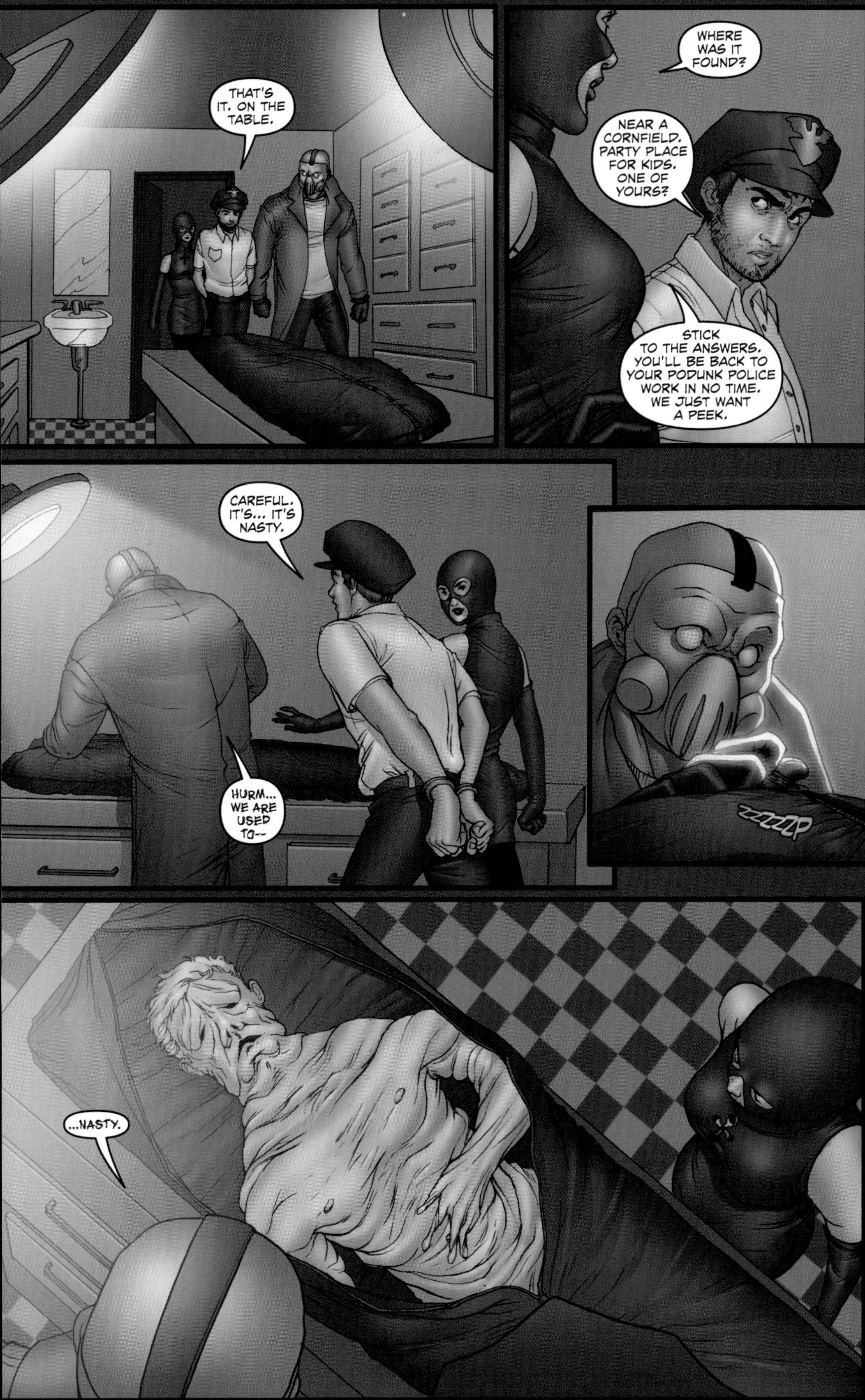
THAT'S IT. ON THE TABLE.
WHERE WAS IT FOUND?
NEAR A CORNFIELD. PARTY PLACE FOR KIDS. ONE OF YOURS?
STICK TO THE ANSWERS. YOU'LL BE BACK TO YOUR PODUNK POLICE WORK IN NO TIME. WE JUST WANT A PEEK.
CAREFUL. IT'S... IT'S NASTY.
HURM... WE ARE USED TO--
ZZZZZP
...NASTY.

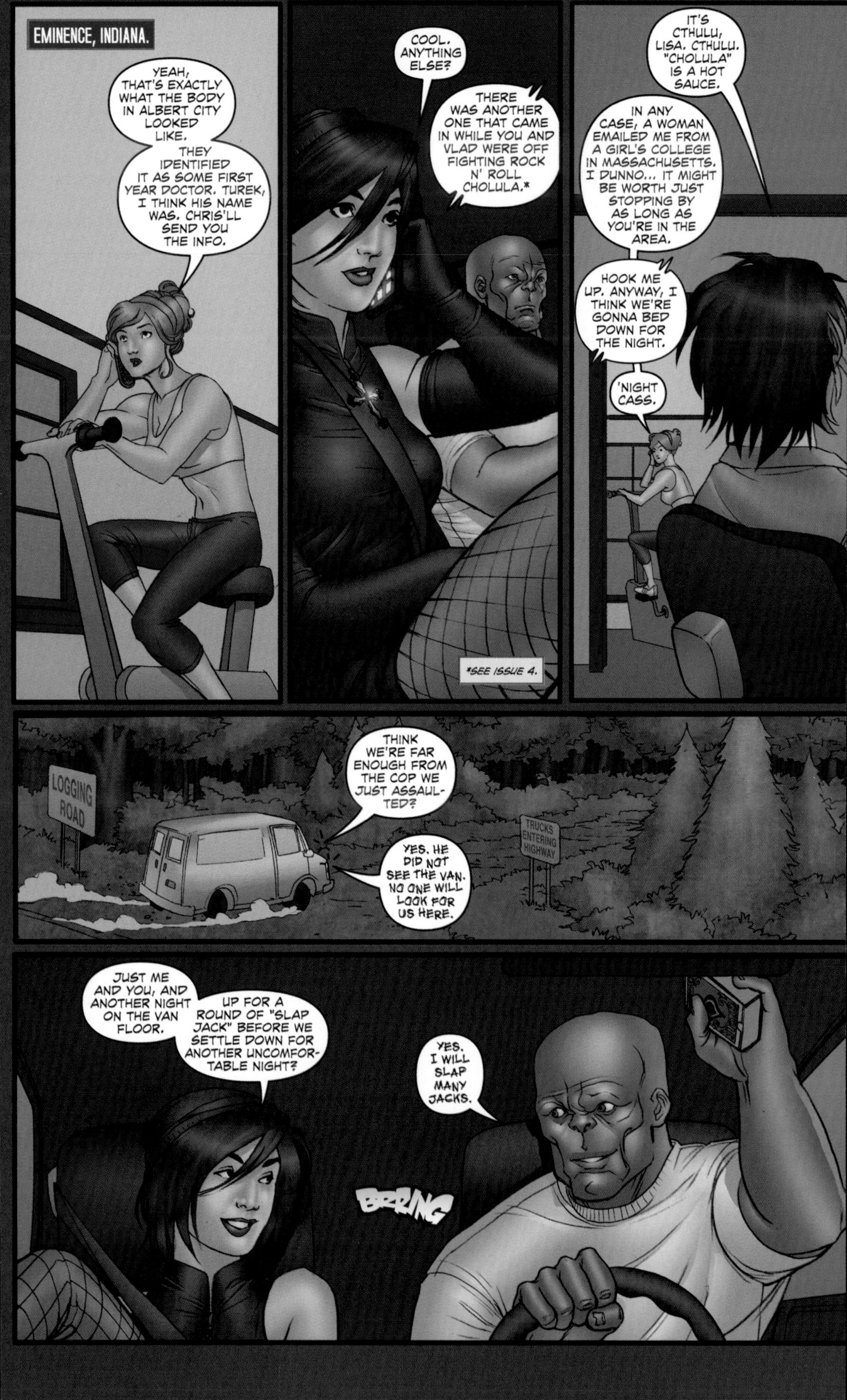
EMINENCE, INDIANA.
YEAH, THAT'S EXACTLY WHAT THE BODY IN ALBERT CITY LOOKED LIKE.
THEY IDENTIFIED IT AS SOME FIRST YEAR DOCTOR. TUREK, I THINK HIS NAME WAS. CHRIS'LL SEND YOU THE INFO.
COOL. ANYTHING ELSE?
THERE WAS ANOTHER ONE THAT CAME IN WHILE YOU AND VLAD WERE OFF FIGHTING ROCK N' ROLL CHOLULA.*
*SEE ISSUE 4.
IT'S CTHULU, LISA. CTHULU. "CHOLULA" IS A HOT SAUCE.
IN ANY CASE, A WOMAN EMAILED ME FROM A GIRL'S COLLEGE IN MASSACHUSETTS. I DUNNO... IT MIGHT BE WORTH JUST STOPPING BY AS LONG AS YOU'RE IN THE AREA.
HOOK ME UP. ANYWAY, I THINK WE'RE GONNA BED DOWN FOR THE NIGHT.
'NIGHT CASS.
LOGGING ROAD
THINK WE'RE FAR ENOUGH FROM THE COP WE JUST ASSAUL-TED?
TRUCKS ENTERING HIGHWAY
YES. HE DID NOT SEE THE VAN. NO ONE WILL LOOK FOR US HERE.
JUST ME AND YOU, AND ANOTHER NIGHT ON THE VAN FLOOR.
UP FOR A ROUND OF "SLAP JACK" BEFORE WE SETTLE DOWN FOR ANOTHER UNCOMFOR-TABLE NIGHT?
YES. I WILL SLAP MANY JACKS.
BRRING

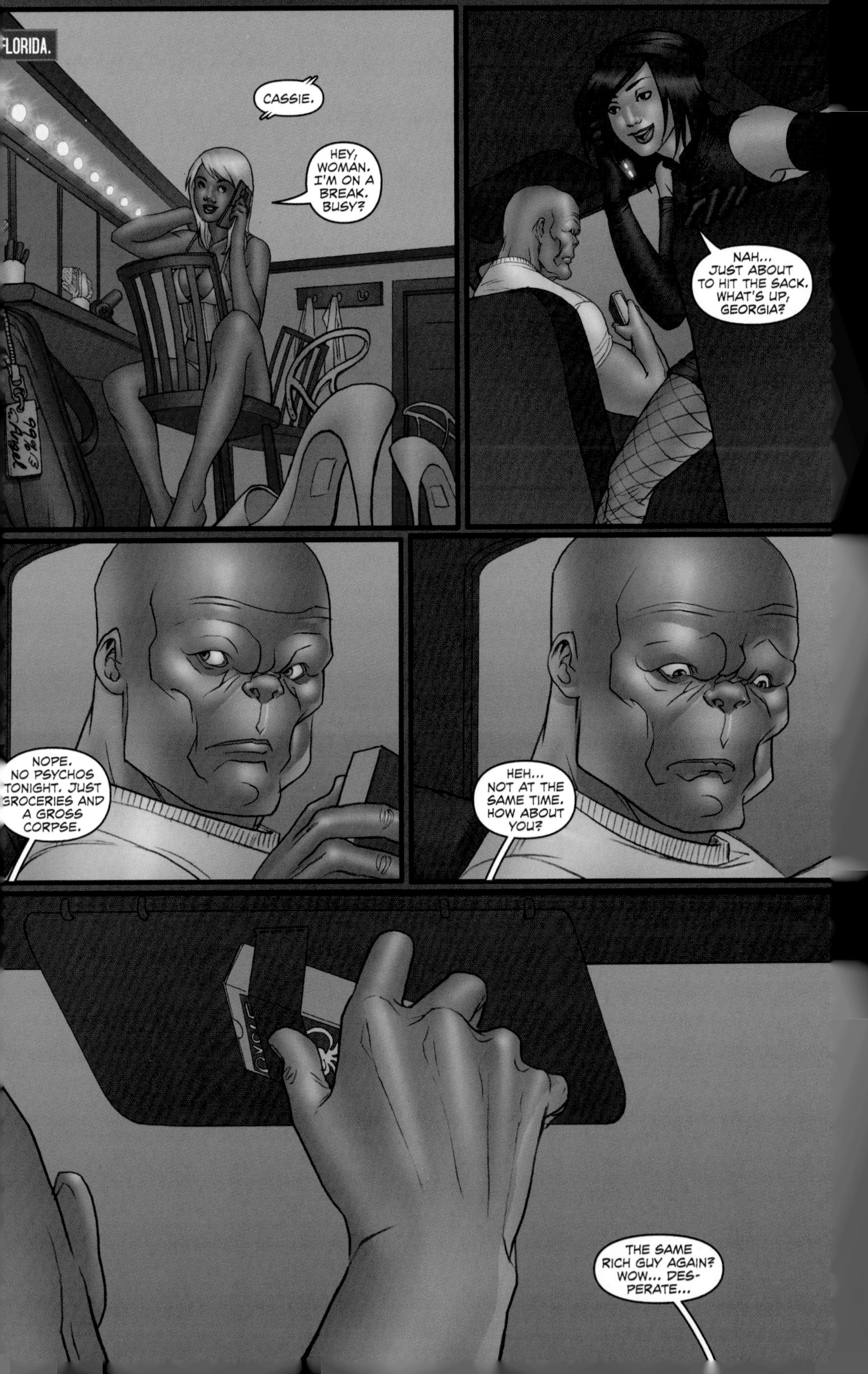
FLORIDA.
CASSIE.
HEY, WOMAN. I'M ON A BREAK. BUSY?
99% 13 Angel
NAH... JUST ABOUT TO HIT THE SACK. WHAT'S UP, GEORGIA?
NOPE. NO PSYCHOS TONIGHT. JUST GROCERIES AND A GROSS CORPSE.
HEH... NOT AT THE SAME TIME. HOW ABOUT YOU?
THE SAME RICH GUY AGAIN? WOW... DES-PERATE...

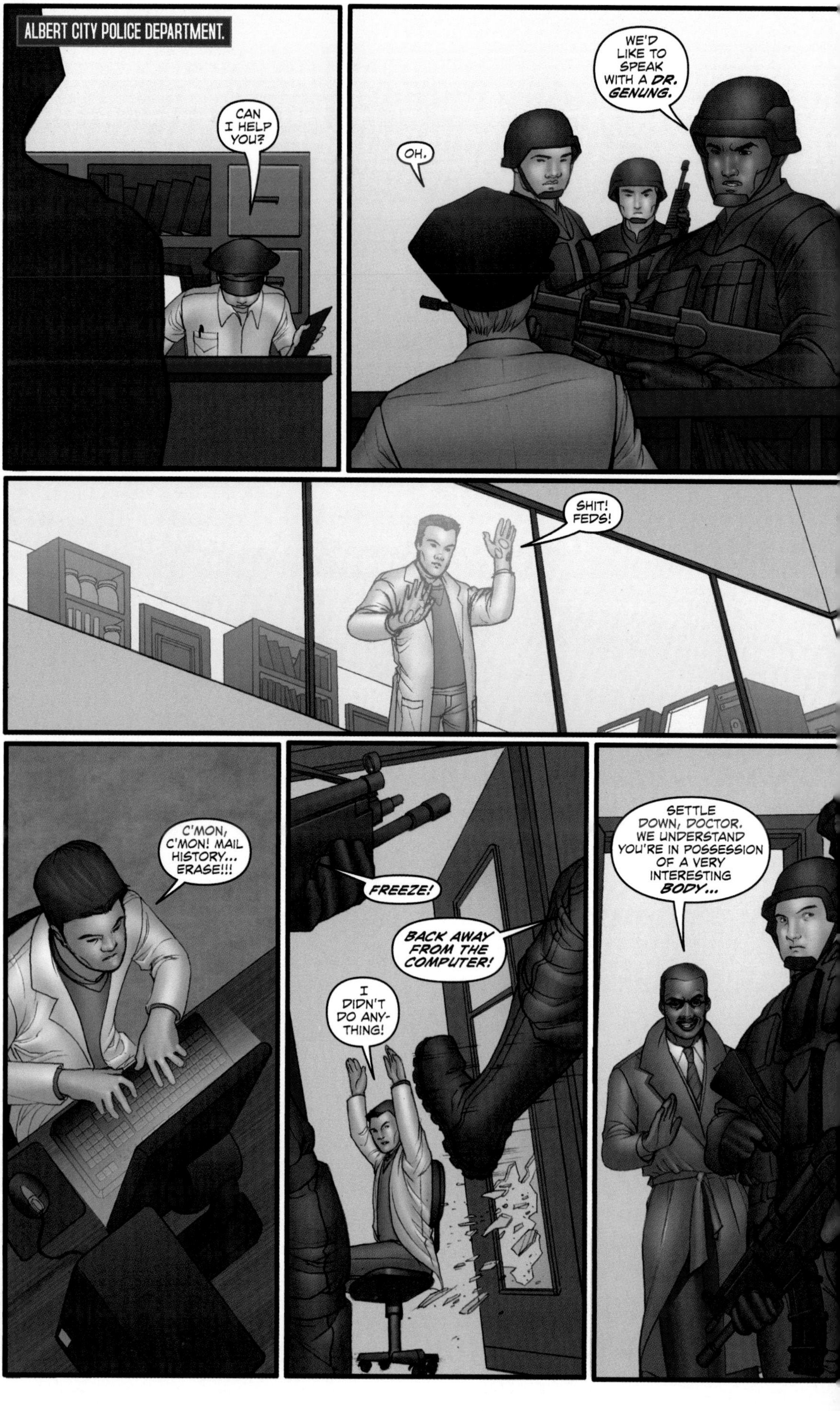
ALBERT CITY POLICE DEPARTMENT.
CAN I HELP YOU?
WE'D LIKE TO SPEAK WITH A DR. GENUNG.
OH.
SHIT! FEDS!
C'MON, C'MON! MAIL HISTORY... ERASE!!!
FREEZE!
BACK AWAY FROM THE COMPUTER!
I DIDN'T DO ANYTHING!
SETTLE DOWN, DOCTOR. WE UNDERSTAND YOU'RE IN POSSESSION OF A VERY INTERESTING BODY...

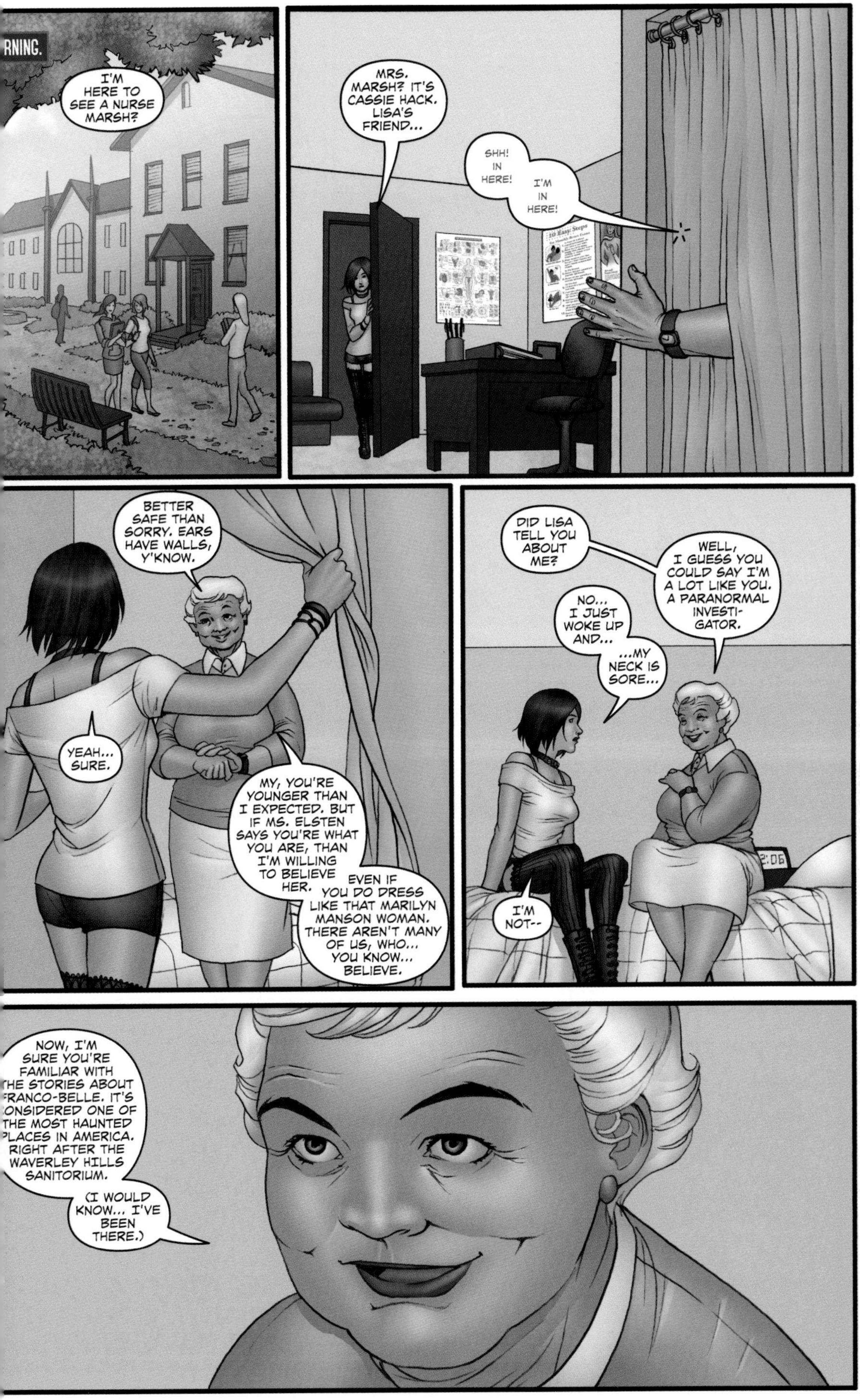
RNING.
I'M HERE TO SEE A NURSE MARSH?
MRS. MARSH? IT'S CASSIE HACK. LISA'S FRIEND...
SHH! IN HERE!
I'M IN HERE!
BETTER SAFE THAN SORRY. EARS HAVE WALLS, Y'KNOW.
YEAH... SURE.
MY, YOU'RE YOUNGER THAN I EXPECTED. BUT IF MS. ELSTEN SAYS YOU'RE WHAT YOU ARE, THAN I'M WILLING TO BELIEVE HER.
EVEN IF YOU DO DRESS LIKE THAT MARILYN MANSON WOMAN. THERE AREN'T MANY OF US, WHO... YOU KNOW... BELIEVE.
DID LISA TELL YOU ABOUT ME?
WELL, I GUESS YOU COULD SAY I'M A LOT LIKE YOU. A PARANORMAL INVESTI-GATOR.
NO... I JUST WOKE UP AND...
...MY NECK IS SORE...
I'M NOT--
NOW, I'M SURE YOU'RE FAMILIAR WITH THE STORIES ABOUT FRANCO-BELLE. IT'S CONSIDERED ONE OF THE MOST HAUNTED PLACES IN AMERICA. RIGHT AFTER THE WAVERLEY HILLS SANITORIUM.
(I WOULD KNOW... I'VE BEEN THERE.)

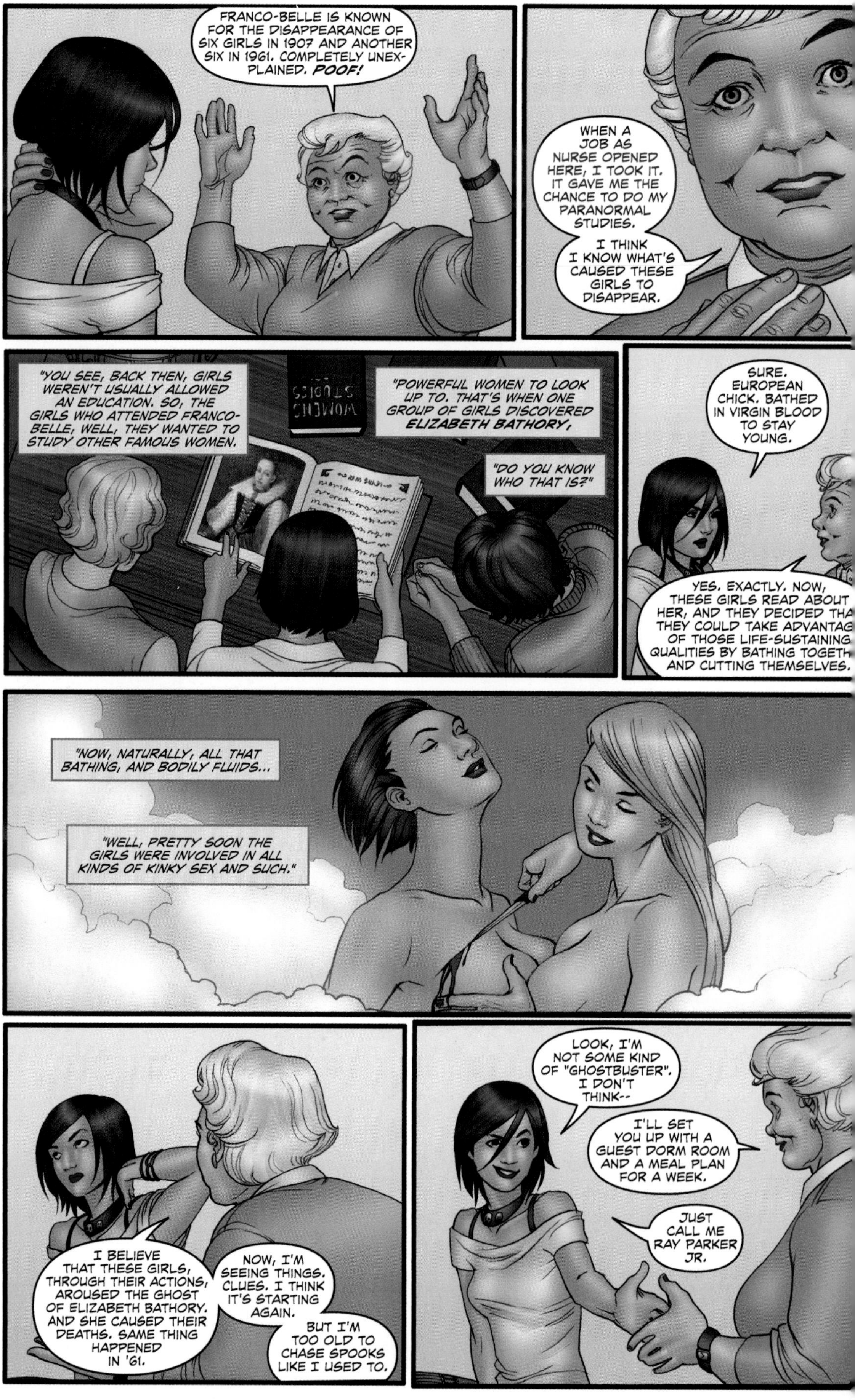
FRANCO-BELLE IS KNOWN FOR THE DISAPPEARANCE OF SIX GIRLS IN 1907 AND ANOTHER SIX IN 1961. COMPLETELY UNEX-PLAINED. POOF!
WHEN A JOB AS NURSE OPENED HERE, I TOOK IT. IT GAVE ME THE CHANCE TO DO MY PARANORMAL STUDIES.
I THINK I KNOW WHAT'S CAUSED THESE GIRLS TO DISAPPEAR.
"YOU SEE, BACK THEN, GIRLS WEREN'T USUALLY ALLOWED AN EDUCATION. SO, THE GIRLS WHO ATTENDED FRANCO-BELLE, WELL, THEY WANTED TO STUDY OTHER FAMOUS WOMEN.
"POWERFUL WOMEN TO LOOK UP TO. THAT'S WHEN ONE GROUP OF GIRLS DISCOVERED ELIZABETH BATHORY,
"DO YOU KNOW WHO THAT IS?"
SURE. EUROPEAN CHICK. BATHED IN VIRGIN BLOOD TO STAY YOUNG.
YES. EXACTLY. NOW, THESE GIRLS READ ABOUT HER, AND THEY DECIDED THA THEY COULD TAKE ADVANTAG OF THOSE LIFE-SUSTAINING QUALITIES BY BATHING TOGETH AND CUTTING THEMSELVES.
"NOW, NATURALLY, ALL THAT BATHING, AND BODILY FLUIDS...
"WELL, PRETTY SOON THE GIRLS WERE INVOLVED IN ALL KINDS OF KINKY SEX AND SUCH."
I BELIEVE THAT THESE GIRLS, THROUGH THEIR ACTIONS, AROUSED THE GHOST OF ELIZABETH BATHORY. AND SHE CAUSED THEIR DEATHS. SAME THING HAPPENED IN '61.
NOW, I'M SEEING THINGS. CLUES. I THINK IT'S STARTING AGAIN.
BUT I'M TOO OLD TO CHASE SPOOKS LIKE I USED TO.
LOOK, I'M NOT SOME KIND OF "GHOSTBUSTER". I DON'T THINK--
I'LL SET YOU UP WITH A GUEST DORM ROOM AND A MEAL PLAN FOR A WEEK.
JUST CALL ME RAY PARKER JR.

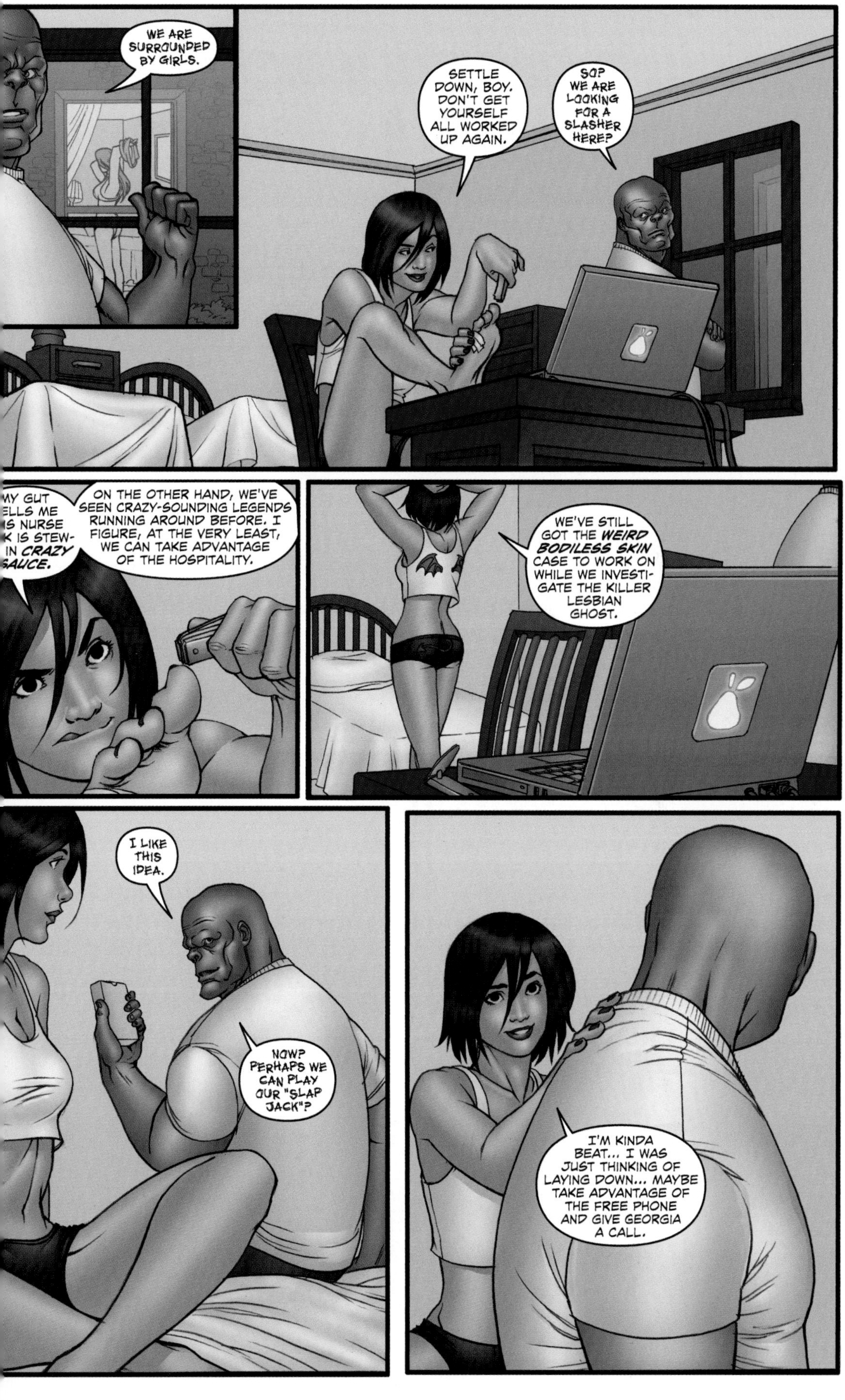
WE ARE SURROUNDED BY GIRLS.
SETTLE DOWN, BOY. DON'T GET YOURSELF ALL WORKED UP AGAIN.
SO? WE ARE LOOKING FOR A SLASHER HERE?
MY GUT ELLS ME S NURSE K IS STEW- IN *CRAZY* SAUCE.
ON THE OTHER HAND, WE'VE SEEN CRAZY-SOUNDING LEGENDS RUNNING AROUND BEFORE. I FIGURE, AT THE VERY LEAST, WE CAN TAKE ADVANTAGE OF THE HOSPITALITY.
WE'VE STILL GOT THE *WEIRD BODILESS SKIN* CASE TO WORK ON WHILE WE INVESTI-GATE THE KILLER LESBIAN GHOST.
I LIKE THIS IDEA.
NOW? PERHAPS WE CAN PLAY OUR "SLAP JACK"?
I'M KINDA BEAT... I WAS JUST THINKING OF LAYING DOWN... MAYBE TAKE ADVANTAGE OF THE FREE PHONE AND GIVE GEORGIA A CALL.

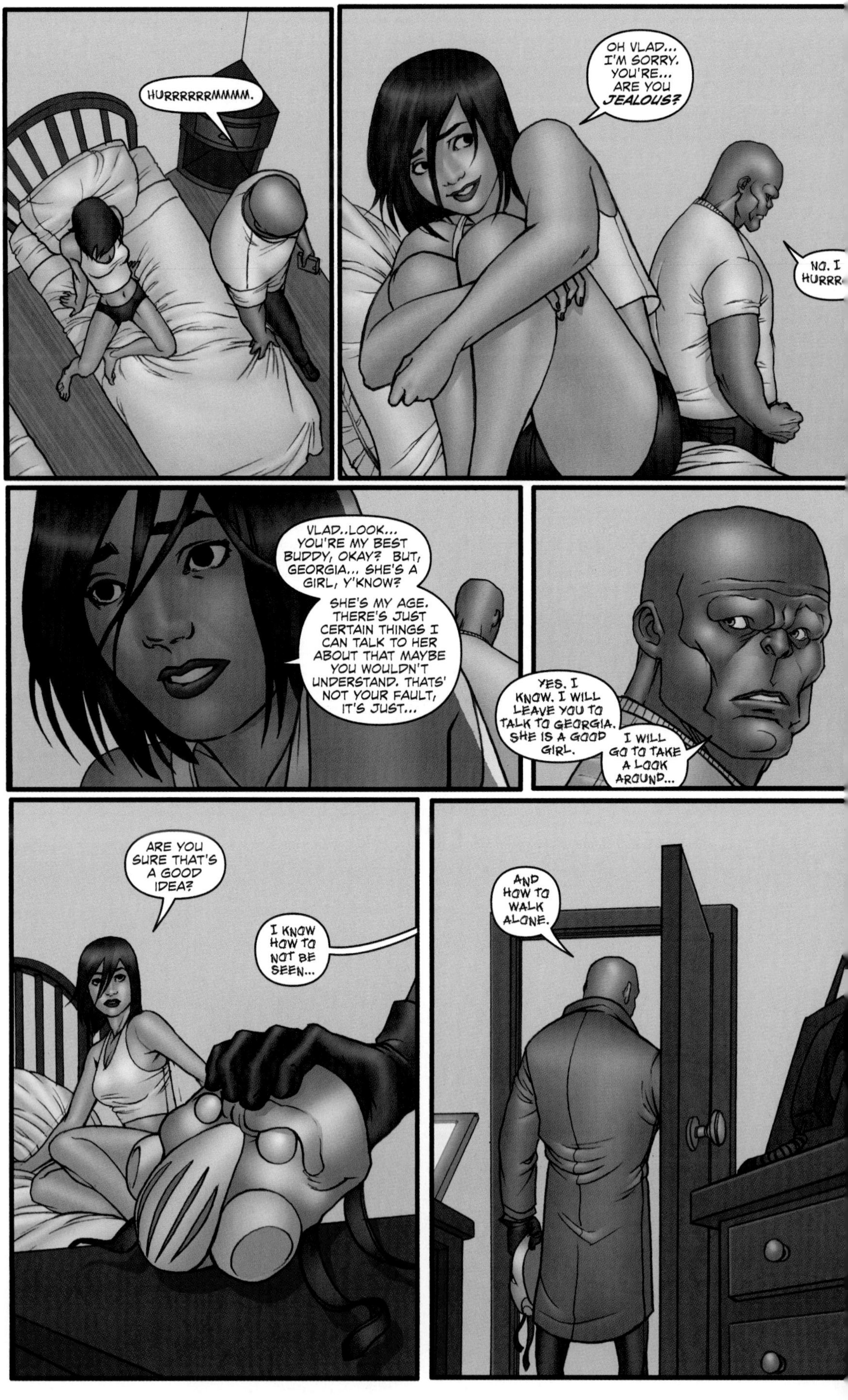
HURRRRRRMMMM.
OH VLAD... I'M SORRY. YOU'RE... ARE YOU JEALOUS?
NO. I HURR
VLAD..LOOK... YOU'RE MY BEST BUDDY, OKAY? BUT, GEORGIA... SHE'S A GIRL, Y'KNOW?
SHE'S MY AGE. THERE'S JUST CERTAIN THINGS I CAN TALK TO HER ABOUT THAT MAYBE YOU WOULDN'T UNDERSTAND. THATS' NOT YOUR FAULT, IT'S JUST...
YES. I KNOW. I WILL LEAVE YOU TO TALK TO GEORGIA. SHE IS A GOOD GIRL.
I WILL GO TO TAKE A LOOK AROUND...
ARE YOU SURE THAT'S A GOOD IDEA?
I KNOW HOW TO NOT BE SEEN...
AND HOW TO WALK ALONE.

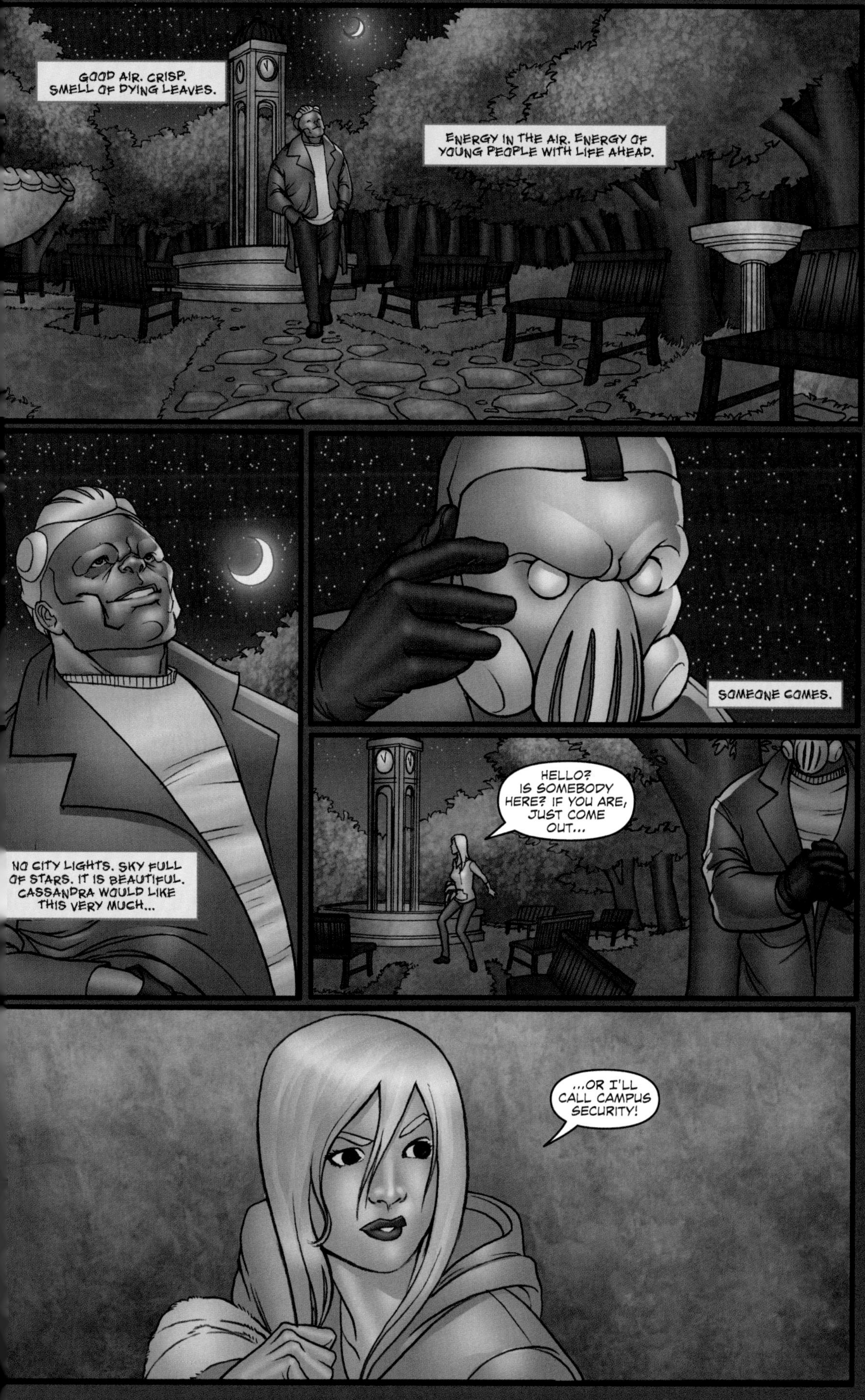
GOOD AIR. CRISP. SMELL OF DYING LEAVES.
ENERGY IN THE AIR. ENERGY OF YOUNG PEOPLE WITH LIFE AHEAD.
NO CITY LIGHTS. SKY FULL OF STARS. IT IS BEAUTIFUL. CASSANDRA WOULD LIKE THIS VERY MUCH...
SOMEONE COMES.
HELLO? IS SOMEBODY HERE? IF YOU ARE, JUST COME OUT...
...OR I'LL CALL CAMPUS SECURITY!

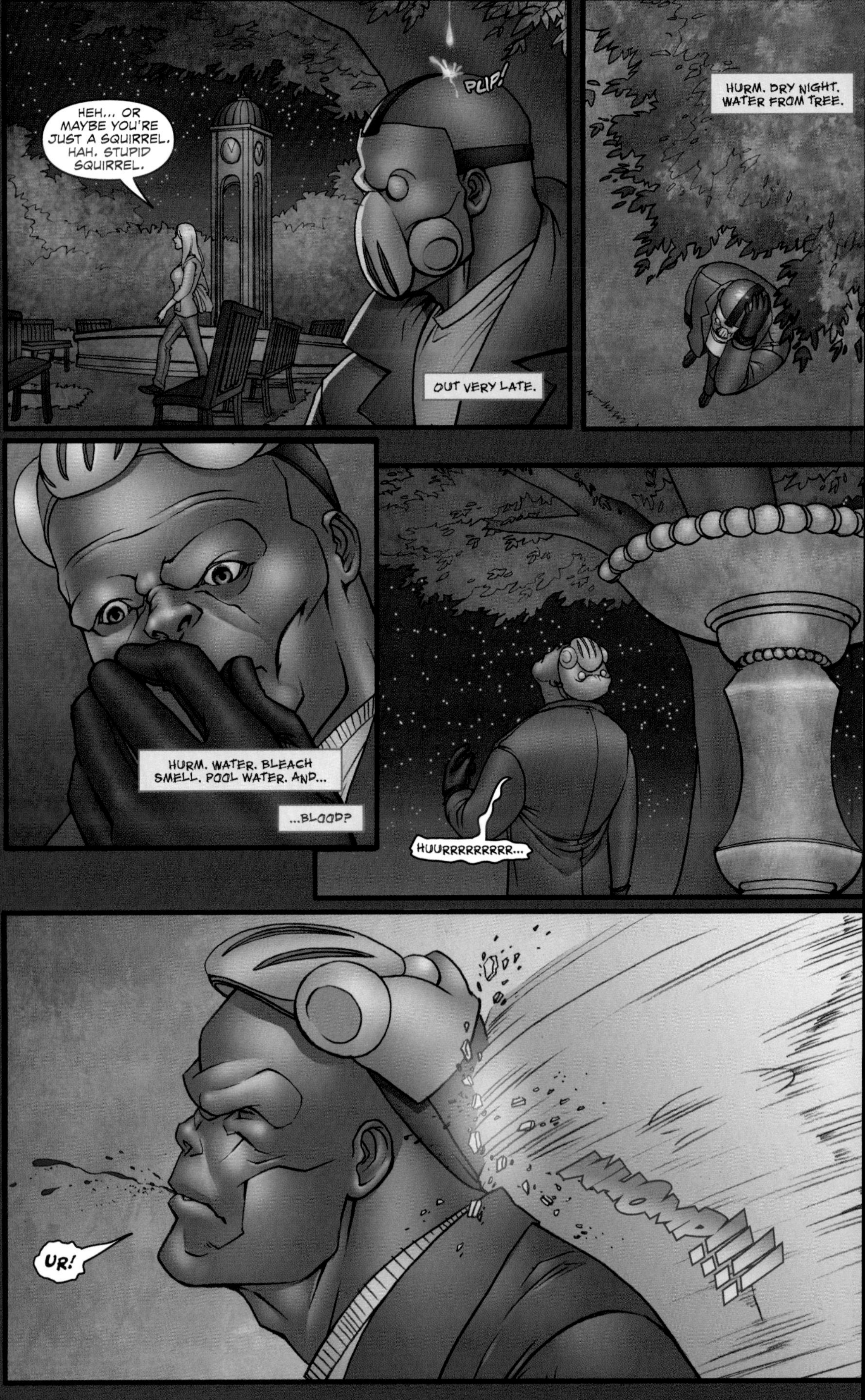
HEH... OR MAYBE YOU'RE JUST A SQUIRREL. HAH. STUPID SQUIRREL.
PLIP!
OUT VERY LATE.
HURM. DRY NIGHT. WATER FROM TREE.
HURM. WATER. BLEACH SMELL. POOL WATER. AND...
...BLOOD?
HUURRRRRRRRR...
UR!
WHOMP!!!

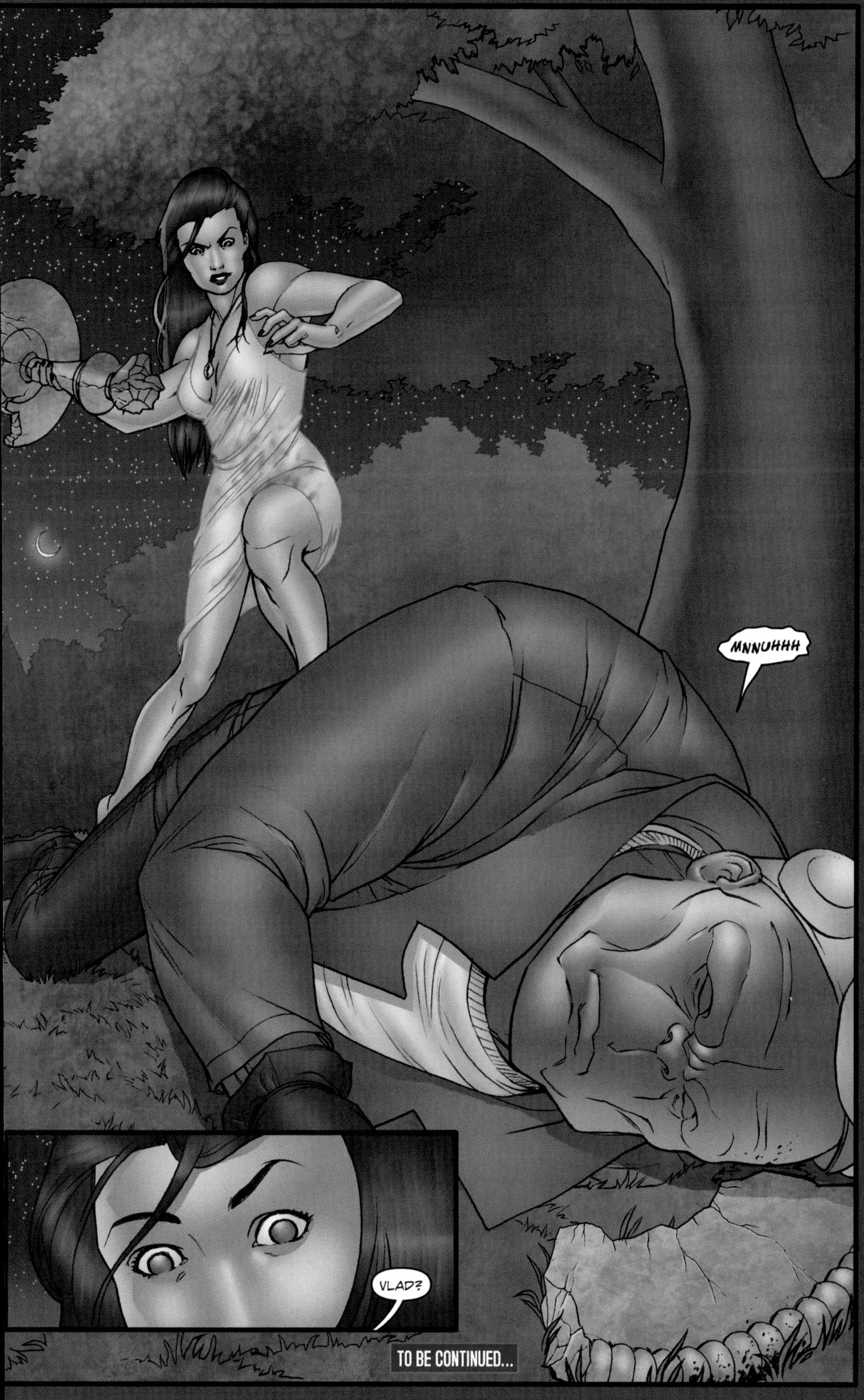
MNNUHHH
VLAD?
TO BE CONTINUED...

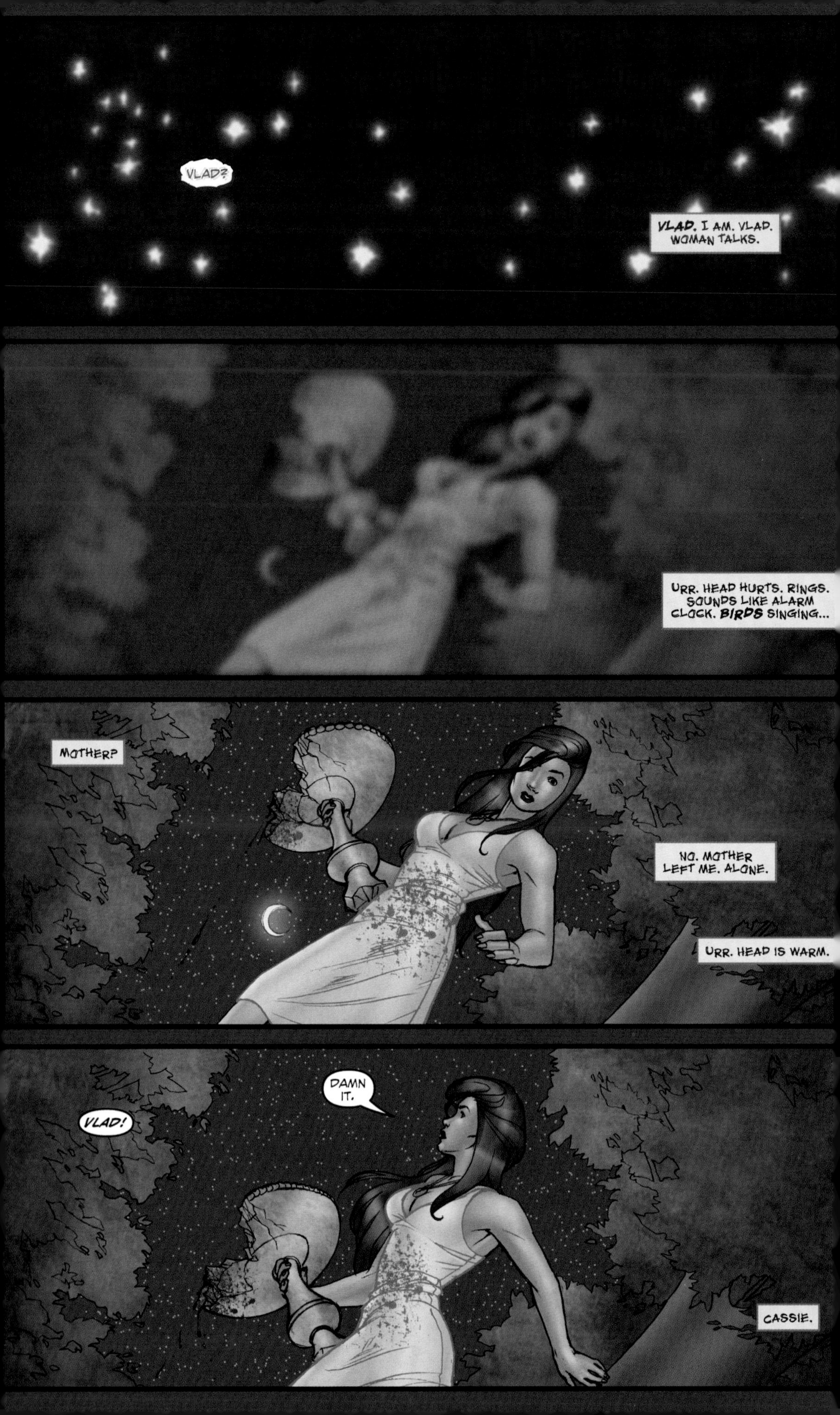
VLAD?
VLAD. I AM. VLAD. WOMAN TALKS.
URR. HEAD HURTS. RINGS. SOUNDS LIKE ALARM CLOCK. BIRDS SINGING...
MOTHER?
NO. MOTHER LEFT ME. ALONE.
URR. HEAD IS WARM.
VLAD!
DAMN IT.
CASSIE.

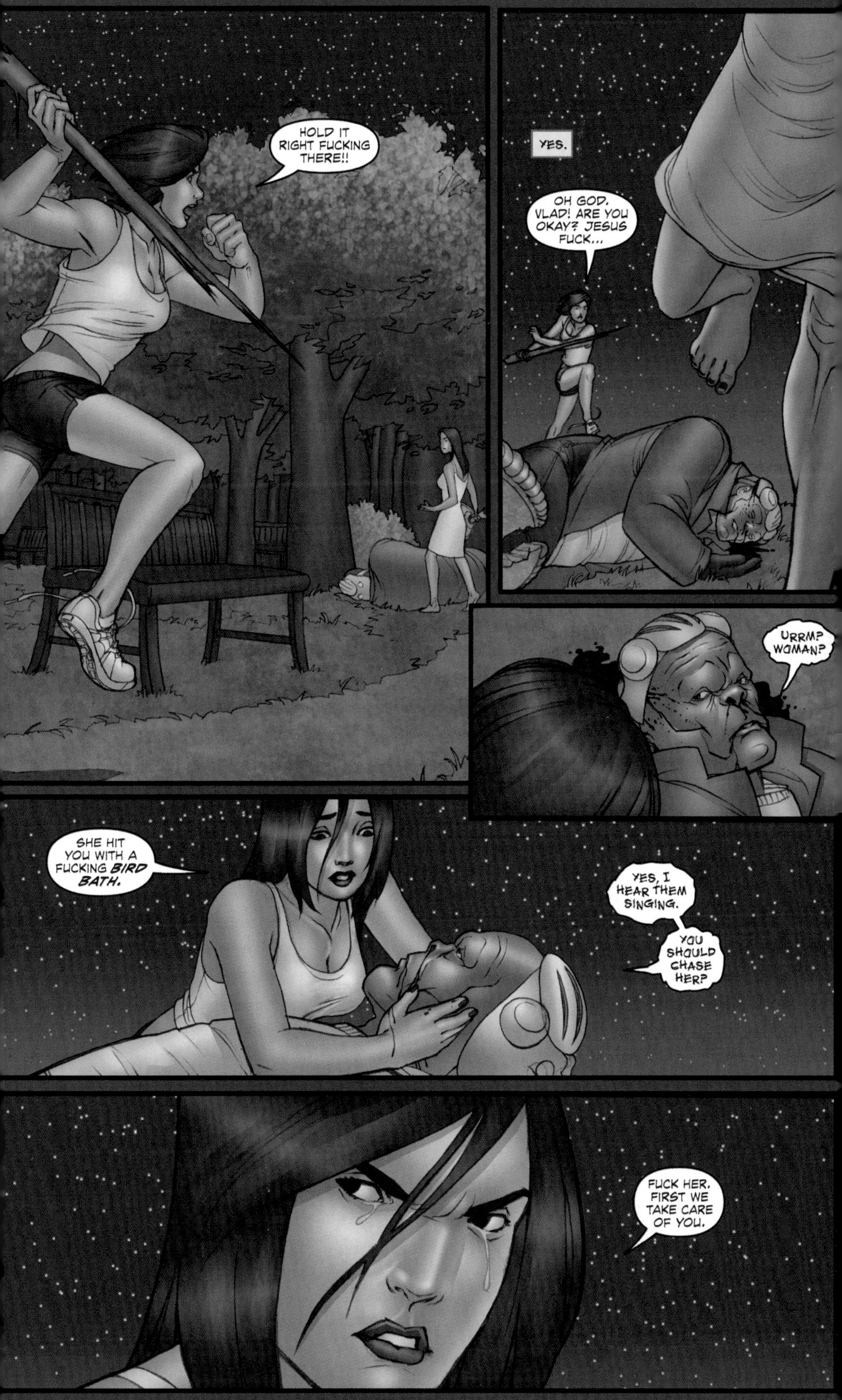
HOLD IT RIGHT FUCKING THERE!!
YES.
OH GOD, VLAD! ARE YOU OKAY? JESUS FUCK...
URRM? WOMAN?
SHE HIT YOU WITH A FUCKING *BIRD BATH.*
YES, I HEAR THEM SINGING.
YOU SHOULD CHASE HER?
FUCK HER. FIRST WE TAKE CARE OF YOU.

IS HE OKAY?!

YES, I BELIEVE SO.

YOUR FRIEND IS BLESSED WITH THE GOOD KIND OF "THICK HEADEDNESS" THAT COMES IN VERY HANDY IN SITUATIONS LIKE THIS.

WISH IT WAS THE KIND MY HUSBAND HAD.

DID YOU GET A GOOD LOOK AT ATTACKER

NO. BUT WHEN I FIND HER, I'M GONNA SHOVE THAT BIRD BATH RIGHT UP HER ASS.

IN THE MEANTIME, VLAD MAY BE SUFFERING FROM A CONCUSSION, IN WHICH CASE, I DON'T RECOMMEND HE SLEEP.

SO, KEEP HIM AWAKE. THE MORE TALKING, THE BETTER.

I'M SURE THAT WON'T BE TOO HARD OLD FRIENDS LIKE YO TWO SHOULD BE ABL TO GAB LIKE GIRLS AT A *SLUMBER PARTY*.

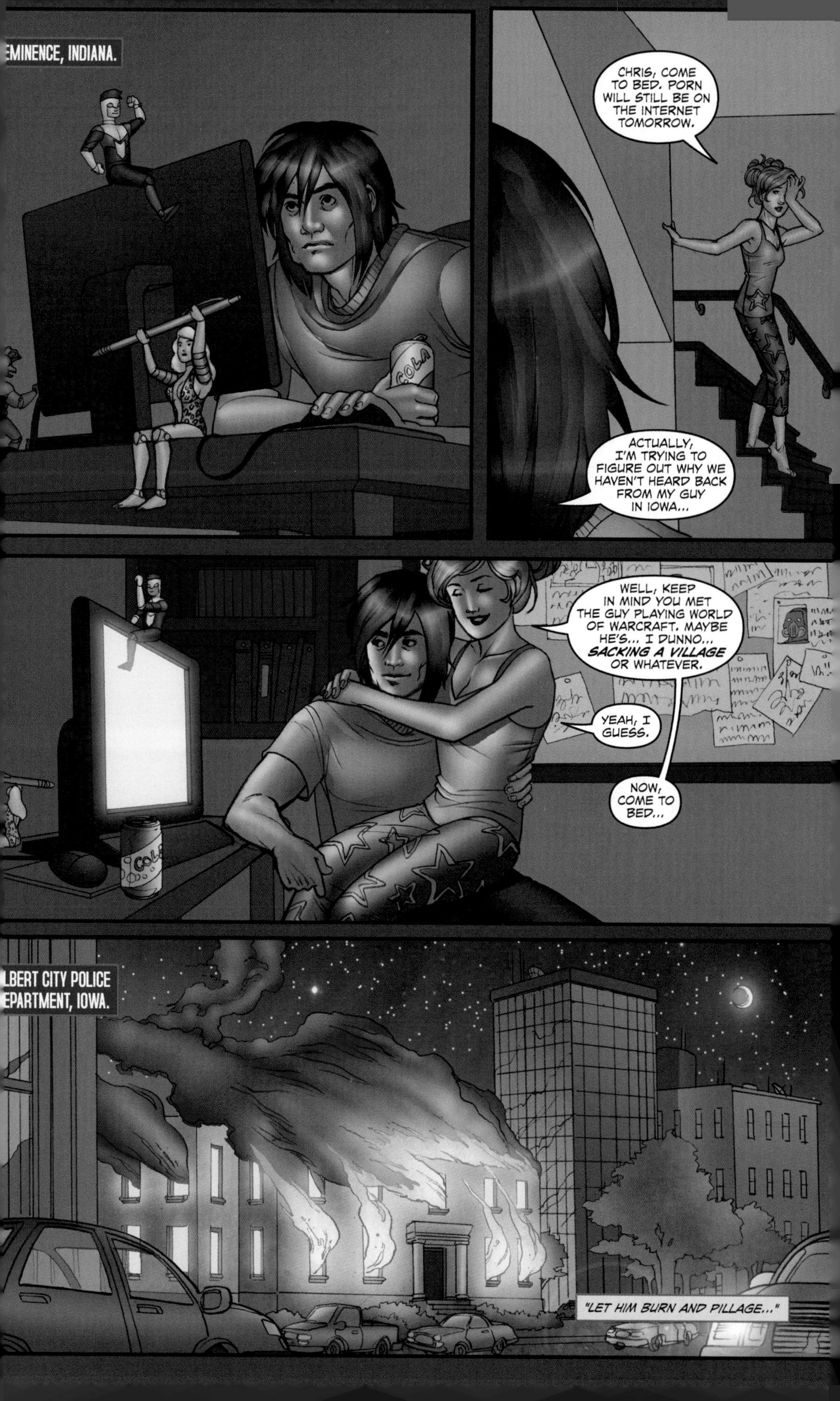
EMINENCE, INDIANA.
CHRIS, COME TO BED. PORN WILL STILL BE ON THE INTERNET TOMORROW.
ACTUALLY, I'M TRYING TO FIGURE OUT WHY WE HAVEN'T HEARD BACK FROM MY GUY IN IOWA...
COLA
WELL, KEEP IN MIND YOU MET THE GUY PLAYING WORLD OF WARCRAFT. MAYBE HE'S... I DUNNO... ***SACKING A VILLAGE*** OR WHATEVER.
YEAH, I GUESS.
NOW, COME TO BED...
LBERT CITY POLICE EPARTMENT, IOWA.
"LET HIM BURN AND PILLAGE..."

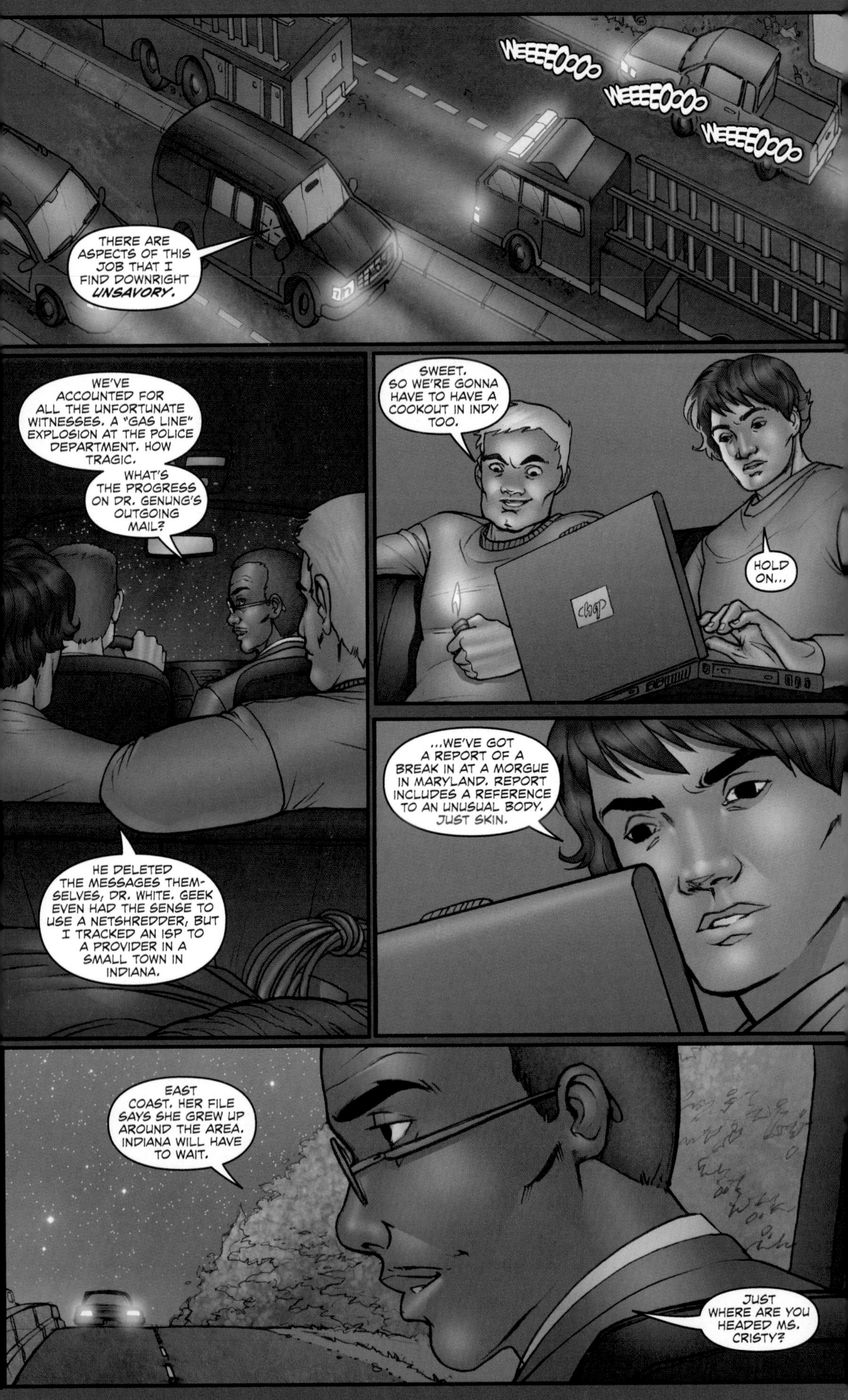
WEEEEOOOO
WEEEEOOOO
WEEEEOOOO
THERE ARE ASPECTS OF THIS JOB THAT I FIND DOWNRIGHT *UNSAVORY.*
WE'VE ACCOUNTED FOR ALL THE UNFORTUNATE WITNESSES. A "GAS LINE" EXPLOSION AT THE POLICE DEPARTMENT. HOW TRAGIC.
WHAT'S THE PROGRESS ON DR. GENUNG'S OUTGOING MAIL?
HE DELETED THE MESSAGES THEMSELVES, DR. WHITE. GEEK EVEN HAD THE SENSE TO USE A NETSHREDDER, BUT I TRACKED AN ISP TO A PROVIDER IN A SMALL TOWN IN INDIANA.
SWEET. SO WE'RE GONNA HAVE TO HAVE A COOKOUT IN INDY TOO.
HOLD ON...
...WE'VE GOT A REPORT OF A BREAK IN AT A MORGUE IN MARYLAND. REPORT INCLUDES A REFERENCE TO AN UNUSUAL BODY. JUST SKIN.
EAST COAST. HER FILE SAYS SHE GREW UP AROUND THE AREA. INDIANA WILL HAVE TO WAIT.
JUST WHERE ARE YOU HEADED MS. CRISTY?

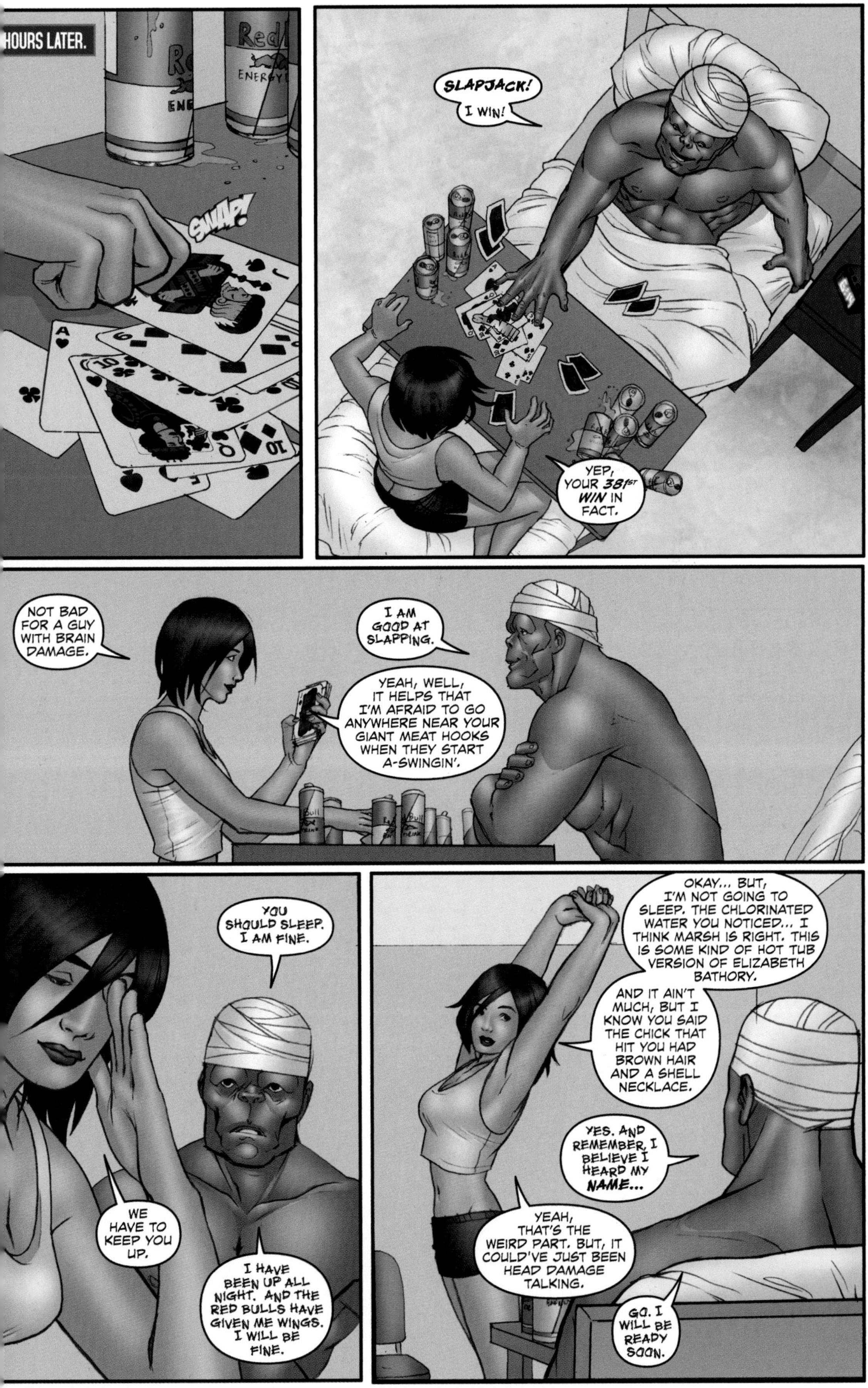
HOURS LATER.
SWAP!
SLAPJACK! I WIN!
YEP, YOUR 381ST WIN IN FACT.
NOT BAD FOR A GUY WITH BRAIN DAMAGE.
I AM GOOD AT SLAPPING.
YEAH, WELL, IT HELPS THAT I'M AFRAID TO GO ANYWHERE NEAR YOUR GIANT MEAT HOOKS WHEN THEY START A-SWINGIN'.
YOU SHOULD SLEEP. I AM FINE.
WE HAVE TO KEEP YOU UP.
I HAVE BEEN UP ALL NIGHT. AND THE RED BULLS HAVE GIVEN ME WINGS. I WILL BE FINE.
OKAY... BUT, I'M NOT GOING TO SLEEP. THE CHLORINATED WATER YOU NOTICED... I THINK MARSH IS RIGHT. THIS IS SOME KIND OF HOT TUB VERSION OF ELIZABETH BATHORY.
AND IT AIN'T MUCH, BUT I KNOW YOU SAID THE CHICK THAT HIT YOU HAD BROWN HAIR AND A SHELL NECKLACE.
YES. AND REMEMBER, I BELIEVE I HEARD MY NAME...
YEAH, THAT'S THE WEIRD PART. BUT, IT COULD'VE JUST BEEN HEAD DAMAGE TALKING.
GO. I WILL BE READY SOON.

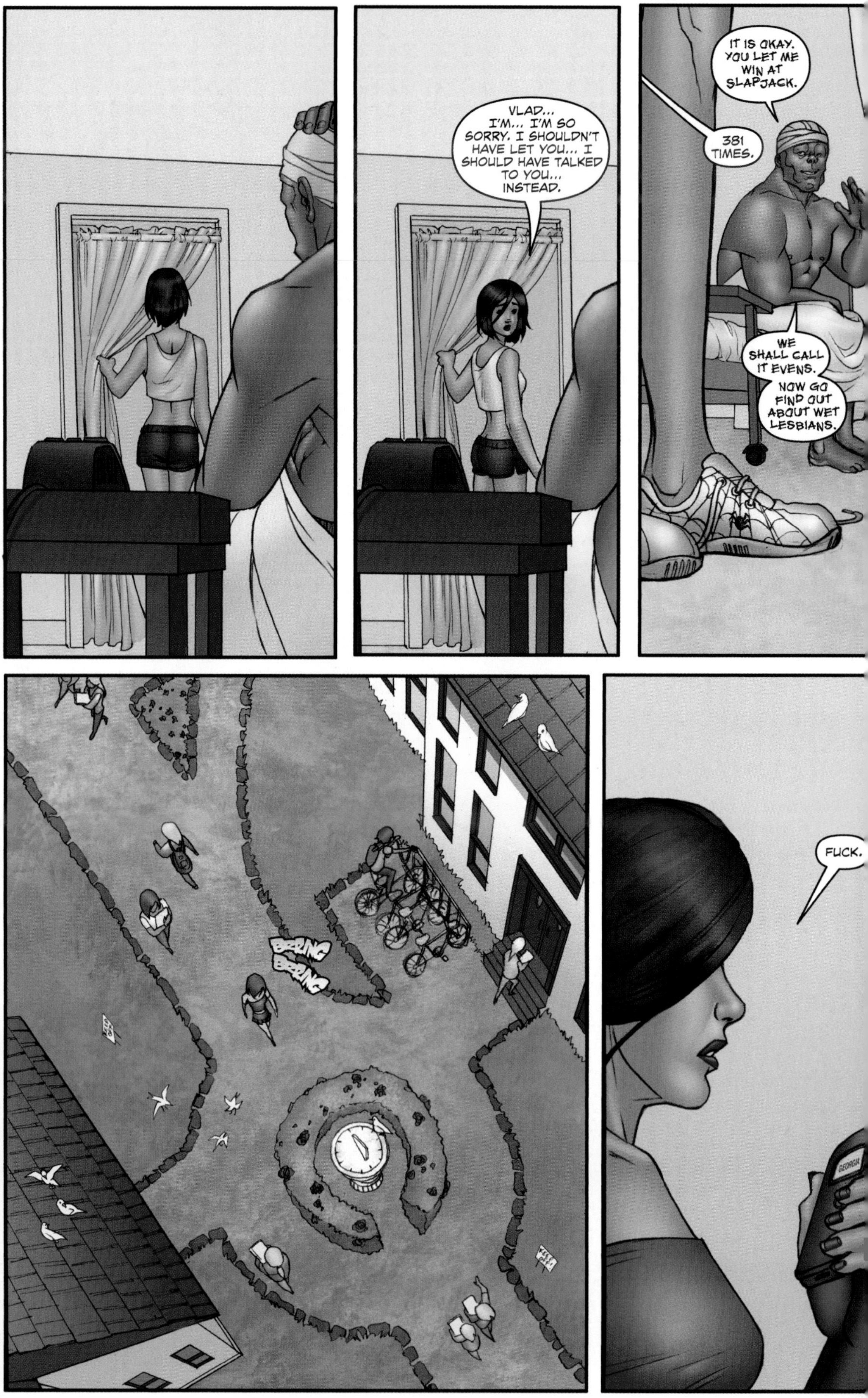
VLAD... I'M... I'M SO SORRY. I SHOULDN'T HAVE LET YOU... I SHOULD HAVE TALKED TO YOU... INSTEAD.
IT IS OKAY. YOU LET ME WIN AT SLAPJACK.
381 TIMES.
WE SHALL CALL IT EVENS.
NOW GO FIND OUT ABOUT WET LESBIANS.
BRRING
BRRING
KEEP OFF
FUCK.
GEORGIA

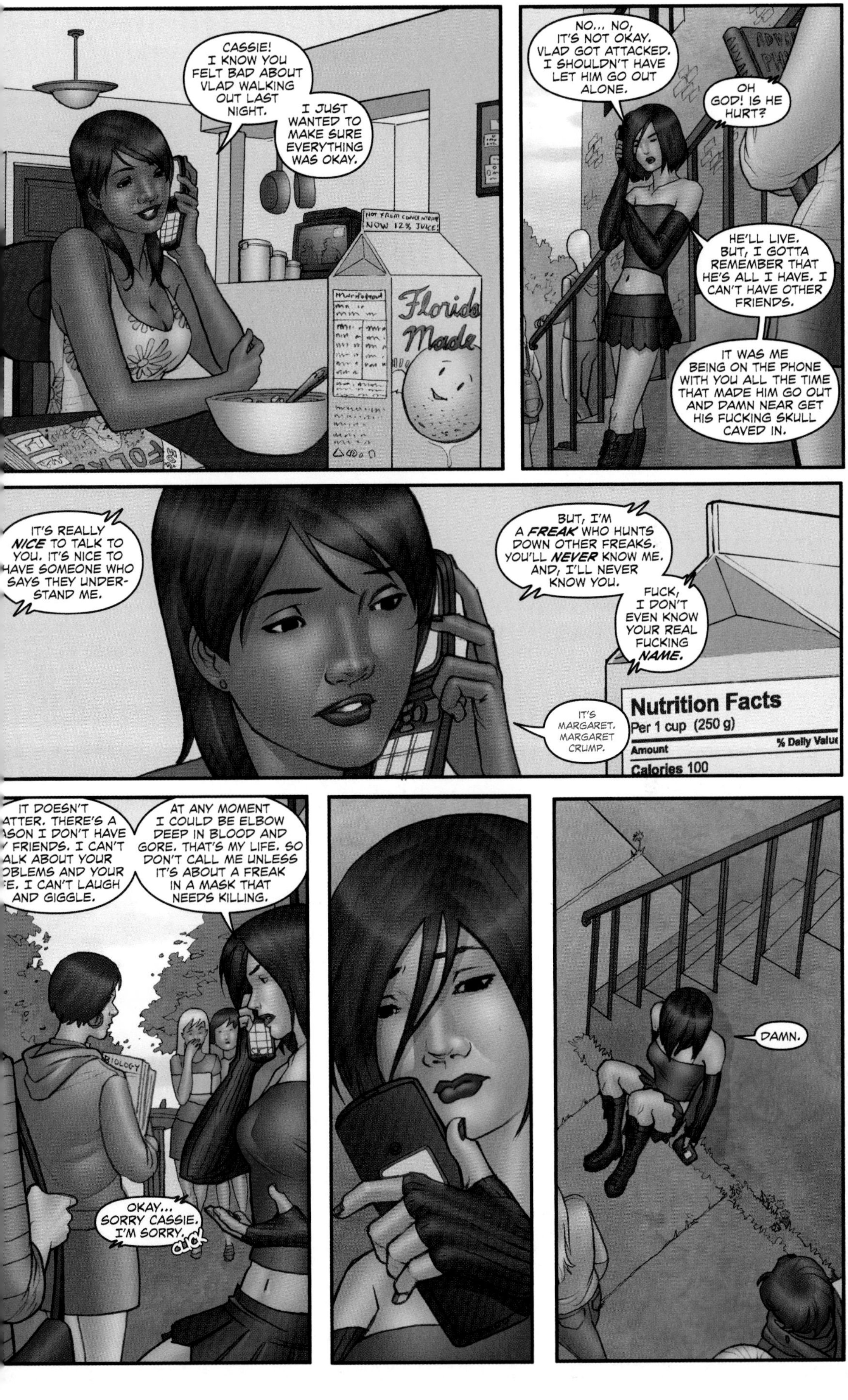
CASSIE! I KNOW YOU FELT BAD ABOUT VLAD WALKING OUT LAST NIGHT.
I JUST WANTED TO MAKE SURE EVERYTHING WAS OKAY.
NOT FROM CONCENTRATE NOW 12% JUICE!
Florida Made
NO... NO, IT'S NOT OKAY. VLAD GOT ATTACKED. I SHOULDN'T HAVE LET HIM GO OUT ALONE.
OH GOD! IS HE HURT?
HE'LL LIVE. BUT, I GOTTA REMEMBER THAT HE'S ALL I HAVE. I CAN'T HAVE OTHER FRIENDS.
IT WAS ME BEING ON THE PHONE WITH YOU ALL THE TIME THAT MADE HIM GO OUT AND DAMN NEAR GET HIS FUCKING SKULL CAVED IN.
IT'S REALLY *NICE* TO TALK TO YOU. IT'S NICE TO HAVE SOMEONE WHO SAYS THEY UNDER-STAND ME.
BUT, I'M A ***FREAK*** WHO HUNTS DOWN OTHER FREAKS. YOU'LL ***NEVER*** KNOW ME. AND, I'LL NEVER KNOW YOU.
FUCK, I DON'T EVEN KNOW YOUR REAL FUCKING ***NAME.***
IT'S MARGARET. MARGARET CRUMP.
Nutrition Facts
Per 1 cup (250 g)
Amount
% Daily Valu
Calories 100
IT DOESN'T ATTER. THERE'S A ASON I DON'T HAVE FRIENDS. I CAN'T ALK ABOUT YOUR OBLEMS AND YOUR FE. I CAN'T LAUGH AND GIGGLE.
AT ANY MOMENT I COULD BE ELBOW DEEP IN BLOOD AND GORE. THAT'S MY LIFE. SO DON'T CALL ME UNLESS IT'S ABOUT A FREAK IN A MASK THAT NEEDS KILLING.
BIOLOGY
OKAY... SORRY CASSIE. I'M SORRY.
CLICK
DAMN.

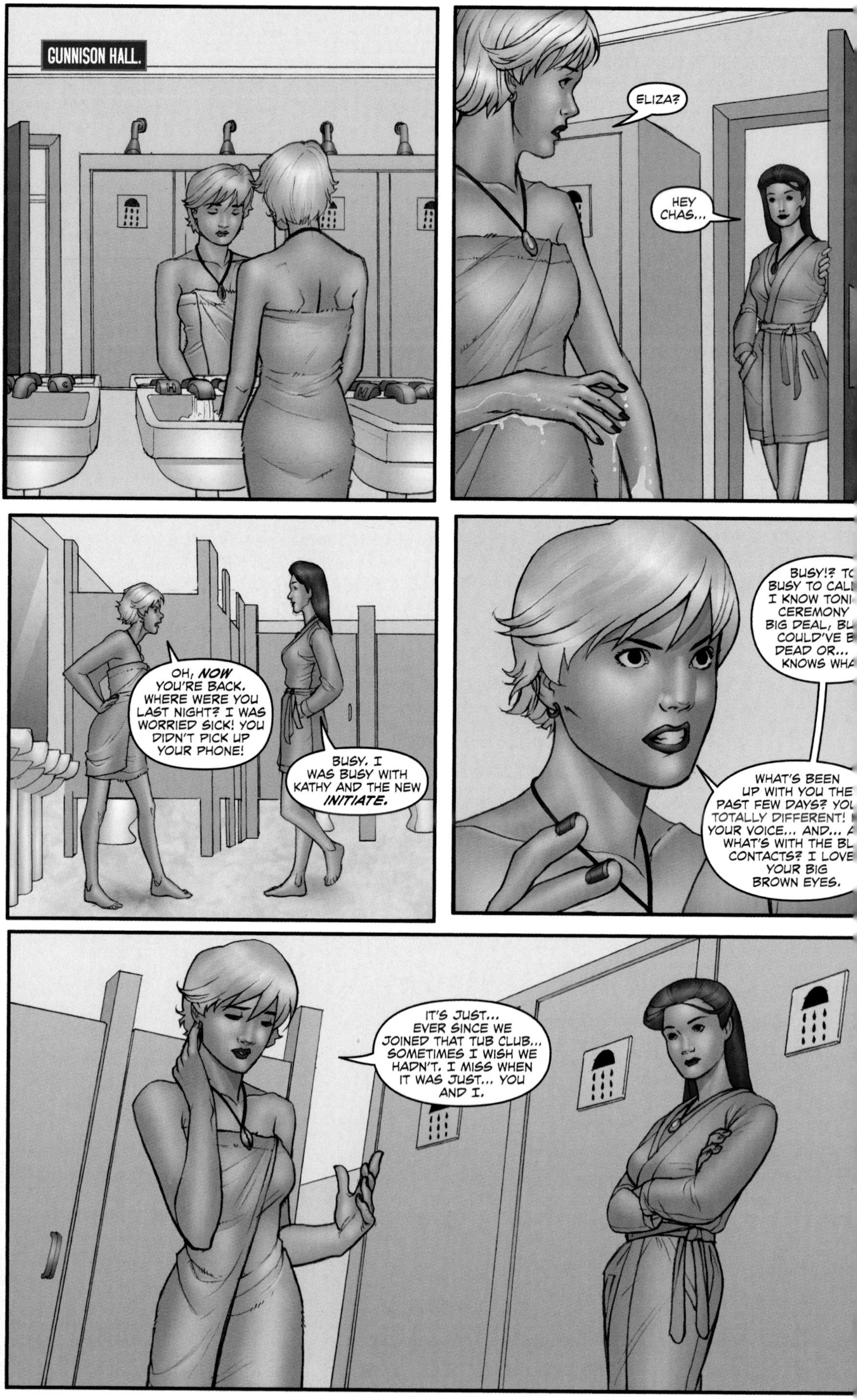
GUNNISON HALL.
ELIZA?
HEY CHAS...
OH, NOW YOU'RE BACK. WHERE WERE YOU LAST NIGHT? I WAS WORRIED SICK! YOU DIDN'T PICK UP YOUR PHONE!
BUSY. I WAS BUSY WITH KATHY AND THE NEW INITIATE.
BUSY!? TO BUSY TO CAL I KNOW TONI CEREMONY BIG DEAL, BU COULD'VE B DEAD OR... KNOWS WHA
WHAT'S BEEN UP WITH YOU THE PAST FEW DAYS? YOU TOTALLY DIFFERENT! YOUR VOICE... AND... WHAT'S WITH THE BL CONTACTS? I LOVE YOUR BIG BROWN EYES.
IT'S JUST... EVER SINCE WE JOINED THAT TUB CLUB... SOMETIMES I WISH WE HADN'T. I MISS WHEN IT WAS JUST... YOU AND I.

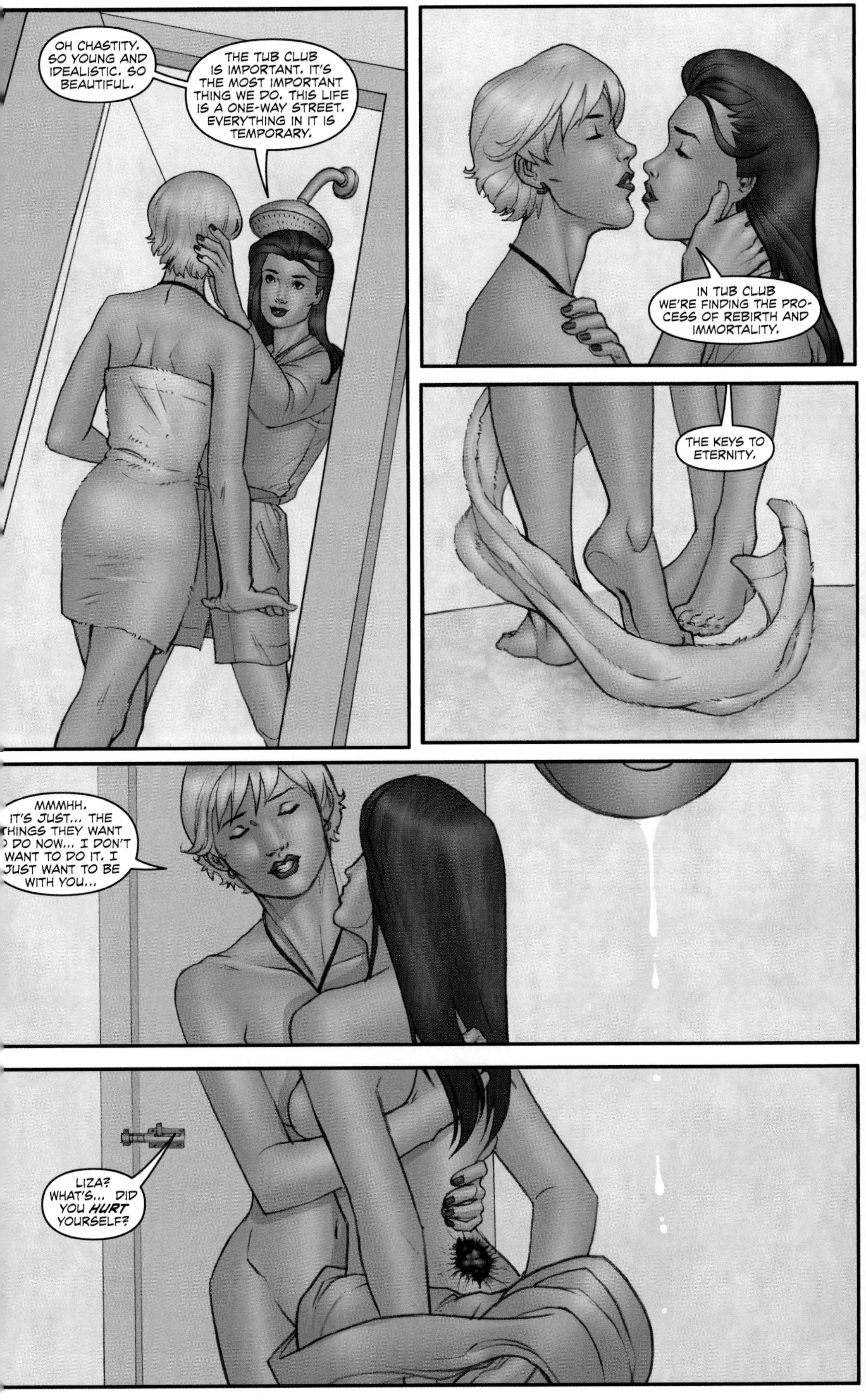
OH CHASTITY. SO YOUNG AND IDEALISTIC. SO BEAUTIFUL.
THE TUB CLUB IS IMPORTANT. IT'S THE MOST IMPORTANT THING WE DO. THIS LIFE IS A ONE-WAY STREET. EVERYTHING IN IT IS TEMPORARY.
IN TUB CLUB WE'RE FINDING THE PROCESS OF REBIRTH AND IMMORTALITY.
THE KEYS TO ETERNITY.
MMMHH. IT'S JUST... THE THINGS THEY WANT O DO NOW... I DON'T WANT TO DO IT. I JUST WANT TO BE WITH YOU...
LIZA? WHAT'S... DID YOU *HURT* YOURSELF?

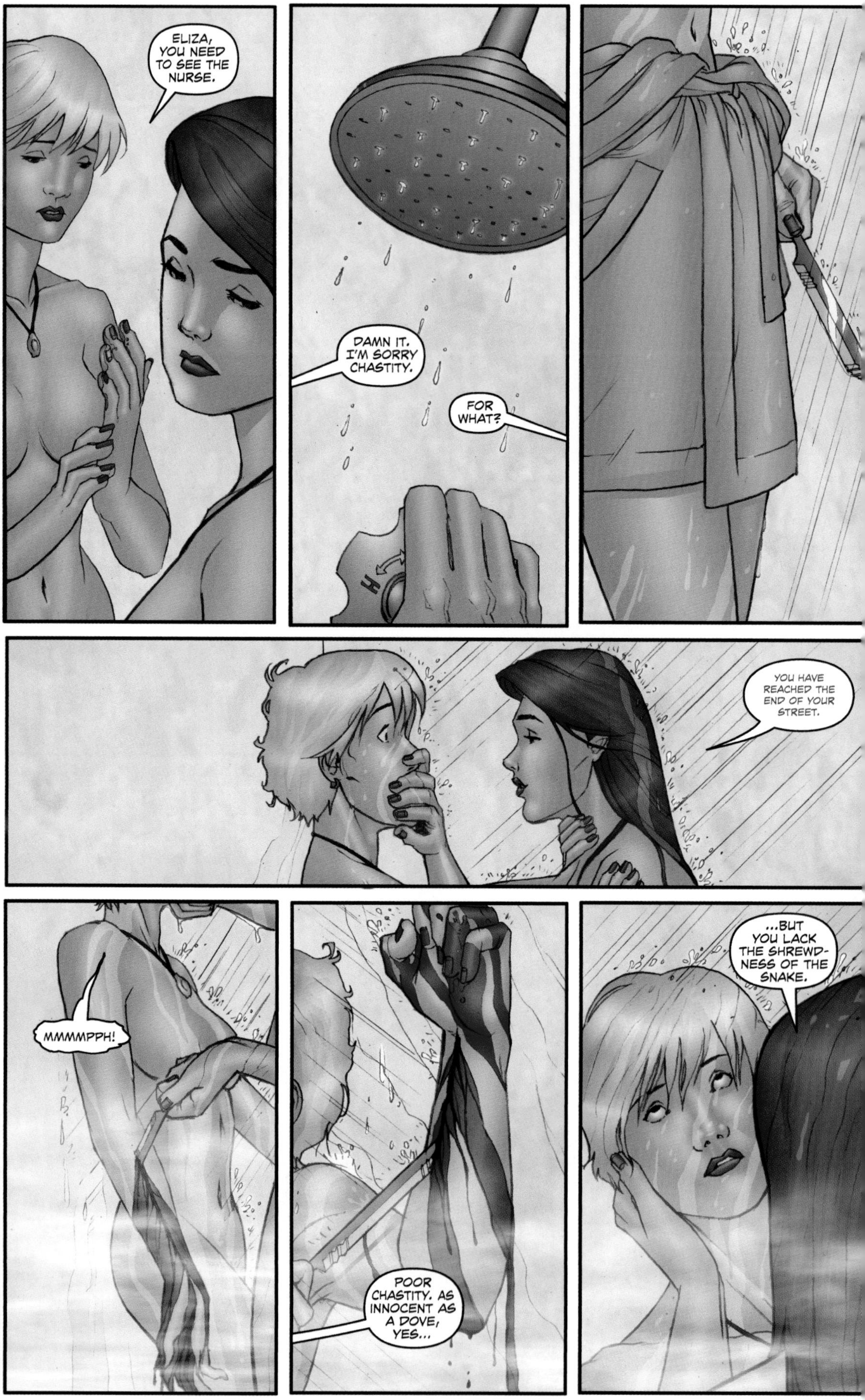
ELIZA, YOU NEED TO SEE THE NURSE.
DAMN IT. I'M SORRY CHASTITY.
FOR WHAT?
YOU HAVE REACHED THE END OF YOUR STREET.
MMMMPPH!
POOR CHASTITY. AS INNOCENT AS A DOVE, YES...
...BUT YOU LACK THE SHREWD-NESS OF THE SNAKE.

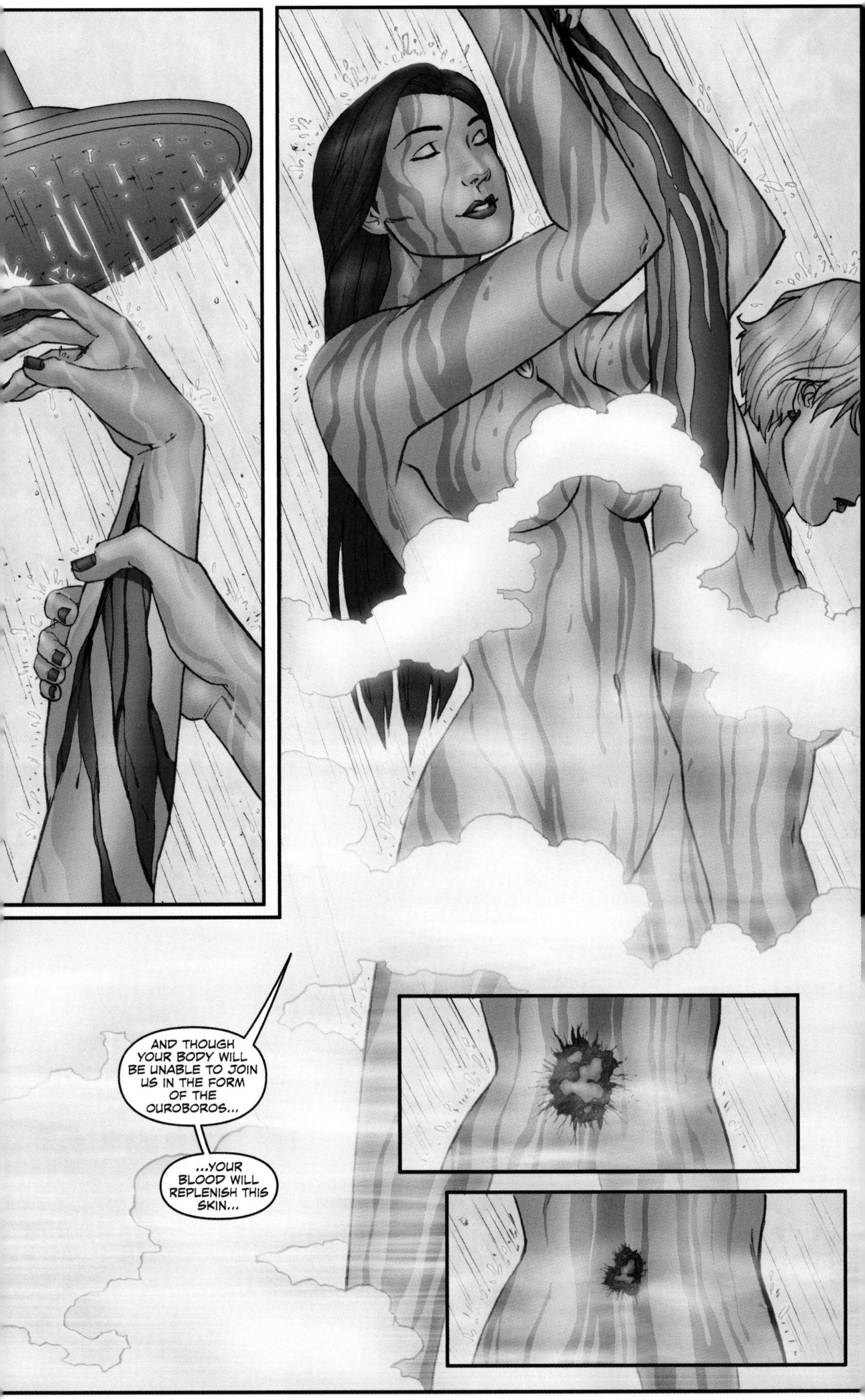
AND THOUGH YOUR BODY WILL BE UNABLE TO JOIN US IN THE FORM OF THE OUROBOROS...
...YOUR BLOOD WILL REPLENISH THIS SKIN...

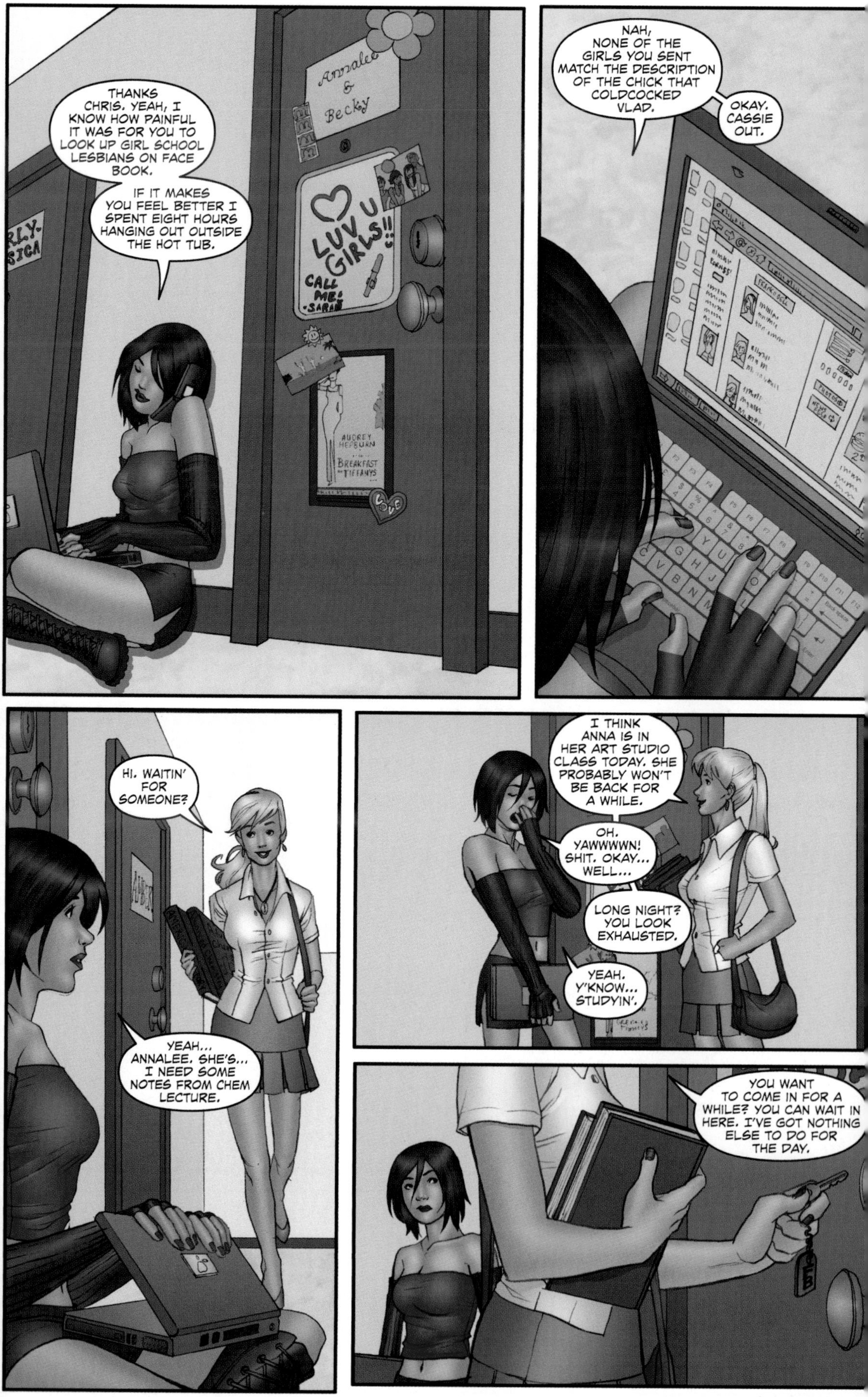
THANKS CHRIS. YEAH, I KNOW HOW PAINFUL IT WAS FOR YOU TO LOOK UP GIRL SCHOOL LESBIANS ON FACE BOOK.
IF IT MAKES YOU FEEL BETTER I SPENT EIGHT HOURS HANGING OUT OUTSIDE THE HOT TUB.
Annalee & Becky
LUV U GIRLS!! CALL ME! -SARAH
AUDREY HEPBURN BREAKFAST AT TIFFANYS
NAH, NONE OF THE GIRLS YOU SENT MATCH THE DESCRIPTION OF THE CHICK THAT COLDCOCKED VLAD.
OKAY. CASSIE OUT.
HI. WAITIN' FOR SOMEONE?
YEAH... ANNALEE. SHE'S... I NEED SOME NOTES FROM CHEM LECTURE.
I THINK ANNA IS IN HER ART STUDIO CLASS TODAY. SHE PROBABLY WON'T BE BACK FOR A WHILE.
OH. YAWWWWN! SHIT. OKAY... WELL...
LONG NIGHT? YOU LOOK EXHAUSTED.
YEAH. Y'KNOW... STUDYIN'.
YOU WANT TO COME IN FOR A WHILE? YOU CAN WAIT IN HERE. I'VE GOT NOTHING ELSE TO DO FOR THE DAY.

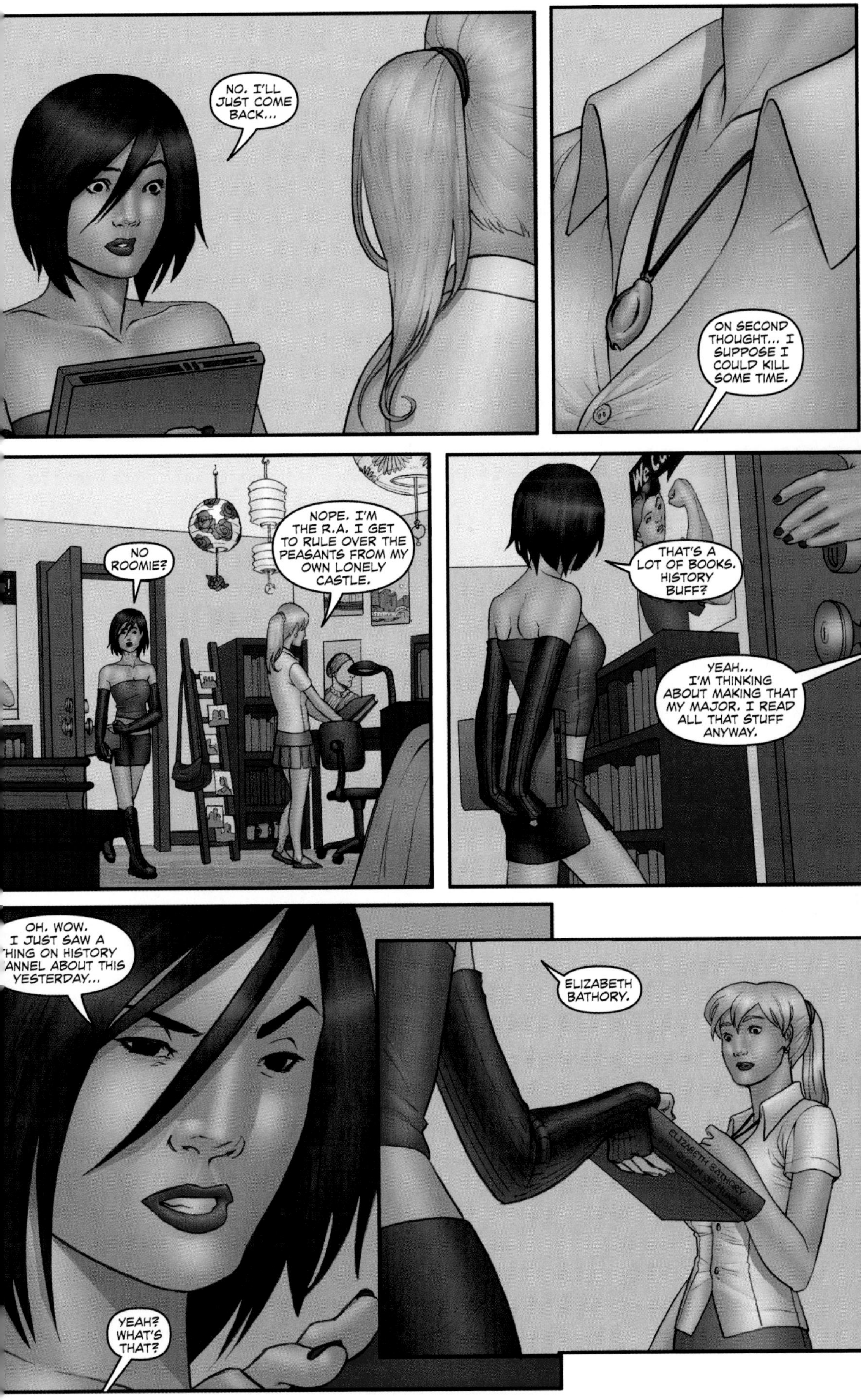
NO. I'LL JUST COME BACK...
ON SECOND THOUGHT... I SUPPOSE I COULD KILL SOME TIME.
NO ROOMIE?
NOPE. I'M THE R.A. I GET TO RULE OVER THE PEASANTS FROM MY OWN LONELY CASTLE.
THAT'S A LOT OF BOOKS. HISTORY BUFF?
YEAH... I'M THINKING ABOUT MAKING THAT MY MAJOR. I READ ALL THAT STUFF ANYWAY.
OH. WOW. I JUST SAW A THING ON HISTORY CHANNEL ABOUT THIS YESTERDAY...
YEAH? WHAT'S THAT?
ELIZABETH BATHORY.
ELIZABETH BATHORY

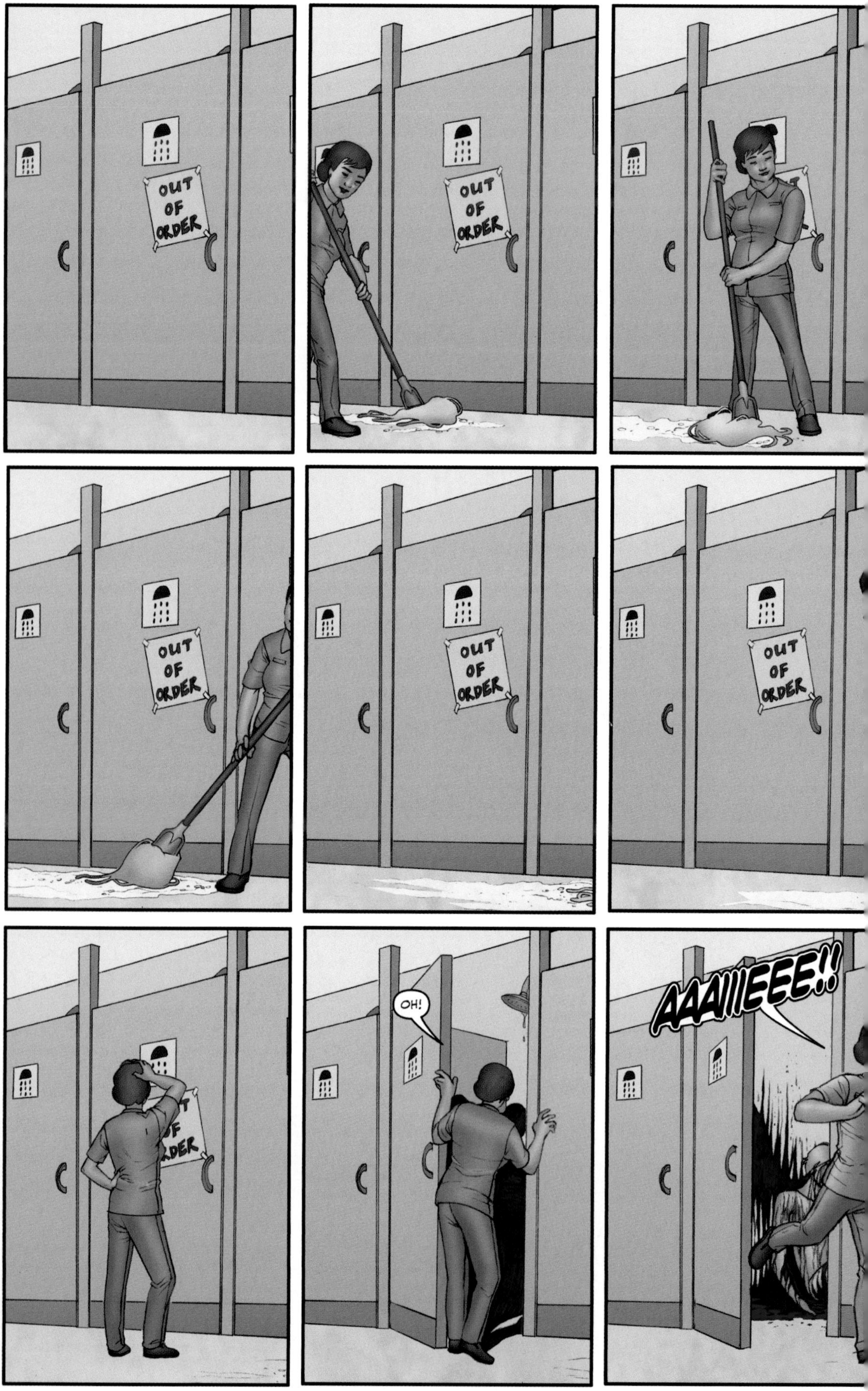
OUT OF ORDER
OUT OF ORDER
OUT OF ORDER
OUT OF ORDER
OUT OF ORDER
OUT OF ORDER
OH!
AAAIIIEEEE!!

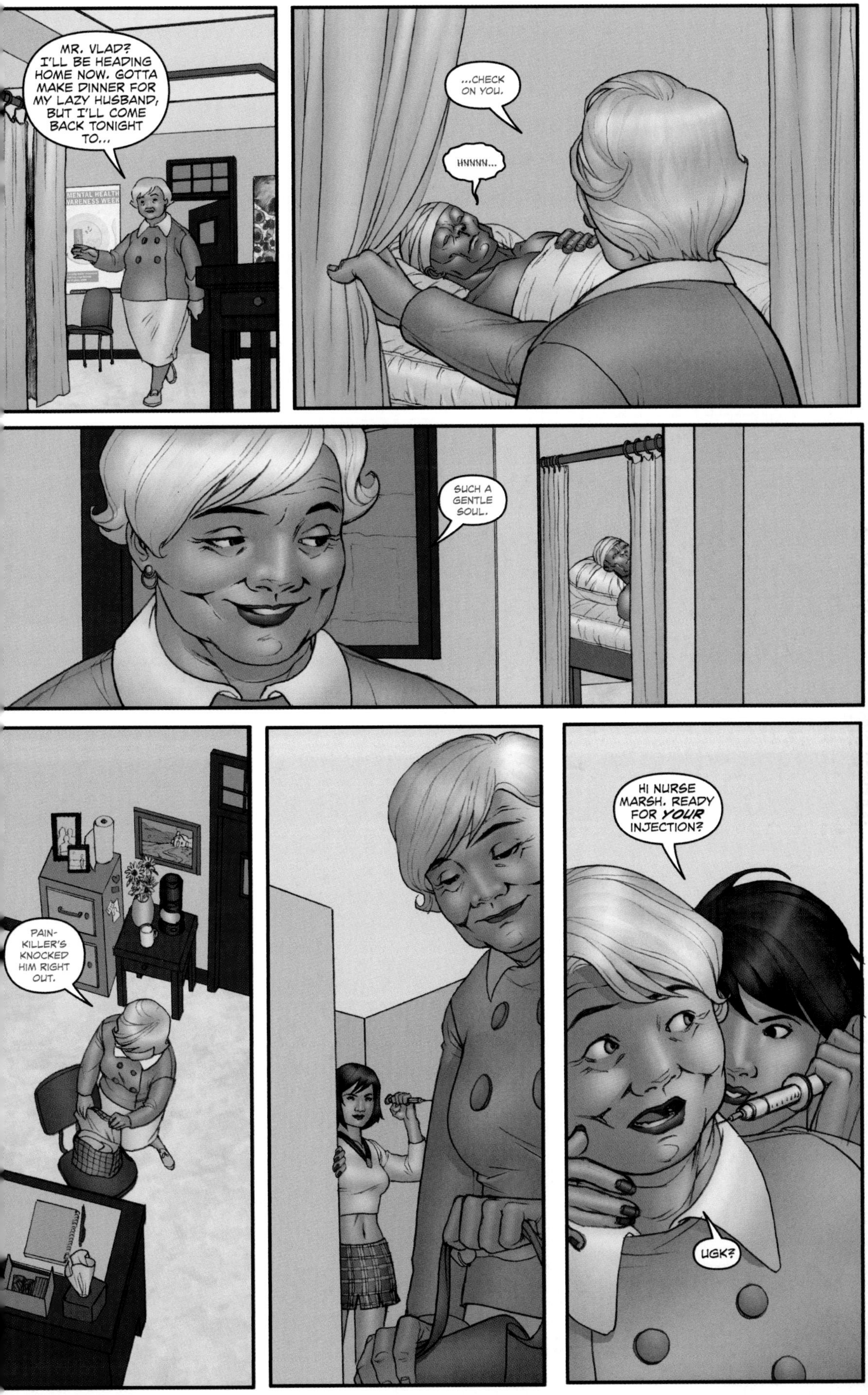
MR. VLAD? I'LL BE HEADING HOME NOW. GOTTA MAKE DINNER FOR MY LAZY HUSBAND, BUT I'LL COME BACK TONIGHT TO...
MENTAL HEALTH AWARENESS WEEK
...CHECK ON YOU.
HNNNN...
SUCH A GENTLE SOUL.
PAIN-KILLER'S KNOCKED HIM RIGHT OUT.
HI NURSE MARSH. READY FOR YOUR INJECTION?
UGK?

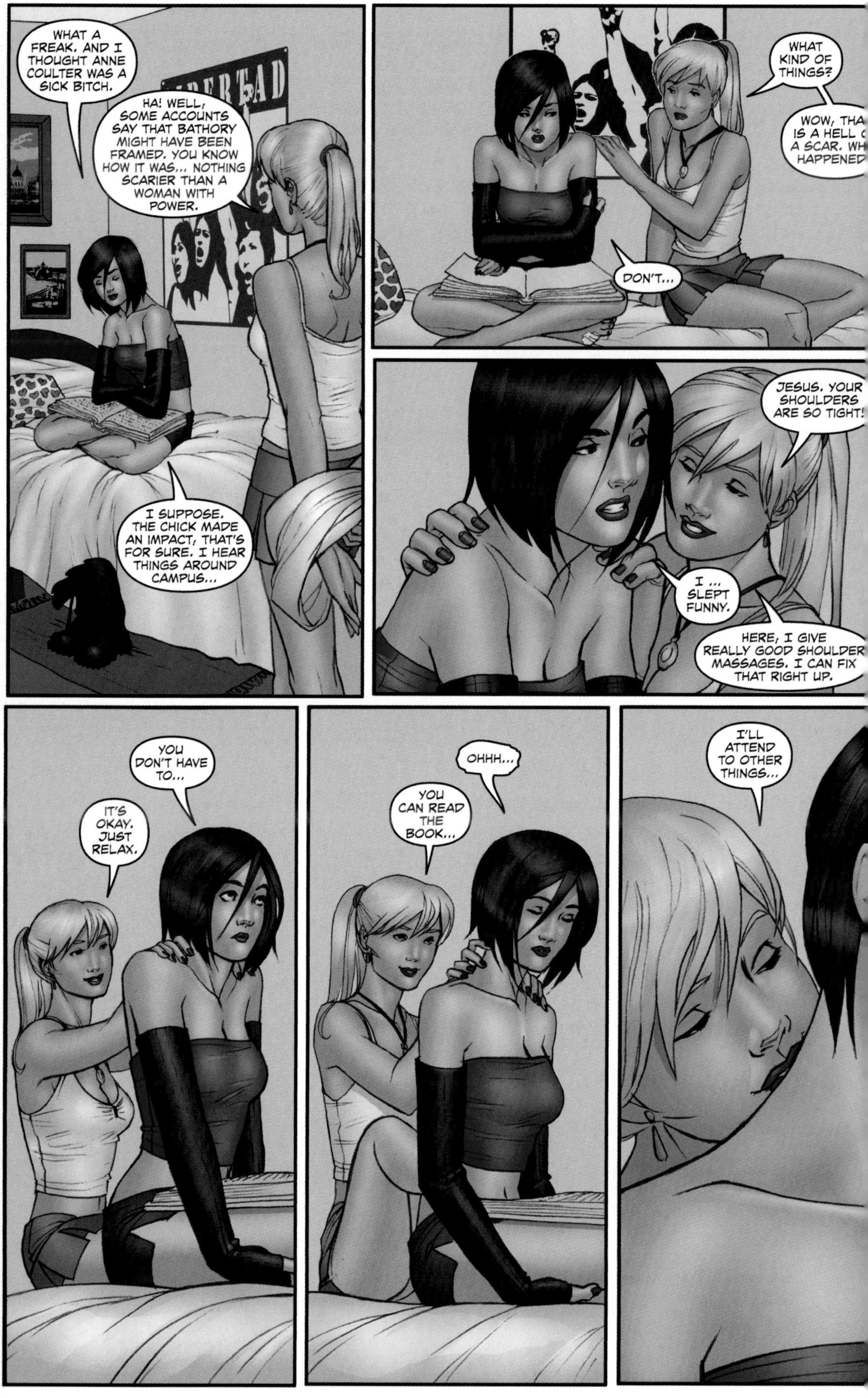
WHAT A FREAK. AND I THOUGHT ANNE COULTER WAS A SICK BITCH.
HA! WELL, SOME ACCOUNTS SAY THAT BATHORY MIGHT HAVE BEEN FRAMED. YOU KNOW HOW IT WAS... NOTHING SCARIER THAN A WOMAN WITH POWER.
I SUPPOSE. THE CHICK MADE AN IMPACT, THAT'S FOR SURE. I HEAR THINGS AROUND CAMPUS...
WHAT KIND OF THINGS?
WOW, THA IS A HELL A SCAR. WH HAPPENED
DON'T...
JESUS. YOUR SHOULDERS ARE SO TIGHT
I ... SLEPT FUNNY.
HERE, I GIVE REALLY GOOD SHOULDER MASSAGES. I CAN FIX THAT RIGHT UP.
YOU DON'T HAVE TO...
IT'S OKAY. JUST RELAX.
OHHH...
YOU CAN READ THE BOOK...
I'LL ATTEND TO OTHER THINGS...

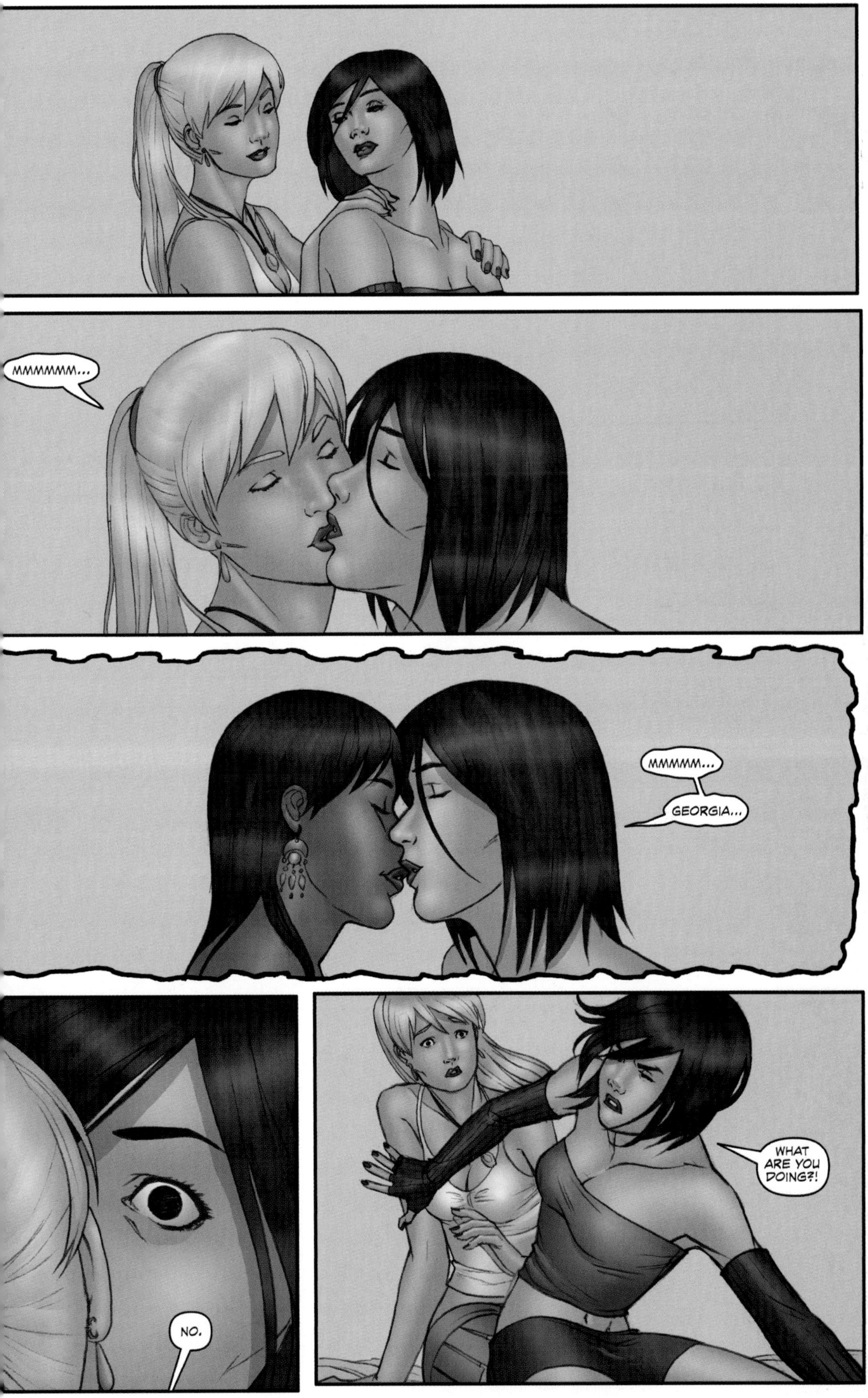
MMMMMM...
MMMMM...
GEORGIA...
NO.
WHAT ARE YOU DOING?!

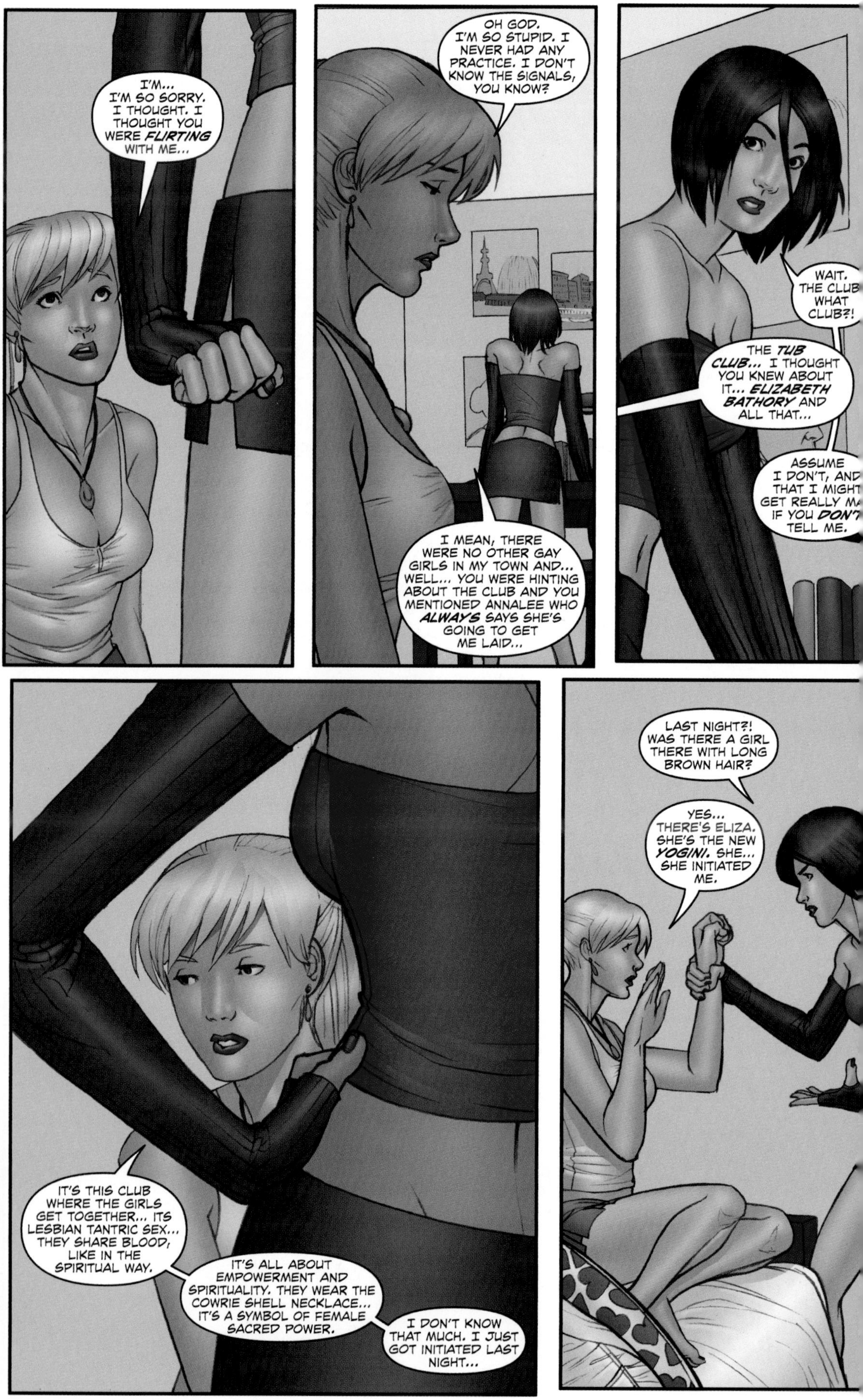
I'M... I'M SO SORRY. I THOUGHT. I THOUGHT YOU WERE *FLIRTING* WITH ME...
OH GOD. I'M SO STUPID. I NEVER HAD ANY PRACTICE. I DON'T KNOW THE SIGNALS, YOU KNOW?
I MEAN, THERE WERE NO OTHER GAY GIRLS IN MY TOWN AND... WELL... YOU WERE HINTING ABOUT THE CLUB AND YOU MENTIONED ANNALEE WHO *ALWAYS* SAYS SHE'S GOING TO GET ME LAID...
WAIT. THE CLUB WHAT CLUB?!
THE *TUB CLUB*... I THOUGHT YOU KNEW ABOUT IT... *ELIZABETH BATHORY* AND ALL THAT...
ASSUME I DON'T, AND THAT I MIGHT GET REALLY MA IF YOU *DON'T* TELL ME.
IT'S THIS CLUB WHERE THE GIRLS GET TOGETHER... ITS LESBIAN TANTRIC SEX... THEY SHARE BLOOD, LIKE IN THE SPIRITUAL WAY.
IT'S ALL ABOUT EMPOWERMENT AND SPIRITUALITY. THEY WEAR THE COWRIE SHELL NECKLACE... IT'S A SYMBOL OF FEMALE SACRED POWER.
I DON'T KNOW THAT MUCH. I JUST GOT INITIATED LAST NIGHT...
LAST NIGHT?! WAS THERE A GIRL THERE WITH LONG BROWN HAIR?
YES... THERE'S ELIZA. SHE'S THE NEW *YOGINI*. SHE... SHE INITIATED ME.

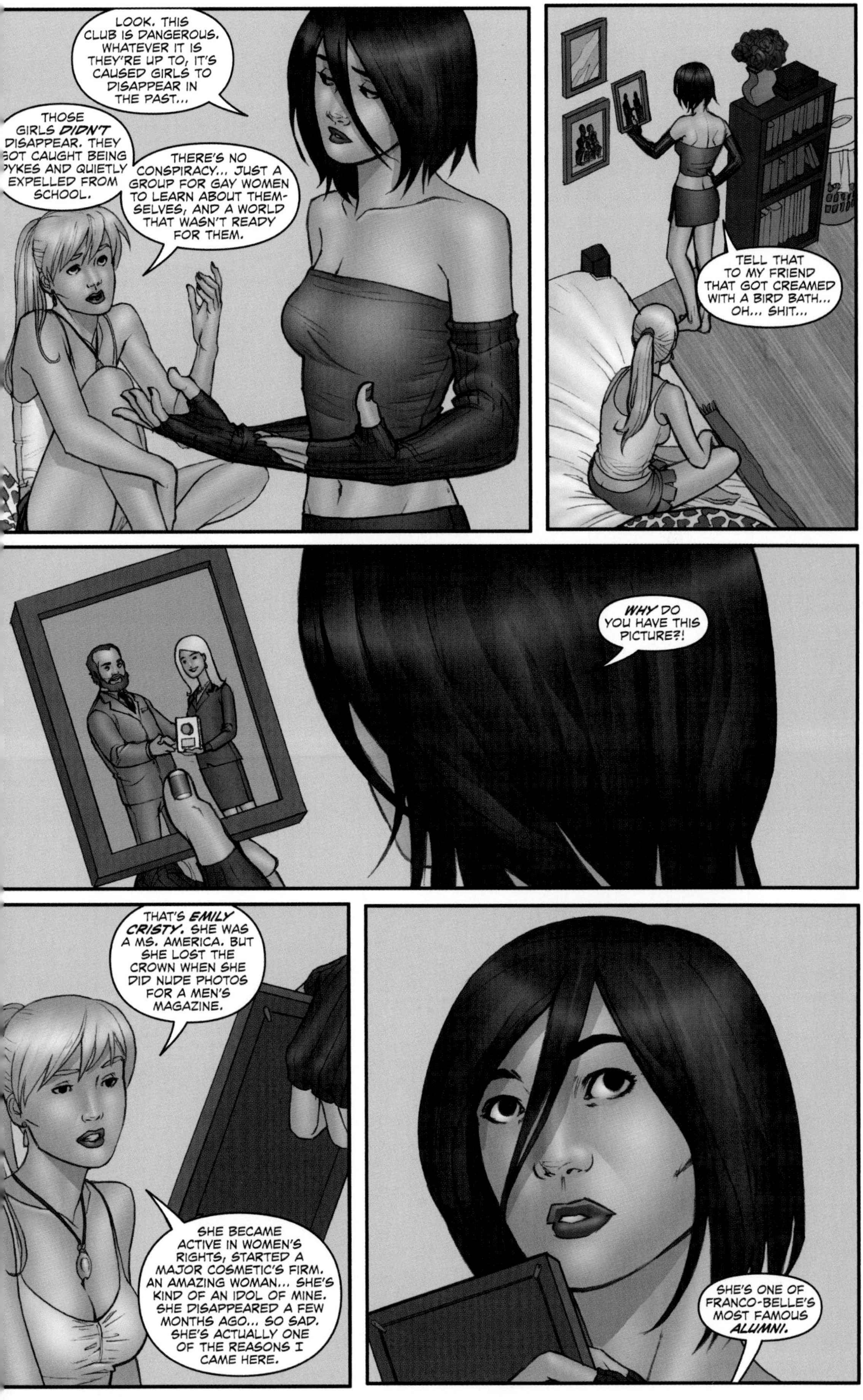
LOOK. THIS CLUB IS DANGEROUS. WHATEVER IT IS THEY'RE UP TO, IT'S CAUSED GIRLS TO DISAPPEAR IN THE PAST...
THOSE GIRLS DIDN'T DISAPPEAR. THEY GOT CAUGHT BEING DYKES AND QUIETLY EXPELLED FROM SCHOOL.
THERE'S NO CONSPIRACY... JUST A GROUP FOR GAY WOMEN TO LEARN ABOUT THEMSELVES, AND A WORLD THAT WASN'T READY FOR THEM.
TELL THAT TO MY FRIEND THAT GOT CREAMED WITH A BIRD BATH... OH... SHIT...
WHY DO YOU HAVE THIS PICTURE?!
THAT'S EMILY CRISTY. SHE WAS A MS. AMERICA. BUT SHE LOST THE CROWN WHEN SHE DID NUDE PHOTOS FOR A MEN'S MAGAZINE.
SHE BECAME ACTIVE IN WOMEN'S RIGHTS, STARTED A MAJOR COSMETIC'S FIRM. AN AMAZING WOMAN... SHE'S KIND OF AN IDOL OF MINE. SHE DISAPPEARED A FEW MONTHS AGO... SO SAD. SHE'S ACTUALLY ONE OF THE REASONS I CAME HERE.
SHE'S ONE OF FRANCO-BELLE'S MOST FAMOUS ALUMNI.

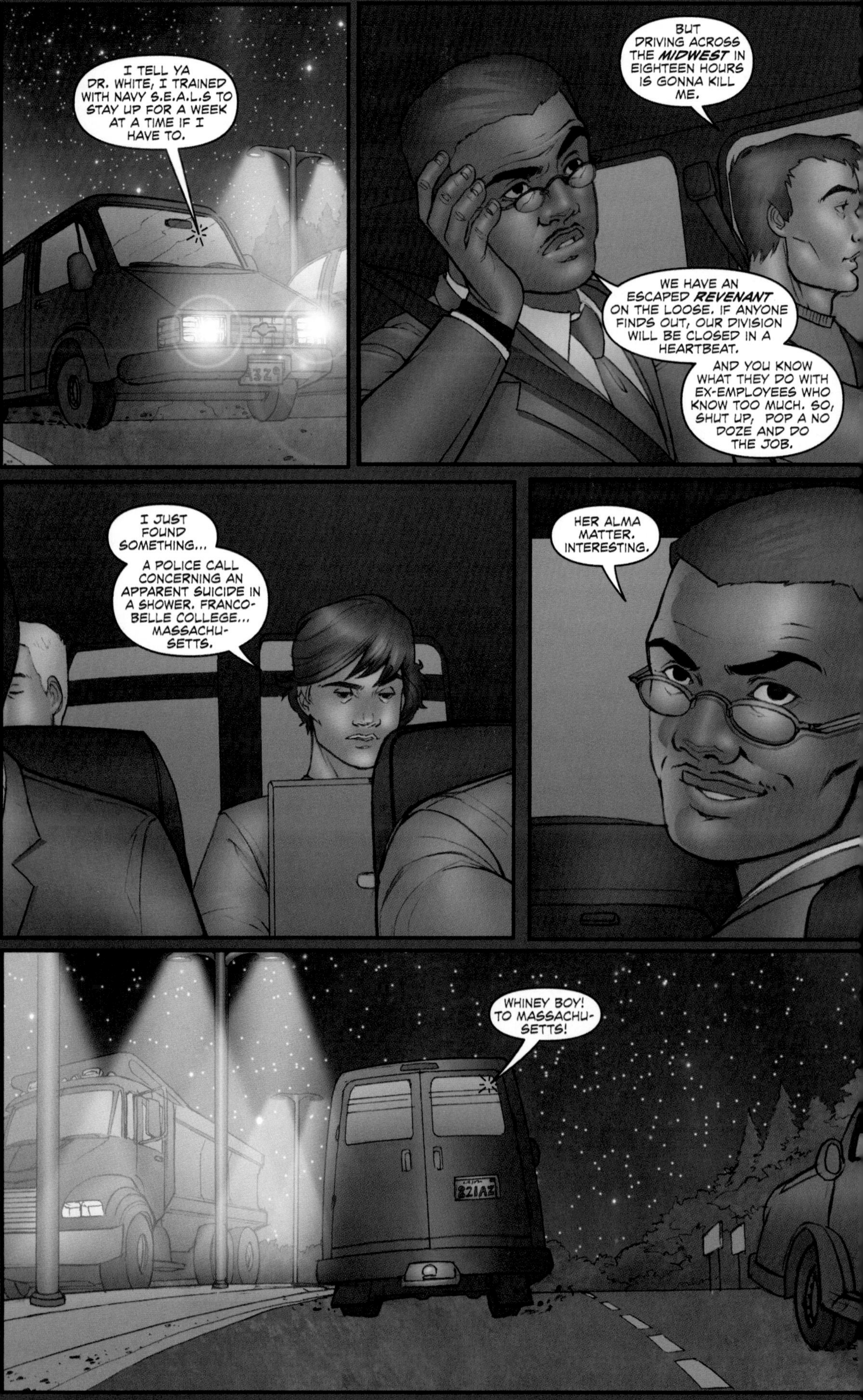
I TELL YA DR. WHITE, I TRAINED WITH NAVY S.E.A.L.S TO STAY UP FOR A WEEK AT A TIME IF I HAVE TO.
BUT DRIVING ACROSS THE *MIDWEST* IN EIGHTEEN HOURS IS GONNA KILL ME.
WE HAVE AN ESCAPED *REVENANT* ON THE LOOSE. IF ANYONE FINDS OUT, OUR DIVISION WILL BE CLOSED IN A HEARTBEAT.
AND YOU KNOW WHAT THEY DO WITH EX-EMPLOYEES WHO KNOW TOO MUCH. SO, SHUT UP, POP A NO DOZE AND DO THE JOB.
I JUST FOUND SOMETHING...
A POLICE CALL CONCERNING AN APPARENT SUICIDE IN A SHOWER. FRANCO-BELLE COLLEGE... MASSACHU-SETTS.
HER ALMA MATTER. INTERESTING.
WHINEY BOY! TO MASSACHU-SETTS!

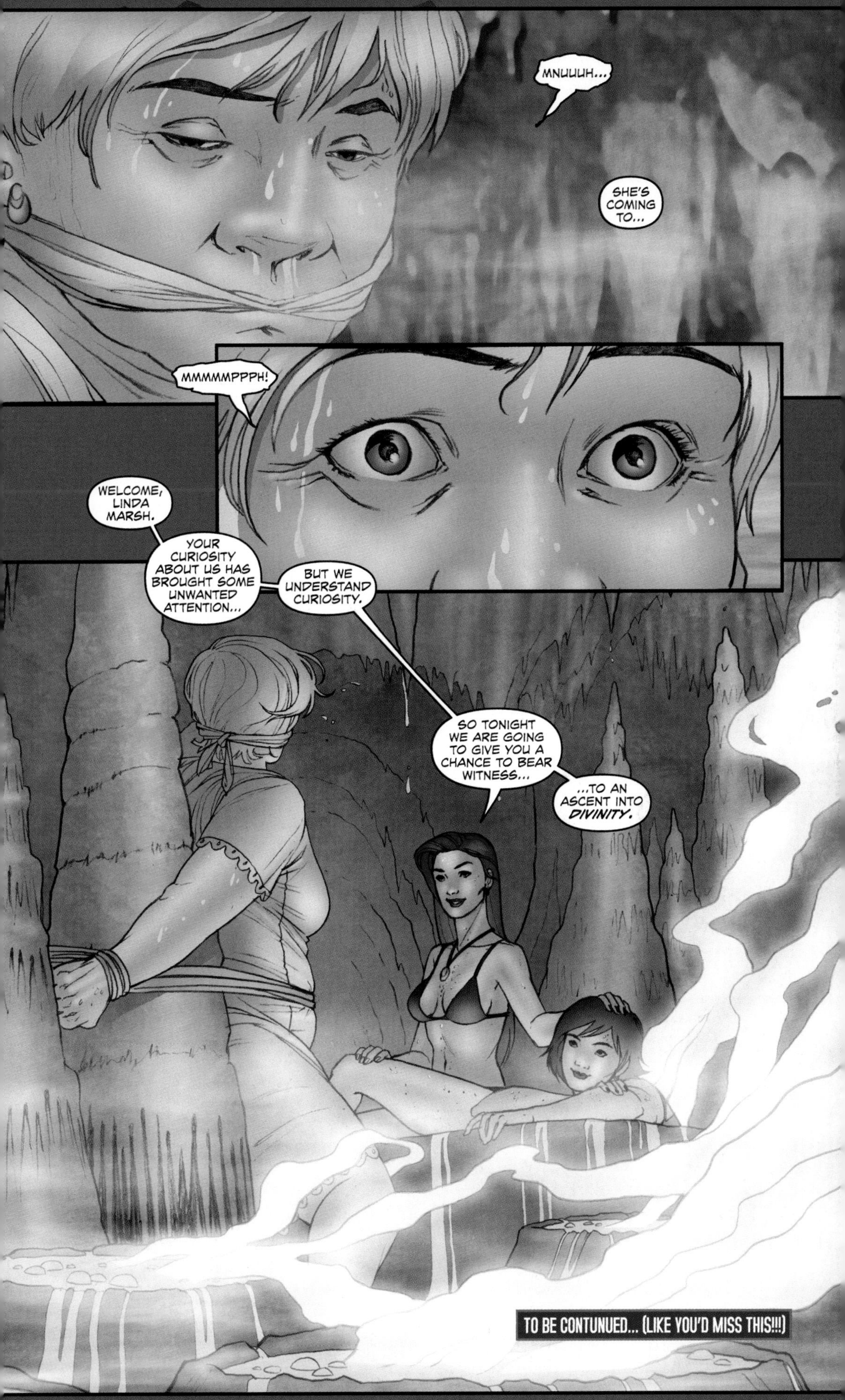
MNUUUH...
SHE'S COMING TO...
MMMMMPPPH!
WELCOME, LINDA MARSH.
YOUR CURIOSITY ABOUT US HAS BROUGHT SOME UNWANTED ATTENTION...
BUT WE UNDERSTAND CURIOSITY.
SO TONIGHT WE ARE GOING TO GIVE YOU A CHANCE TO BEAR WITNESS...
...TO AN ASCENT INTO *DIVINITY*.
TO BE CONTUNUED... (LIKE YOU'D MISS THIS!!!)

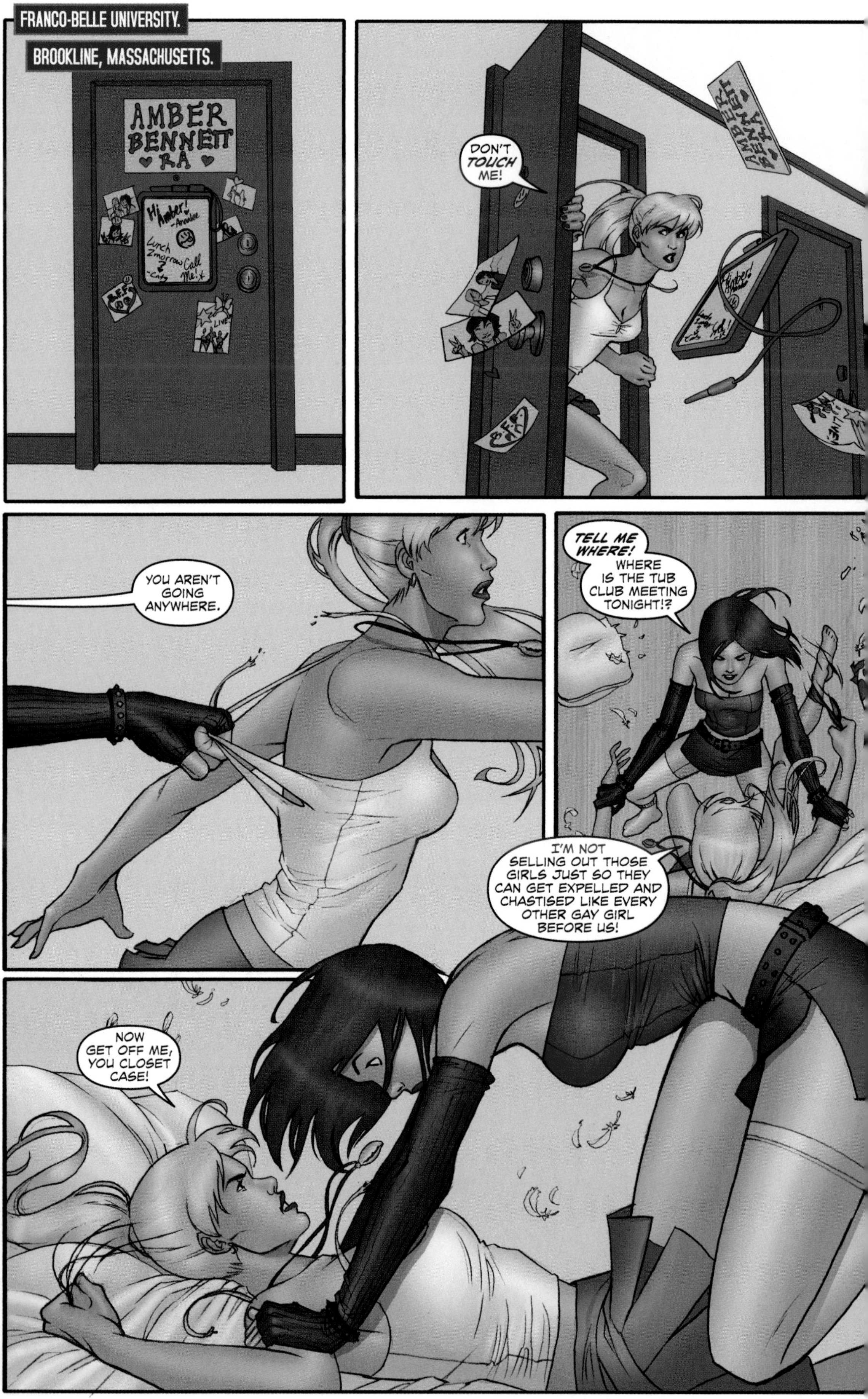
FRANCO-BELLE UNIVERSITY.
BROOKLINE, MASSACHUSETTS.
AMBER BENNETT RA
DON'T TOUCH ME!
YOU AREN'T GOING ANYWHERE.
TELL ME WHERE! WHERE IS THE TUB CLUB MEETING TONIGHT!?
I'M NOT SELLING OUT THOSE GIRLS JUST SO THEY CAN GET EXPELLED AND CHASTISED LIKE EVERY OTHER GAY GIRL BEFORE US!
NOW GET OFF ME, YOU CLOSET CASE!

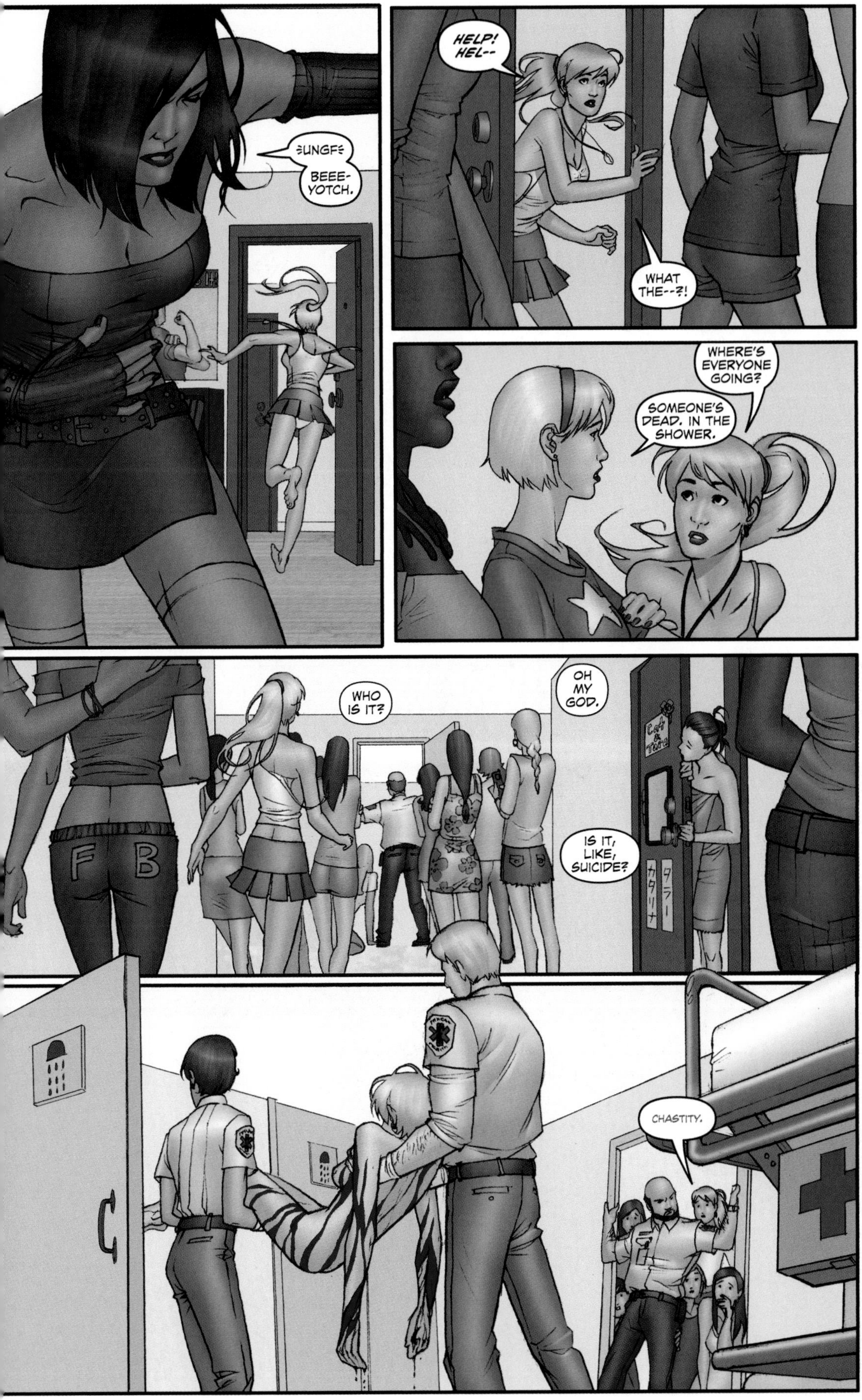
UNGF
BEEE-YOTCH.
HELP! HEL--
WHAT THE--?!
WHERE'S EVERYONE GOING?
SOMEONE'S DEAD. IN THE SHOWER.
WHO IS IT?
OH MY GOD.
IS IT, LIKE, SUICIDE?
CHASTITY.

OH GOD. CHASTITY.

IF YOU DON'T TELL ME WHERE THAT MEETING IS...

...ALL YOUR FRIENDS ARE GOING TO END UP *JUST* LIKE THAT.

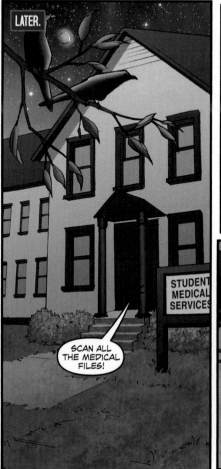

LATER.

STUDENT MEDICAL SERVICES

SCAN ALL THE MEDICAL FILES!

WE NEED ANY REFERENCES TO BLOOD LOSS OR SKIN ABNORMALITIES. IF CRISTY IS HERE, SHE MAY BE RESIDING IN THE SKIN OF ONE OF THE STUDENTS.

RUN THE NAME OF THE "SUICIDE VICTIM" ALSO. AS SOON AS LOCAL LAW ENFORCE- MENT--

SIR?

I'VE GOT BLOOD...

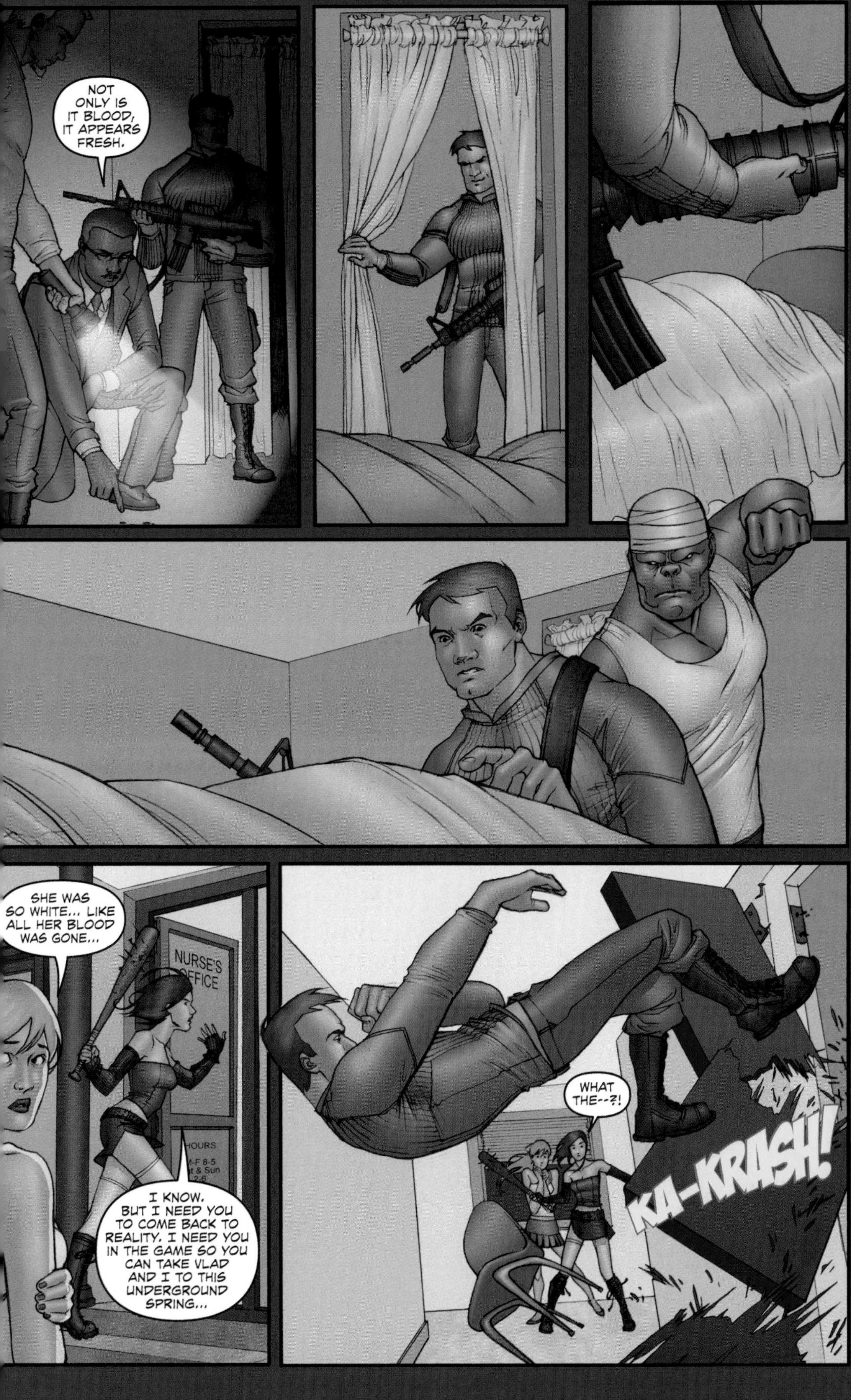
NOT ONLY IS IT BLOOD, IT APPEARS FRESH.
SHE WAS SO WHITE... LIKE ALL HER BLOOD WAS GONE...
NURSE'S OFFICE
I KNOW. BUT I NEED YOU TO COME BACK TO REALITY. I NEED YOU IN THE GAME SO YOU CAN TAKE VLAD AND I TO THIS UNDERGROUND SPRING...
WHAT THE--?!
KA-KRASH!

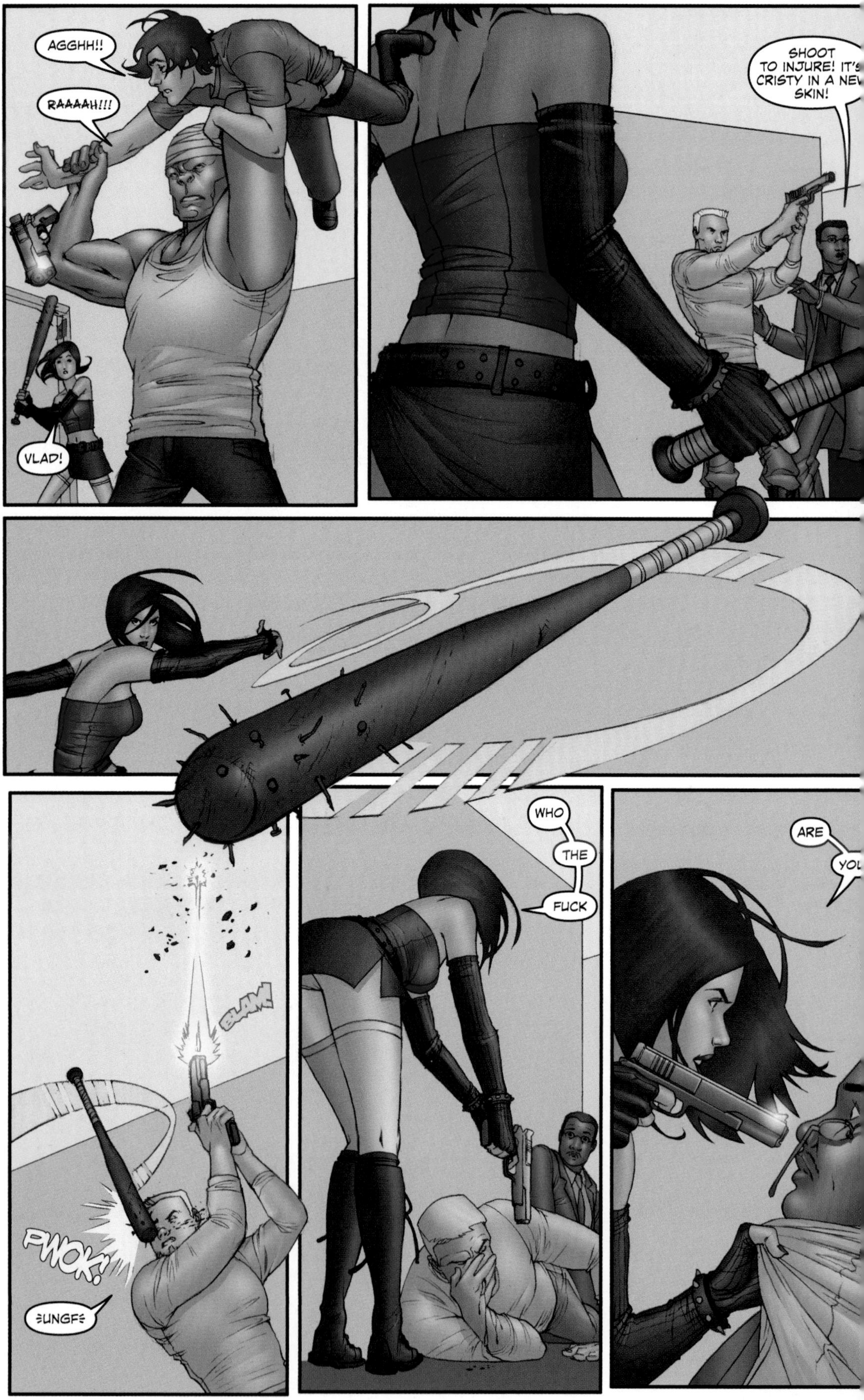
AGGHH!!
RAAAAH!!!
VLAD!
SHOOT TO INJURE! IT'S CRISTY IN A NEW SKIN!
BLAM!
PWOK!
UNGF
WHO
THE
FUCK
ARE

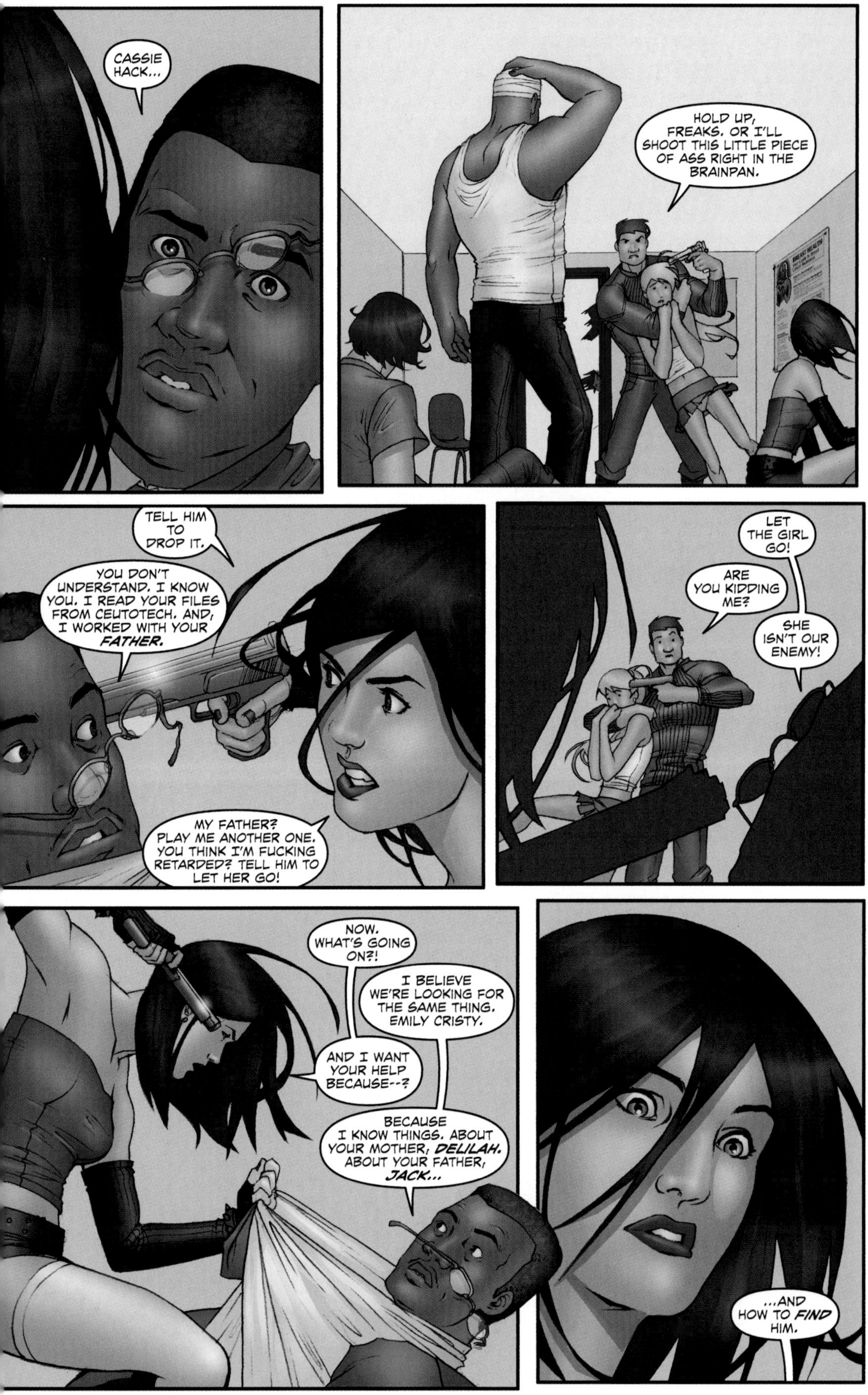
CASSIE HACK...
HOLD UP, FREAKS, OR I'LL SHOOT THIS LITTLE PIECE OF ASS RIGHT IN THE BRAINPAN.
TELL HIM TO DROP IT.
YOU DON'T UNDERSTAND. I KNOW YOU. I READ YOUR FILES FROM CEUTOTECH. AND, I WORKED WITH YOUR FATHER.
MY FATHER? PLAY ME ANOTHER ONE. YOU THINK I'M FUCKING RETARDED? TELL HIM TO LET HER GO!
LET THE GIRL GO!
ARE YOU KIDDING ME?
SHE ISN'T OUR ENEMY!
NOW. WHAT'S GOING ON?!
I BELIEVE WE'RE LOOKING FOR THE SAME THING. EMILY CRISTY.
AND I WANT YOUR HELP BECAUSE--?
BECAUSE I KNOW THINGS. ABOUT YOUR MOTHER, DELILAH. ABOUT YOUR FATHER, JACK...
...AND HOW TO FIND HIM.

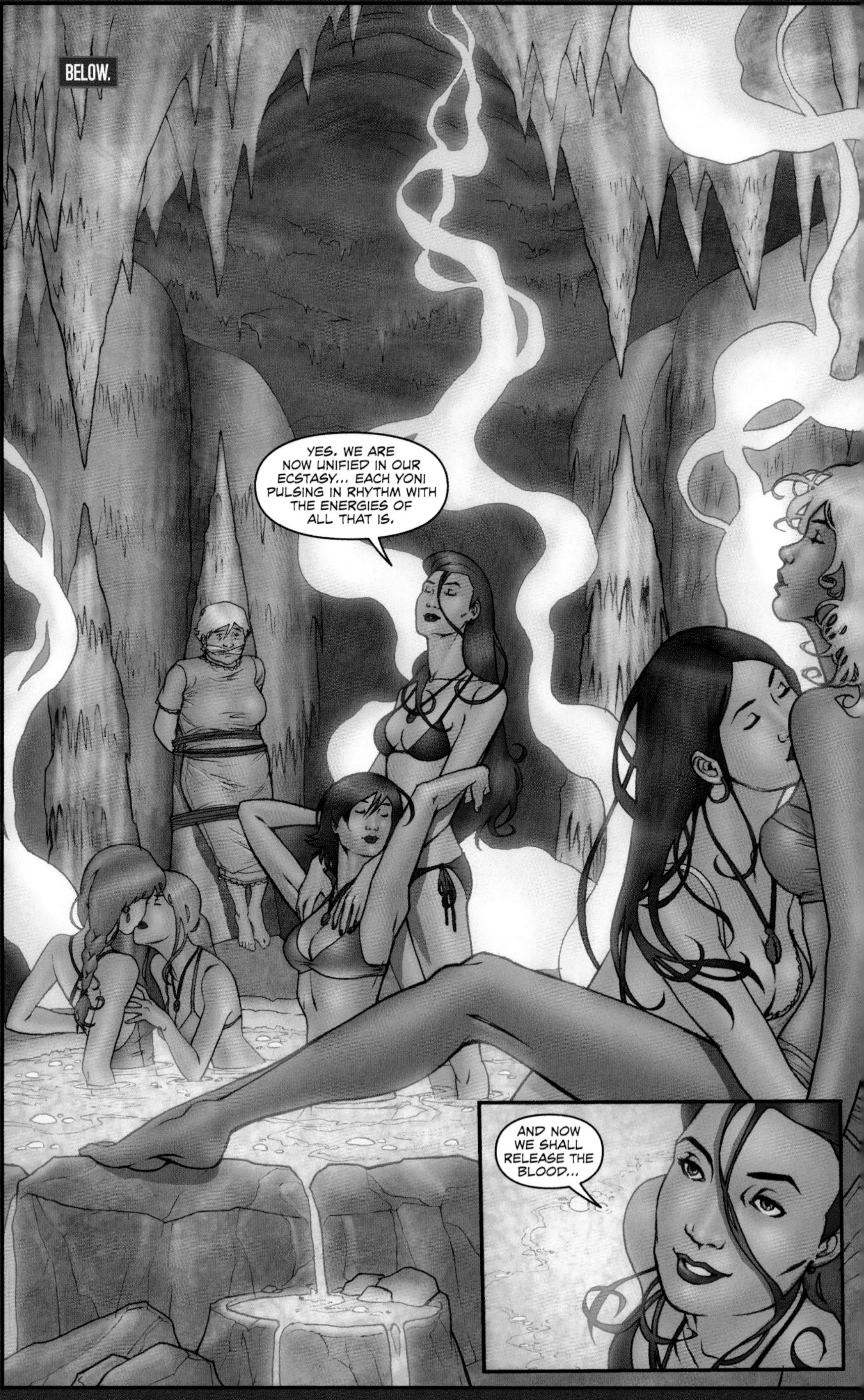
BELOW.
YES. WE ARE NOW UNIFIED IN OUR ECSTASY... EACH YONI PULSING IN RHYTHM WITH THE ENERGIES OF ALL THAT IS.
AND NOW WE SHALL RELEASE THE BLOOD...

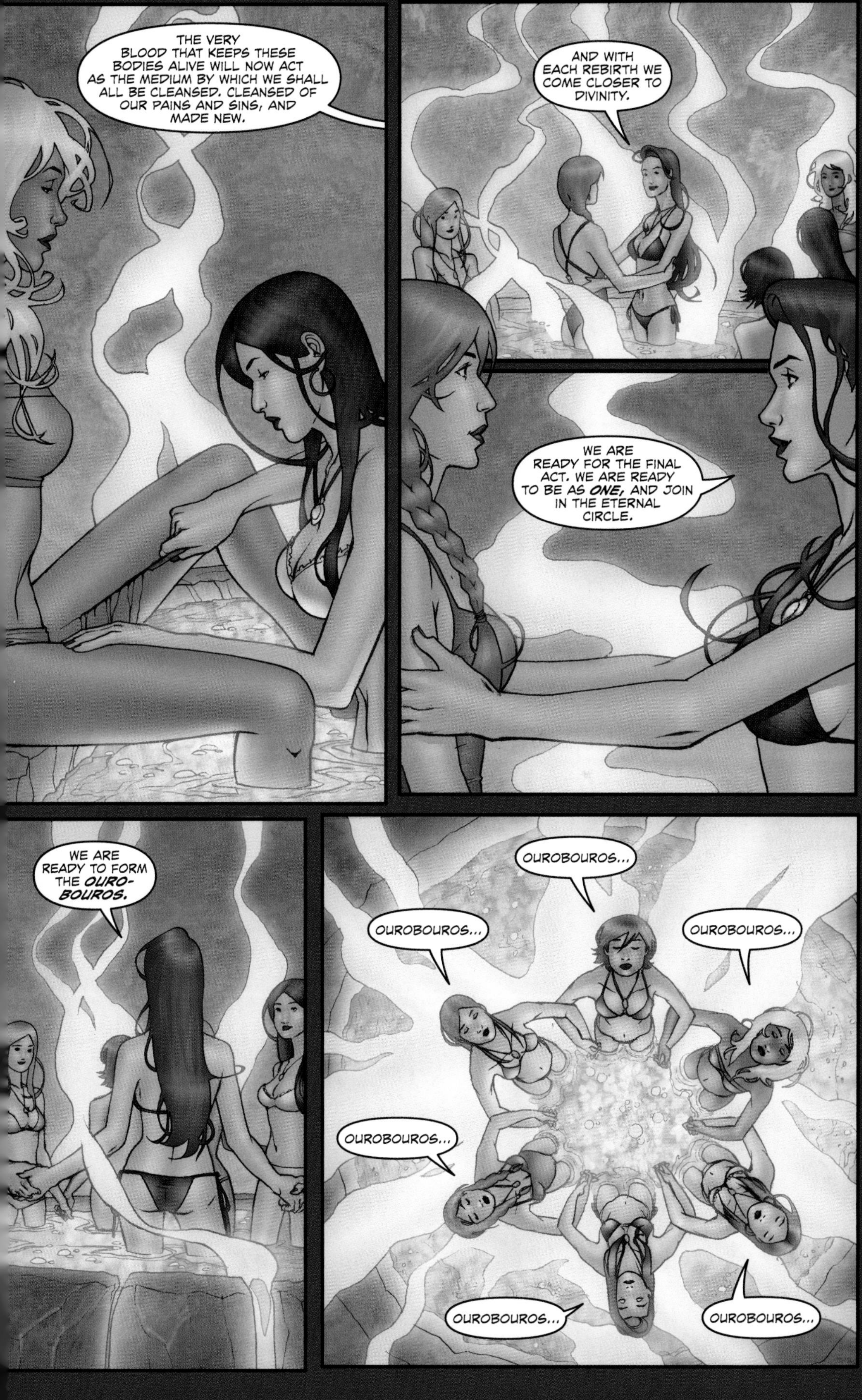
THE VERY BLOOD THAT KEEPS THESE BODIES ALIVE WILL NOW ACT AS THE MEDIUM BY WHICH WE SHALL ALL BE CLEANSED. CLEANSED OF OUR PAINS AND SINS, AND MADE NEW.
AND WITH EACH REBIRTH WE COME CLOSER TO DIVINITY.
WE ARE READY FOR THE FINAL ACT. WE ARE READY TO BE AS *ONE,* AND JOIN IN THE ETERNAL CIRCLE.
WE ARE READY TO FORM THE *OURO-BOUROS.*
OUROBOUROS...
OUROBOUROS...
OUROBOUROS...
OUROBOUROS...
OUROBOUROS...
OUROBOUROS...

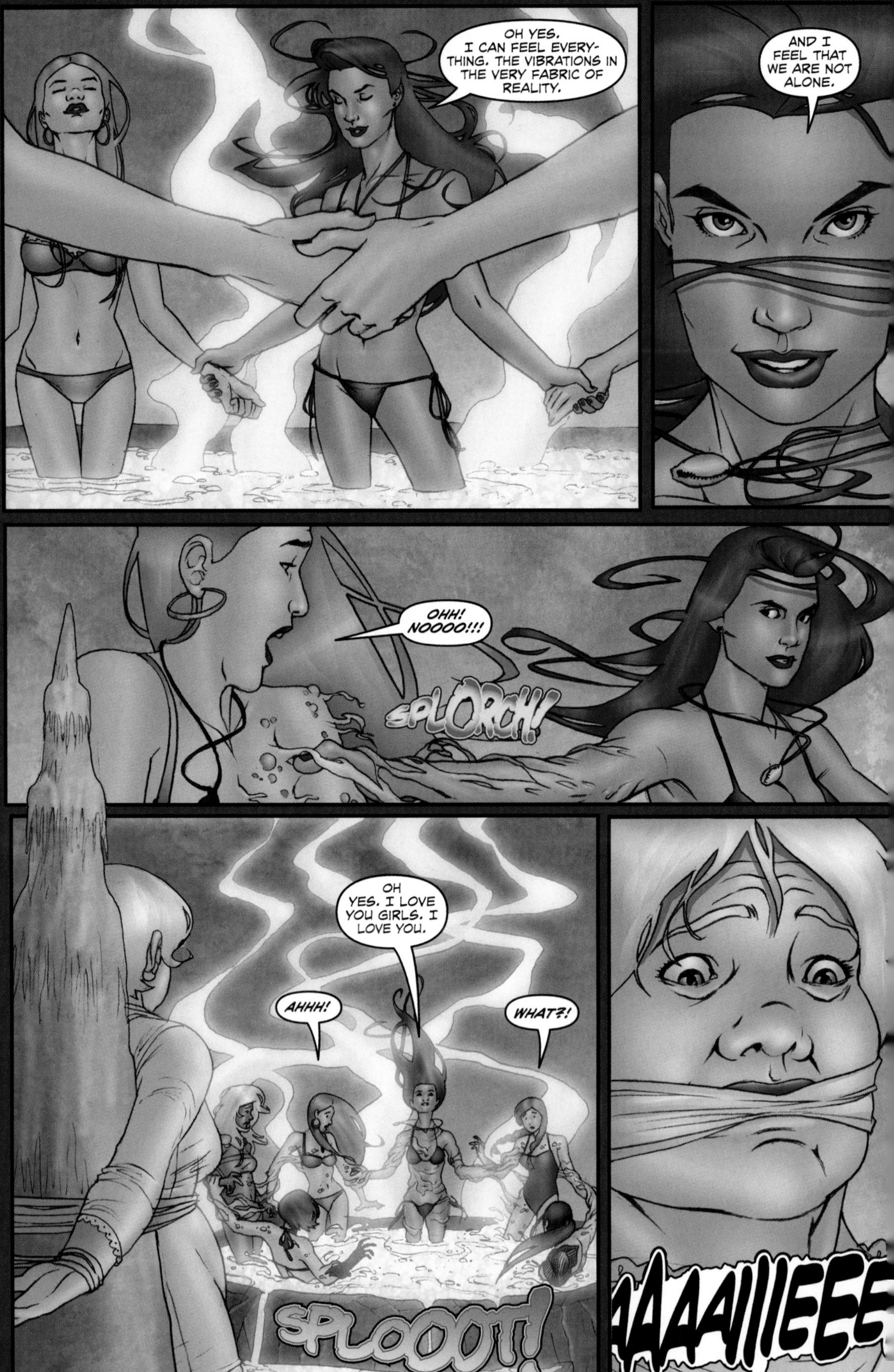
OH YES. I CAN FEEL EVERY-THING. THE VIBRATIONS IN THE VERY FABRIC OF REALITY.
AND I FEEL THAT WE ARE NOT ALONE.
OHH! NOOOO!!!
SPLORCH!
OH YES. I LOVE YOU GIRLS. I LOVE YOU.
AHHH!
WHAT?!
SPLOOOT!
AAAAIIIEEEE

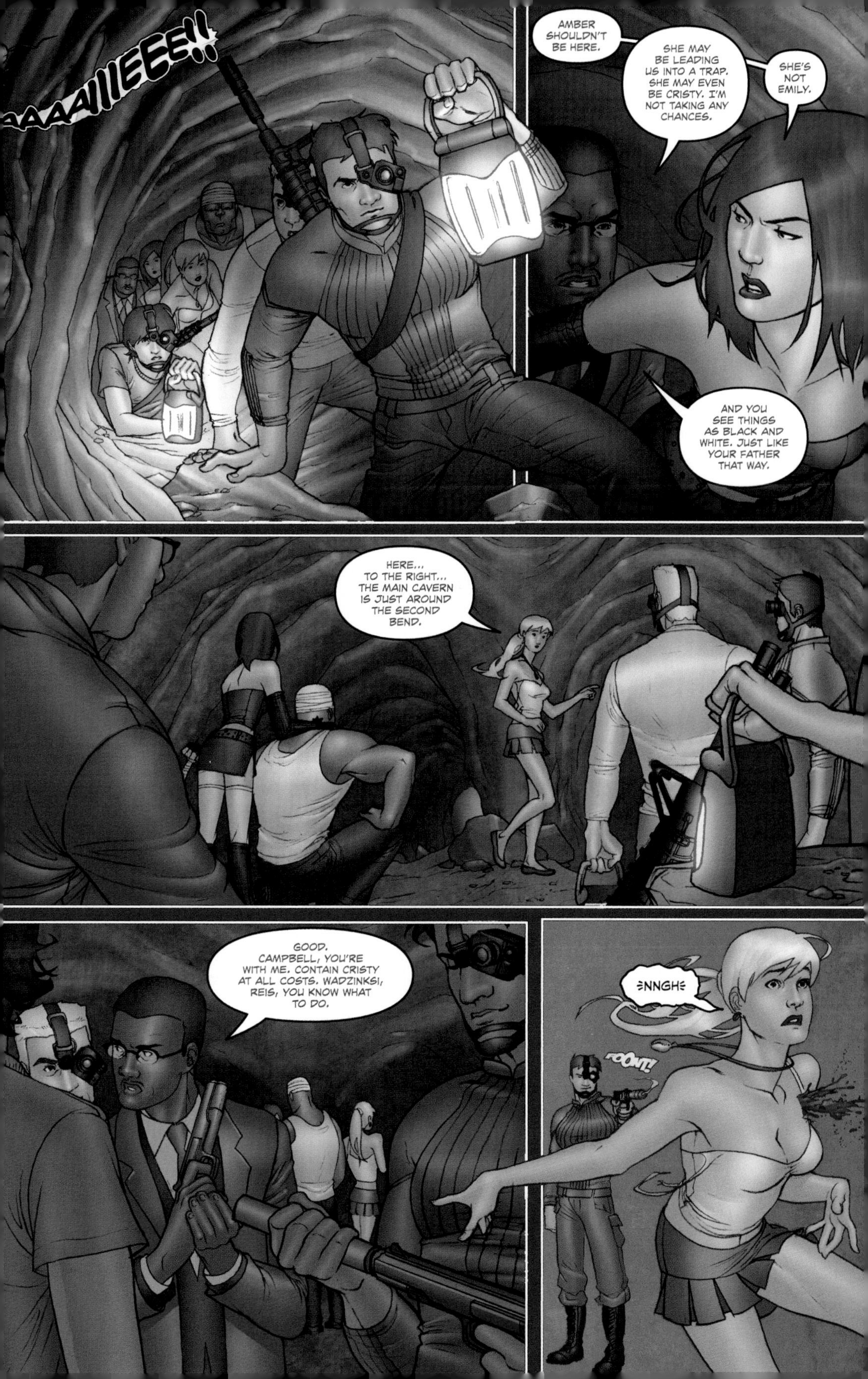
AAAAIIIEEEE!!
AMBER SHOULDN'T BE HERE.
SHE MAY BE LEADING US INTO A TRAP. SHE MAY EVEN BE CRISTY. I'M NOT TAKING ANY CHANCES.
SHE'S NOT EMILY.
AND YOU SEE THINGS AS BLACK AND WHITE. JUST LIKE YOUR FATHER THAT WAY.
HERE... TO THE RIGHT... THE MAIN CAVERN IS JUST AROUND THE SECOND BEND.
GOOD. CAMPBELL, YOU'RE WITH ME. CONTAIN CRISTY AT ALL COSTS. WADZINKSI, REIS, YOU KNOW WHAT TO DO.
NNGH
FOOMT!

OH GOD! AMBER!

WHO WANTS TO WATCH WHO GO? I'M ITCHIN' TO POP THE BIG GUY FIRST.

WHICK!

NUHN!

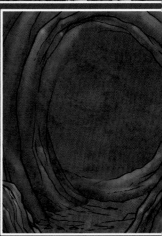

YOU MOTHE- FUCKER

I TRULY AM SORRY, MS. HACK. THIS CASE DEMANDS THERE BE NO WITNESSES.

BUT, I DO WANT YOU TO KNOW, YOUR FATHER TRULY WAS A GOOD AND HONORABLE. MAN.

EVEN IF THE WORK HE DID WAS NOT.

CAMPBELL! THERE'S-- CAMPBELL!

FOONT!

FOONT!

FOONT!

SPLUTCH!!!

AAAIIIGHHH!!

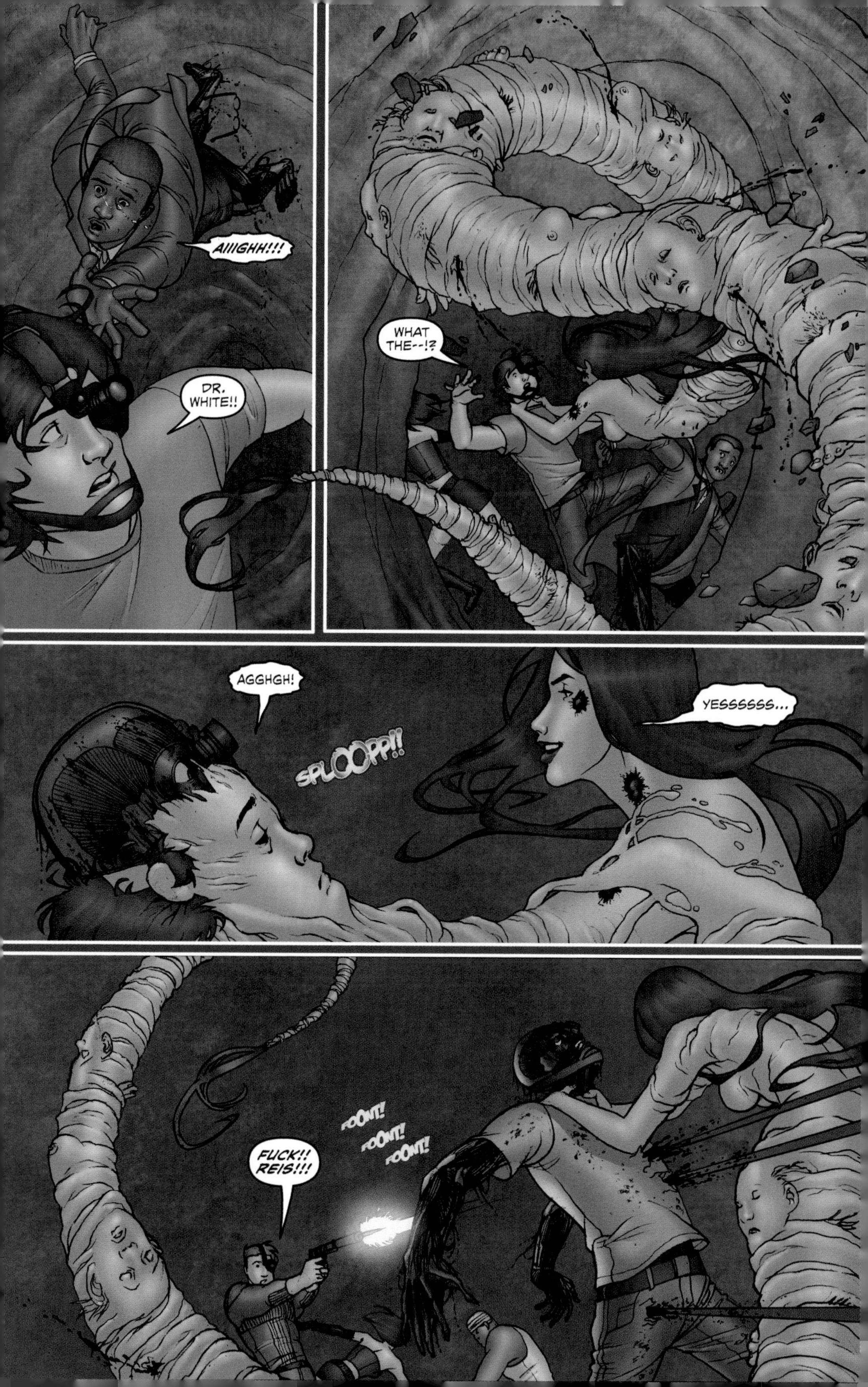
AIIIGHH!!!
DR. WHITE!!
WHAT THE--!?
AGGHGH!
SPLOOPP!!
YESSSSSS...
FUCK!! REIS!!!
FOONT!
FOONT!
FOONT!

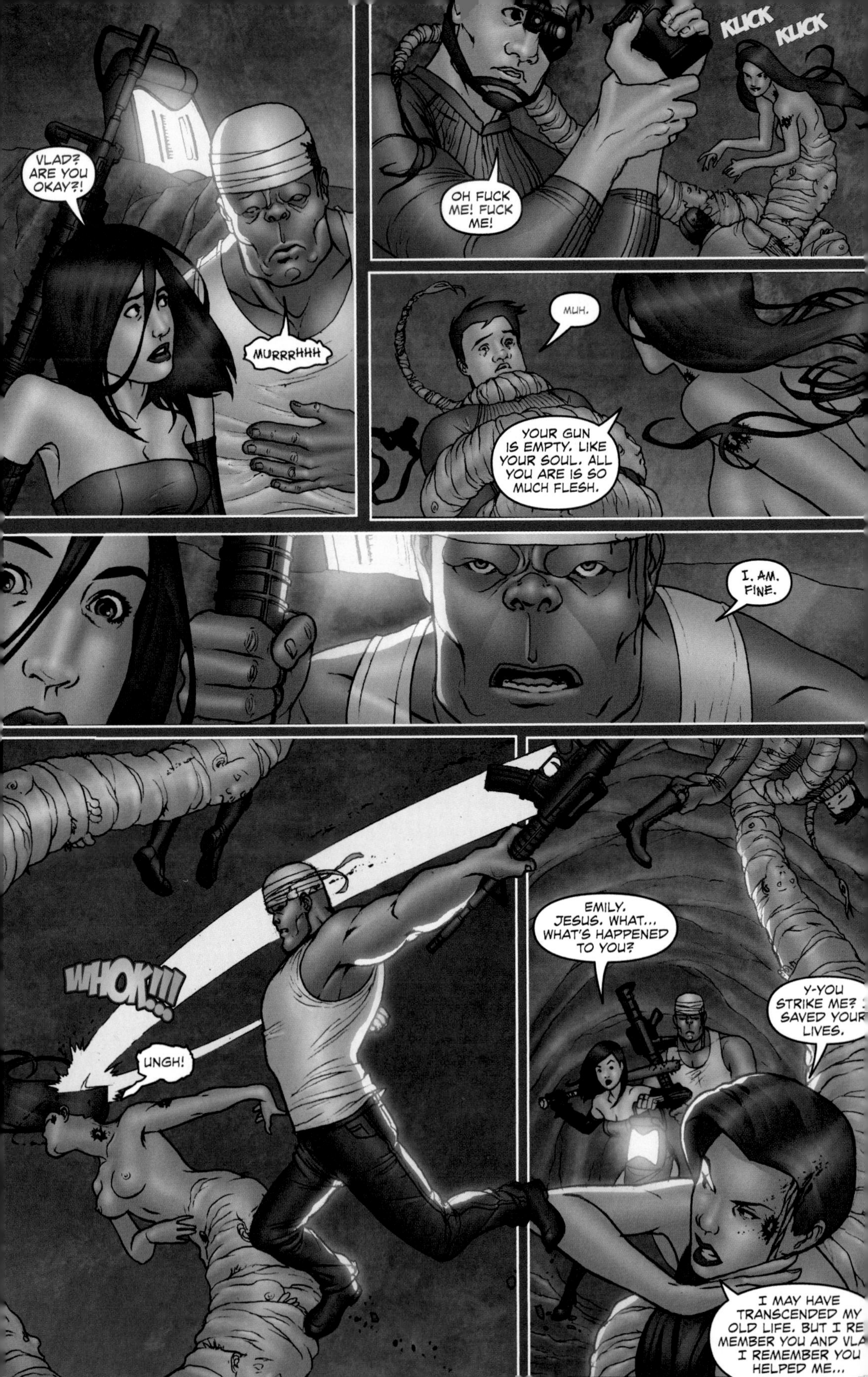
VLAD? ARE YOU OKAY?!
MURRRHHH
KLICK
KLICK
OH FUCK ME! FUCK ME!
MUH.
YOUR GUN IS EMPTY. LIKE YOUR SOUL. ALL YOU ARE IS SO MUCH FLESH.
I. AM. FINE.
WHOK!!!
UNGH!
EMILY. JESUS. WHAT... WHAT'S HAPPENED TO YOU?
Y-YOU STRIKE ME? SAVED YOUR LIVES.
I MAY HAVE TRANSCENDED MY OLD LIFE. BUT I RE MEMBER YOU AND VLA I REMEMBER YOU HELPED ME...

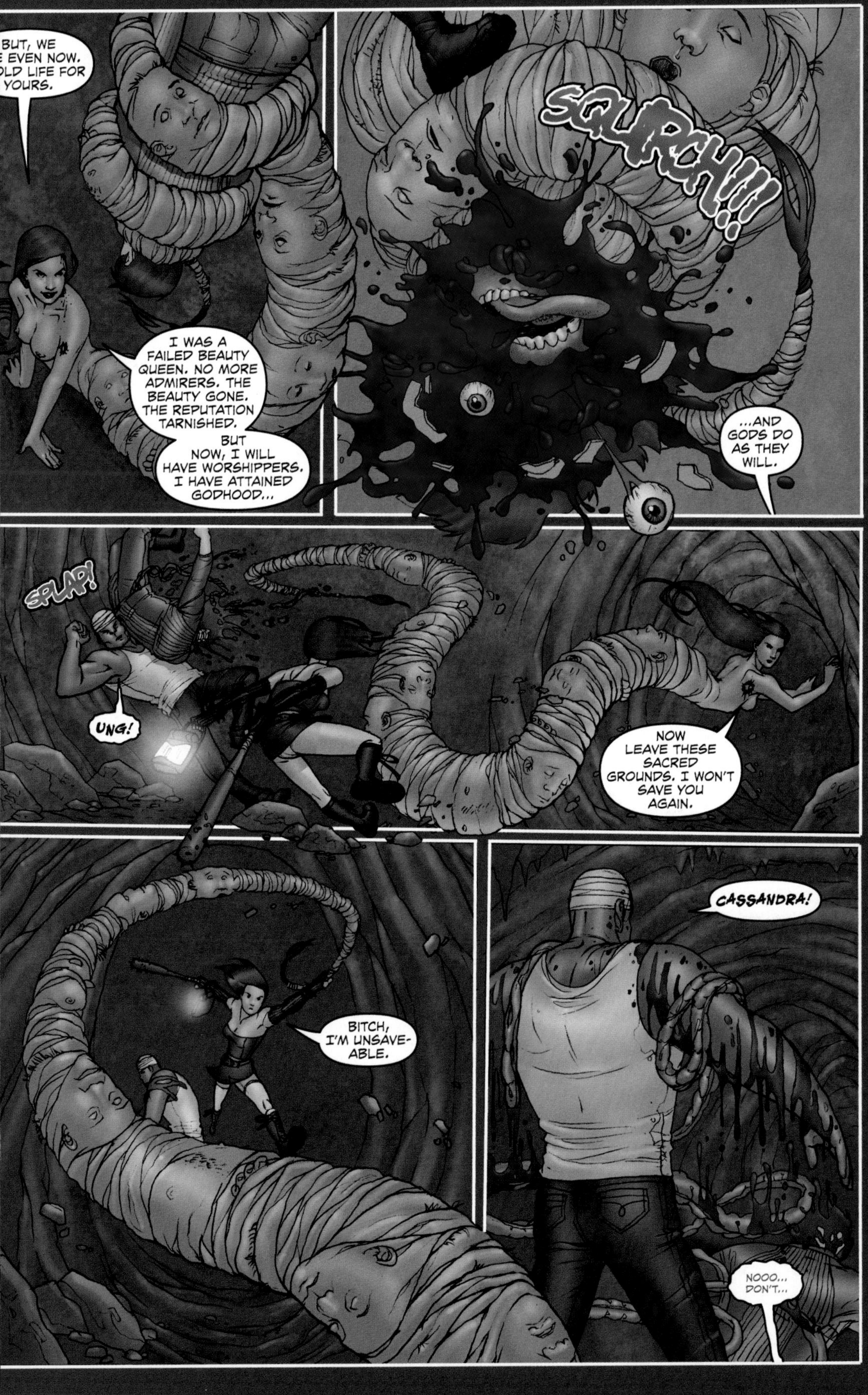
BUT, WE
E EVEN NOW.
OLD LIFE FOR
YOURS.
SQUARCH!!!
I WAS A FAILED BEAUTY QUEEN. NO MORE ADMIRERS. THE BEAUTY GONE. THE REPUTATION TARNISHED.
BUT NOW, I WILL HAVE WORSHIPPERS. I HAVE ATTAINED GODHOOD...
...AND GODS DO AS THEY WILL.
SPLAP!
UNG!
NOW LEAVE THESE SACRED GROUNDS. I WON'T SAVE YOU AGAIN.
BITCH, I'M UNSAVE-ABLE.
CASSANDRA!
NOOO... DON'T...

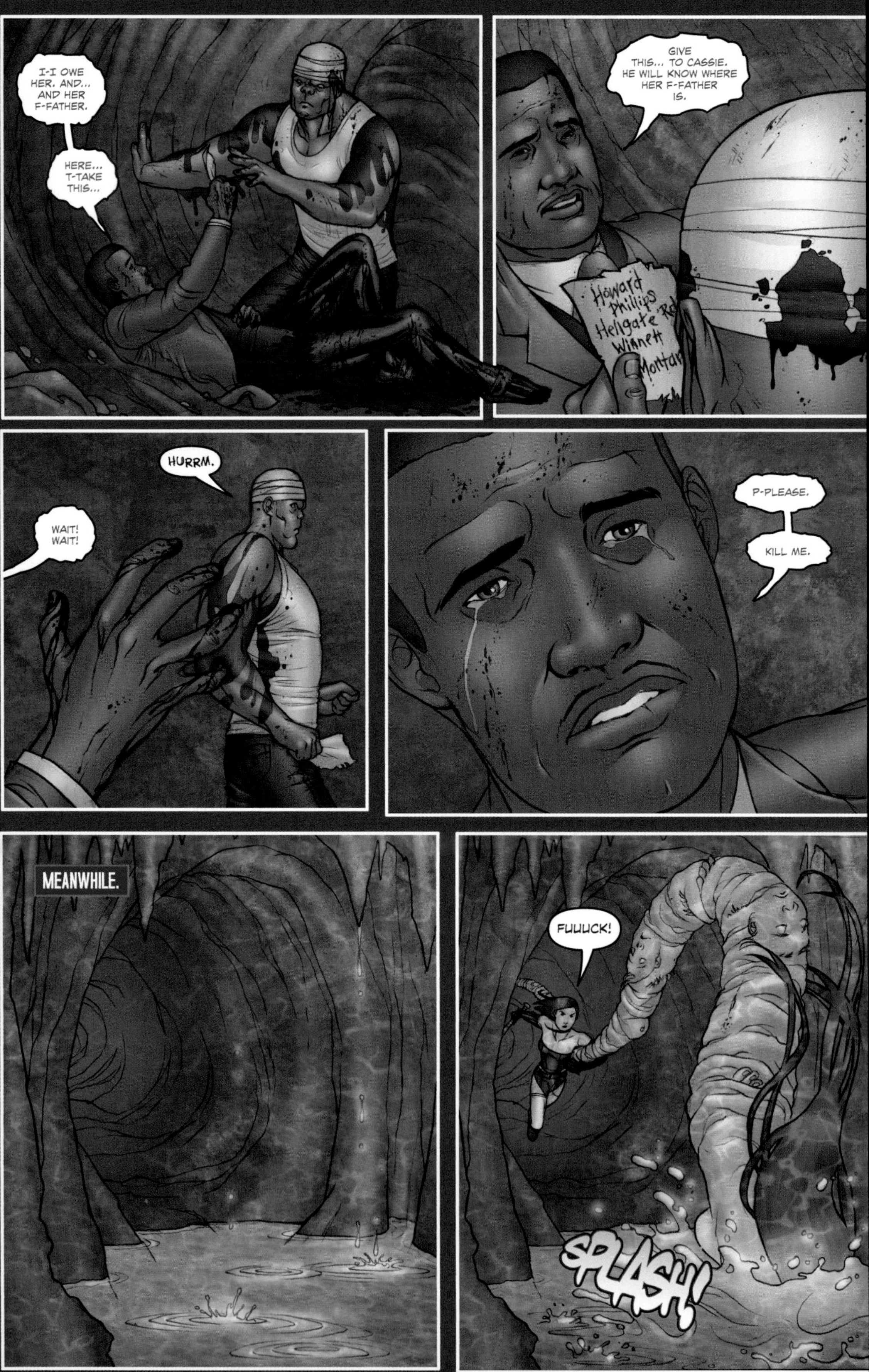
I-I OWE HER. AND... AND HER F-FATHER.
HERE... T-TAKE THIS...
GIVE THIS... TO CASSIE. HE WILL KNOW WHERE HER F-FATHER IS.
Howard Phillips
Hellgate Rd
Winnett
Montan
HURRM.
WAIT! WAIT!
P-PLEASE.
KILL ME.
MEANWHILE.
FUUUCK!
SPLASH!

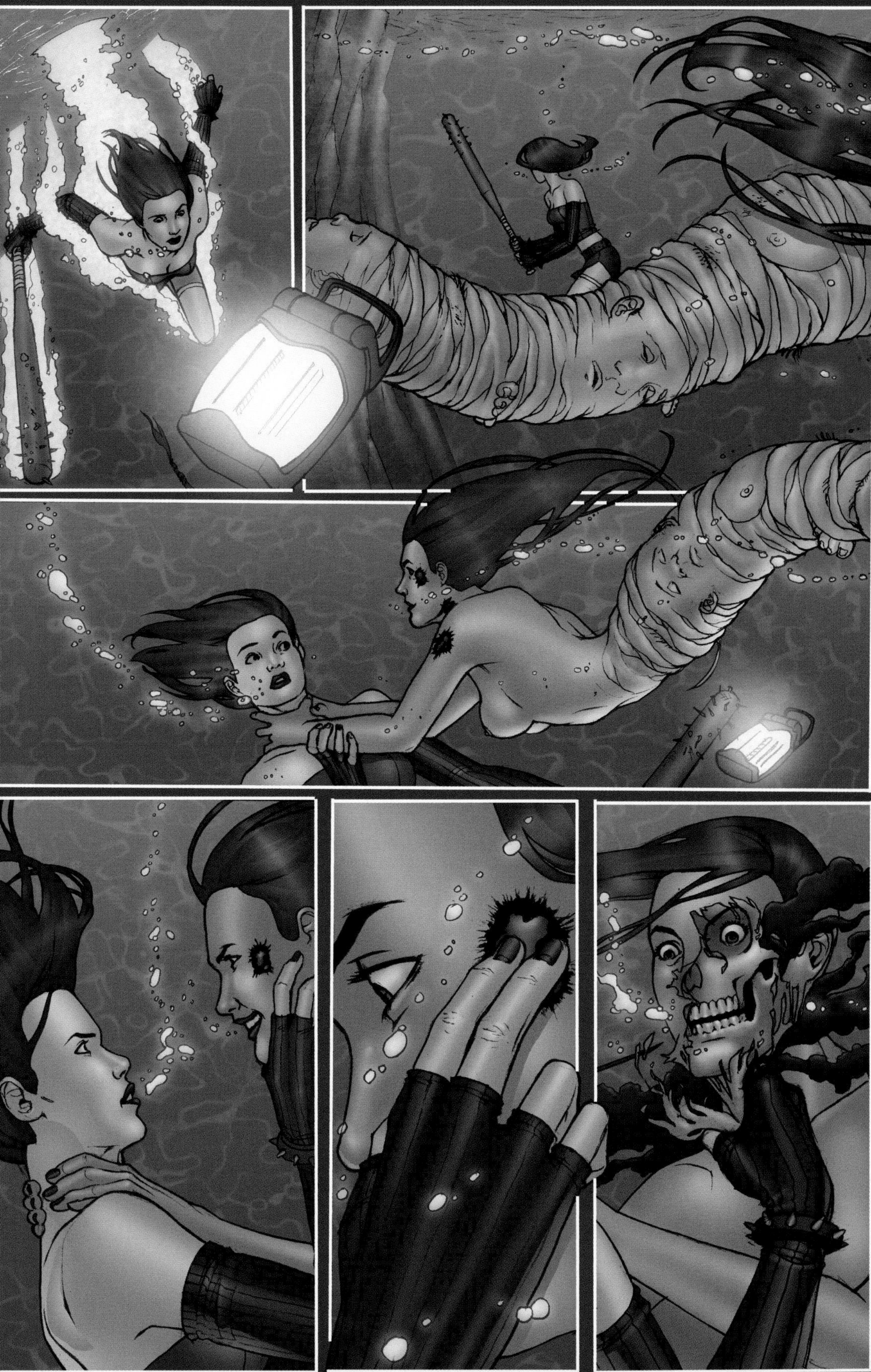

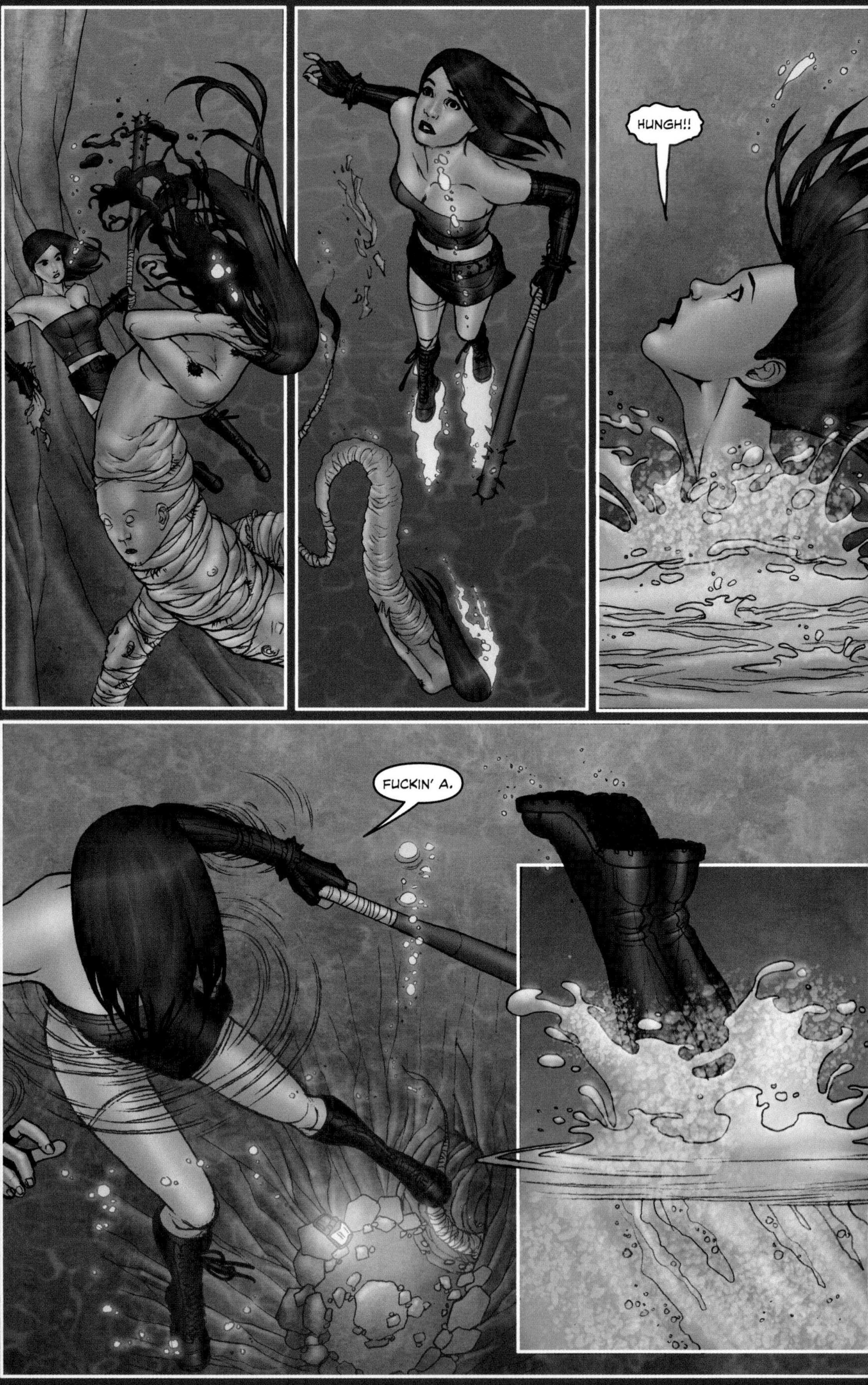
HUNGH!!
FUCKIN' A.

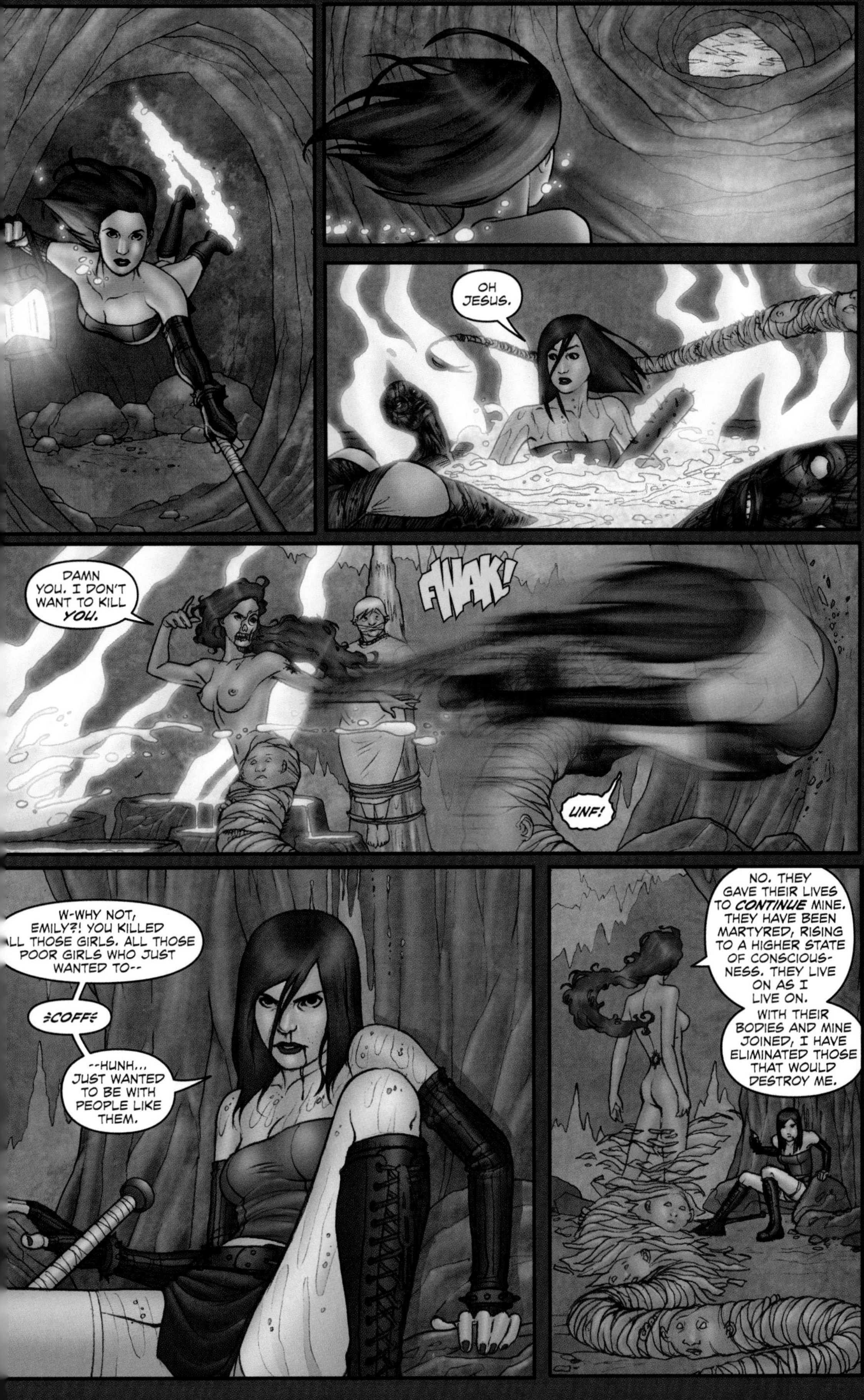
OH JESUS.
DAMN YOU. I DON'T WANT TO KILL YOU.
FWAK!
UNF!
W-WHY NOT, EMILY?! YOU KILLED ALL THOSE GIRLS. ALL THOSE POOR GIRLS WHO JUST WANTED TO--
COFF
--HUNH... JUST WANTED TO BE WITH PEOPLE LIKE THEM.
NO. THEY GAVE THEIR LIVES TO CONTINUE MINE. THEY HAVE BEEN MARTYRED, RISING TO A HIGHER STATE OF CONSCIOUSNESS. THEY LIVE ON AS I LIVE ON.
WITH THEIR BODIES AND MINE JOINED, I HAVE ELIMINATED THOSE THAT WOULD DESTROY ME.

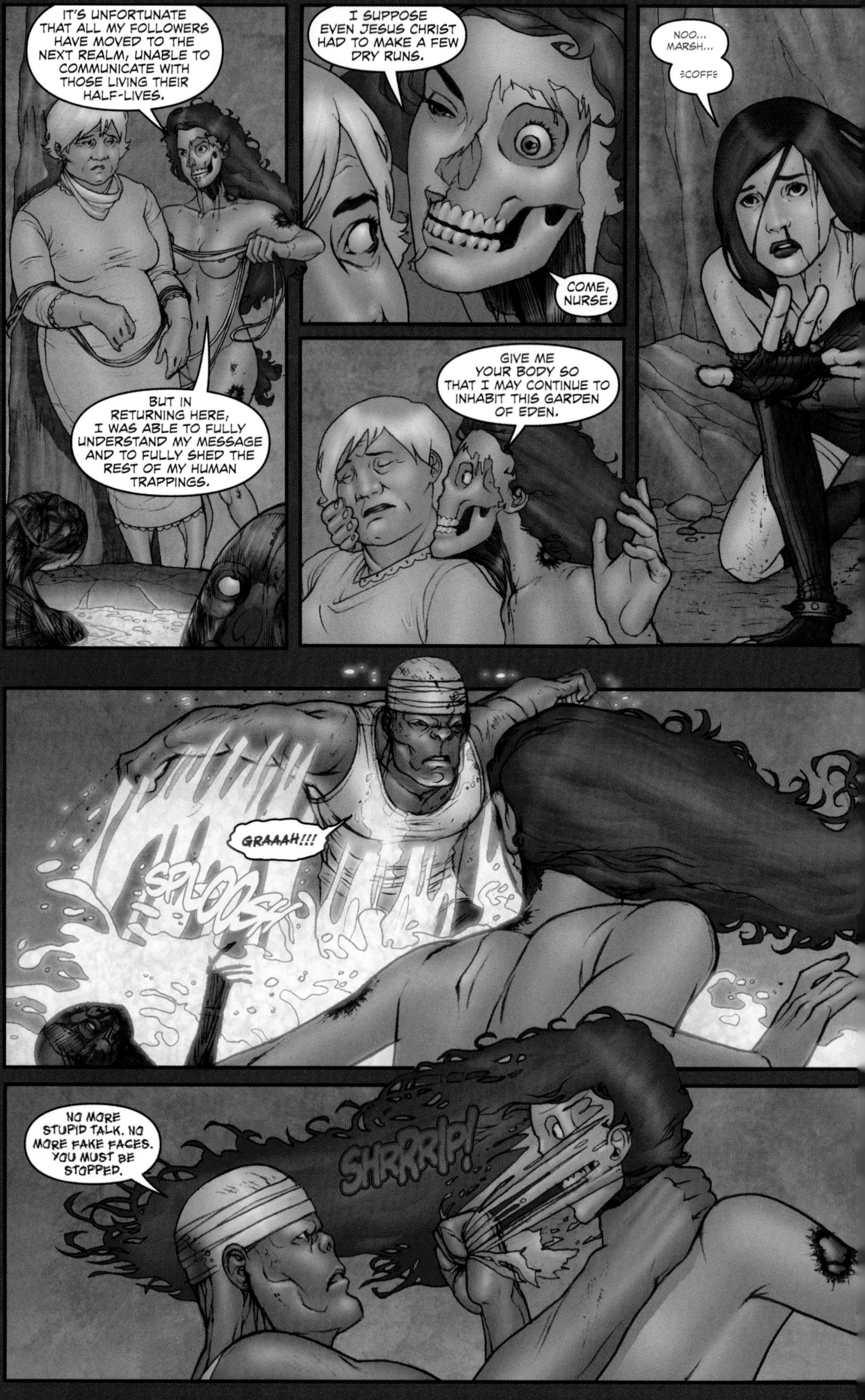
IT'S UNFORTUNATE THAT ALL MY FOLLOWERS HAVE MOVED TO THE NEXT REALM, UNABLE TO COMMUNICATE WITH THOSE LIVING THEIR HALF-LIVES.
BUT IN RETURNING HERE, I WAS ABLE TO FULLY UNDERSTAND MY MESSAGE AND TO FULLY SHED THE REST OF MY HUMAN TRAPPINGS.
I SUPPOSE EVEN JESUS CHRIST HAD TO MAKE A FEW DRY RUNS.
COME, NURSE.
GIVE ME YOUR BODY SO THAT I MAY CONTINUE TO INHABIT THIS GARDEN OF EDEN.
NOO... MARSH...
COFF
GRAAAH!!!
SPLOOSH
NO MORE STUPID TALK. NO MORE FAKE FACES. YOU MUST BE STOPPED.
SHRRRIP!

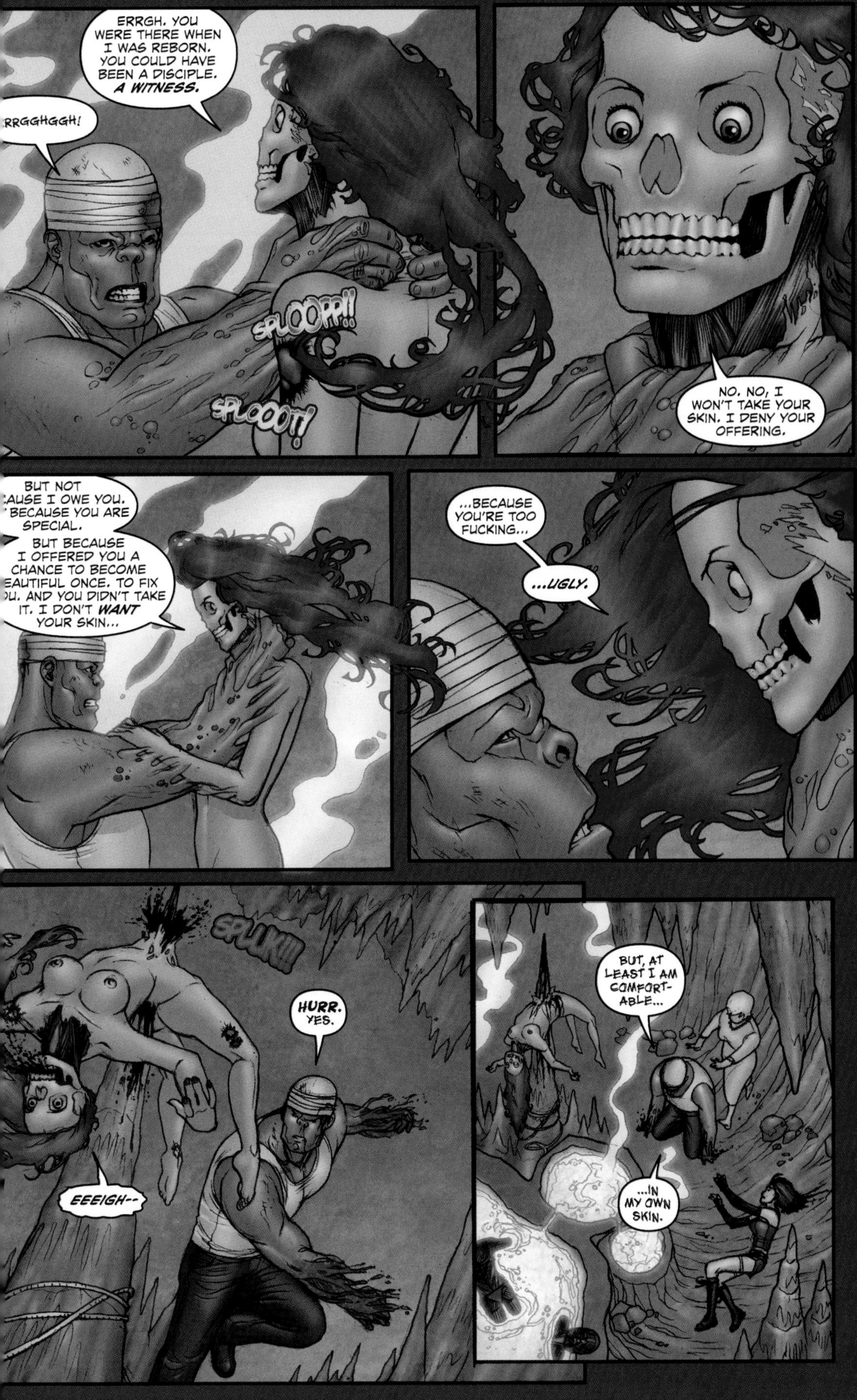
ERRGH. YOU WERE THERE WHEN I WAS REBORN. YOU COULD HAVE BEEN A DISCIPLE. *A WITNESS.*
RRGGHGGH!
SPLOOPP!!
SPLOOOT!
NO. NO, I WON'T TAKE YOUR SKIN. I DENY YOUR OFFERING.
BUT NOT CAUSE I OWE YOU. BECAUSE YOU ARE SPECIAL.
BUT BECAUSE I OFFERED YOU A CHANCE TO BECOME EAUTIFUL ONCE. TO FIX OU. AND YOU DIDN'T TAKE IT. I DON'T *WANT* YOUR SKIN...
...BECAUSE YOU'RE TOO FUCKING...
...UGLY.
SPLUK!!!
HURR. YES.
EEEIGH--
BUT, AT LEAST I AM COMFORT-ABLE...
...IN MY OWN SKIN.

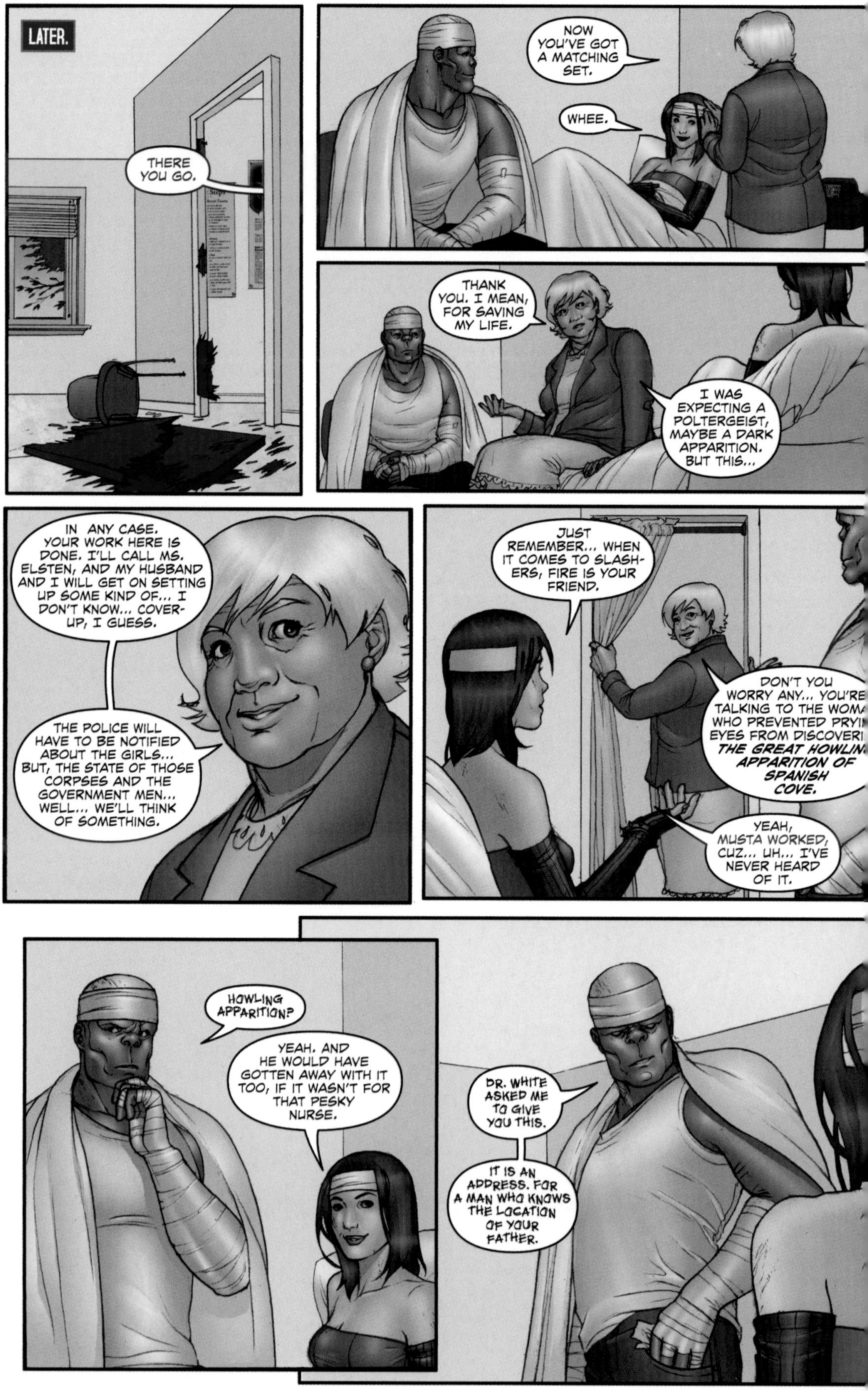
LATER.
THERE YOU GO.
NOW YOU'VE GOT A MATCHING SET.
WHEE.
THANK YOU. I MEAN, FOR SAVING MY LIFE.
I WAS EXPECTING A POLTERGEIST, MAYBE A DARK APPARITION. BUT THIS...
IN ANY CASE. YOUR WORK HERE IS DONE. I'LL CALL MS. ELSTEN, AND MY HUSBAND AND I WILL GET ON SETTING UP SOME KIND OF... I DON'T KNOW... COVER-UP, I GUESS.
THE POLICE WILL HAVE TO BE NOTIFIED ABOUT THE GIRLS... BUT, THE STATE OF THOSE CORPSES AND THE GOVERNMENT MEN... WELL... WE'LL THINK OF SOMETHING.
JUST REMEMBER... WHEN IT COMES TO SLASHERS, FIRE IS YOUR FRIEND.
DON'T YOU WORRY ANY... YOU'RE TALKING TO THE WOMA WHO PREVENTED PRYI EYES FROM DISCOVERI *THE GREAT HOWLIN APPARITION OF SPANISH COVE.*
YEAH, MUSTA WORKED, CUZ... UH... I'VE NEVER HEARD OF IT.
HOWLING APPARITION?
YEAH. AND HE WOULD HAVE GOTTEN AWAY WITH IT TOO, IF IT WASN'T FOR THAT PESKY NURSE.
DR. WHITE ASKED ME TO GIVE YOU THIS.
IT IS AN ADDRESS. FOR A MAN WHO KNOWS THE LOCATION OF YOUR FATHER.

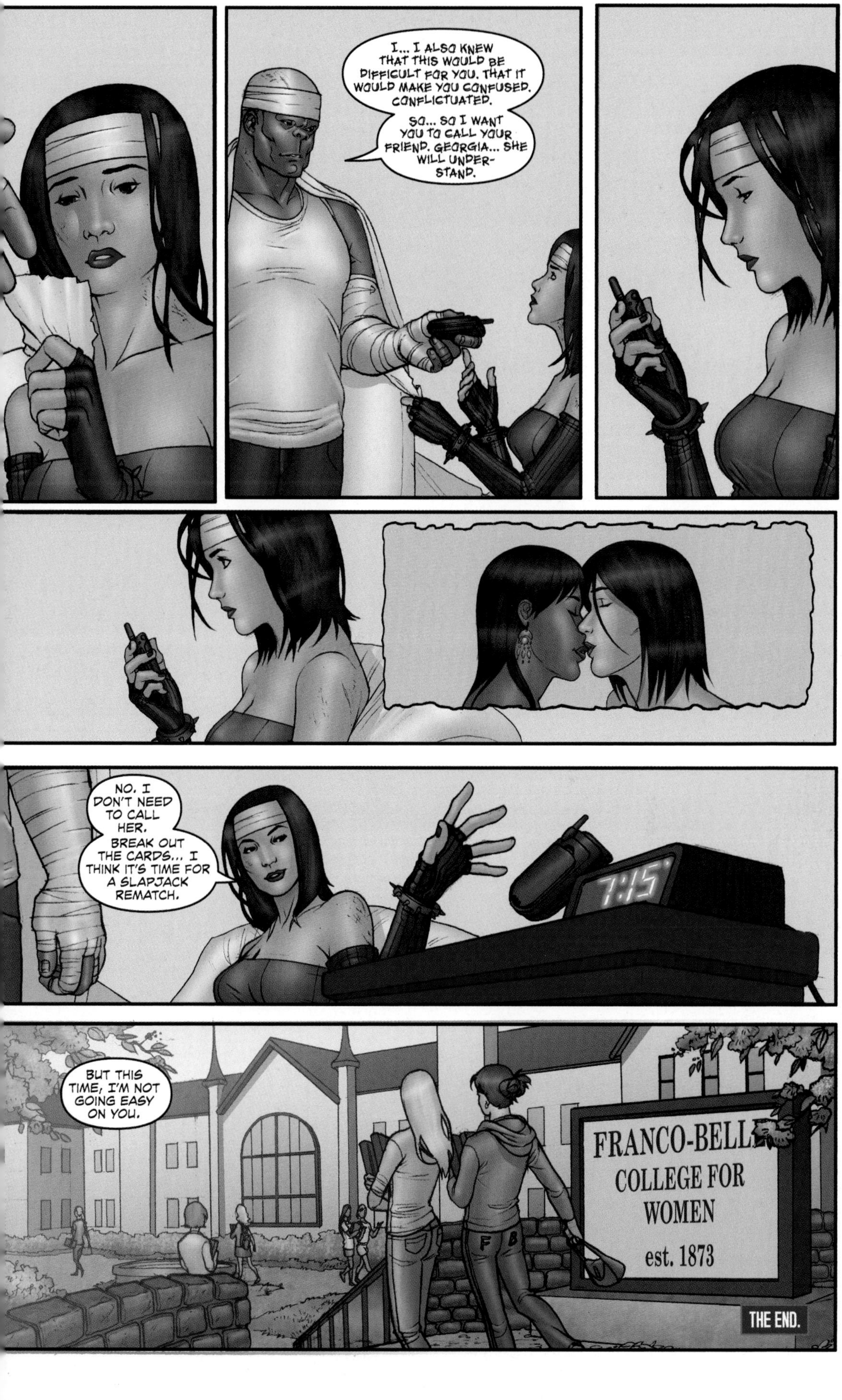
I... I ALSO KNEW THAT THIS WOULD BE DIFFICULT FOR YOU. THAT IT WOULD MAKE YOU CONFUSED. CONFLICTUATED.
SO... SO I WANT YOU TO CALL YOUR FRIEND. GEORGIA... SHE WILL UNDER-STAND.
NO. I DON'T NEED TO CALL HER.
BREAK OUT THE CARDS... I THINK IT'S TIME FOR A SLAPJACK REMATCH.
7:15
BUT THIS TIME, I'M NOT GOING EASY ON YOU.
FRANCO-BELL
COLLEGE FOR WOMEN
est. 1873
F B
THE END.

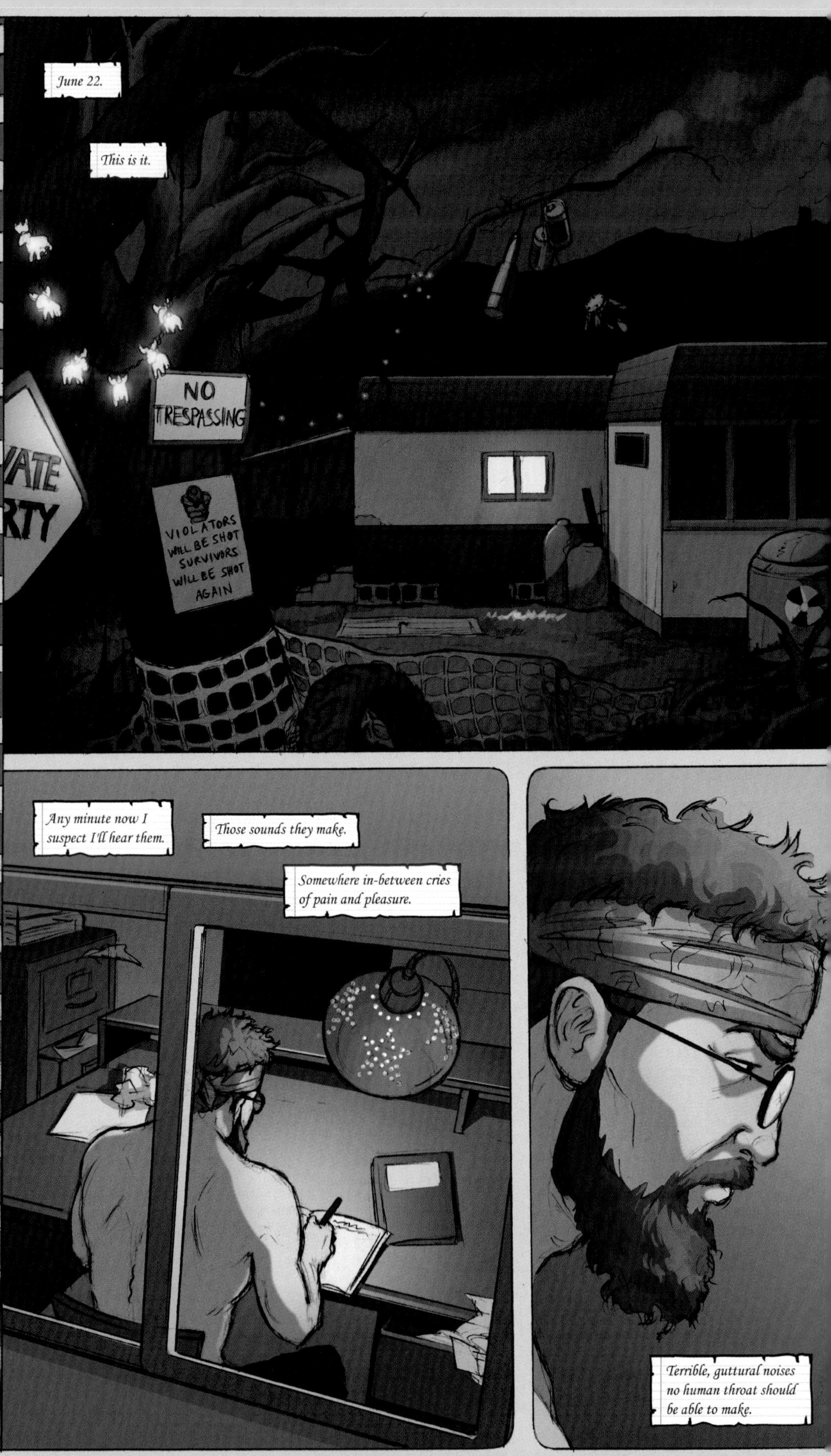
June 22.
This is it.
NO TRESPASSING
VIOLATORS WILL BE SHOT SURVIVORS WILL BE SHOT AGAIN
Any minute now I suspect I'll hear them.
Those sounds they make.
Somewhere in-between cries of pain and pleasure.
Terrible, guttural noises no human throat should be able to make.

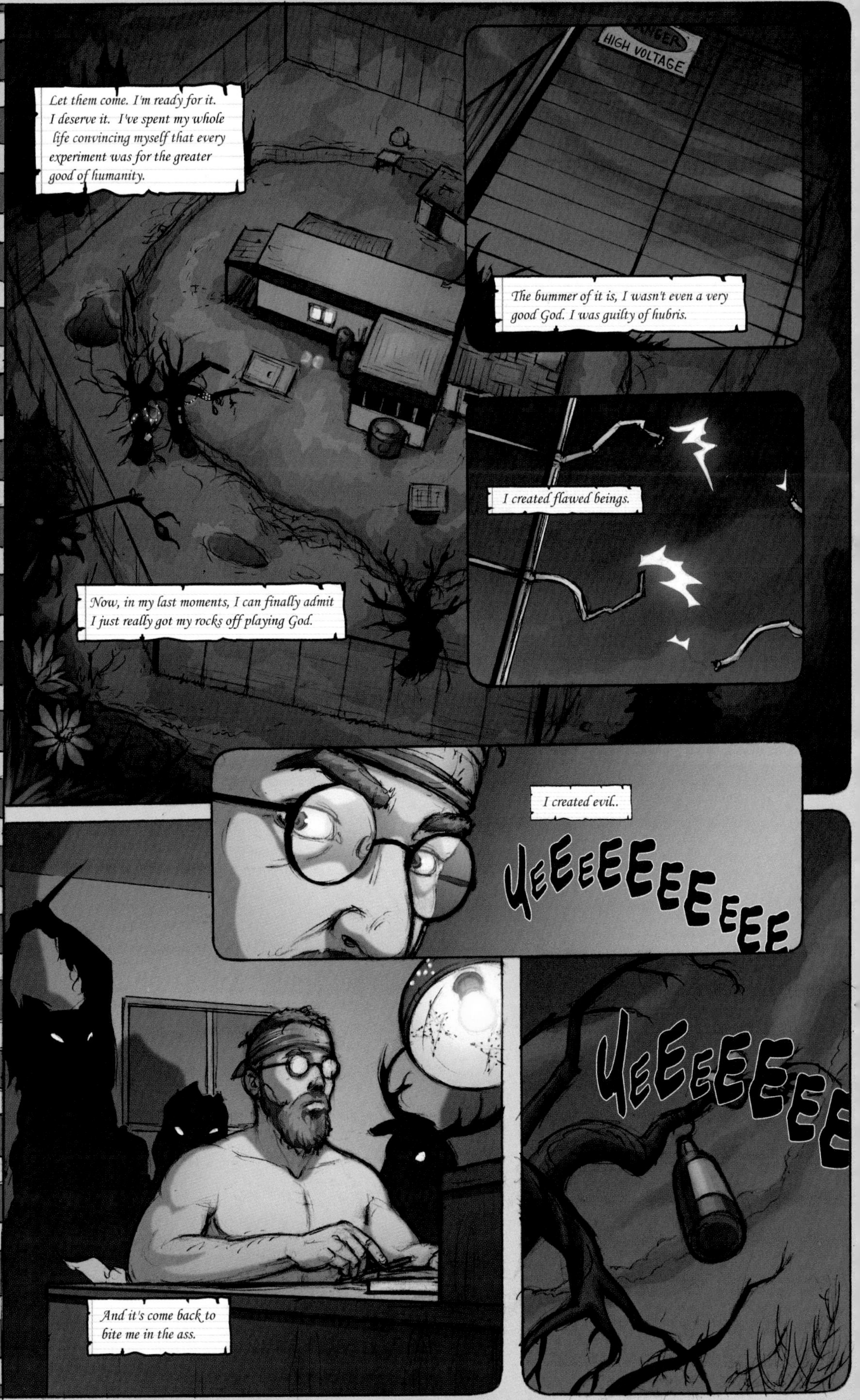
DANGER
HIGH VOLTAGE
Let them come. I'm ready for it. I deserve it. I've spent my whole life convincing myself that every experiment was for the greater good of humanity.
The bummer of it is, I wasn't even a very good God. I was guilty of hubris.
I created flawed beings.
Now, in my last moments, I can finally admit I just really got my rocks off playing God.
I created evil..
UEEEEEEEEEEE
And it's come back to bite me in the ass.
UEEEEEEEEE

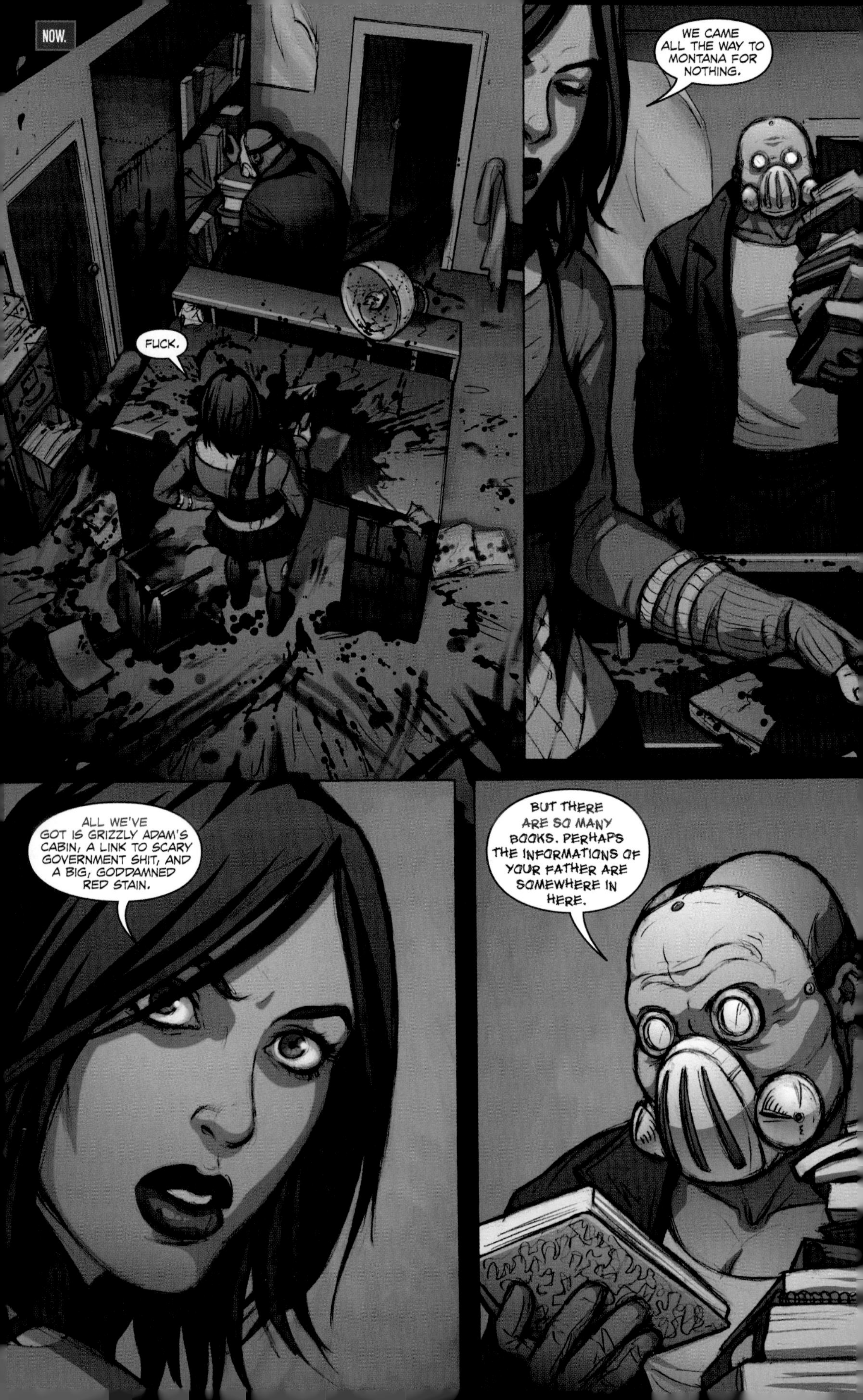
NOW.
FUCK.
WE CAME ALL THE WAY TO MONTANA FOR NOTHING.
ALL WE'VE GOT IS GRIZZLY ADAM'S CABIN, A LINK TO SCARY GOVERNMENT SHIT, AND A BIG, GODDAMNED RED STAIN.
BUT THERE ARE SO MANY BOOKS. PERHAPS THE INFORMATIONS OF YOUR FATHER ARE SOMEWHERE IN HERE.

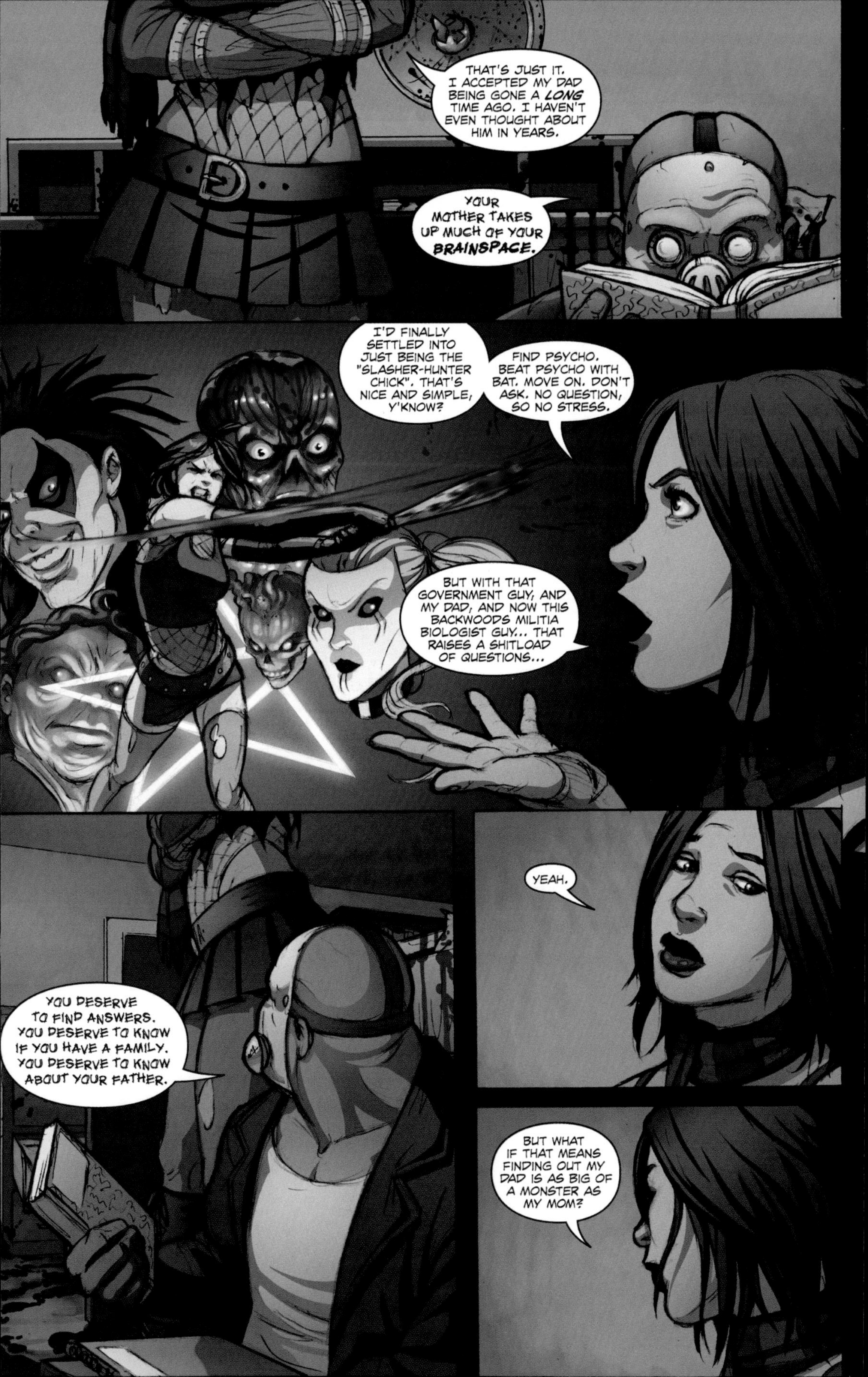
THAT'S JUST IT. I ACCEPTED MY DAD BEING GONE A LONG TIME AGO. I HAVEN'T EVEN THOUGHT ABOUT HIM IN YEARS.
YOUR MOTHER TAKES UP MUCH OF YOUR BRAINSPACE.
I'D FINALLY SETTLED INTO JUST BEING THE "SLASHER-HUNTER CHICK". THAT'S NICE AND SIMPLE, Y'KNOW?
FIND PSYCHO. BEAT PSYCHO WITH BAT. MOVE ON. DON'T ASK. NO QUESTION, SO NO STRESS.
BUT WITH THAT GOVERNMENT GUY, AND MY DAD, AND NOW THIS BACKWOODS MILITIA BIOLOGIST GUY... THAT RAISES A SHITLOAD OF QUESTIONS...
YEAH.
YOU DESERVE TO FIND ANSWERS. YOU DESERVE TO KNOW IF YOU HAVE A FAMILY. YOU DESERVE TO KNOW ABOUT YOUR FATHER.
BUT WHAT IF THAT MEANS FINDING OUT MY DAD IS AS BIG OF A MONSTER AS MY MOM?

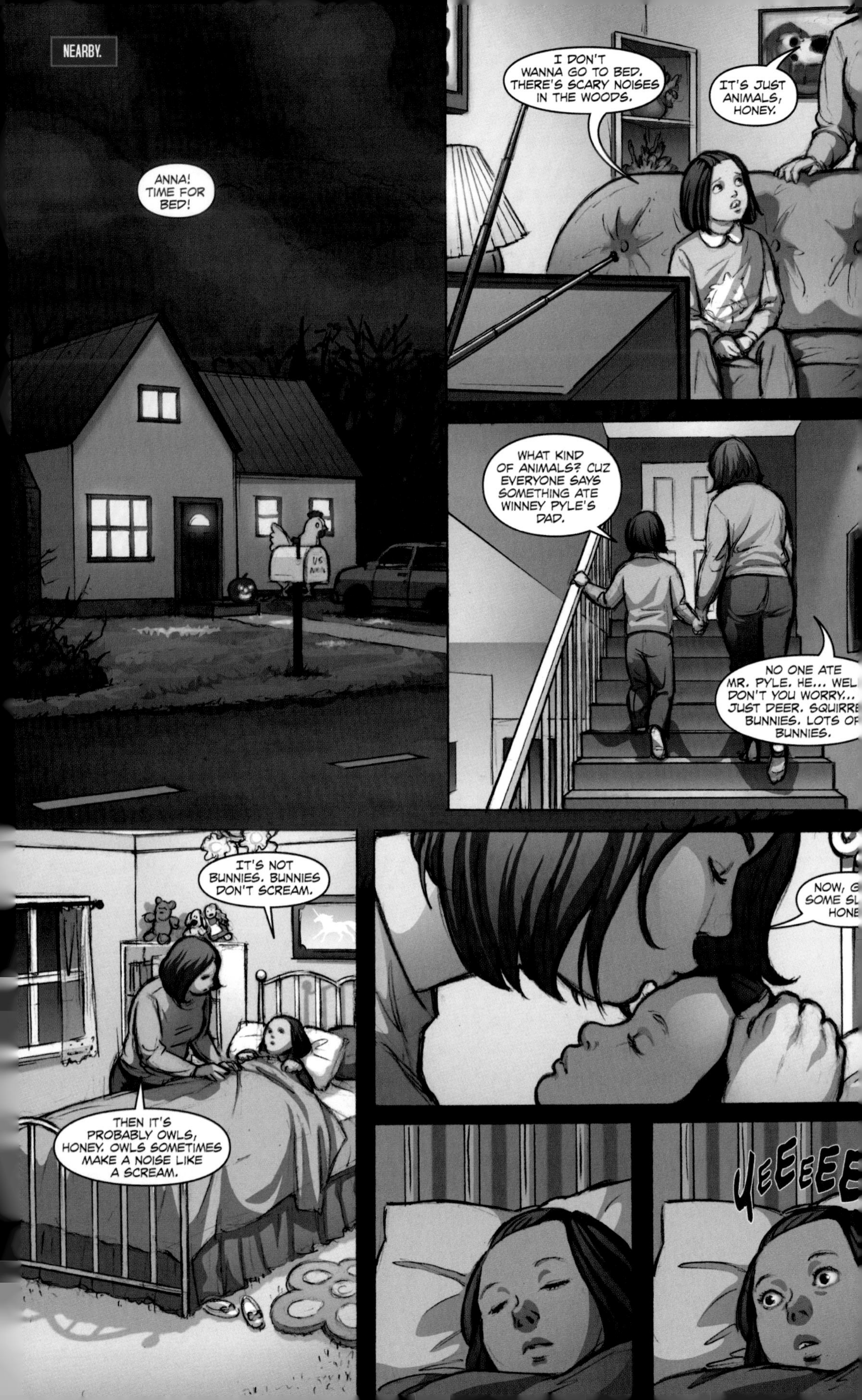
NEARBY.
ANNA! TIME FOR BED!
I DON'T WANNA GO TO BED. THERE'S SCARY NOISES IN THE WOODS.
IT'S JUST ANIMALS, HONEY.
WHAT KIND OF ANIMALS? CUZ EVERYONE SAYS SOMETHING ATE WINNEY PYLE'S DAD.
NO ONE ATE MR. PYLE. HE... WEL DON'T YOU WORRY... JUST DEER. SQUIRRE BUNNIES. LOTS OF BUNNIES.
IT'S NOT BUNNIES. BUNNIES DON'T SCREAM.
THEN IT'S PROBABLY OWLS, HONEY. OWLS SOMETIMES MAKE A NOISE LIKE A SCREAM.
NOW, G SOME SL HONE
UEEEEE

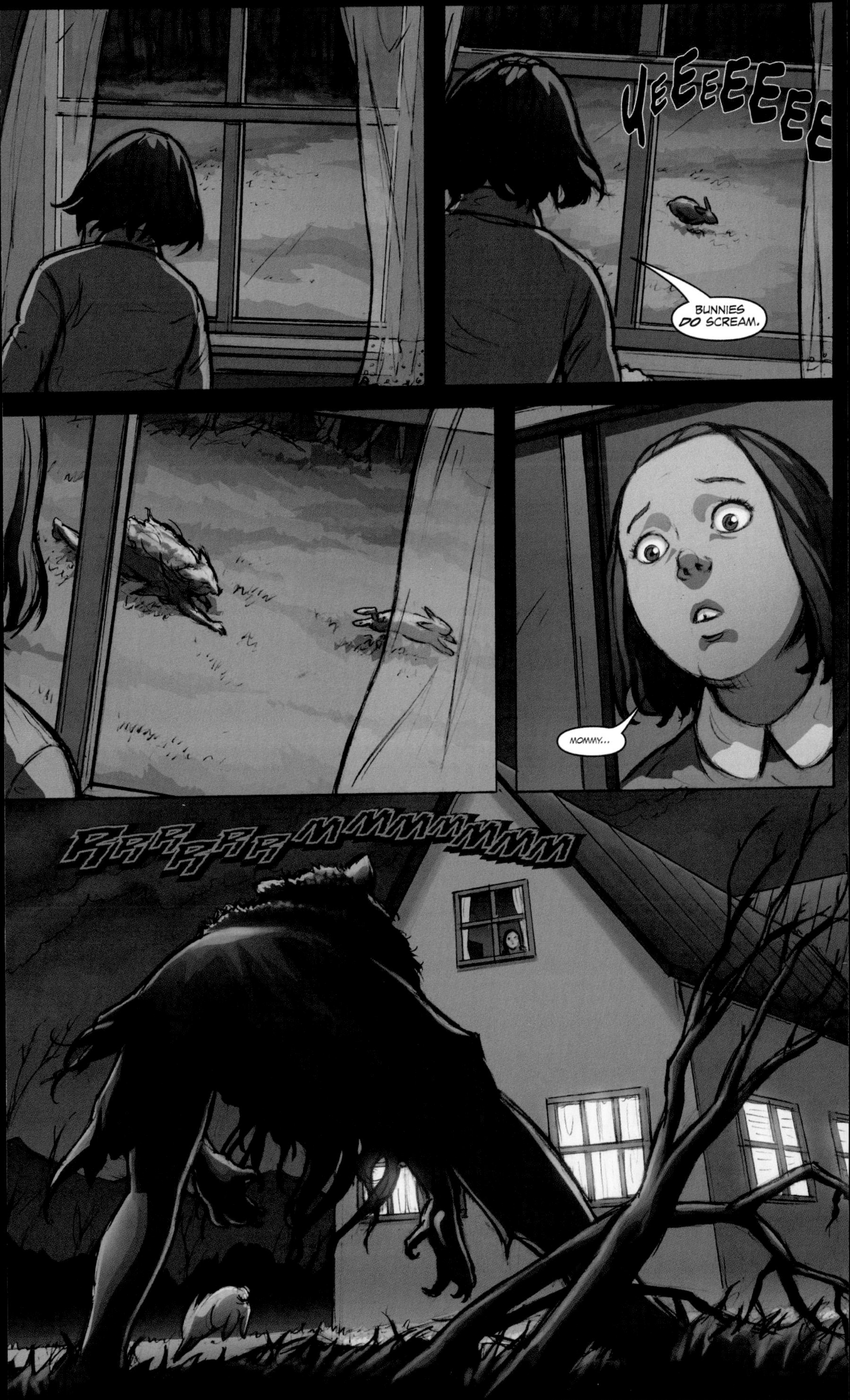
YEEEEEEE
BUNNIES DO SCREAM.
MOMMY...
RRRRRRRMMMMMMMM

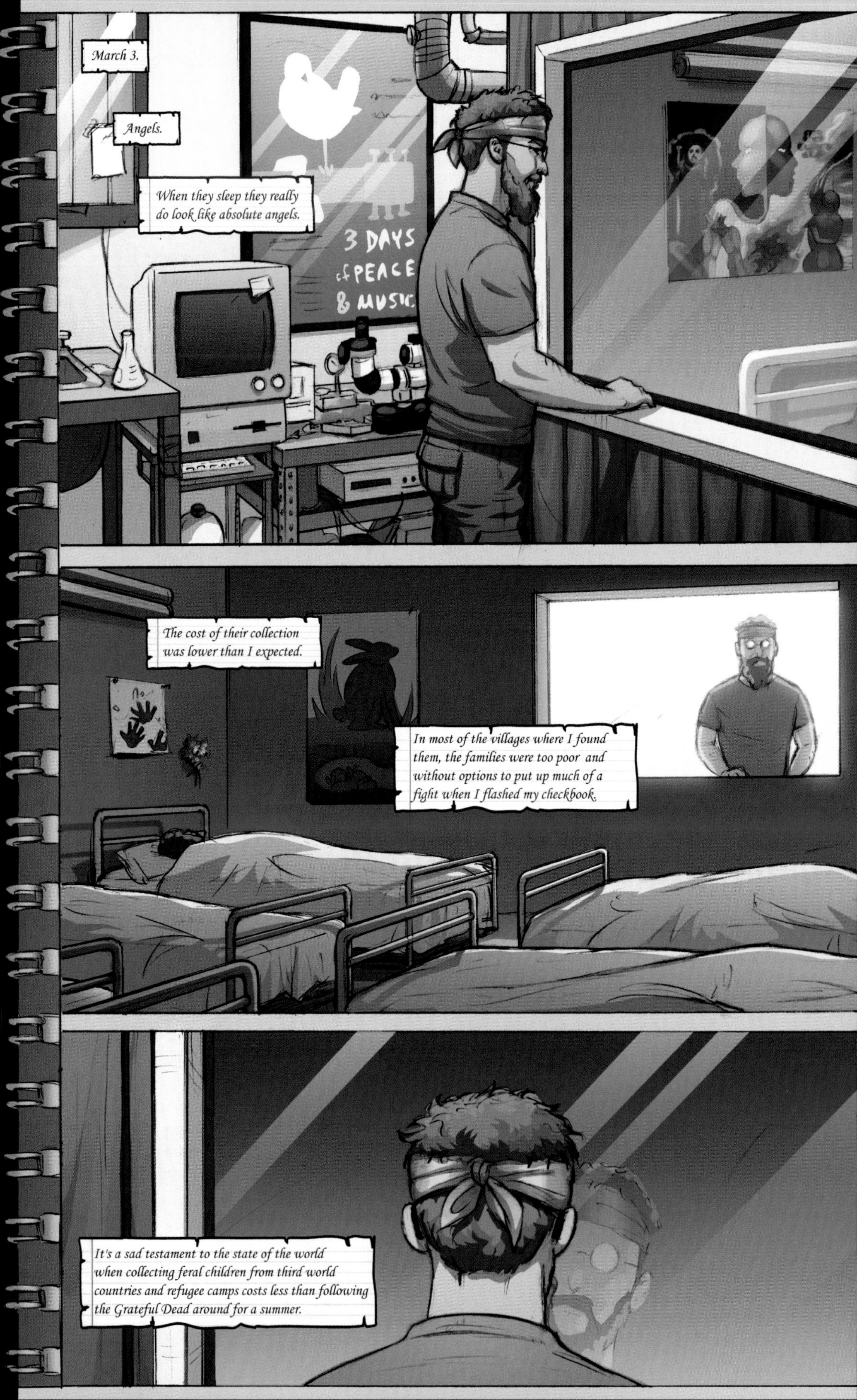
March 3.
Angels.
When they sleep they really do look like absolute angels.
3 DAYS of PEACE & MUSIC
The cost of their collection was lower than I expected.
In most of the villages where I found them, the families were too poor and without options to put up much of a fight when I flashed my checkbook.
It's a sad testament to the state of the world when collecting feral children from third world countries and refugee camps costs less than following the Grateful Dead around for a summer.

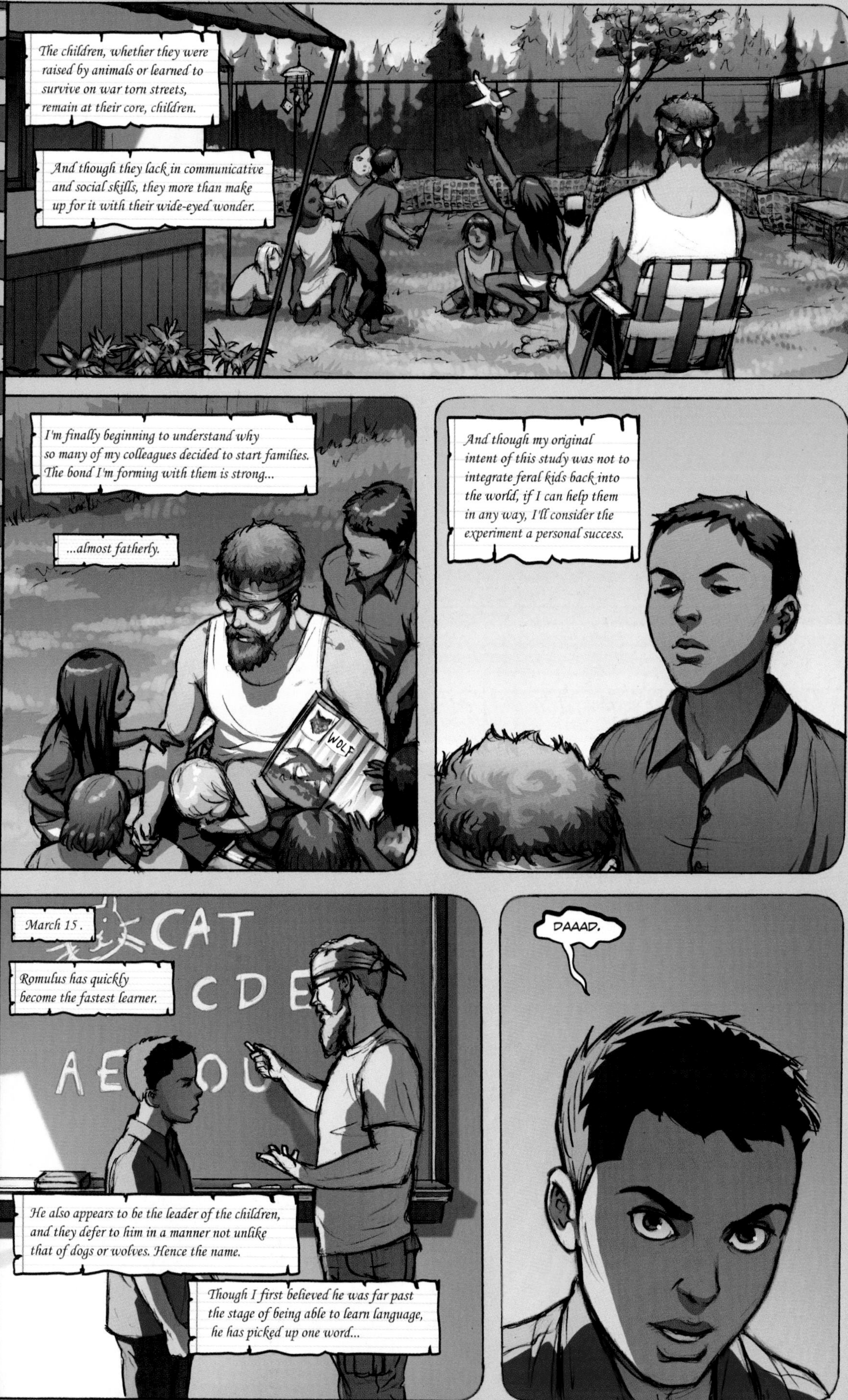
The children, whether they were raised by animals or learned to survive on war torn streets, remain at their core, children.
And though they lack in communicative and social skills, they more than make up for it with their wide-eyed wonder.
I'm finally beginning to understand why so many of my colleagues decided to start families. The bond I'm forming with them is strong...
...almost fatherly.
WOLF
And though my original intent of this study was not to integrate feral kids back into the world, if I can help them in any way, I'll consider the experiment a personal success.
March 15 .
CAT
Romulus has quickly become the fastest learner.
CDE
AE OU
He also appears to be the leader of the children, and they defer to him in a manner not unlike that of dogs or wolves. Hence the name.
Though I first believed he was far past the stage of being able to learn language, he has picked up one word...
DAAAD.

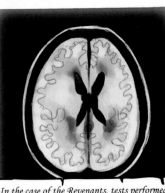

March 19.

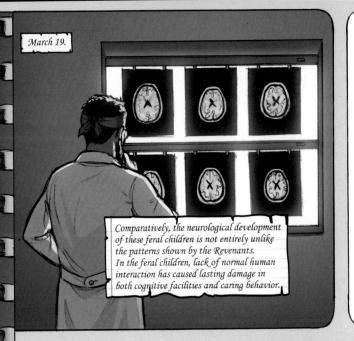

Comparatively, the neurological development of these feral children is not entirely unlike the patterns shown by the Revenants.
In the feral children, lack of normal human interaction has caused lasting damage in both cognitive facilities and caring behavior.

In the case of the Revenants, tests performed after a post-mortem reactivation show a lack of regenerative biology in the brain, whereas the rest of the body has undergone a major metamorphosis.

The brain, especially parts known to deal with moral and social interaction, has actually seemed to degrade.

Within the week, I will be ready to test my Rev-D, which I believe may be able to reverse the downward curve of the children's development, and provide answers regarding Revenants.

April 1.

I let my guard down.

The children had been progressing so well. I decided to relax. In the time it took me to listen to side A of Bitch's Brew and smoke one joint, a massive social upheaval had befallen the kids.

Apparently, Romulus felt Remus had challenged him for his role as leader.

Romulus tore out his throat with his teeth.

I believe the Rev-D has increased his feral urges rather than restrained them.

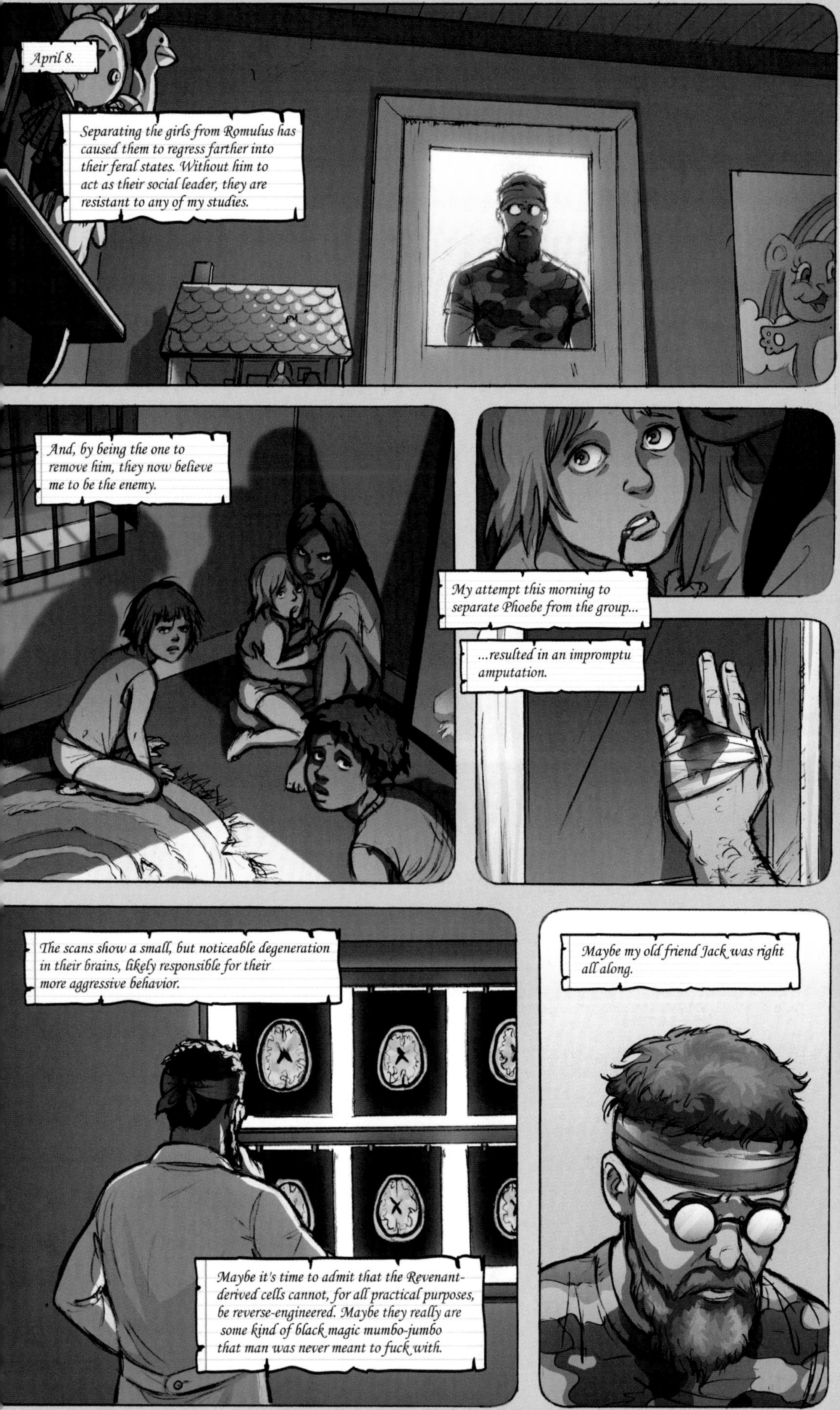

April 8.
Separating the girls from Romulus has caused them to regress farther into their feral states. Without him to act as their social leader, they are resistant to any of my studies.
And, by being the one to remove him, they now believe me to be the enemy.
My attempt this morning to separate Phoebe from the group...
...resulted in an impromptu amputation.
The scans show a small, but noticeable degeneration in their brains, likely responsible for their more aggressive behavior.
Maybe it's time to admit that the Revenant-derived cells cannot, for all practical purposes, be reverse-engineered. Maybe they really are some kind of black magic mumbo-jumbo that man was never meant to fuck with.
Maybe my old friend Jack was right all along.

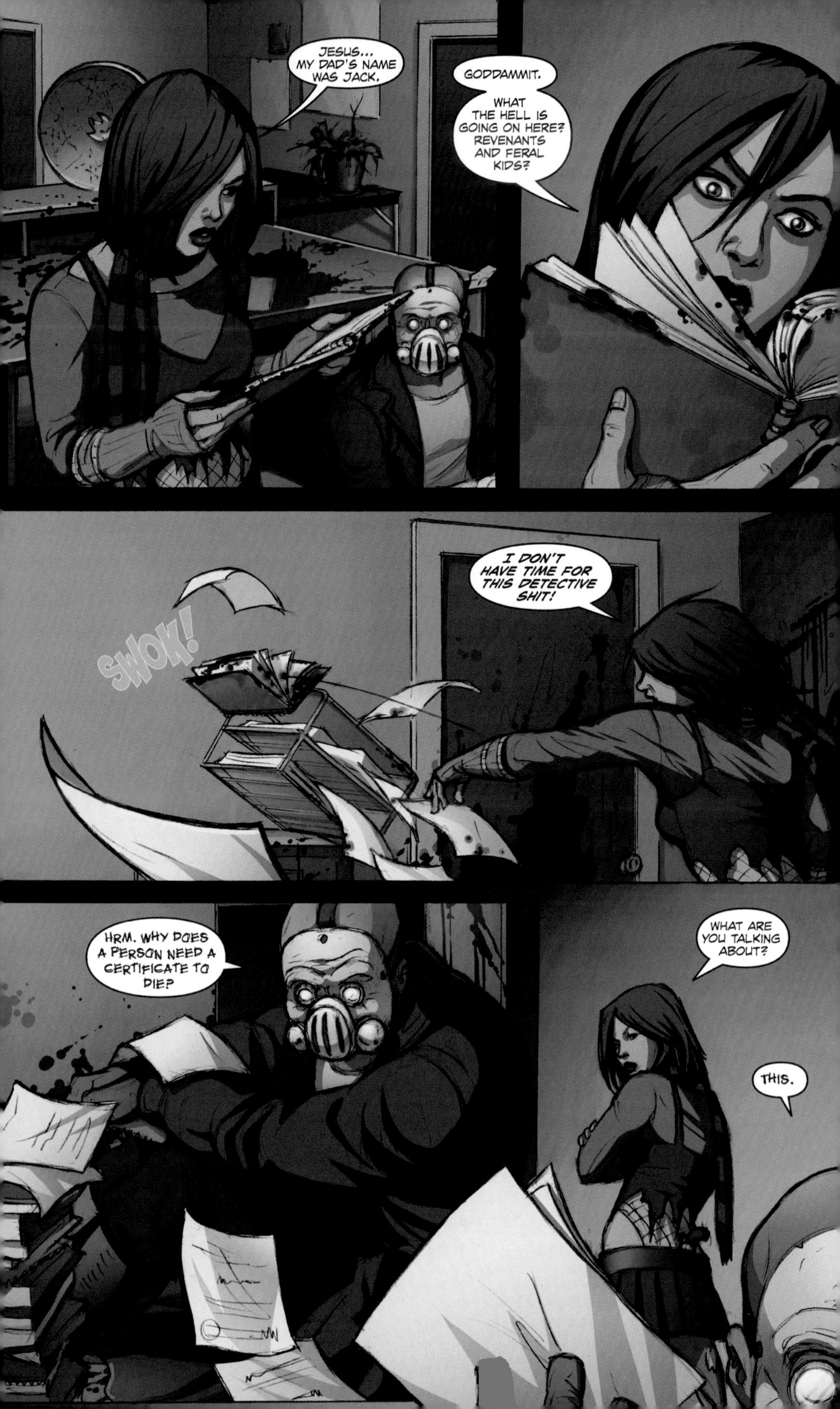
JESUS... MY DAD'S NAME WAS JACK.
GODDAMMIT.
WHAT THE HELL IS GOING ON HERE? REVENANTS AND FERAL KIDS?
I DON'T HAVE TIME FOR THIS DETECTIVE SHIT!
SWOK!
HRM. WHY DOES A PERSON NEED A CERTIFICATE TO DIE?
WHAT ARE YOU TALKING ABOUT?
THIS.

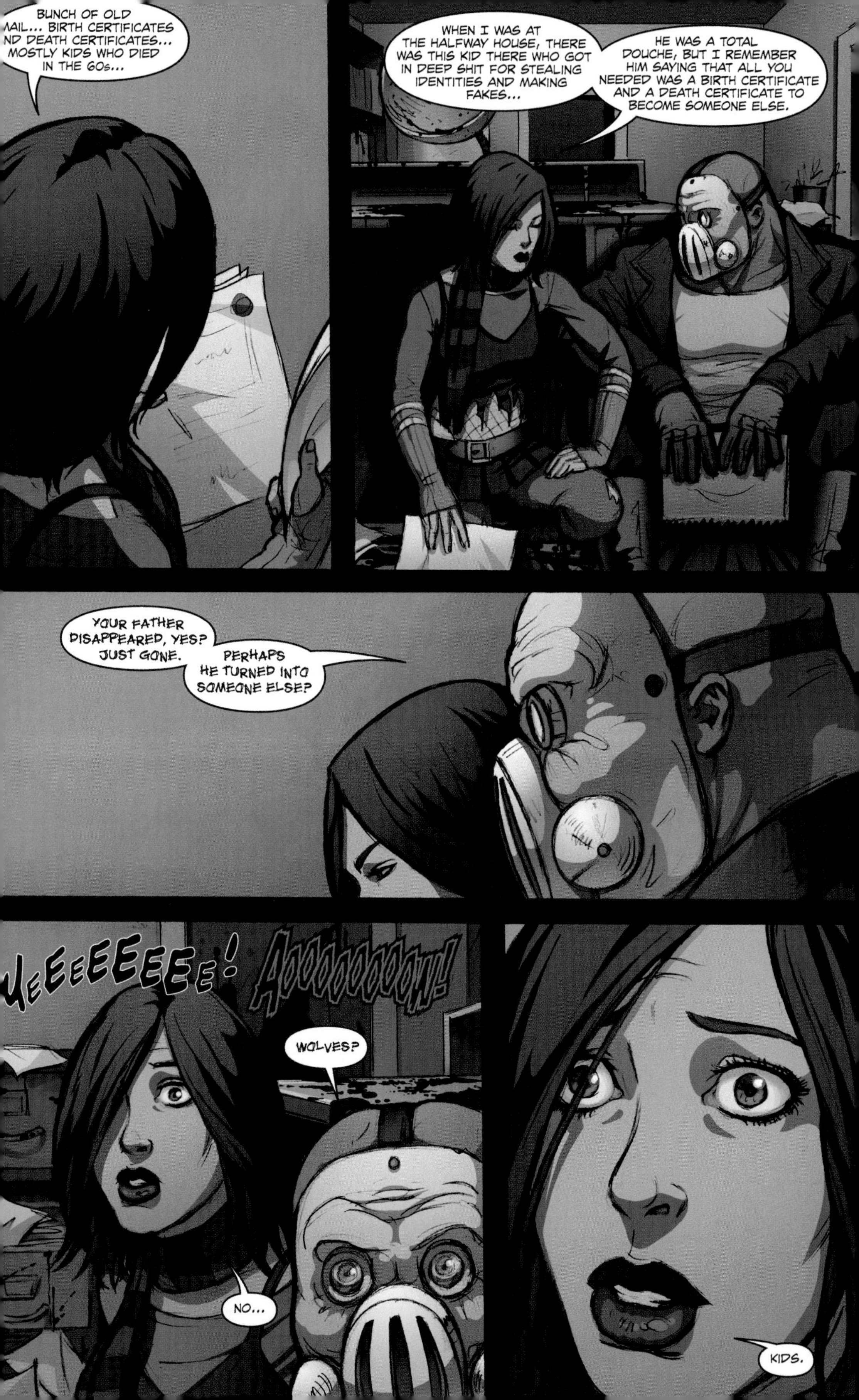
BUNCH OF OLD MAIL... BIRTH CERTIFICATES ND DEATH CERTIFICATES... MOSTLY KIDS WHO DIED IN THE 60s...
WHEN I WAS AT THE HALFWAY HOUSE, THERE WAS THIS KID THERE WHO GOT IN DEEP SHIT FOR STEALING IDENTITIES AND MAKING FAKES...
HE WAS A TOTAL DOUCHE, BUT I REMEMBER HIM SAYING THAT ALL YOU NEEDED WAS A BIRTH CERTIFICATE AND A DEATH CERTIFICATE TO BECOME SOMEONE ELSE.
YOUR FATHER DISAPPEARED, YES? JUST GONE.
PERHAPS HE TURNED INTO SOMEONE ELSE?
UEEEEEEEEE!
AOOOOOOOOW!
WOLVES?
NO...
KIDS.

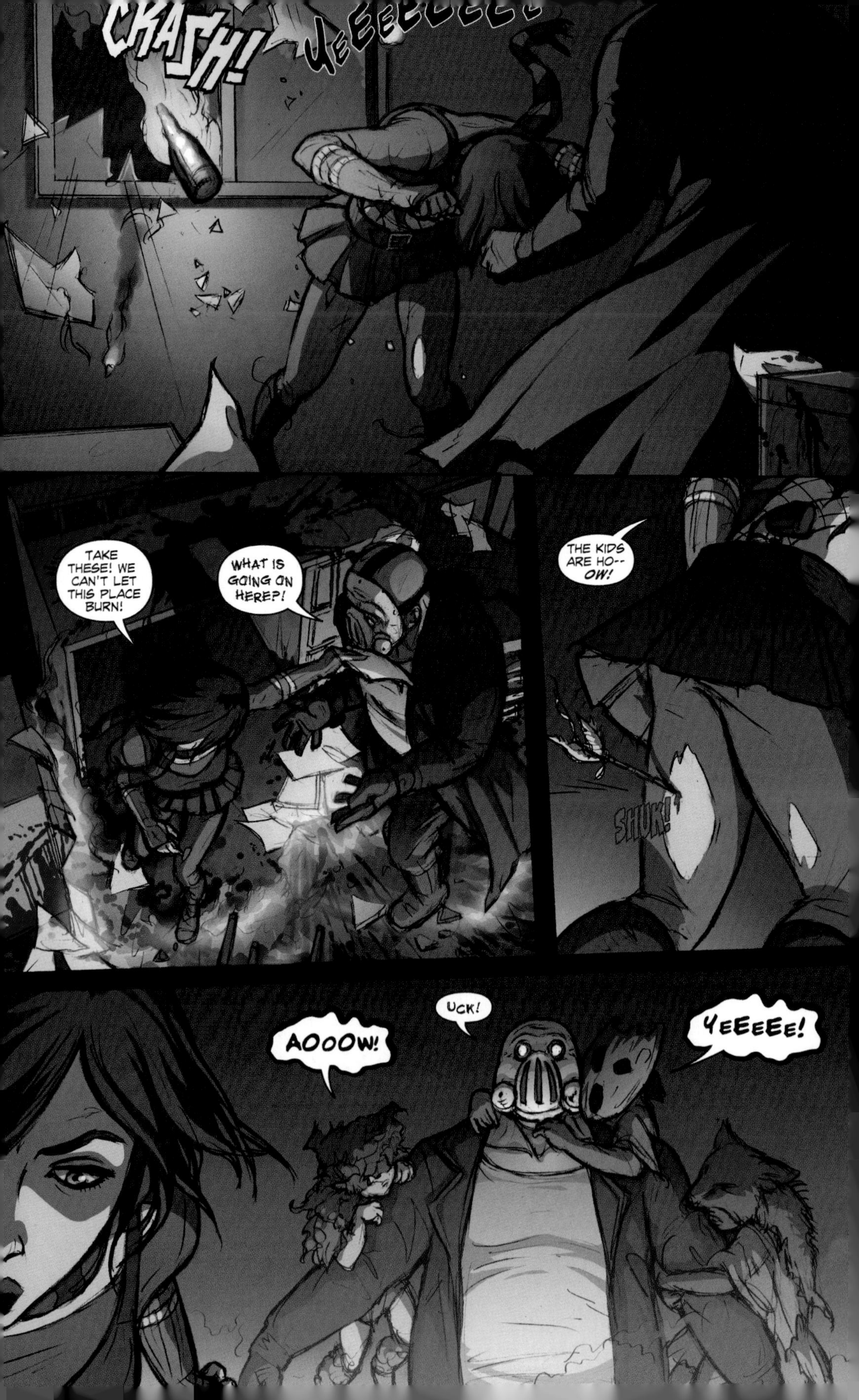
CRASH!
TAKE THESE! WE CAN'T LET THIS PLACE BURN!
WHAT IS GOING ON HERE?!
THE KIDS ARE HO-- OW!
SHUK!
AOOOW!
UCK!
YEEEEE!

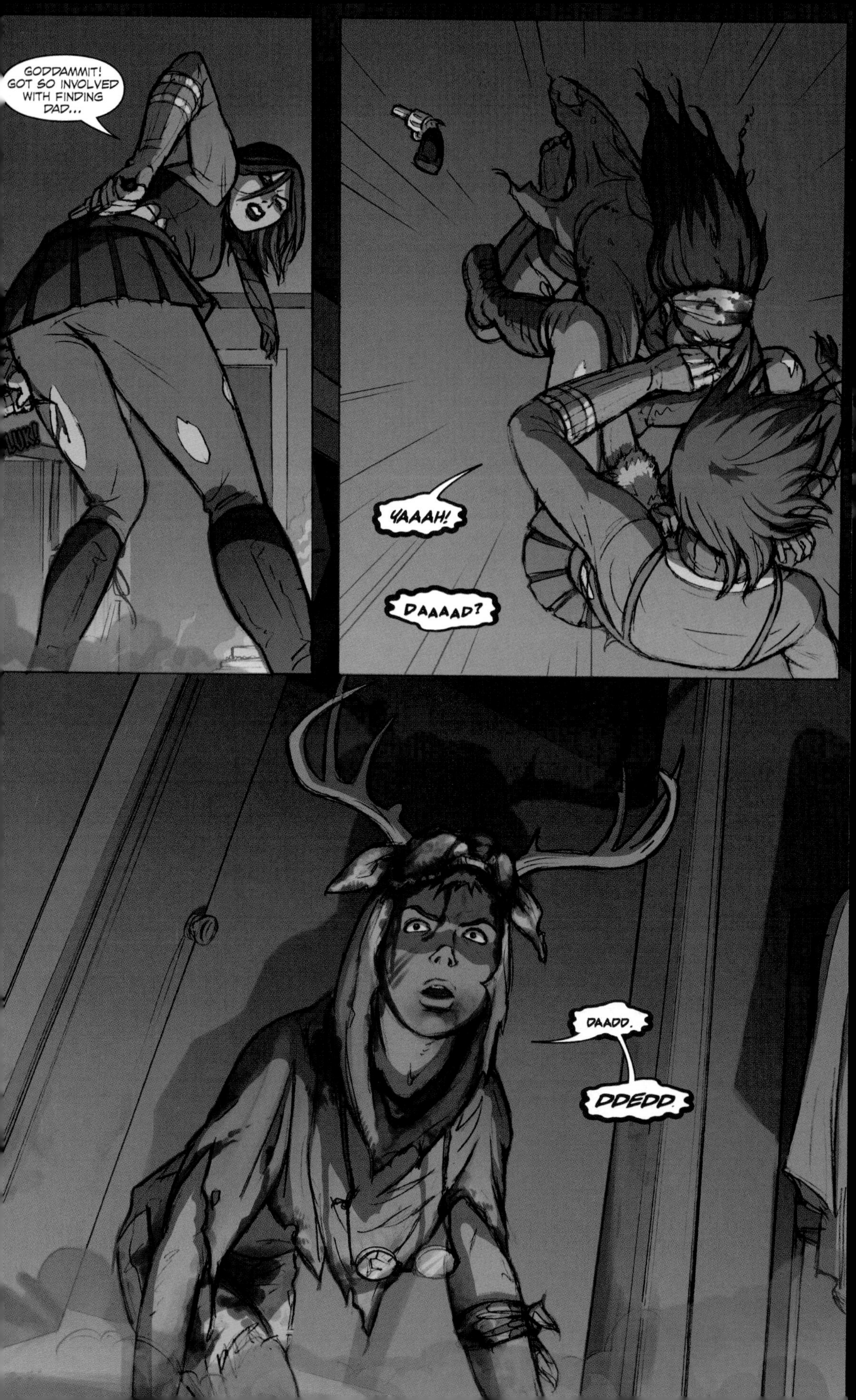
GODDAMMIT! GOT SO INVOLVED WITH FINDING DAD...
YAAAH!
DAAAAD?
DAADD.
DDEDD.

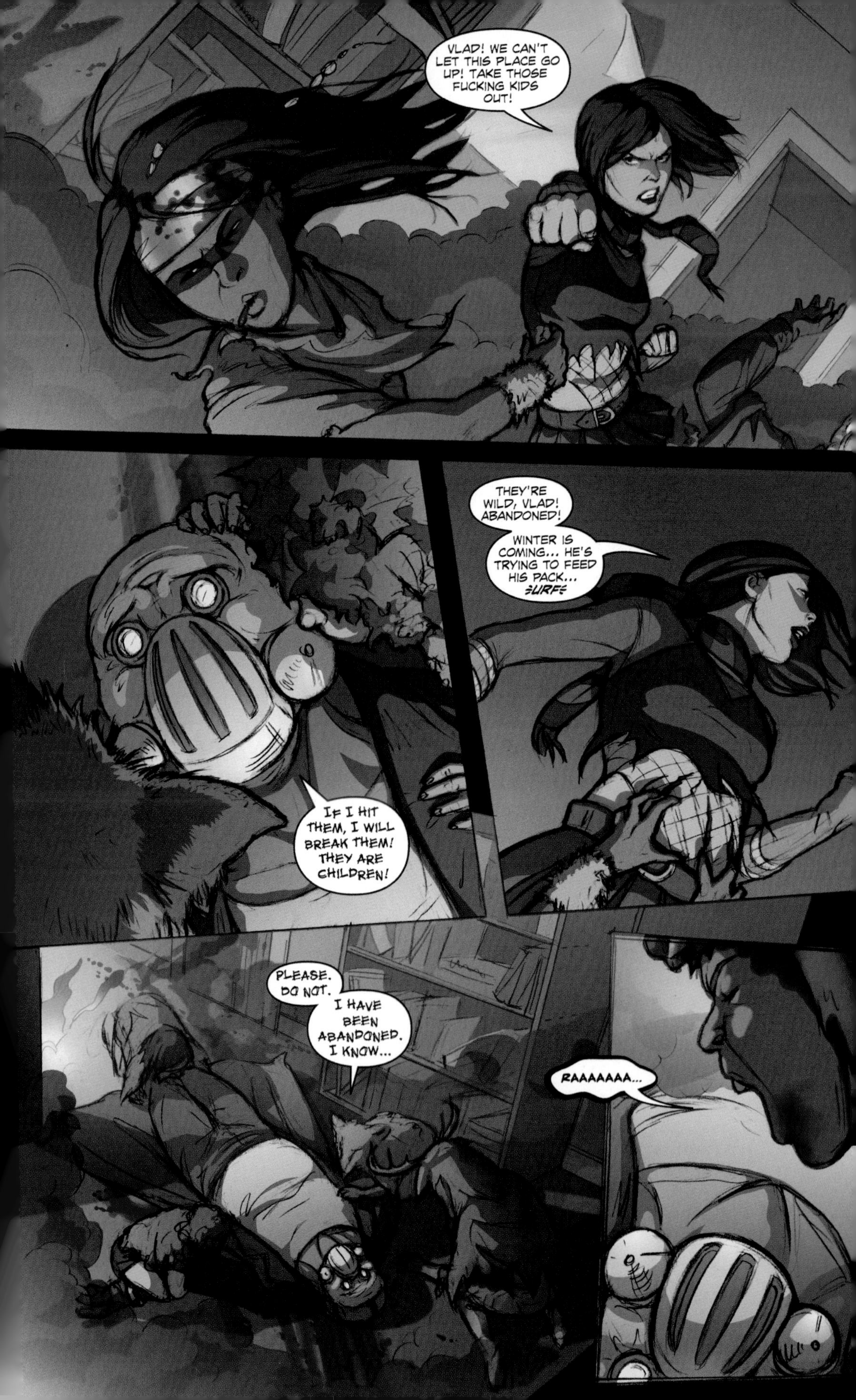
VLAD! WE CAN'T LET THIS PLACE GO UP! TAKE THOSE FUCKING KIDS OUT!
IF I HIT THEM, I WILL BREAK THEM! THEY ARE CHILDREN!
THEY'RE WILD, VLAD! ABANDONED!
WINTER IS COMING... HE'S TRYING TO FEED HIS PACK...
URF
PLEASE. DO NOT.
I HAVE BEEN ABANDONED. I KNOW...
RAAAAAAA...

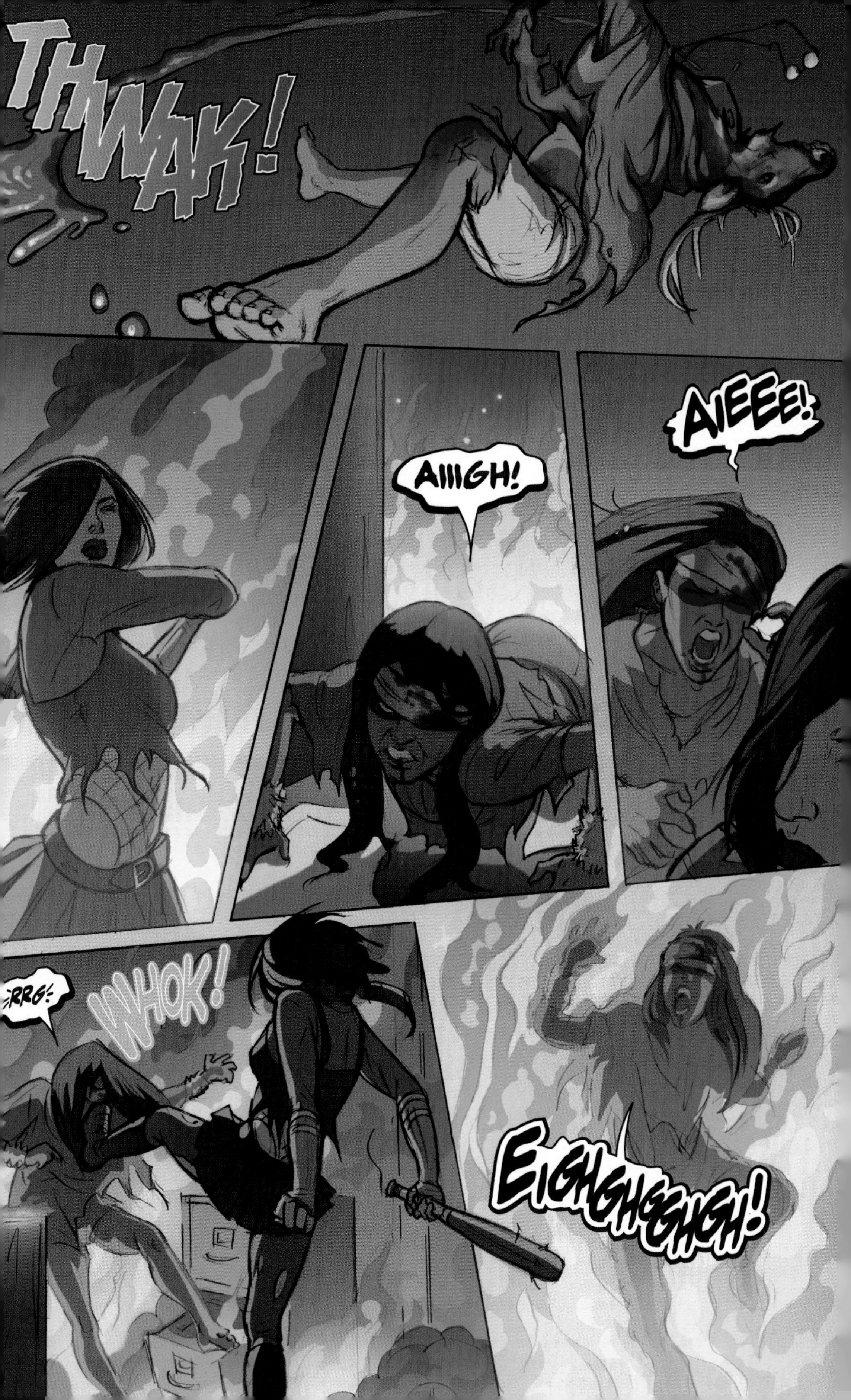
THWAK!
AIIIGH!
AIEEE!
RRG
WHOK!
EIGHGHGGHGH!

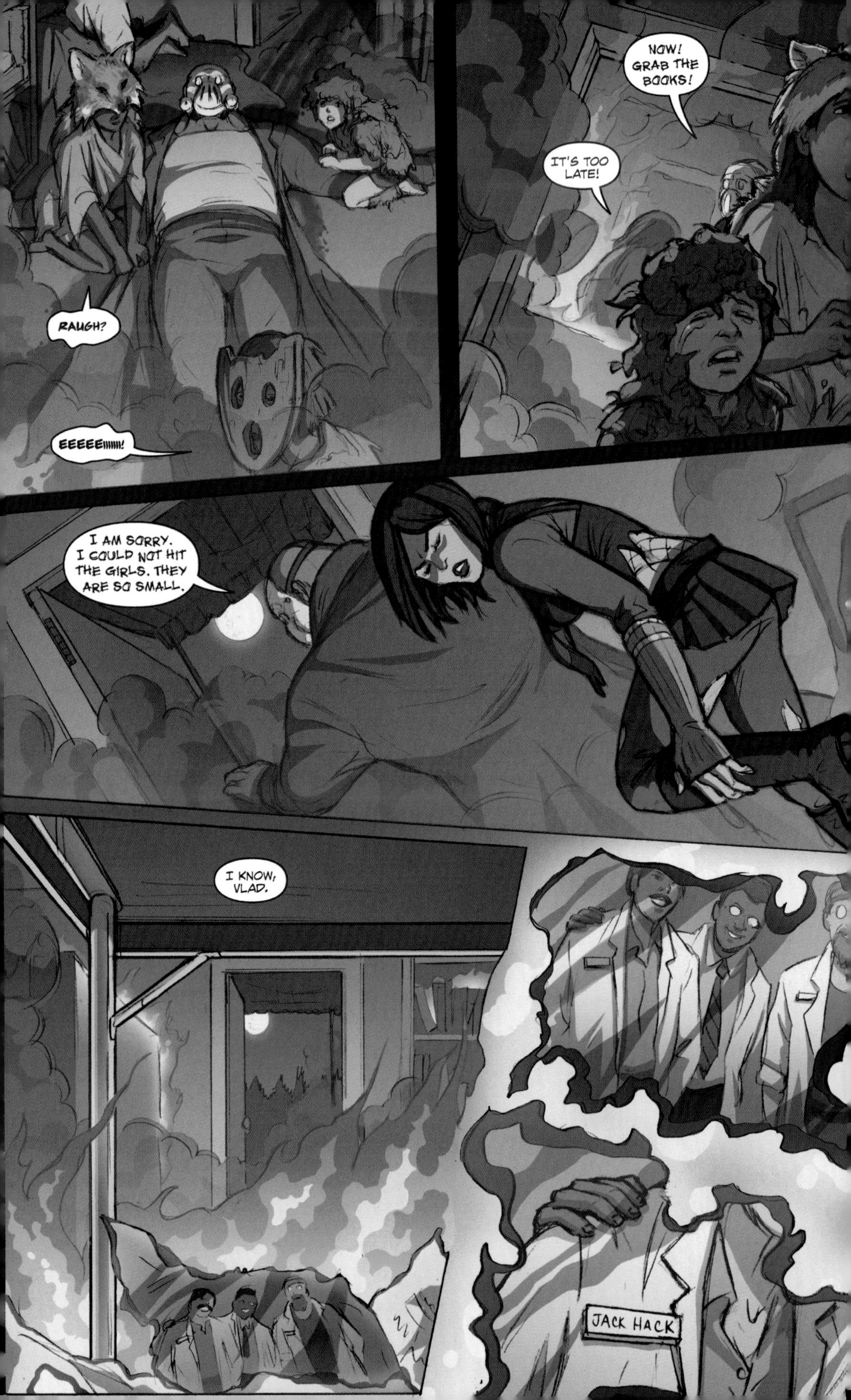
RAUGH?
EEEEEIIIIII!
NOW! GRAB THE BOOKS!
IT'S TOO LATE!
I AM SORRY. I COULD NOT HIT THE GIRLS. THEY ARE SO SMALL.
I KNOW, VLAD.
JACK HACK

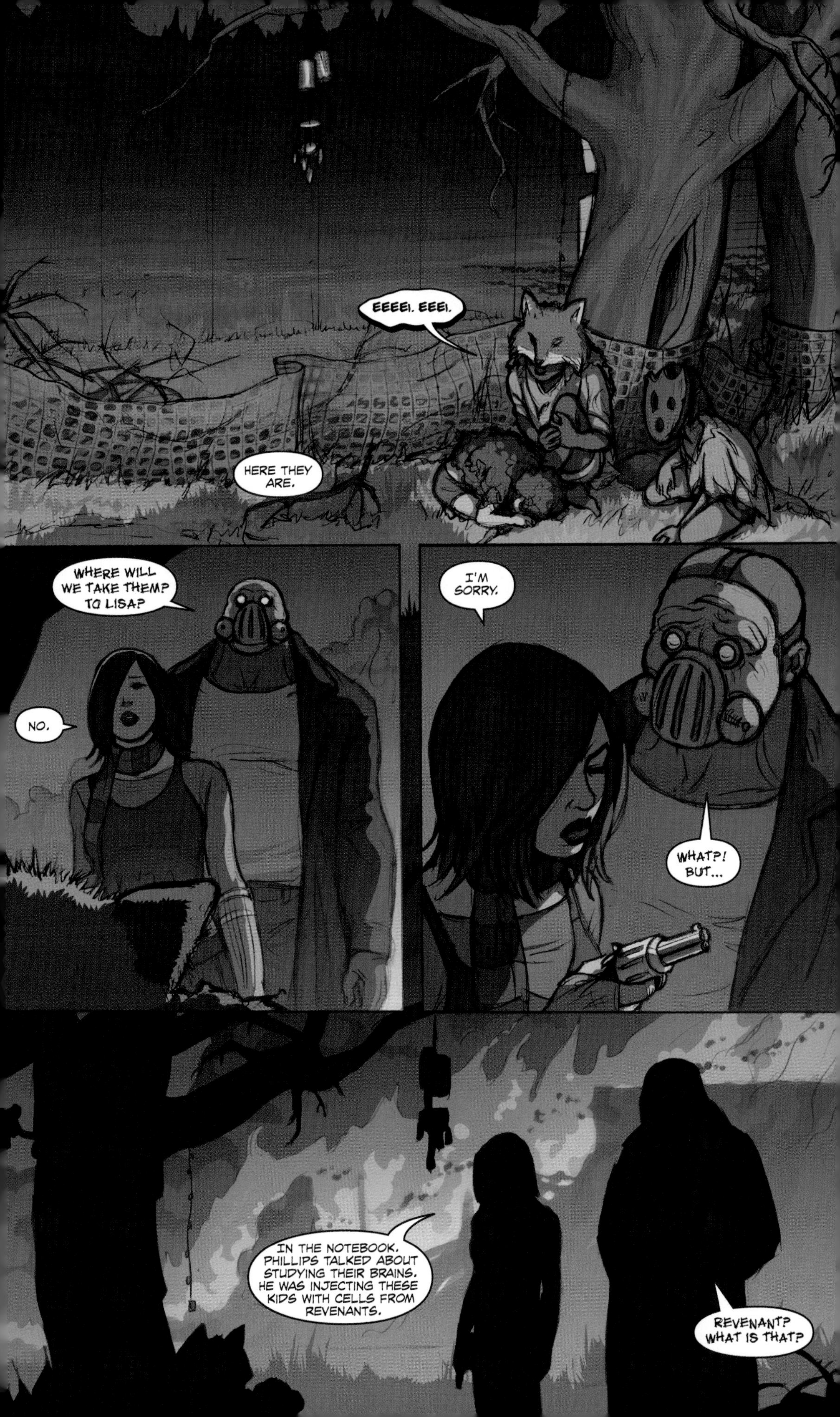
EEEE!. EEE!.
HERE THEY ARE.
WHERE WILL WE TAKE THEM? TO LISA?
NO.
I'M SORRY.
WHAT?! BUT...
IN THE NOTEBOOK, PHILLIPS TALKED ABOUT STUDYING THEIR BRAINS. HE WAS INJECTING THESE KIDS WITH CELLS FROM REVENANTS.
REVENANT? WHAT IS THAT?

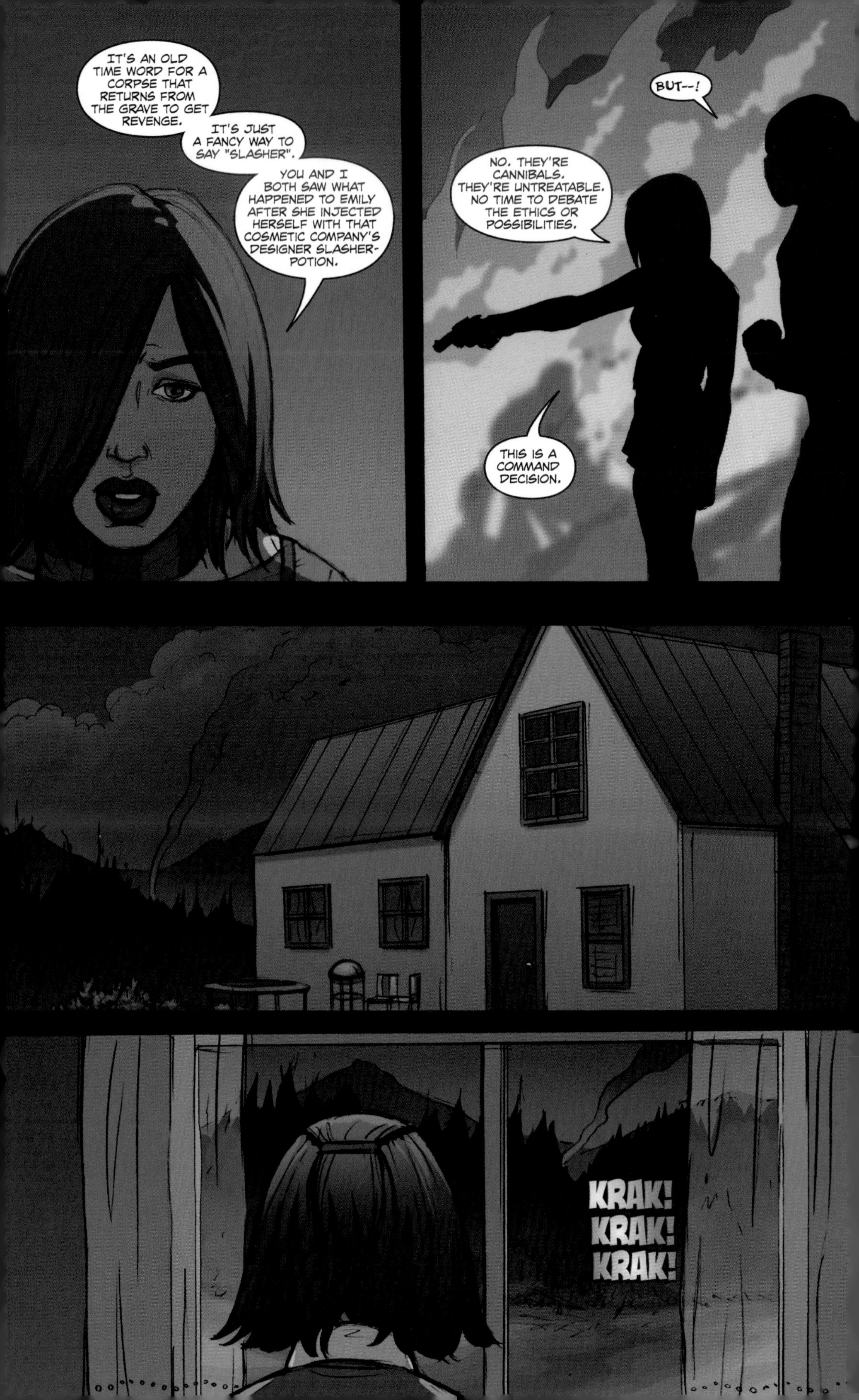

IT'S AN OLD TIME WORD FOR A CORPSE THAT RETURNS FROM THE GRAVE TO GET REVENGE.
IT'S JUST A FANCY WAY TO SAY "SLASHER".
YOU AND I BOTH SAW WHAT HAPPENED TO EMILY AFTER SHE INJECTED HERSELF WITH THAT COSMETIC COMPANY'S DESIGNER SLASHER-POTION.
BUT--!
NO. THEY'RE CANNIBALS. THEY'RE UNTREATABLE. NO TIME TO DEBATE THE ETHICS OR POSSIBILITIES.
THIS IS A COMMAND DECISION.
KRAK! KRAK! KRAK!

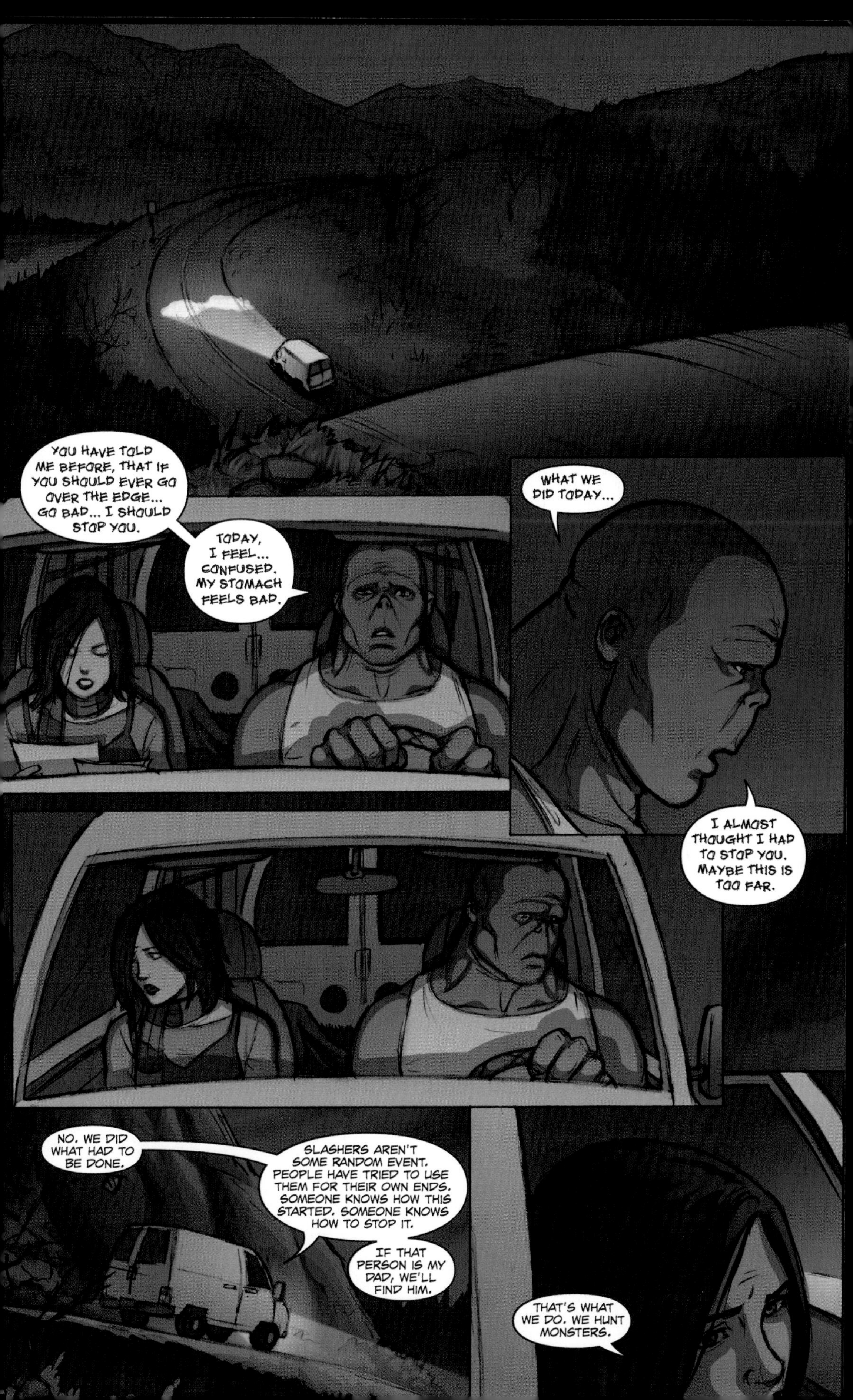
YOU HAVE TOLD ME BEFORE, THAT IF YOU SHOULD EVER GO OVER THE EDGE... GO BAD... I SHOULD STOP YOU.
TODAY, I FEEL... CONFUSED. MY STOMACH FEELS BAD.
WHAT WE DID TODAY...
I ALMOST THOUGHT I HAD TO STOP YOU. MAYBE THIS IS TOO FAR.
NO. WE DID WHAT HAD TO BE DONE.
SLASHERS AREN'T SOME RANDOM EVENT. PEOPLE HAVE TRIED TO USE THEM FOR THEIR OWN ENDS. SOMEONE KNOWS HOW THIS STARTED. SOMEONE KNOWS HOW TO STOP IT.
IF THAT PERSON IS MY DAD, WE'LL FIND HIM.
THAT'S WHAT WE DO. WE HUNT MONSTERS.

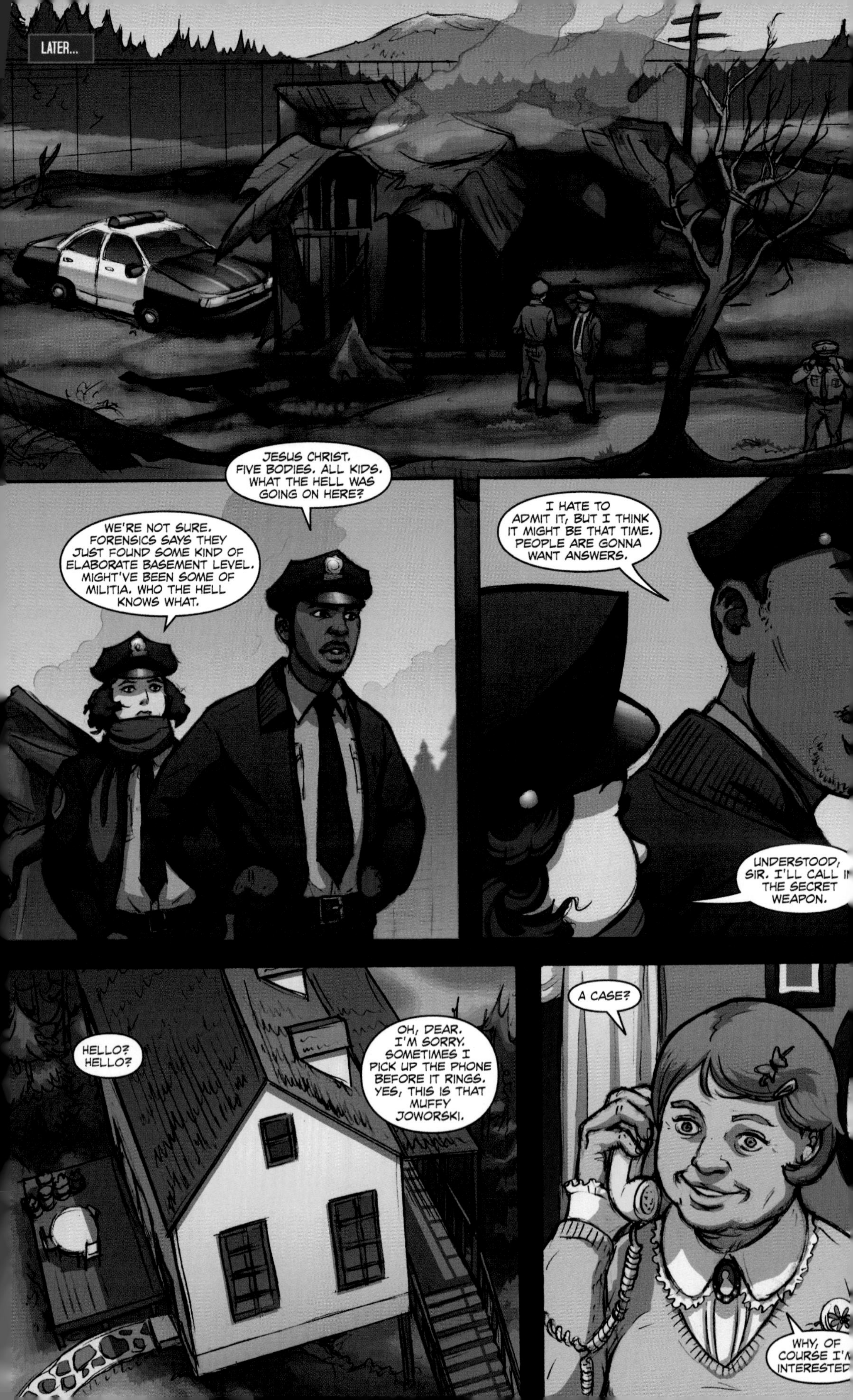
LATER...
JESUS CHRIST. FIVE BODIES. ALL KIDS. WHAT THE HELL WAS GOING ON HERE?
WE'RE NOT SURE. FORENSICS SAYS THEY JUST FOUND SOME KIND OF ELABORATE BASEMENT LEVEL. MIGHT'VE BEEN SOME OF MILITIA. WHO THE HELL KNOWS WHAT.
I HATE TO ADMIT IT, BUT I THINK IT MIGHT BE THAT TIME. PEOPLE ARE GONNA WANT ANSWERS.
UNDERSTOOD, SIR. I'LL CALL IN THE SECRET WEAPON.
HELLO? HELLO?
OH, DEAR. I'M SORRY. SOMETIMES I PICK UP THE PHONE BEFORE IT RINGS. YES, THIS IS THAT MUFFY JOWORSKI.
A CASE?
WHY, OF COURSE I'M INTERESTED

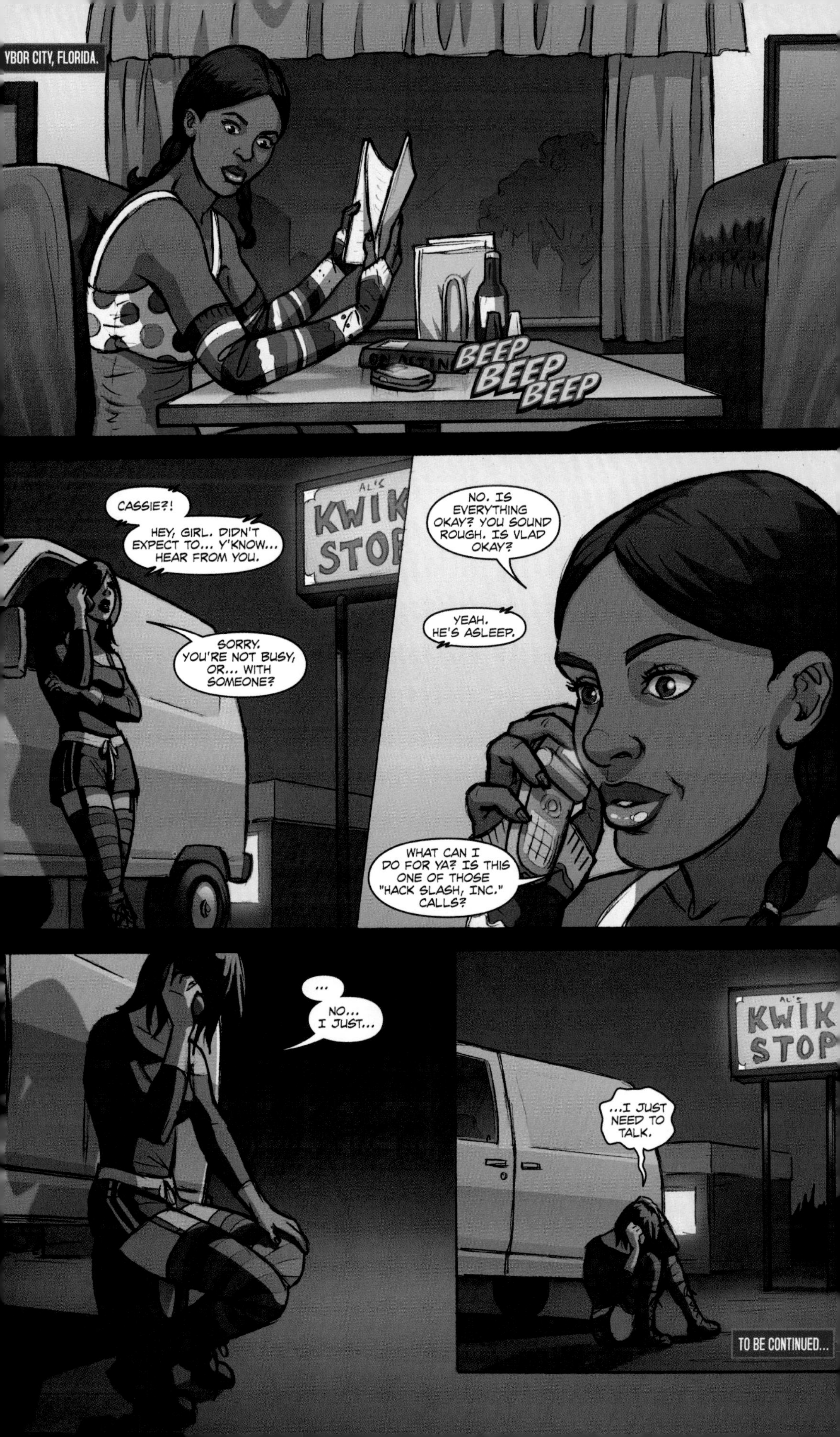

YBOR CITY, FLORIDA.
BEEP BEEP BEEP
CASSIE?!
HEY, GIRL. DIDN'T EXPECT TO... Y'KNOW... HEAR FROM YOU.
AL'S KWIK STOP
NO. IS EVERYTHING OKAY? YOU SOUND ROUGH. IS VLAD OKAY?
SORRY. YOU'RE NOT BUSY, OR... WITH SOMEONE?
YEAH. HE'S ASLEEP.
WHAT CAN I DO FOR YA? IS THIS ONE OF THOSE "HACK SLASH, INC." CALLS?
... NO... I JUST...
AL'S KWIK STOP
...I JUST NEED TO TALK.
TO BE CONTINUED...

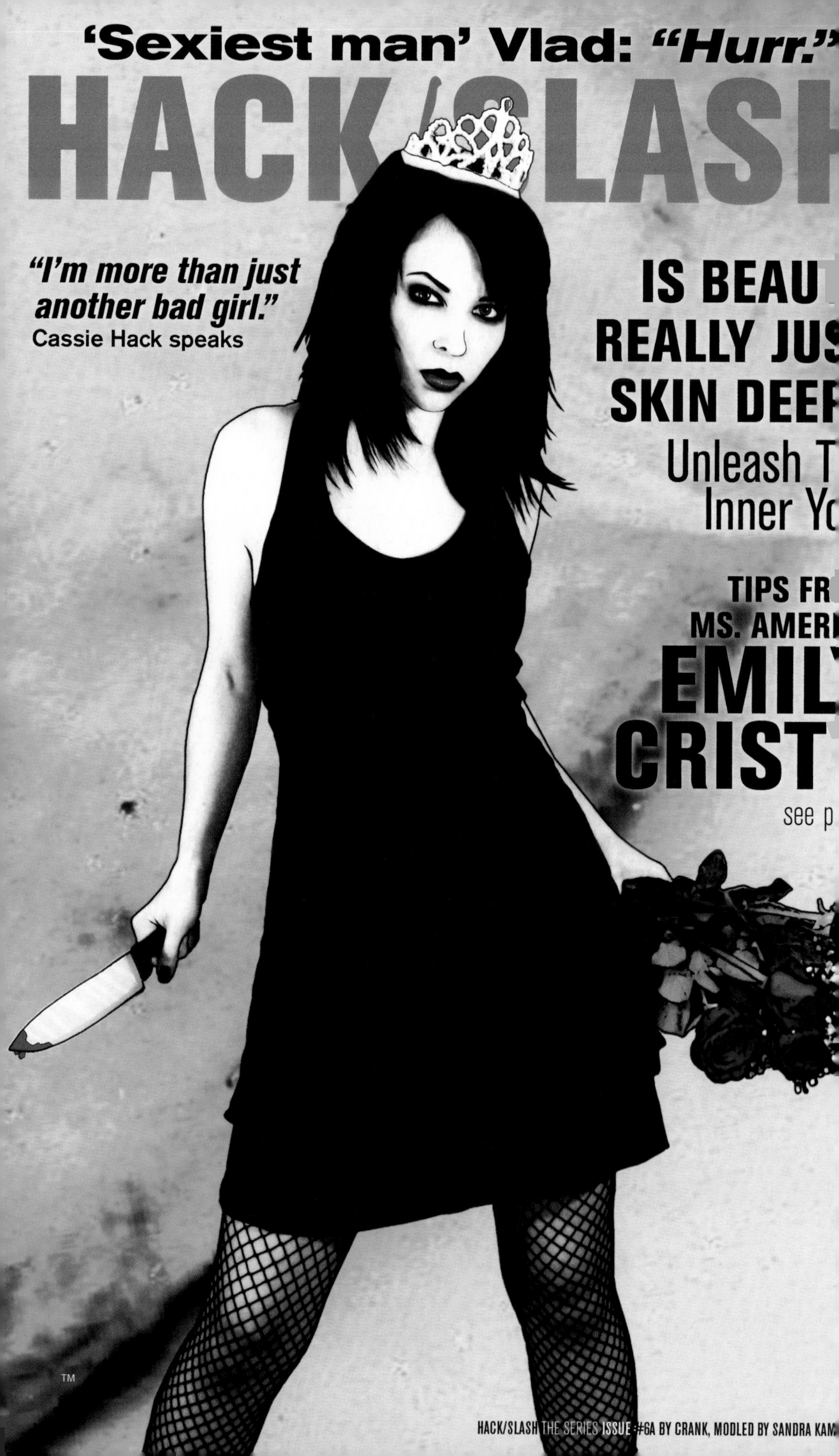

'Sexiest man' Vlad: "Hurr."
HACK/SLASH
"I'm more than just another bad girl."
Cassie Hack speaks
IS BEAU
REALLY JUS
SKIN DEEP
Unleash T
Inner Yo
TIPS FR
MS. AMERI
EMIL
CRIST
see p
TM
HACK/SLASH THE SERIES ISSUE #6A BY CRANK, MODLED BY SANDRA KAM

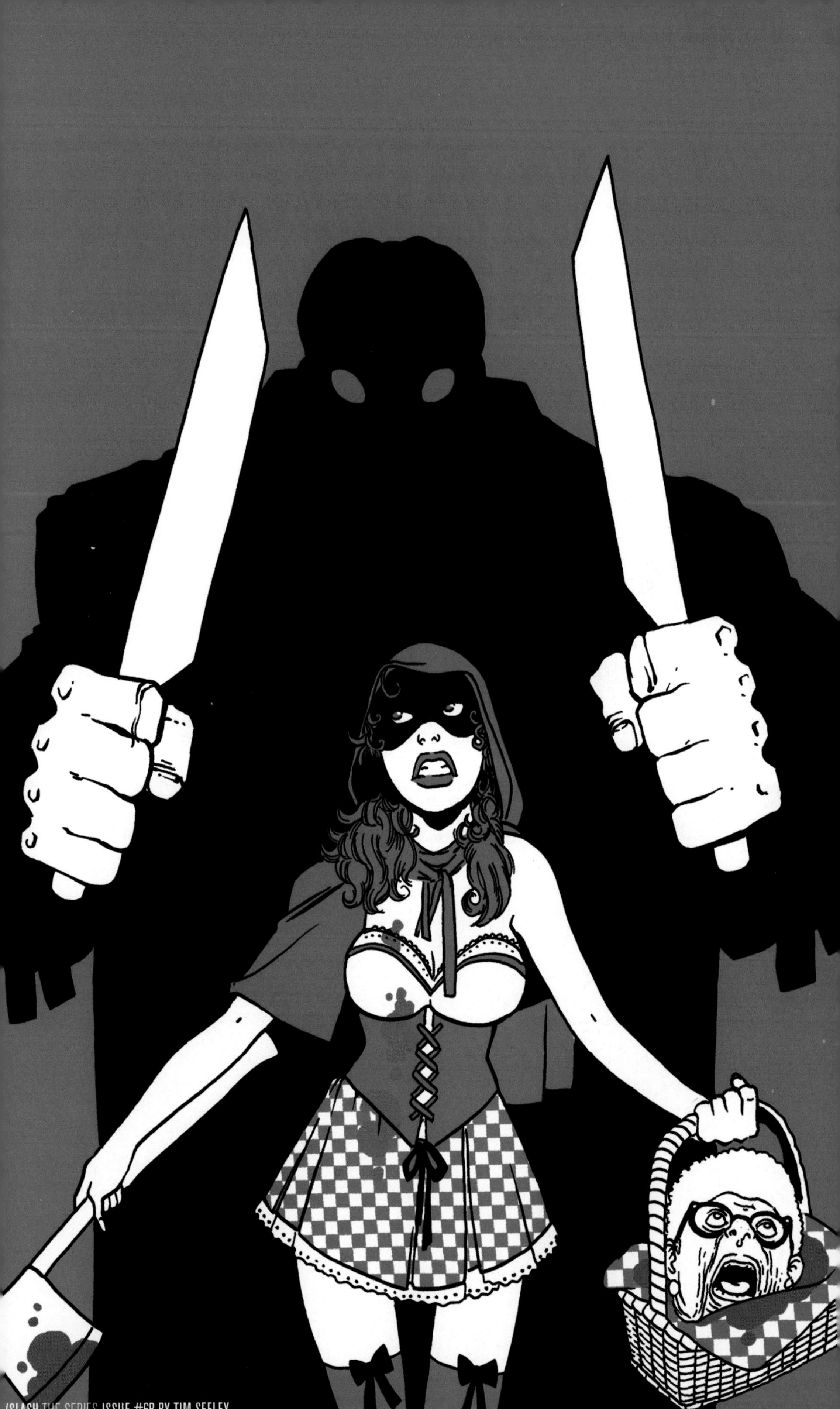

/SLASH THE SERIES ISSUE #6B BY TIM SEELEY

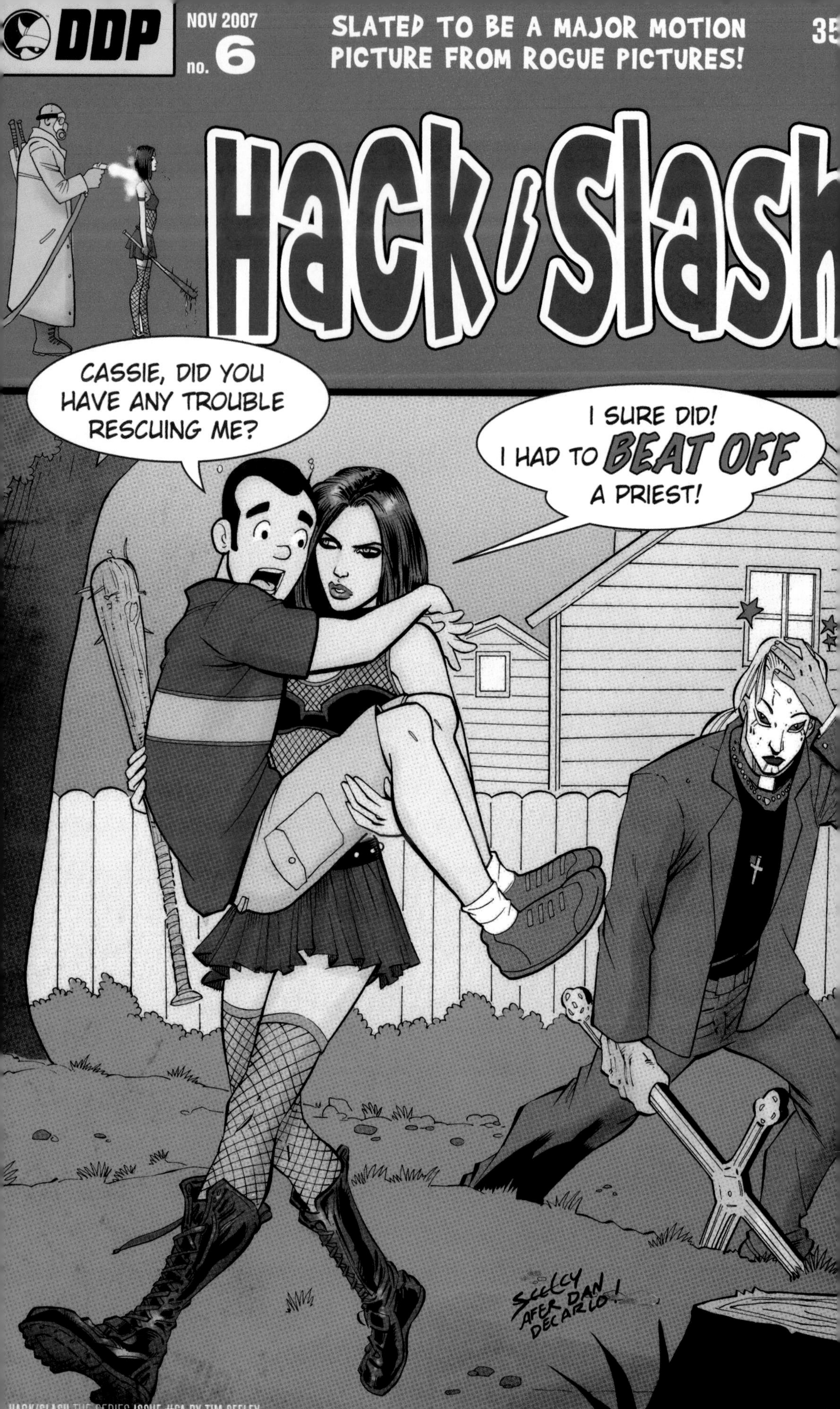
DDP
NOV 2007
no. 6
SLATED TO BE A MAJOR MOTION PICTURE FROM ROGUE PICTURES!
Hack/Slash
CASSIE, DID YOU HAVE ANY TROUBLE RESCUING ME?
I SURE DID! I HAD TO BEAT OFF A PRIEST!
SEELEY AFER DAN DECARLO!

HACK/SLASH THE SERIES ISSUE #6A BY TIM SEELEY

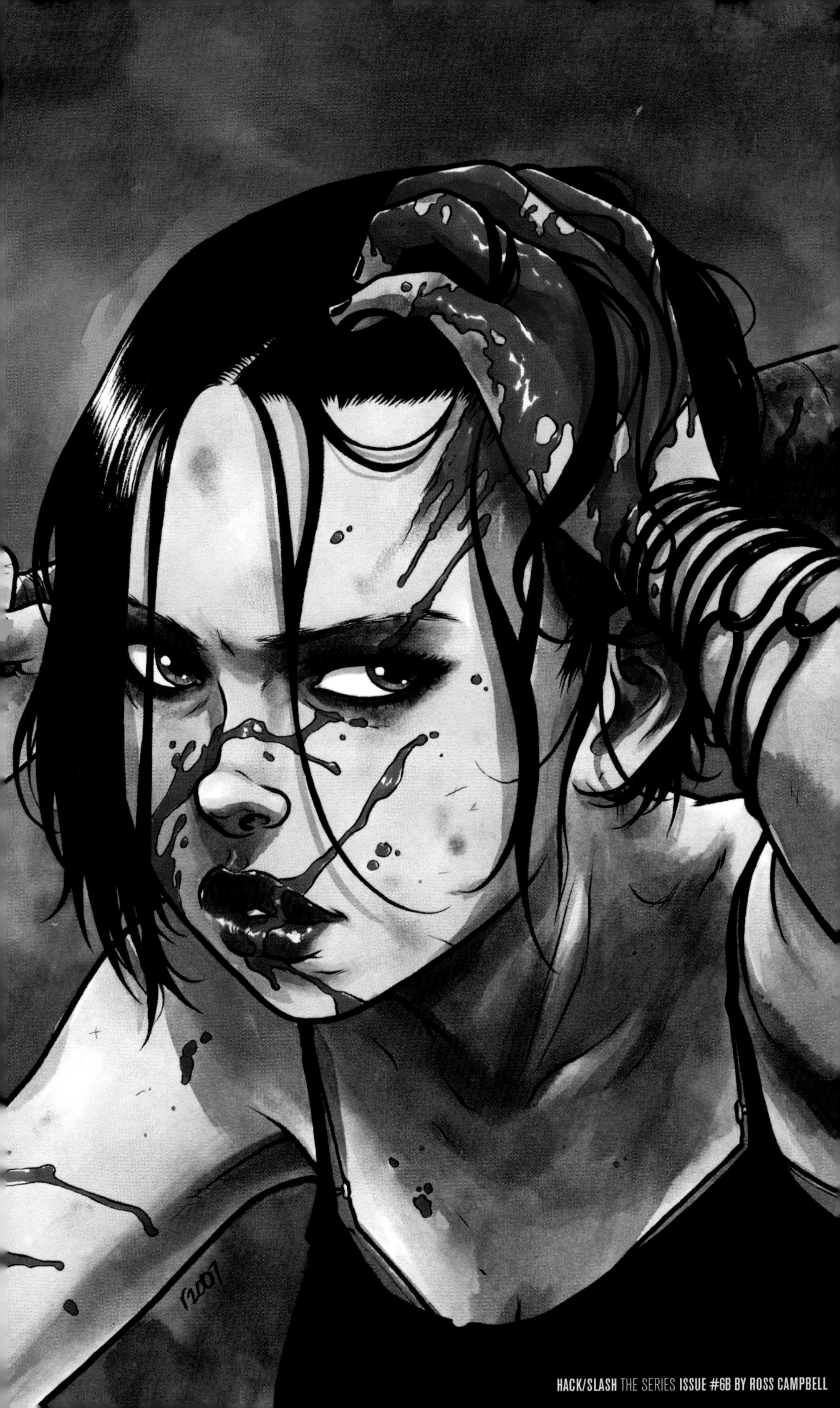
r2007

HACK/SLASH THE SERIES **ISSUE #6B BY ROSS CAMPBELL**

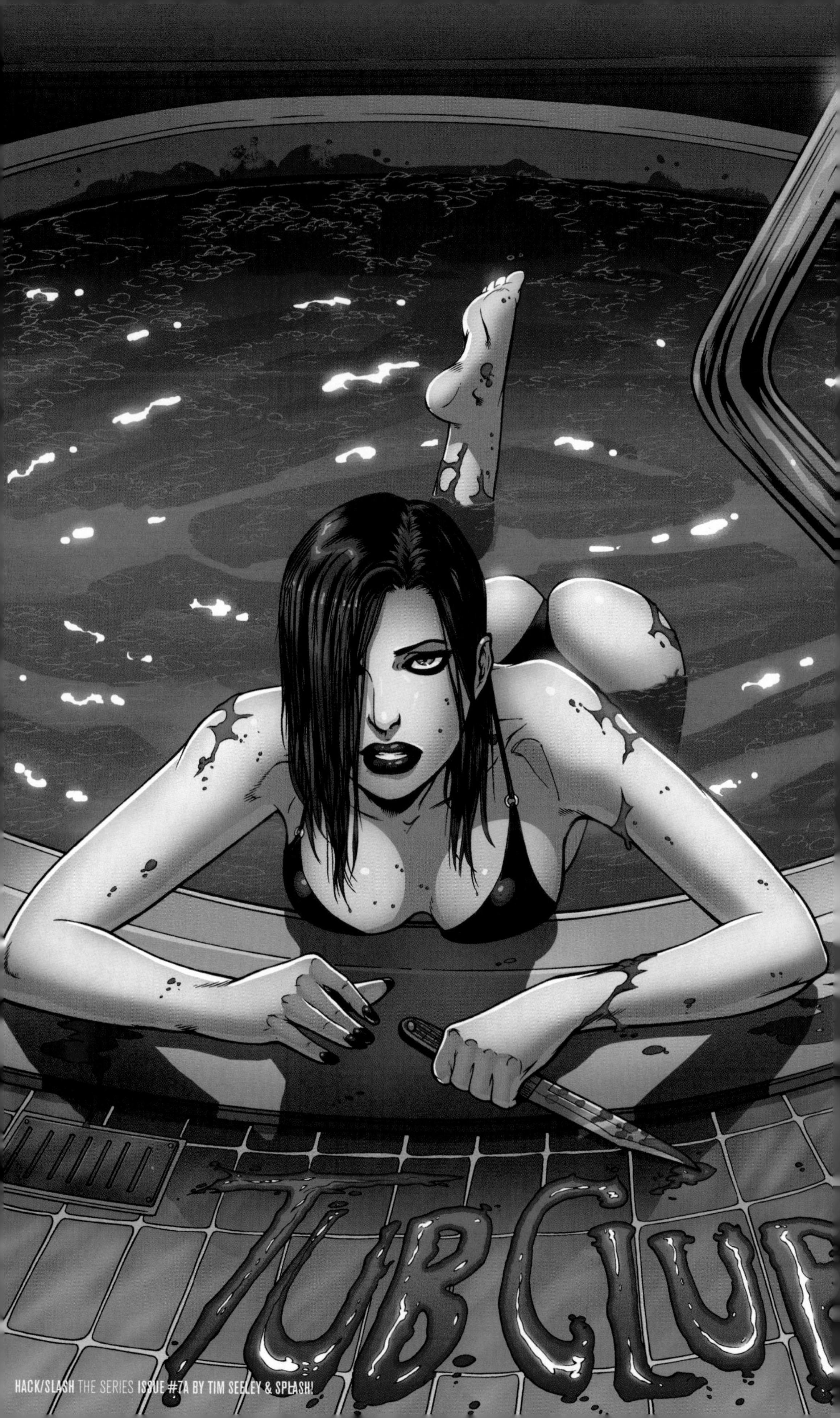
TUB CLUB

HACK/SLASH THE SERIES ISSUE #7A BY TIM SEELEY & SPLASH!

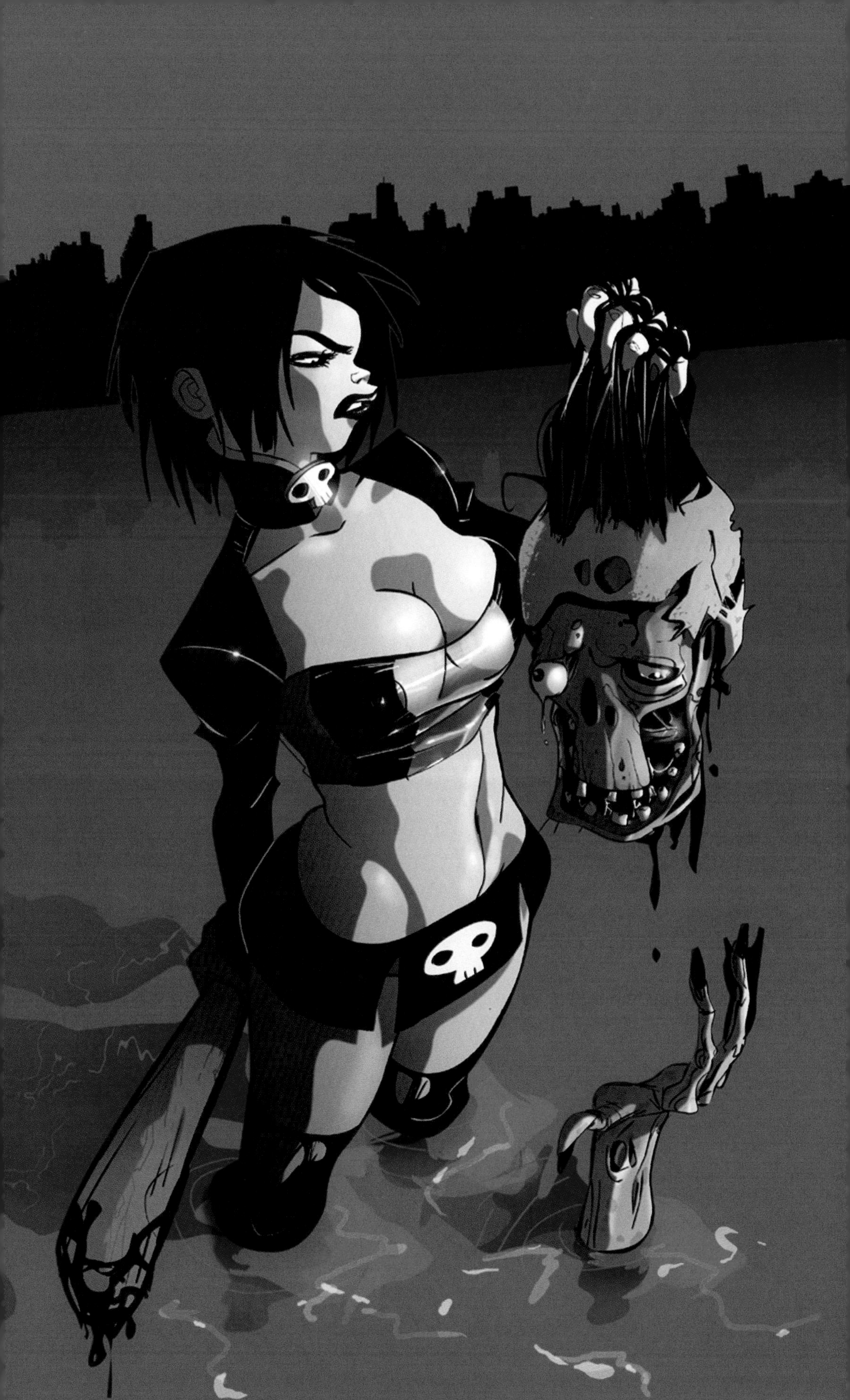

HACK/SLASH THE SERIES ISSUE #7B BY SARA PICHELLI

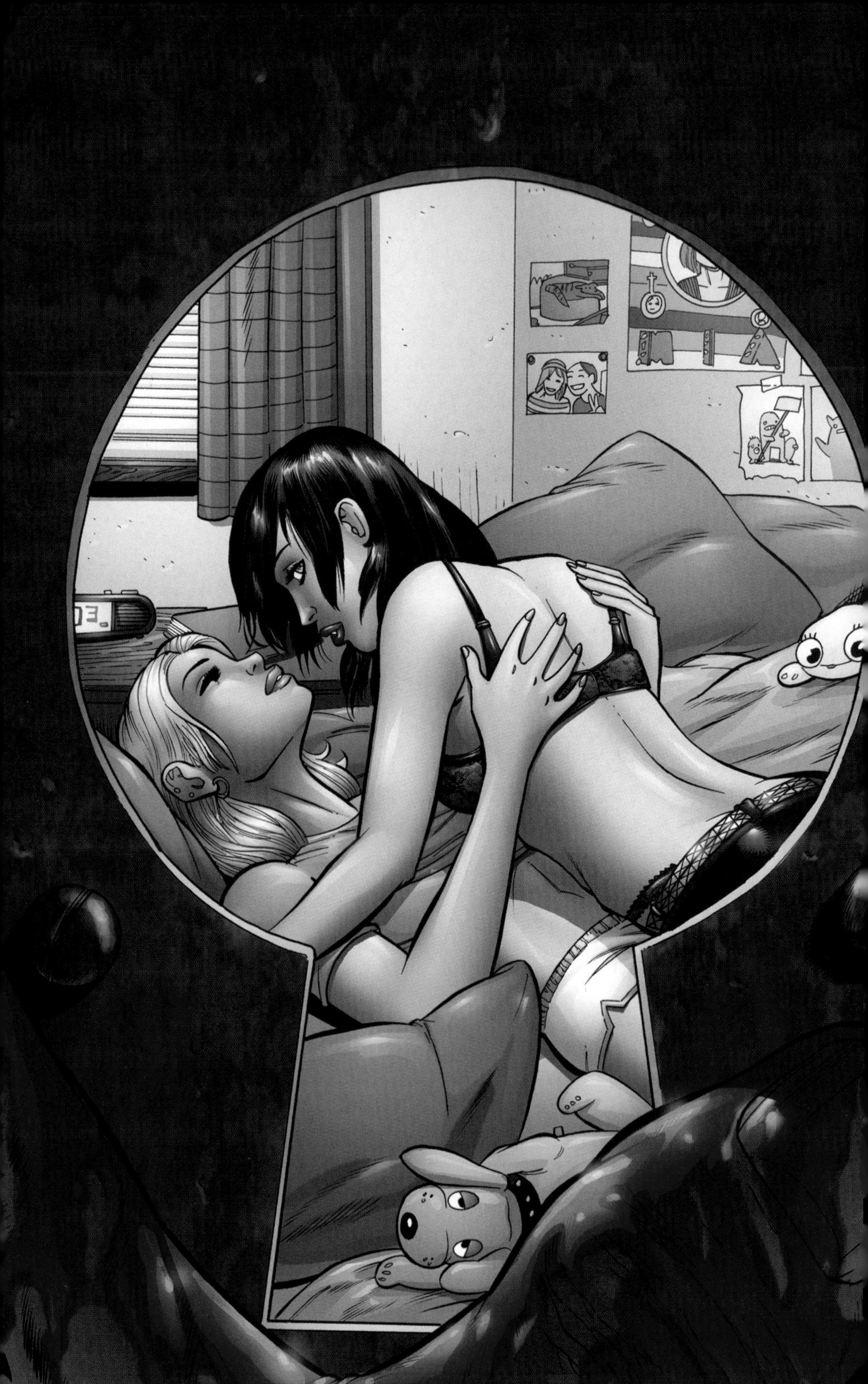

HACK/SLASH THE SERIES ISSUE #8A BY TIM SEELEY & WES DZIOBA

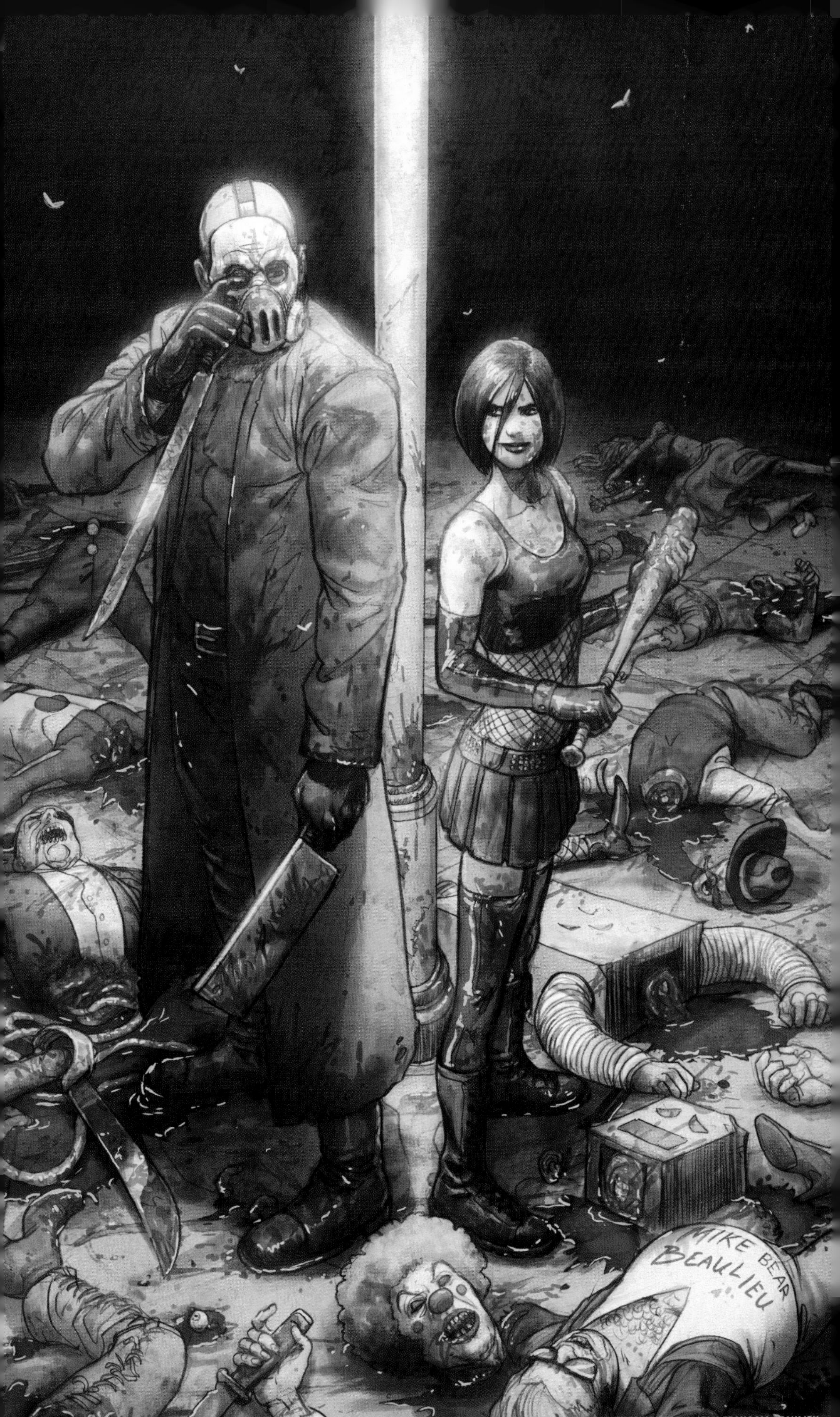
MIKE BEAR
BEAULIEU
HACK/SLASH THE SERIES ISSUE #8B BY MIKE BEAR & JEAN-FRANCOIS BEAULIEU

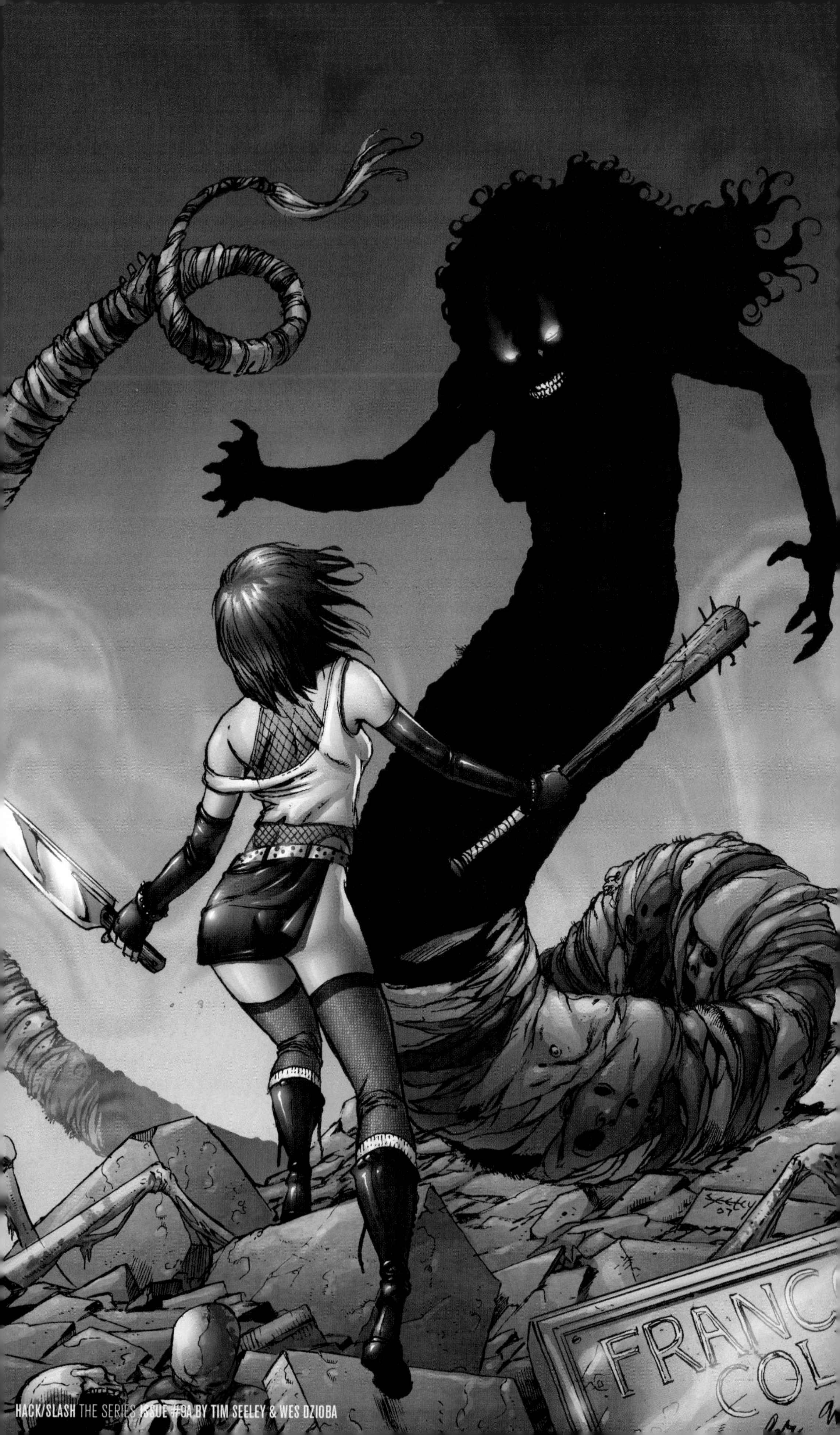
FRANC
COL
HACK/SLASH THE SERIES ISSUE #9A BY TIM SEELEY & WES DZIOBA

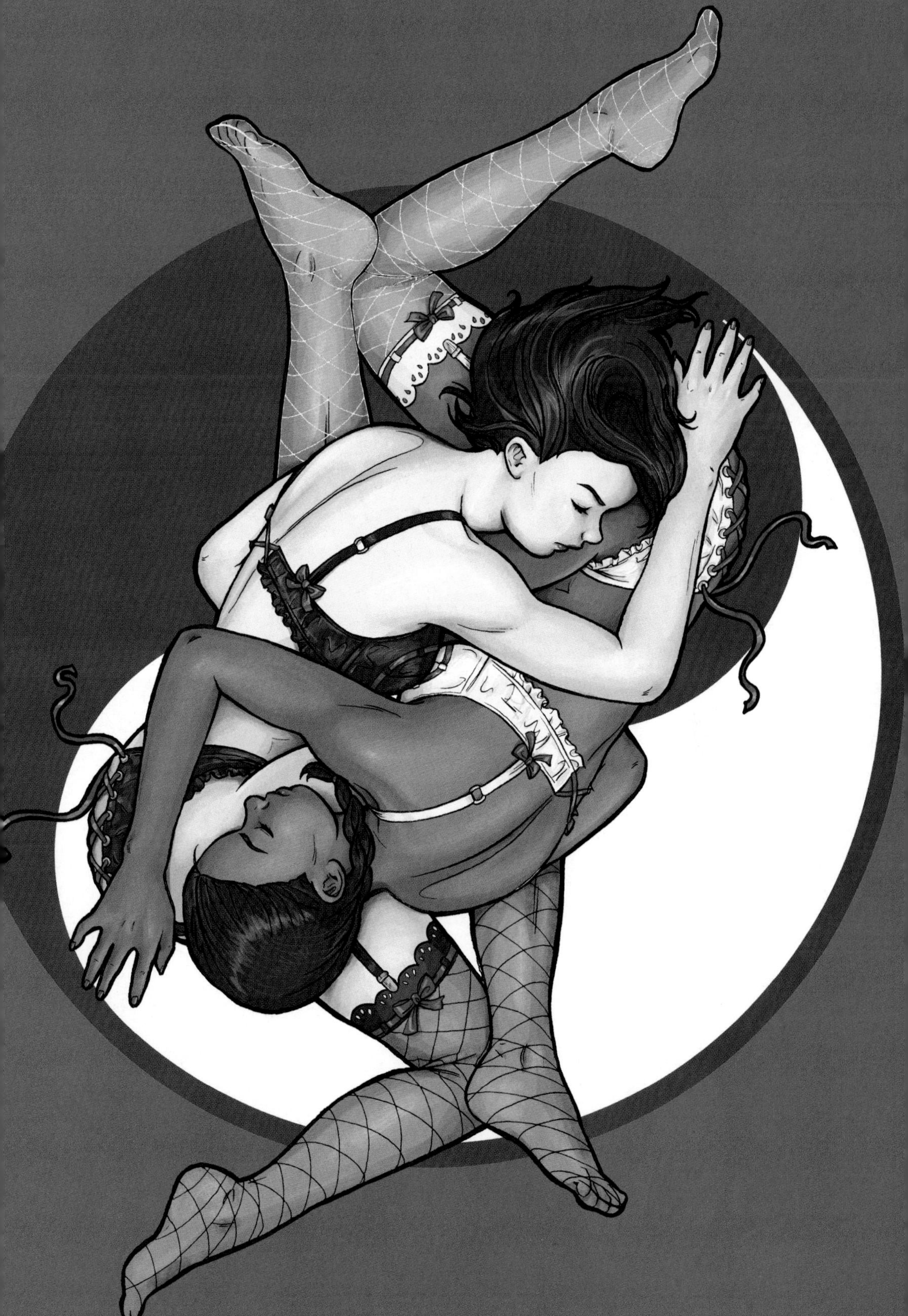

HACK/SLASH THE SERIES ISSUE #9B BY EMILY STONE

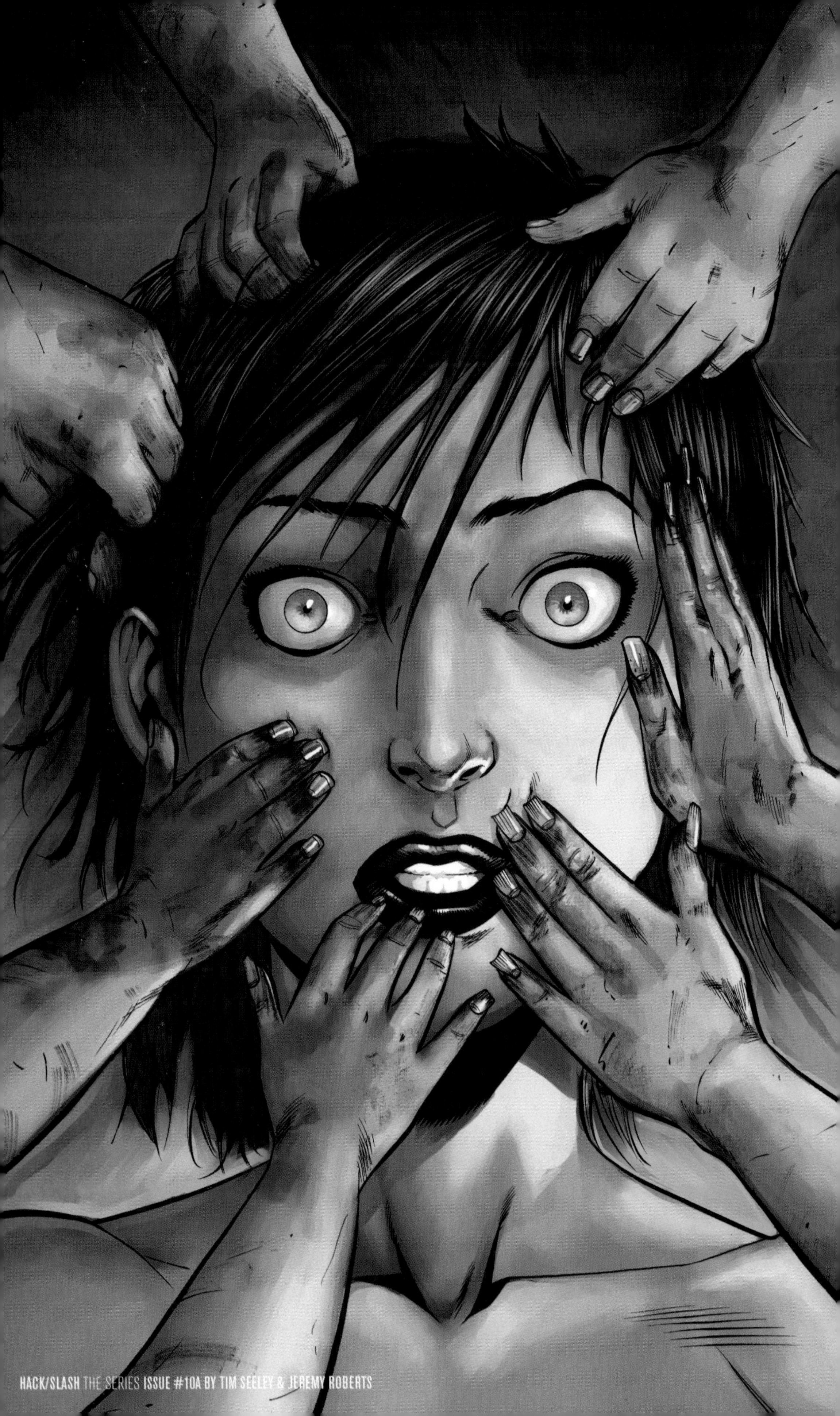
HACK/SLASH THE SERIES ISSUE #10A BY TIM SEELEY & JEREMY ROBERTS

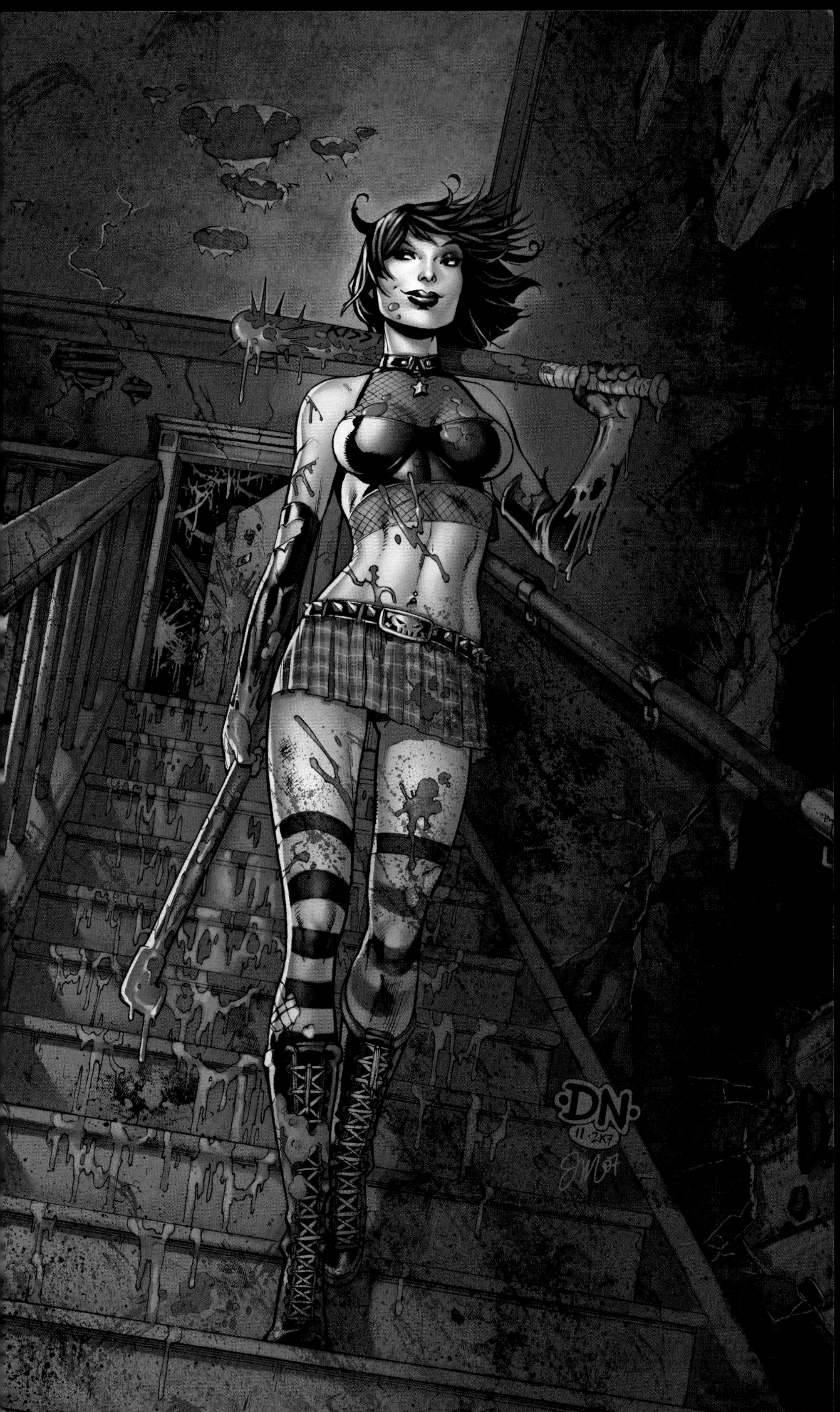

HACK/SLASH THE SERIES ISSUE #2A BY DAVID NAKAYAMA & EMILY WARREN

EMILY CRISTY

Real Name: Emily Cristy
Aliases: The Ourobouros
Death by: Stabbing
Pre-Slasher Occupation: Head Researcher, Ceutotech Inc., Former Ms. America winner. Former nude model
Slasher type: Vengeful ghoul

Special abilities:
Superhuman strength, Regeneration, resistance to damage, and the ability to absorb the skins of others and use them as her own.

Slasher weapon: None

Body Count: 12

The story: While studying Biology at Franco-Belle University. She took various small jobs to pay for school, at one point modeling nude. Eventually her good looks and personality got her as far as the Ms.America pageant, which she won. Shortly thereafter he nude photos resurfaced and were published by GIRLIE magazine. This of course caused a large controversy, and Cristy was eventually forced to give up her crown. Determined to help women, and utilize her intelligence, she eventually took a job at Ceutotech, Inc, a cosmetics firm she had once been a spokes model for. Cristy headed the Regenerative Research Division tasked with studying the regenerative qualities of slashers and the potential youth restoring effects that could be derived from them. During a breakout, The slasher known as Acid Angel stabbed Emily, a wound which eventually caused her to bleed to death, but not before she injected herself with the concentrated slasher-derived chemical called "Hate Juice." When Emily later returned to life, she discovered she could steal the skin of others. She escaped from a government lab and returned to her alma matter to kill again.

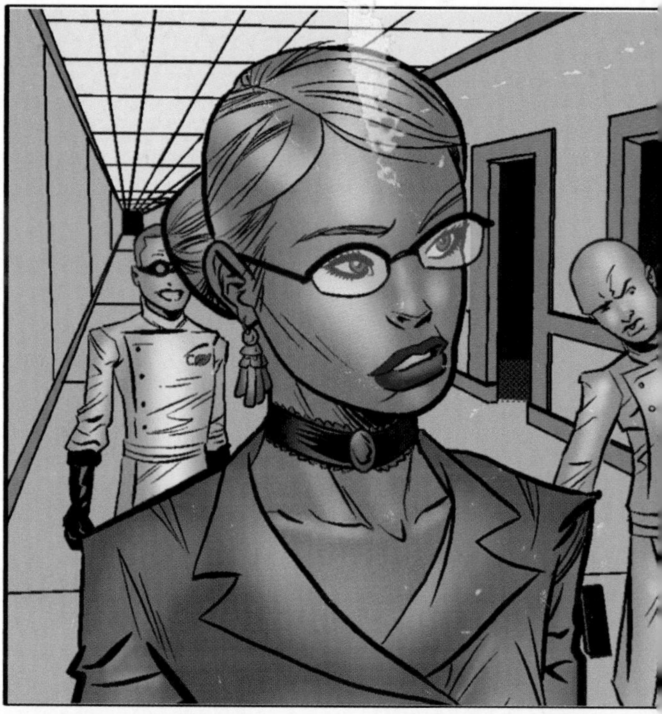

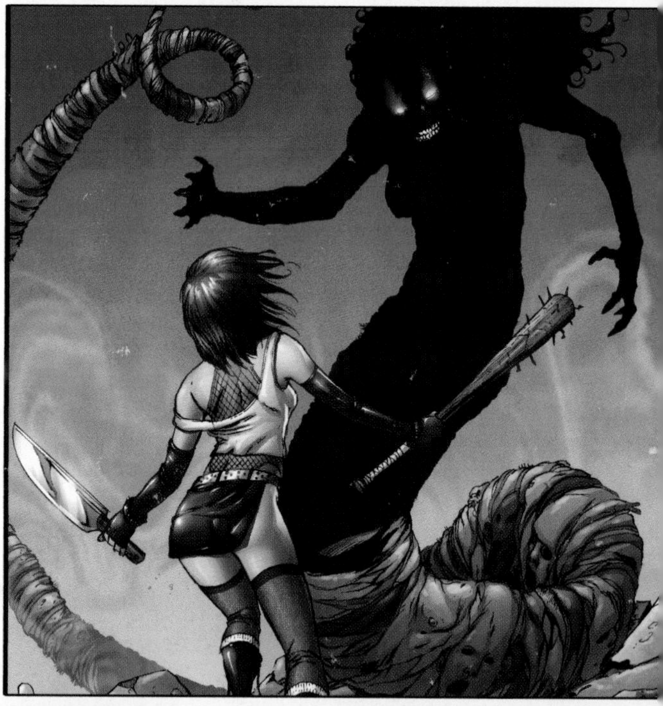

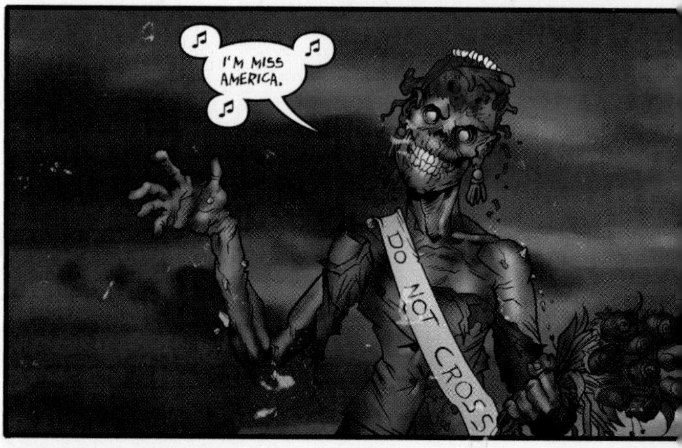
I'M MISS AMERICA.
DO NOT CROSS

ATHER WRATH 2

al Name: Samuel Lawrence
ath by: N/A
e-Slasher Occupation: Preacher's sistant
asher type: Obsessive Nutjobl

ecial abilities: None

asher weapon: Cross

dy Count: 3

e story: The story: Samuel wrence was the nephew and assis- t to the original Father Wrath. ıen his uncle tried to sexually sault him, he responded by blud- oning the man to death. Disillu- ned he became a drug abuser and oholic. Eventually, he decided the rld was a lesser place without his cle and decided to take up his title d appearance and punish sinners.

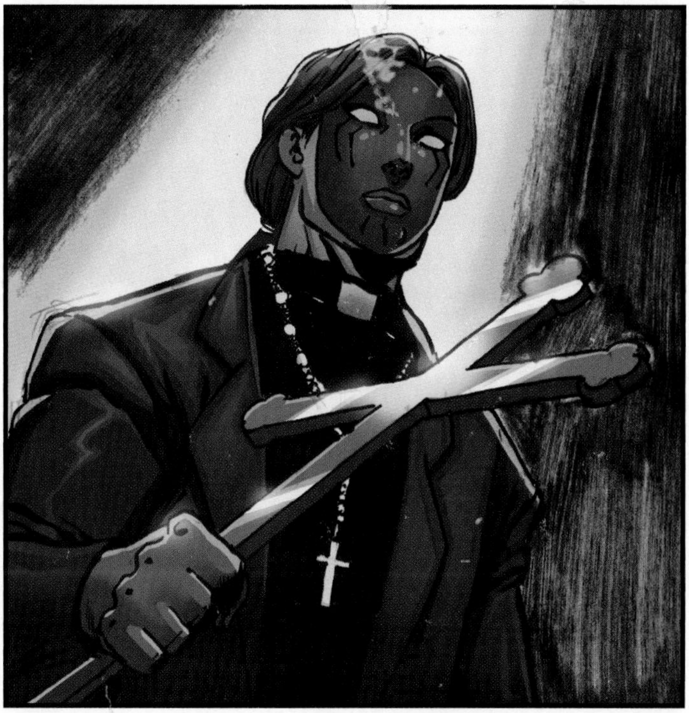

HE CHILDREN

al Name: Unknown. Dr. Phillips ned them Romulus, Remus, Phoebe, oa, Artemis, and Sonia.
ath by: N/A
-Slasher Occupation: N/A
asher type: Backwoods Psychos

ecial abilities: None

asher weapon: None

dy Count: Undetermined. At least 2

e story: The children were an assort- nt of feral kids, collected from ious places around the world. Dr. ward Phillips' attempt to cure them h slasher derived cells only further volved them, creating fierce, canni- istic creatures who lived in a wolf ck-like organization.

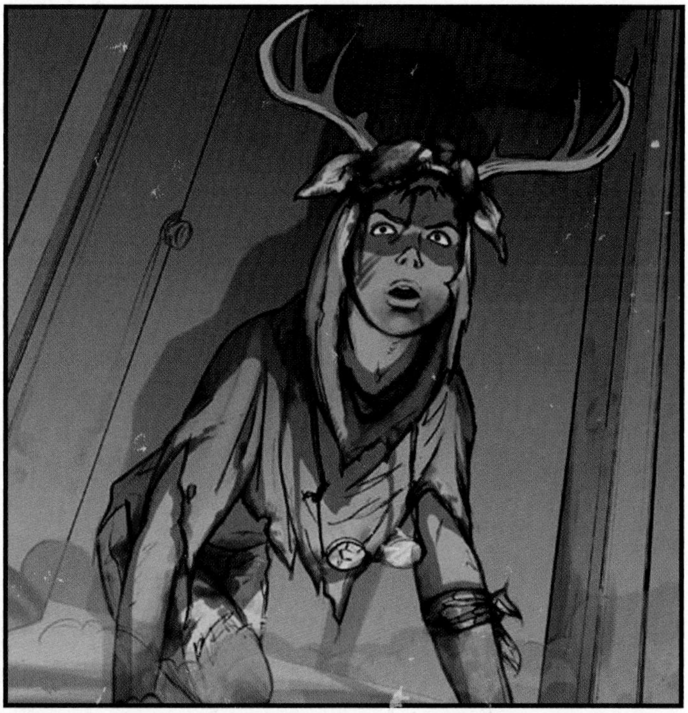

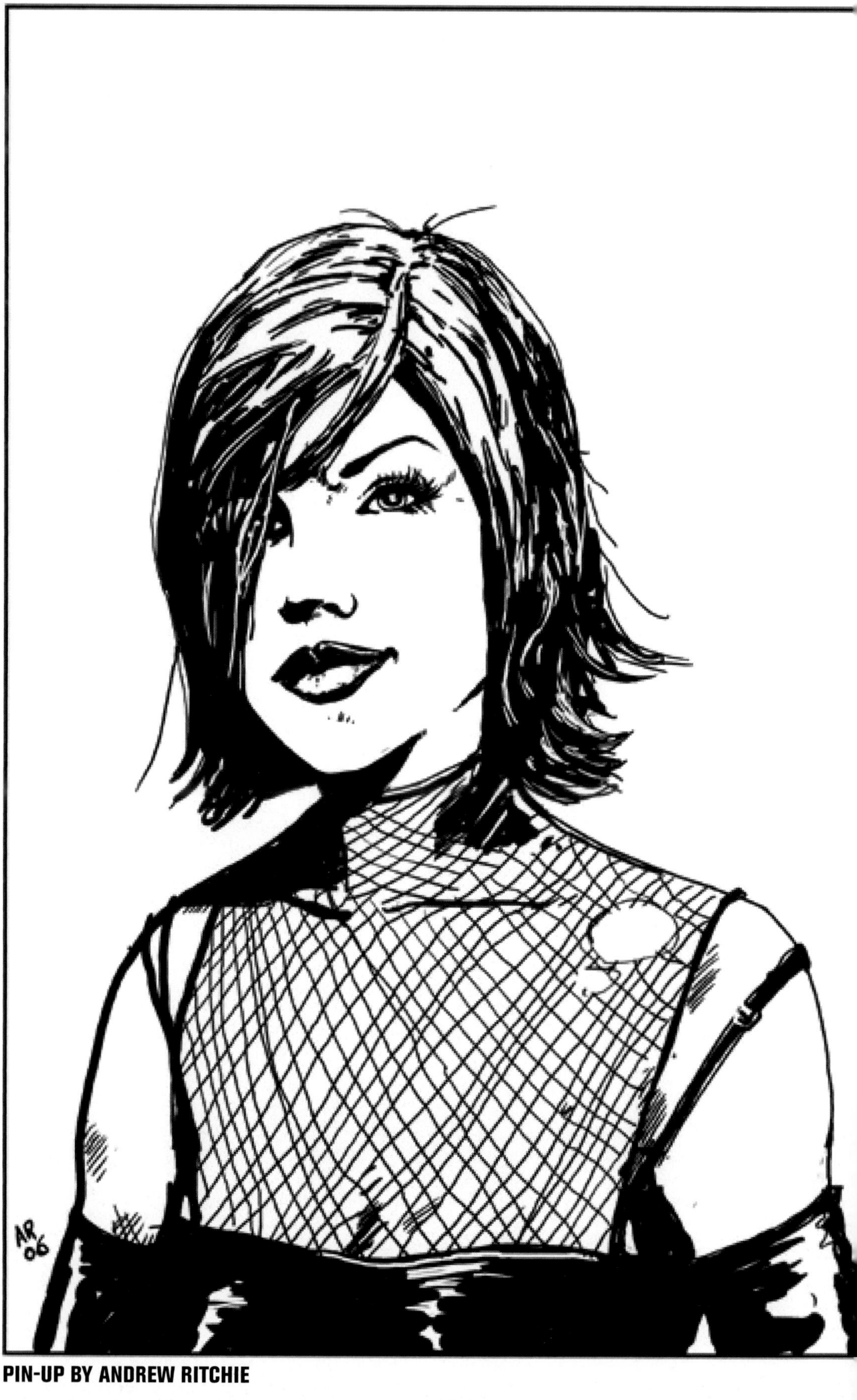

PIN-UP BY ANDREW RITCHIE

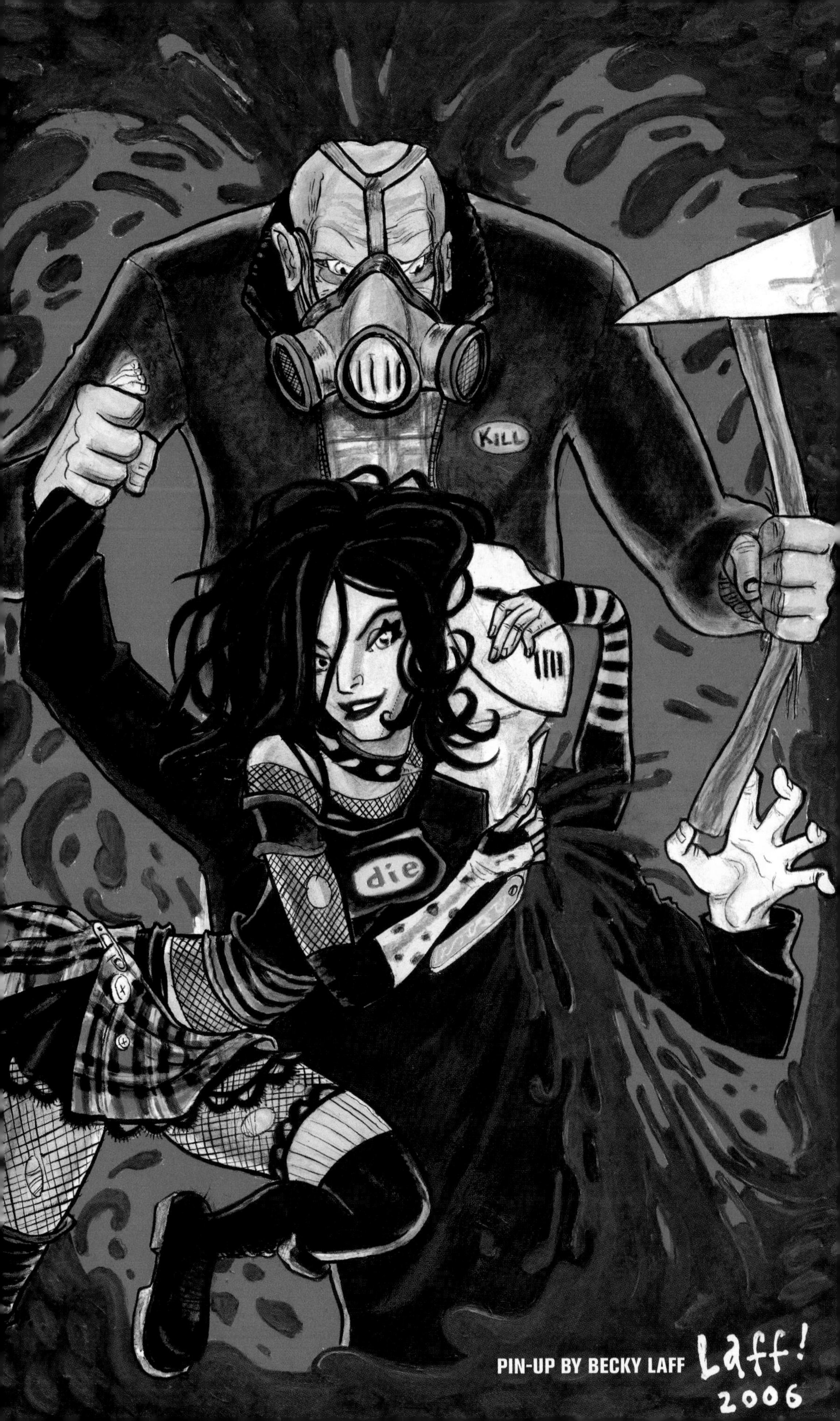
KILL
die
Laff!
2006
PIN-UP BY BECKY LAFF

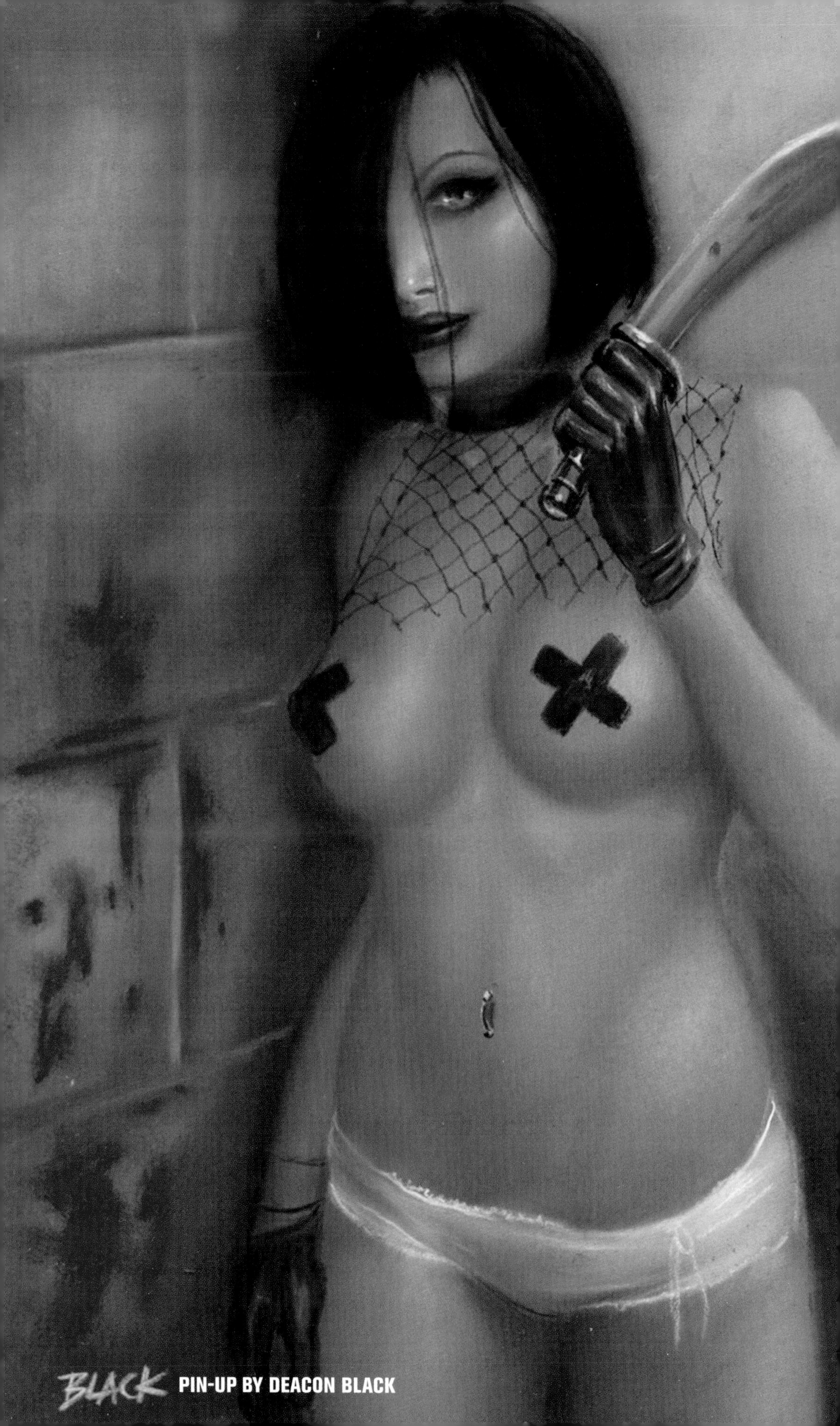
BLACK
PIN-UP BY DEACON BLACK